VOLUNTARY SIMPLICITY

the poetic alternative to consumer culture

edited by samuel alexander

stead & daughters ltd

Voluntary Simplicity: The Poetic Alternative to Consumer Culture
This anthology first published by Stead & Daughters Ltd © 2009
Stead & Daughters Ltd
60 Guyton Street
Whanganui 4500
New Zealand
www.steadanddaughters.com

978-0-9864537-0-0

Cataloguing-in-Publication Data: a catalogue record for this book is available from the National Library of New Zealand.

Typeset in Rotis Semi Serif
Cover utilises Kingthings Printingkit thanks to www,kingthingsfont.co.uk

Printed and bound by Astra Print, New Zealand.

This book utilises chain of custody certified stock. Stead & Daughters Ltd is committed to responsible forest management and environmental business practices.

CONTENTS

ACKNOWLEDGEMENTS

This book is dedicated to all those free spirits who have joined the Life Poets' Simplicity Collective and who are, this very moment, participating in the quiet revolution. Let our Collective take responsibility for creatively advancing the Voluntary Simplicity Movement – humbly, passionately, and in the spirit of celebration. From the very depths of my nature, thank you and Godspeed. (www.simplicitycollective.com)

This publication was partially funded by the Office for Environmental Programs (O.E.P.) and the Centre for Resources, Energy and Environmental Law (C.R.E.E.L.), University of Melbourne, Australia. I am extremely grateful for the financial support I received from these progressive institutions, as well as for the administrative support I received from their wonderful staff, Pete Morgan (O.E.P.) especially. Special thanks also to Professor Lee Godden, my doctoral supervisor and Director of the O.E.P. (07/08), for being an inexhaustible source of kindness, encouragement, and inspiration. I would also like to extend my appreciation to Melbourne Law School for providing such a stimulating environment in which to lecture, study, and think up new projects.

Most of the contributions that comprise this anthology have been published (with minor variations) elsewhere. My thanks to the following authors / publishers / copyright holders both for their enthusiasm for this not-for-profit project and for their generous permission to reprint the following material:

Chapter One, 'Voluntary Simplicity: The "Middle Way" to Sustainability," by Mark A. Burch, originally appeared in his book *Stepping Lightly: Simplicity for People and the Planet* (Gabriola Island: New Society Publishers, 2000); Chapter Two, 'A New Social Movement?' by Amatai Etzioni, originally appeared (as 'Voluntary Simplicity: A New Social Movement?') in William E. Halal and Kenneth B. Taylor (eds.), *21st Century Economics: Perspectives of Socioeconomics for a Changing World* (New York: Palgrave Macmillan, 1999); Chapter Three, 'Two Ways of Thinking About Money,' by Jerome M. Segal, originally appeared in his book *Graceful Simplicity: The Philosophy and Politics of the Alternative American Dream* (Berkeley: University of California Press, 1999); Chapter Four, 'What is Affluenza?', by Clive Hamilton and Richard Denniss, originally appeared in their book *Affluenza: When Too Much is Never Enough* (Crows Nest: Allen & Unwin, 2005); CHAPTER FIVE, 'The Conundrum of Consumption,' by Alan Durning, originally appeared in *How Much Is Enough? The Consumer Society and the Future of the Earth* (New York: W.W.. Norton, 1992) a Worldwatch Institute publication (www.Worldwatch.org); CHAPTER SIX, 'The Value of Voluntary Simplicity,' by Richard Gregg, originally appeared as *The Value of Voluntary Simplicity* (Wallingford, Pennsylvania: Pendle Hill Publications, Pendle Hill Pamphlet #3, 1936.); it was also published in the Indian Journal *Visva-Bharati Quarterly* (1936); the complete essay can be read online at www.pendlehill.org; CHAPTER SEVEN, 'Less is More,' by Philip Cafaro, an extended version of which originally appeared in *Global Bioethics* 14 (2001) 46–59; thanks also to the University of Georgia Press as well as the Center for American Architecture & Design at the University of Texas for permission to reprint this article; CHAPTER EIGHT, 'Building the Case for Global Living,' by Jim Merkel, originally appeared in *Radical Simplicity: Small Footprints on a Finite Planet* (Gabriola Island: New Society Publishers, 2003); CHAPTER NINE, 'Voluntary Simplicity,' by Duane Elgin and Arnold Mitchell, originally appeared in the *Co-Evolution Quarterly* (Summer, 1977); the complete essay can be read online at www.awakeningearth.org/articles; CHAPTER TEN, 'Thoreau's Alternative Economics,' by Philip Cafaro, originally appeared (as 'Economy') in *Thoreau's Living Ethics:* Walden *and the Pursuit of Virtue* (Athens: University of Georgia, 2004); CHAPTER ELEVEN, 'Why Simplify?', by Mark A. Burch, originally appeared (as 'Why Voluntary Simplicity?') in *Simplicity: Notes, Stories, and Exercises for Developing Unimaginable Wealth* (Gabriola Island: New Society Publishers, 1995); CHAPTER TWELVE, 'Sharing the Earth,' by Jim Merkel, originally appeared in *Radical Simplicity: Small Footprints on a Finite Planet* (Gabriola Island: New Society Publishers, 2003); CHAPTER THIRTEEN, 'The Downshifters,' by Clive Hamilton and Richard Denniss, originally appeared in *Affluenza: When Too Much is Never Enough* (Crows Nest: Allen & Unwin, 2005); CHAPTER FOURTEEN, 'A Culture of Permanence,' by Alan Durning, originally appeared in *How Much Is Enough? The Consumer Society and the Future of the Earth* (New York: W.W. Norton, 1992) a Worldwatch Institute publication (www.Worldwatch.org); CHAPTER FIFTEEN, 'Simplicity, Community, and Private Land,' by Eric T. Freyfogle, was written specifically for this anthology and has not been previously published. Copyright remains vested with the author; CHAPTER SIXTEEN, 'The New Politics of Consumption,' by Juliet Schor, originally appeared in *Boston Review* (Summer, 1999); CHAPTER SEVENTEEN, 'Political Prescriptions,' by John de Graaf, a version of which originally appeared in his book (coauthored with David Wann and Thomas H. Naylor) *Affluenza: The All-consuming Epidemic* (San Francisco: Berrett-Koehler Publishers, 2005); CHAPTER EIGHTEEN, 'Extending the Movement,' by Mary Grigsby, originally appeared in *Buying Time and Getting By: The Voluntary Simplicity Movement* (Albany:

State University of New York Press, 2004); CHAPTER NINETEEN, 'Transcendental Simplicity,' David Shi, originally appeared in *The Simple Life: Plain Living and High Thinking in American Culture* (Oxford: Oxford University Press, 1985). Thanks also to François Schneider and Research & Degrowth (www.degrowth.net) for permission to reprint the Declaration on Degrowth (APPENDIX THREE).

(Every effort has been made to ensure that all copyright holders have been contacted regarding the not-for-profit publication of the material in this volume. In the unlikely event that there has been an oversight, please bring this to the attention of the editor of this volume so that some arrangement can be explored.)

On a more personal note, thanks to my good friends Derek Baron, Aaron Brenneman, Andrew Doodson, Andy Gibson, Brian Harmon, Mathieu Papazzoni, and my friend-enemy Simon Ussher, for dignifying me with thoughtful criticism, advice, and assistance during the preparation of this volume. Much love and gratitude to the Gatehouse Gang, especially for letting me live in the backyard. Thanks to my smallest friend, Laurie Duckham, for insisting that I engage life with the seriousness of a child at play. Thanks also – and especially! – to my friend and publisher, Renée Stead, and Stead & Daughters Ltd, for believing in this project and for agreeing, without hesitation, to publish it on a not-for-profit basis. Thanks, yet again, to my parents for their love, tolerance, and endless support. And, finally, to the beautiful Helen, for improving my writing and ideas, for always encouraging me to find my own way, and for enriching my life in ways unimagined. Words cannot express the unsayable, but I hope that I am understood.

Getting and spending, we lay waste our powers.

– William Wordsworth

INTRODUCTION

Samuel Alexander

Is consumer culture the ultimate fulfillment of human destiny? Or are we entitled to hope for something more? Our current use of language, it must be said, does not bode well for those of us who live in hope, for consider what today is proudly called the 'developed world': In the face of extreme poverty we see gross overconsumption; in the face of environmental degradation we see a fetishistic obsession with economic growth; in the face of social decay and spiritual malaise we see a vast corporate wasteland eating away at the future of humanity. Our collective imagination lies dormant. *What is to be done? How now shall we live?*

Intended as an invitation to an alternative way of life, this anthology brings together some of the most important literature on the post-consumerist living strategy known as 'voluntary simplicity.' Our planet urgently needs us to explore alternative ways to live, and one promising way to lessen our impact on nature is to voluntarily embrace 'a simpler life' of reduced consumption. From various perspectives, the chapters explore what this way of life might involve and, just as importantly, what it does not involve. They also consider what potential or significance it has as a quietly emerging people's movement, and what its limitations might be. The central message of this book is that by *lowering* our 'standard of living' we can actually *increase* our 'quality of life.' Paradoxical though it may sound, voluntary simplicity is about living more with less.

Since there may be some who are unfamiliar with the term 'voluntary simplicity,' I thought I should begin this introduction by offering a preliminary definition of the basic idea. After doing so I will outline various ways that voluntary simplicity can be *justified* as a way of life, and I will also spend a short time discussing the *practice* of simplicity and the *attitudes* that make the practice of simplicity possible.

How one should respond to these issues is a creative and intimately personal matter – the following pages contain more questions than answers – but I wish to highlight the point that voluntary simplicity is an expression of human freedom and an affirmation of life, and I believe that this book requires evaluation in these terms.

All these matters and many more will be explored in detail throughout this comprehensive collection of celebrated writing. I will conclude this introduction by providing a brief overview of each chapter.

What Is Voluntary Simplicity?

Allow me to spend a moment laying some groundwork and trying to put this discussion in some context.

The economic problem of how to provide for ourselves and our families, of how to secure the necessaries of life, has been solved for the vast majority of ordinary people in western society. We are fabulously wealthy when considered in the context of all known history or when compared to the three billion human beings who today subsist on one or two dollars per day. As one leading economist has noted, 'Most westerners today are prosperous beyond the dreams of their grandparents.'[1] The houses of typical families are bigger than ever and they are each filled with untold numbers of consumer products, like multiple TVs, racks of unused clothes, washing machines, dishwashers, dryers, vacuum cleaners, kitchen gadgets, garages full of 'stuff,' etc. Houses are often centrally heated and have air-conditioning, with spare rooms, and two cars parked outside. It is nothing for an average parent to spend one hundred dollars on a present for a child or to buy them a personal mobile phone. Most of us have spare income to spend on take-out food, alcohol, going to the movies, books, taking holidays, etc. We generally have access to sophisticated health care and free primary and secondary education. On top of all this, we live in a democracy, our water is clean, and almost nobody goes hungry.

All this is indicative of a society that has attained unprecedented wealth, which I am not about to suggest is a bad thing, necessarily. But it is a prosperity which has proven extremely easy to take for granted, leaving many in the global middleclass still complaining about the hardness of their lot, and feeling deprived despite their plenty.

What I am suggesting is that western society is, at last, rich enough to be truly free, free from material want; although, as I have implied, not many people seem willing to accept that this is so. Is it because the prospect of freedom is terrifying? Perhaps it is terrifying because, once we recognize the sufficiency of our material situations and are able to quench the upward creep of material desire, we are forced to give an answer to that great question of what to *do* with the radical freedom that material sufficiency provides – a freedom which I believe is on offer to us today. But rather than facing this ultimate human question, many people today seem to have climbed or fallen upon a consumerist treadmill, and become enslaved, consciously or unconsciously, to a lifestyle in which too much consumption is never enough. There is no end to consumer cravings, for as soon as one is satisfied, two pop up. The goal in life does not seem to be material sufficiency, but material excess. In such cases, it seems to me, a life of freedom does not often arise. That so few recognize this is my greatest temptation to despair.

Despite the fact that western society is several times richer than it was in the 50s, at the beginning of the 21st century we are confronted by what Clive Hamilton (a contributor to this anthology) has called an 'awful fact.' Despite the unprecedented levels of material wealth, there is a growing body of social science which indicates that people today are no more satisfied with their lives than people were in the 50s and 60s.[2] In other words, it seems that increases in personal and social wealth have stopped increasing our wellbeing. *Getting richer is no longer making us any happier.* It is troubling, therefore, to see that our whole society is geared towards *maximizing wealth.* As Henry David Thoreau would say, 'We labor under a mistake.'

Is it possible that we have reached a stage in our economic development where the process of getting richer is now causing the very problems that we seem to think getting richer will solve? As one of Thoreau's disciples, I wish to suggest that we have. I wish to suggest that, however suitable the pursuit of more wealth and higher standards of living were in the past, today that pursuit has become not just wasteful but dangerously counter-productive – fetishistic, even. Consumer culture, which everyday is being globalized further, has failed and is still failing to fulfill its promise of a better life. It has even begun taking away many of things upon which our wellbeing depends, such as community life, a work/life balance, spiritual and aesthetic experience, and a healthy natural environment. We can no longer just fall in line, then, and continue the march 'business as usual.' We must explore alternative ways to live. We must experiment creatively, like the artist. *We must be the poets of our own lives and of a new generation.*

That is the invitation/incitation embodied in this book.

A Preliminary Definition

Voluntary simplicity is a post-consumerist living strategy that *rejects* the materialistic lifestyle of consumer culture and *affirms* what is often just called 'the simple life,' or 'downshifting.' The rejection of consumerism arises from the recognition that ordinary western consumption habits are destroying the planet; that lives of high consumption are unethical in a world of great human need; and that the meaning of life does not and cannot consist in the consumption or accumulation of material things. Extravagance and acquisitiveness are thus considered a despairing waste of life, not so much sad as foolish, and certainly not deserving of the social status and admiration they seem to attract today. The affirmation of simplicity arises from the recognition that very little is needed to live well – that abundance is a state of mind, not a quantity of consumer products, nor attainable through them.

Sometimes called 'the quiet revolution,' this approach to life involves providing for material needs as simply and directly as possible, minimizing expenditure on consumer goods and services, and directing progressively more time and energy towards pursuing non-materialistic sources of satisfaction and meaning. This generally means accepting a lower income and a lower level of consumption, in exchange for more time and freedom to pursue other life goals, such as community or social engagements, family time, artistic or intellectual projects, more fulfilling employment, political participation, sustainable living, spiritual exploration, reading, conversation, contemplation, relaxation, pleasure-seeking, love, and so on – none of which need to rely on money. The grounding assumption of voluntary simplicity is that human beings are inherently capable of living meaningful, free, happy, and infinitely diverse lives, while consuming no more than an equitable share of nature. Ancient but ever-new, the message is that those who know they have enough are rich.

According to this view, personal and social progress is measured not by the conspicuous display of wealth or status, but by increases in the qualitative richness of daily living, the cultivation of relationships, and the development of social, intellectual, aesthetic, and spiritual potentials. As Duane Elgin (a contributor to this anthology) has famously defined it, voluntary simplicity is 'a manner of living that is outwardly simple and inwardly rich, ... a deliberate choice to live with less in the belief that more life will be returned to us in the process.'[3]

Voluntary simplicity does *not*, however, mean living in poverty, becoming an ascetic monk, or indiscriminately renouncing all the advantages of science and technology. It does not involve regressing to a primitive state or becoming a self-righteous puritan. And it is not some escapist fad reserved for saints, hippies, or eccentric outsiders. Rather, by examining afresh our relationship with money, material possessions, the planet, ourselves and each other, 'the simple life' of voluntary simplicity is about discovering the freedom and contentment that comes with knowing how much consumption is truly 'enough.' And this might be a theme that has something to say to everyone, especially those of us who are everyday bombarded with thousands of cultural and institutional messages insisting that 'more is always better.' Voluntary simplicity is an art of living that is aglow with the insight that 'just enough is plenty.'

The spirit of late capitalist society, however, cries out like a banshee for us to expend our lives pursuing middleclass luxuries and colored paper, for us to become faceless bodies dedicated to no higher purpose than the acquisition of nice things. We can embrace that comfortable unfreedom if we wish, that bourgeois compromise. But it is not the only way to live.

Voluntary simplicity presents an alternative.

What Voluntary Simplicity Is Not

So as not to be misunderstood, I now wish to clarify and elaborate on a few points that I have just made, by distinguishing voluntary simplicity from what it is *not.*

Voluntary simplicity is not a glorification of poverty. Nor does it deny that a small percentage of people in western society, and a large percentage around the rest of the world, still live lives oppressed by material deprivation. Far from glorifying or ignoring poverty, voluntary simplicity is about the importance of understanding and attaining material *sufficiency*, a concept that is all but unthinkable in a culture that generally assumes that 'more is always better.' My point is that living simply involves having an honest answer to the question of 'How much consumption is enough?', and then honestly attaining that much, and not bothering with superfluities. And the Voluntary Simplicity Movement is demonstrating, through the lives of millions of participants, that surprisingly little is needed to live well and to be free, if only life is approached with the right attitude.

Just as voluntary simplicity does not mean living in poverty, nor does it imply that people must leave the city to live to the country or join a hippie commune. Although some may decide that, for example, the life of an independent, self-sufficient rural farmer is a very good and natural way to live, it will not be for everybody; nor will joining a hippie commune. Indeed, learning how to live more sustainably in an urban setting strikes me as one of the greatest challenges of our age, especially since our political and economic institutions and our social infrastructure make urban simple living, especially, much more difficult than it needs to be, a point which I will touch on again later. For now, suffice it to say that voluntary simplicity is not synonymous with the 'back to the land movement' or the countercultures that arose in the 60s and 70s. I should note, however, that these movements do share some common ideals with voluntary simplicity, such as anti-consumerism, a reverence for nature, and non-violent resistance to unjust features of our society.

Voluntary simplicity, furthermore, does not mean indiscriminately renouncing all the advantages of science and technology. It does not mean living in a cave, giving up electricity, or rejecting modern medicine. But it does question the assumption that science and technology are the only paths to health, happiness, and freedom. To live simply, as I am using the phrase, is to at least put one's mind to the question of whether some new technology or scientific discovery actually improves our lives, or whether, on the contrary, it ultimately costs us more than it comes to, in terms of 'life.' Furthermore, the simple liver might come to see that there is a certain elegance and sophistication to the clothesline or the bicycle that the washing machine and the automobile decidedly lack. The simple liver will not build a ten billion dollar, hi-tech, desalination plant. The simple liver will install a water tank and think up ways to use less water. Rather than using central heating, the simple liver will be inclined to put on a sweater. And so on and so forth. Soon enough a new form of life emerges.

Why Simplify?

Now that I have offered a preliminary definition of voluntary simplicity, I wish to say a few words on why, exactly, we might want to adopt voluntary simplicity, why we might want to step out of the rush and begin shaping a simple life of our own.

I have divided my discussion of this question into four overlapping sections – personal, social, environmental, and spiritual.

Personal

Consumer culture can distract us from what is best in our lives, and it functions to keep many locked in a work-and-spend cycle that has no end and attains no lasting satisfaction. But if we rethink our relationship with money and possessions, we may be able to free up more time and energy for the pursuit of what truly inspires us and makes us happy, whatever that may be. In this way voluntary simplicity can be seen to enhance the meaning of our lives.

I begin with this point not because it is the most important, necessarily, but because I believe that if the Voluntary Simplicity Movement is to expand, it must be shown that simple living does not generate deprivations, but actually frees people from an insidiously addictive consumerism and an unhealthy relationship with money and 'stuff.'

Rather than dedicating one's life to the pursuit of riches or status, simple livers are more likely to have a balanced working life or even work part-time, and are more likely to seek fulfilling employment and accept a modest income, rather than get too hung up about a high salary. With less time devoted to acquiring expensive things, simple livers will have more time to spend with friends and family, and more time to spend pursuing their private passions or enjoying their civic responsibilities. The point is that disciplined and enlightened moderation with respect to our material lives will not tend to give rise to any sense of deprivation, but will ultimately lead to a happiness, a satisfaction, and a freedom far greater than that which is ordinarily known in the hectic, dead-end lifestyles of consumer culture. In short, many are drawn to simplicity because they want to escape the rat race and live more with less.

Social

Although there are indeed many personal incentives for adopting voluntary simplicity, it would be an impoverished philosophy that sought to justify itself only in relation to personal self-interest. For that reason, it is important to recognize that there are also many *social* and *humanitarian* reasons for adopting voluntary simplicity. Living simply can be a powerful lifestyle response to social injustices, and many people are drawn to simplicity because it can be understood to be an act of sharing, an act of human solidarity. It can therefore foster a heightened sense of human community, both locally and globally.

One obvious way to share with others is simply to take less, to try to take only what one needs for a dignified life, and no more. This may not be easy, but it could be said that before the problem of global poverty can ever be solved, those in the consuming middleclass will need to show some enlightened, compassionate restraint in relation to their material lives, and accept that in a world of great human need the wasteful consumption of material things is an unambiguous act of violence.

The global population is expected to approach ten billion by the end of this century, and trends indicate that most of these extra souls will find themselves born into the Third World. This, among other factors, has lead the United Nations to publish several urgent and strongly worded warnings to the effect that if First World attitudes to consumption persist, then future generations not so far away should expect humanitarian crises beyond what we have ever experienced.[4]

Fortunately, at least part of the solution is at hand. As Mahatma Gandhi once said, 'Live simply so that others may simply live.'

Environmental

As well as personal and social reasons for simplifying, there are, of course, also *environmental* reasons. It is becoming increasingly obvious to more and more people that simpler living, in some form or another, is needed to save our planet from real ecological disaster, and that lifestyles of reduced consumption will be a necessary part of any sustainable future for human civilization. We know this very well, I suspect, both in our heads and in our hearts, so I need not review the details of the environmental predicament which is beginning to define our age. Let me just assert, then, that simple living is one very promising way – if not *the* most promising way – to personally confront global environmental problems such as climate change, pollution, and the overconsumption of non-renewable resources. And given what is at stake here – the health of the life-support system we call Earth – perhaps this should be justification enough for everyone.

Spiritual

Finally, for immediate purposes, there are what could be called *spiritual* reasons for living simply. I acknowledge that I am now touching on a very private matter – 'private,' not because spiritual exploration must be done alone, but because nobody can do it for us. By shifting attention from the material to the non-material side of life, voluntary simplicity can facilitate a deeper awareness of the spiritual dimension of being. I will not now argue this point, however, since it is one that I suspect can only be experienced, not explained; at least, not explained by me. I will only say this: That if we take time to isolate ourselves from consumer culture for long enough to unlearn it, for long enough to rouse ourselves from the daze of unexamined habit and reopen the doors of perception, we just might provoke a surprisingly fresh interpretation of the form of life behind, as well as provoke a new appreciation of the possibilities of an alternative mode of being. In other words, when we let ourselves be enchanted by ordinary experience, it quickly becomes clear that 'a simple life' is a profoundly beautiful life, one that is exciting and worth living. For simplicity is nothing if it is not an affirmative state of mind, an authentic celebration of life, and it is a state of mind that often seems to reflect a mystical interpretation of life and a deep reverence for nature, even if one does not subscribe to any traditional religion nor any crude pantheism.

Earlier generations confronted spiritual questions face to face, we through their eyes. But why, as Emerson would insist, should we not also enjoy an original relation to the universe?

The Practice Of Simplicity

Having now defined voluntary simplicity and offered a few words on why we might embrace it as a living strategy, it is important, I think, to say at least a few words about the *practice* of simplicity, about 'how' exactly one might go about simplifying one's life, and 'how' one might try to *live the idea*, if one were convinced that this way of life was desirable.

I will, however, be very brief on this aspect of simplicity, not because it isn't important. Obviously, it is very important. But the fact is that there is no Doctrine or Code of Simplicity to follow, as such. There is no Method or Equation of Simplicity into which we can plug the facts of our lives and be told how to live. That is precisely what the idea cannot do – but perhaps that suits your disposition as well as it does mine.

Voluntary simplicity, as I have said, is more about questions than answers, which implies that practicing simplicity calls for creative interpretation and personalized application. It is not for me, therefore, or for anyone, to prescribe universal rules on how to live simply. We each live unique lives, and we each find ourselves in different situations, with different capabilities, and different responsibilities. Accordingly, the practice of simplicity by one person, in one situation, will very likely involve different things to a different person, in a different situation. But, as I have implied, I do not think that this practical indeterminacy is an objection to the idea.

With that proviso noted, allow me say a few general and very brief words on what a simple life might look like and how one might begin to live it.

Money

Although living simply is much more than just living cheaply and consuming less, spending wisely plays an important role. The following exercise may surprise you: Over a one month period, record *every* purchase you make, and then categorize your expenses. Multiply each category by twelve to get a rough estimate of the annual cost. Then consider how much of your time and energy you spent obtaining the money required to buy everything you consumed that month. Question not only the *amount* of money you spent on each category, but also the *categories* on which you spent your money. You might find that seemingly little purchases add up to an inordinate amount over a whole year, suggesting that the money might be better spent elsewhere, not at all, or exchanged for more time by working less. One does not have to be a tightwad, as such, only thoughtful. 'The cost of a thing,' after all, 'is the amount of life which is required to be exchanged for it.'[5] You may find that some small changes to your spending habits, rather than inducing any sense of deprivation, will instead be life-affirming.[6]

And when it comes to spending our money we should always bear in mind Vicki Robin's profound democratic insight: That how we spend our money is how we vote on what exists in the world. If this is true, then the global middleclass has the potential to become a non-violent revolutionary class and change the world, simply by changing its spending habits. Money is power, and with this power comes responsibility.

I repeat: How we spend our money is how we vote on what exists in the world.

Shelter

Housing or accommodation is typically life's greatest expense, so we should think especially carefully about where we live and why, and how much of our lives we are prepared to spend seeking a nicer home. Exactly what kind of shelter does one need to live well and to be free? Obviously, we must answer this question for ourselves, but again the words of Henry David Thoreau might give us a moment's pause: 'Most people appear never to have considered what a house is, and are actually though needlessly poor all their lives because they think that they must have such a one as their neighbors have.'[7] The individual or family who today is admired for a large and luxurious house might find that our culture comes to admire those who have learned how to combine functional simplicity and beauty in a smaller, much more modest, home.[8]

Clothing

The historic purpose of clothing, of course, was to keep us warm and, in time, for reasons of modesty. Today its primary purpose seems to be fashion and the conspicuous display of wealth and status. People can, of course, spend thousands and thousands of dollars on clothing if they want, in search of themselves. But we should never forget that functional, second-hand clothing can be obtained extremely cheaply. And those who 'dress down' often express themselves more uniquely than those who are limited to the styles found in shopping malls or who try to imitate celebrities. Many hundreds of billions of dollars are spent each and every year on the fashion industry. Just imagine if even half of that money was redirected towards green energy or humanitarian initiatives? We would lose so little and gain so much.

Once again, how we spend our money is how we vote on what exists in the world.

Food

Eating locally, eating green, eating out in moderation, eating less meat, eating simply and creatively – I know by experience this can be done very cheaply. Given some thought and a little discipline, a good diet can be obtained at a surprisingly low cost, especially if you are able to cultivate your own garden, which is a very natural and strangely satisfying thing to do.

Work

I have just outlined, with a very broad brush, a voluntarily simplistic perspective on acquiring the most basic necessities of life – shelter, clothing, and food. Once upon a time these necessities could be obtained by hunting and gathering in the commons, but in our day and age, of course, they must be obtained through economic transactions in the marketplace, usually through the medium of money, which we must work to acquire. It is important to consider, therefore, however briefly, the question of employment.

When it comes to work, we would do well, I believe, to more carefully put our minds to the question of what our time is worth. For once we have obtained the necessities of life, and have acquired a few comforts appropriate for a dignified life, there is another alternative than to spend our lives working to obtain material superfluities. And that is to pass up those superfluities and instead 'adventure on life now,' as Thoreau would say, 'our vacation from humbler toil having commenced.' From the perspective of voluntary simplicity, this exchange of money for time will often prove to be a very good trade.

If we keep raising our standard of living every time we come into more money, through a raise, for example; or if we keep raising our standard of living every time we become more productive, through some new technological development, for example; then we will never shorten our working week. Most westerners, especially North Americans, are working longer hours today than they were in the 50s,[9] despite being many times richer and many times more productive. Why should we always be working for more consumer products and not sometimes be content with less? Why should we not accept a lower standard of living and work half as much? Who can say what wonders such a cultural style might not bring! The immediate point is simply that if we can embrace the simple life and stop the upward creep of material desire, then we can take some of our pay increases or increases in productivity, not in terms of dollars and things, but in 'freedom' instead. Again, this seems like it would be a very good trade – a no-brainer, even. But history suggests that most westerners will choose otherwise. The ruts of conformity run deep.

A Thumbnail Sketch

A comprehensive guide to simple living would obviously require much more space than is available here, so let me just round off this part of my discussion by summarizing what simple living *tends* to involve. It tends to involve thoughtful thrift and environmentally and socially conscientious spending habits. It can involve recognizing that there is no good reason for desperately trying to 'keep up with the Joneses,' since modest accommodation and few possessions are perfectly sufficient to live a free and happy life. Simple living can involve buying secondhand clothing and furniture, creating one's own style, and rejecting high fashion. It might involve cultivating a garden, eating simply, locally, and creatively, and discovering that doing so can be both cheap and satisfying. And it might involve riding a bike instead of driving a car, choosing a washing line over a dryer, or even something as simple as choosing a book over television. Rather than stay at a luxurious resort, the simple liver might spend $12 a night bush camping in midst of nature. Rather than work long hours to afford a life dedicated to consumption, the simple liver might step out of the rush and reduce working hours, freeing up more time to be creative, play a musical instrument, meditate, spend with friends / family, laugh etc. Rather than choose competition, the simple liver is likely to choose community. Not money, but meaning. And so on and so forth, until the elements of life have been transformed.

Despite these tentative remarks on how to practice simplicity, I wish to reiterate that there is not *one way* to live the simple life, and that anyone who wishes to embrace simplicity must be prepared to think over the idea for oneself, until it takes root in personal experience. I am convinced, however, both by faith and by experience, that if someone is genuinely committed to the idea of simplicity then that person, with a little courage and some imaginative effort, will find a way to shape a simple life of their own. Start with a few small steps, enjoy the adventure, and soon enough your life has changed.

The Call Of Simplicity

From what I have said so far, it should be clear that voluntary simplicity embodies a way of life that is very different from the high consumption, materialistic lifestyle that is widely celebrated in advanced capitalist society today. And it should be of concern to all those who are sympathetic to voluntary simplicity that this way of life is given very little serious attention by politicians and the mass media, two of the most powerful forces in our society. Our politicians and the mass media seem not just indifferent but fundamentally opposed to the idea of voluntary simplicity, despite the occasional lip-service that is paid to the social and environmental problems caused by overconsumption. It is little surprise, then, that to date the Voluntary Simplicity Movement has not entered the mainstream, although perhaps some light is beginning to break through the crust of convention, albeit with much difficulty.

The mass media, in particular, has very little interest in promoting voluntary simplicity, since it is, by in large, made up of privately owned corporations, each of which is driven almost exclusively by the incentive of private profits. Corporate shareholders, by definition, it seems, want us only to consume more and more – never less. Indeed, many of the world's most sophisticated psychologists are today hired by corporations as 'marketers,' and I do not think it misrepresents the situation to say that these marketers spend all day thinking up ways to make us – potential consumers – feel dissatisfied with what we have, despite our plenty, in order to get us buy things we didn't even know we wanted and certainly didn't need. The message they convey in their slick, ever-present advertisements is that more money, more material things, more consumption, is what is needed to improve our lives. And we are easily persuaded.

Disappointingly, we can perceive the very same message in the rhetoric of our so-called 'political representatives.' In the newspapers everyday, on the television news every night, and throughout every political campaign I have ever experienced, political parties seem to assume that it is their overriding objective to maximize economic growth. Almost every political party, whether on the Left or the Right, claims that they will run the economy 'best,' by which it is implied that they will increase our standard of living, make us all richer, and make us better able to buy more things – as if that were the solution to all our problems.

This is a point that has been picked up on and criticized heavily by Clive Hamilton, who I mentioned earlier. To oversimplify slightly, he sums up contemporary public policy as follows: Unemployment is high: only economic growth can create the jobs; schools and hospitals are under-funded: economic growth will improve the budget; protection of the environment is too expensive: the solution is economic growth; poverty is entrenched: economic growth will rescue the poor; income distribution is unequal: economic growth will make everyone better off.[10] Just as with the mass media, the point is that our politicians are telling us that more money and more consumer products are the key to a better life.

Voluntary simplicity rejects this approach. To repeat a phrase mentioned earlier, in stark contrast to the idea that 'more is always better,' voluntary simplicity is an art of living that is aglow with the insight that 'just enough is plenty.' But, whether we like it or not, most of us today have been educated into a materialistic culture that assumes the legitimacy of ever-higher levels of consumption. Even though we are now aware that ordinary western consumption habits are destroying the planet, we think that it is normal and acceptable for the mass media and our politicians to dedicate themselves to encouraging and facilitating ever higher levels of consumption. So embedded are we in consumer culture that these perversities seem natural and inevitable; facts of life; just the way the world is. An alternative is almost unthinkable and largely unspeakable.

When a whole society is geared towards producing and then consuming ever-more consumer products, it can be very difficult for people to live and think differently, even for those of us who want to. As I see it, there is no easy, silver-bullet, solution to this problem. But one step that can be taken is to dedicate more of our attention to exploring alternatives, and that was one motivation I had for publishing this book. Obviously, just *reading* and *talking* about voluntary simplicity is not enough to change our lives and our society, but I am convinced that it is an important and perhaps necessary first step. In a world such as ours, focused so intently on making money, it is important that we occasionally take time to step back and ask ourselves, 'What is money is *for*?" and "What is our economy *for*?" For when we ask ourselves these questions, it quickly becomes apparent that the meaning of life does not and cannot consist in the consumption and accumulation of material things. There is more to life than desiring big houses, new carpet, fine clothing, expensive cars, and luxurious holidays, etc. There is freedom from such desires.

What I am suggesting, and what is discussed in this book, is that 'the simple life' is a viable alternative to consumer culture, one that will improve not only our own lives, but the lives of others, and, at the same time, help save the planet from the environmental catastrophe towards which we are so enthusiastically marching. By reading and talking about voluntary simplicity, I believe we can revolutionize – a term I do not use lightly – the form of life we have inherited from the past. By giving more attention to alternatives to consumer culture, we will discover that there are other, better, more fulfilling ways to live. By acting upon this realization, we can reshape our own lives, improve our culture, and upset the ruts of conformity. We can better face the social and environmental challenges which confront us today, and which will undoubtedly confront us for all of the foreseeable future. What we can be sure of is that the 21st century will be defined, to a large extent, by how we today deal with the problems caused by overconsumption – not only how we deal with them politically and economically, but perhaps most importantly how we deal with them through the everyday decisions we make in our private lives.

And it is for this reason that the idea of voluntary simplicity gives me such hope, because it shows (although perhaps this is obvious) that the power to change the world ultimately lies in the hands of ordinary people. It is a reminder that, in the end, the nature of a society is the product of nothing more or less than the countless number of small decisions made by private individuals.

The corollary of this is that those small decisions, those small acts of simplification – insignificant though they may seem in isolation – can be of revolutionary significance when added up and taken as a whole. And that, I wish to emphasize, is one of the central messages I would like to convey: *That if we are concerned about the direction our society is heading, and if we seek a different way of life, then we must first look to our own lives, and begin making changes there, and not be disheartened by the fact that our social, economic, and political institutions embody outdated materialistic values that we ourselves reject.*

As Gandhi once said, in a phrase that captures the revolutionary spirit of voluntary simplicity: 'Be the change you wish to see in the world.' This inspiring call to personal action complements the call of another great simple liver, Henry David Thoreau, who never tired of reminding us that, 'The individual who goes it alone can start today.' The point, as I understand it, is that there is no reason, nor is there any time, to wait for politicians to deal with the problems that we face. For what the world needs more than anything else is for brave visionaries to quietly step out of the rat race and show, by example, both to themselves and to others, that a different way of life is both possible and desirable.

Let us, then, be pioneers once more.

Chapter Overviews

The contributors to this anthology – all leading figures in the Voluntary Simplicity Movement – are highly distinguished scholars, activists, educators, and artists. Brought together so comprehensively for the first time, the result is a collection of the very best writing on one of today's most important but neglected ideas. The great advantage of an 'anthology' is that by bringing together diverse minds and mixing perspectives and styles, the reader is exposed to a richness, depth, and variety of analysis that makes for a perfect introduction for the student of simplicity, and, at the same time, results in a valuable resource for those who have already studied the literature. That, at least, was my goal in publishing this deliberately long book.

In order to give the reader some insight into how this anthology unfolds and the central themes it addresses, below I have provided short summaries of each chapter. The book will then be left to speak for itself.

1. Voluntary Simplicity: The 'Middle Way' to Sustainability

Mark A. Burch

Since this anthology is intended to be accessible to the reader who is unfamiliar with voluntary simplicity, it made sense to open with a close analysis of what the term means. Accordingly, in Chapter One, Mark A. Burch provides an extended definitional statement of voluntary simplicity and discusses the core ideals and values underpinning it. Addressing issues such as material sufficiency, anti-consumerism, minimalism, self-reliance, and environmental sustainability, Burch shows how 'simple living' is both a humble, personal endeavor, and at the same time a socially, economically, and politically radical form of life. I know of no better introduction to the subject.

2. A New Social Movement?

Amatai Etzioni

In Chapter Two, Amatai Etzioni examines the Voluntary Simplicity Movement with regard to its sociological significance as a possible counterbalance to mainstream capitalist society. Etzioni acknowledges that whether the movement expands will depend a great deal upon whether it is perceived as generating deprivations, or whether it is found to liberate people from an obsessive and possibly addictive consumerism. After critically reviewing a large body of social science, Etzioni is lead to the conclusion that, not far beyond the poverty line, there is only a very weak correlation between having more money and increased wellbeing. In other words, it seems that once human beings have their basic needs securely met, and have acquired a modicum of comforts appropriate for a dignified life, further increases in wealth have a fast diminishing and at times even negative impact on human wellbeing. The far-reaching implications of these mutually reinforcing studies cannot be brushed aside: if increases in income beyond a modest level tend to stop increasing wellbeing, then the pursuit of ever-more wealth quickly begins to look not just wasteful but counter-productive – fetishistic, even. A profound intellectual challenge to the ideology of consumer capitalism, this astute sociological analysis establishes the Voluntary Simplicity Movement as a promising counter-cultural force.

3. Two Ways of Thinking About Money

Jerome Segal

With the preliminary definitions and sociological groundwork complete, in this chapter Jerome Segal takes a closer look at the philosophy and history of voluntary simplicity. 'In Western thought,' observes Segal, 'from the very beginning to the present day, people had doubts about the real value of riches and the things money can buy. There has always been a conflict between the view that "more is better" and the view that "just enough is plenty."' Segal shows that this divide is reflected in two ways of thinking about money, and in two very different visions of the good life. By offering a contemporary interpretation of Aristotle, Segal presents a compelling case for why the vision resting upon the attainment of a simple life is the sounder vision. 'Simple living,' he concludes, 'is not the residue that emerges when one consumes less; it is an achievement. It is what can emerge when as a result of subjecting the material dimension to a larger vision, one succeeds in creating a life that is rich and exciting in its aesthetic, intellectual, spiritual, and social dimensions.'

4. What is Affluenza?

Clive Hamilton and Richard Denniss

Throughout this anthology voluntary simplicity is presented as an 'alternative' to the materialistic form of life widely celebrated within consumer culture. In Chapter Four, Clive Hamilton and Richard Denniss sharpen our understanding of voluntary simplicity by taking a closer look at the form of life it is reacting against. Backed up by extensive sociological research, their provocative thesis is that western society is in the grip of a collective psychological disorder, which they call 'affluenza,' a disorder that deludes people into thinking that they are deprived despite their plenty.

5. The Conundrum of Consumption

Alan Durning

In Chapter Five, Alan Durning discusses what he calls the 'conundrum of consumption.' He points out that the American middleclass is the group that, more than any other, defines and embodies the contemporary international vision of 'the good life.' Yet, that consuming middleclass is among the world's premier environmental problems, and may be the most difficult to solve. Scientific advances, better laws, restructured industries, new treaties, environmental campaigns – all these can help us move closer to a sustainable society. But Durning's forthright conclusion is that, ultimately, what is required is that we change our values. Both sobering and inspiring, this chapter is a reminder that before we can change the world, we must change ourselves.

6. The Value of Voluntary Simplicity

Richard Gregg

Chapter Six is an abridged version of the pioneering 1936 essay by Richard Gregg, who coined the term 'voluntary simplicity.' A disciple of Gandhi's, this properly suggests that there is an intimate link between voluntary simplicity and non-violent resistance. Gregg's essay is especially valuable in that he anticipates many of the *objections* that can be raised against voluntary simplicity, before methodically responding to them in a balanced manner. Always insightful, Gregg approaches voluntary simplicity from various perspectives, including economics, politics, religion, psychology, and aesthetics.

7. Less is More

Philip Cafaro

Voluntary simplicity is built upon the paradox that 'less is more.' In Chapter Seven, Philip Cafaro unravels this paradox and in doing so he undermines the consumerist view that 'more is always better.' Shifting between (and often merging) economic and environmentalist perspectives, Cafaro argues that we should judge consumption by whether it improves or detracts from our lives, and act on that basis, rather than just assume that more consumption is what is needed to improve our lives. With our enlightened self-interest in mind, Cafaro shows that less is often more, particularly for middle and upper class members of wealthy industrialized societies. If all this chapter does is open up the question of whether less is more – if all it does is remind the reader that this is a question, and that our answers to it have important repercussions – then it will have served its purpose.

8. Building the Case for Global Living

Jim Merkel

Jim Merkel begins Chapter Eight with a striking thought experiment. He asks us to imagine we are first in line at a potluck buffet that includes not just food and water, but also the materials needed for shelter, clothing, health-care and education. Six billion people, shoulder to shoulder, form a line with plates in hand, and behind them, the untold millions of other species that in habit the Earth. Further behind still, are the soon-to-be-born children, cubs, larvae, etc. How do we know how much to take? How much would be fair? One answer is that we could just take what seems *normal* to have, but then how much will be left for those who must come after us, those at the end of the line? These are the difficult issues of 'global living' that Merkel tackles in this chapter – not to induce guilt or place blame, but only to share with us his hope for a world in which all life forms, of all generations, have 'enough' to live a simple, dignified life of material sufficiency. Merkel shows that such a world is achievable, but that it will require some restraint by those in the consuming middleclass.

9. Voluntary Simplicity

Duane Elgin and Arnold Mitchell

Chapter Nine is an abridged version of the much celebrated essay, 'Voluntary Simplicity,' by Duane Elgin and Arnold Mitchell. In this essay the authors discuss five prominent features of voluntary simplicity: (1) Material simplicity; (2) Human scale; (3) Self-determination; (4) Ecological awareness; and (5) Personal growth. According to Elgin and Mitchell, our era of relative abundance contrasts sharply with the material poverty of the past, meaning that for the first time in history large numbers of ordinary people can live lives of material sufficiency. On that basis, they think that voluntary simplicity may prove an increasingly powerful economic, social, and political force over coming decades and beyond if large numbers of people of diverse backgrounds come to see it as a workable and purposeful response to many of the critical problems that we face. In living a life that is outwardly simple and inwardly rich, they argue that *the needs of the individual uniquely match the needs of society*. Of what other emergent life patterns can this be said?

10. Thoreau's Alternative Economics

Philip Cafaro

'When we have obtained those things necessary to life,' wrote Henry David Thoreau, 'there is another alternative than to obtain superfluities; and that is to adventure on life now, our vacation from humbler toil having commenced.' In Chapter Ten, Philip Cafaro considers this alternative living strategy of Thoreau's and contrasts it with the living strategy normally employed within advanced capitalist society. What is the best way to earn a living? How much time should we spend at it? How much food and what kind of shelter is necessary to live, or to live well? Through a close reading of Thoreau's *Walden* (see chapter twenty), Cafaro shows that the real importance of our economic lives lies not in how much wealth they create, but what sorts of people they make us, and how they relate us to others.

11. Why Simplify?

Mark A. Burch

Why would anyone want to adopt voluntary simplicity? In Chapter Eleven, Mark A. Burch offers a four-fold answer to this question, aspects of which were summarized earlier. I will not repeat that earlier discussion, which Burch expands upon insightfully and at some length, but only reiterate that there are various personal, social, environmental, and spiritual reasons for embracing the simple life, many of which are mutually reinforcing.

12. Sharing the Earth

Jim Merkel

Environmental sustainability can be broadly defined as follows: *each generation should meet its needs without jeopardizing the prospects of future generations to meet their needs.* There is now an overwhelming consensus among scientists that 'ordinary' western consumption habits are *not* sustainable, and certainly not universalizable. Accordingly, it is time to seriously reconsider the 'ethics of consumption' and reevaluate inherited cultural understandings of 'the good life.' Environmental issues and questions of distributive justice have been discussed already at various places in this anthology, but in this chapter they take center stage, with Jim Merkel tackling urgent ethical questions about how humanity ought to share the Earth. With characteristic eloquence and humility, Merkel considers the consumption and distribution of natural resources from the three perspectives of interspecies equity, interhuman equity, and intergenerational equity.

13. The Downshifters

Clive Hamilton and Richard Denniss

In Chapter Thirteen, Hamilton and Denniss review their research into the class of people they call 'Downshifters' – people exploring the simple life who have made a conscious decision to accept a lower income and a lower level of consumption, in order to pursue other life goals. Who are these people? What are their stories? How many of them are there? And why do they live as they do? These are some of the questions surveyed in this fascinating enquiry into an emerging post-consumerist subculture.

14. A Culture of Permanence

Alan Durning

From this chapter onward, the anthology takes a deliberate turn towards the political, which is meant to acknowledge the limitations of personal action alone. Our choices, notes Alan Durning, are constrained by the social pressures, physical infrastructure, and institutional channels that envelop us. Thus, a strategy for reducing consumption must focus as much on changing the framework in which we make choices as it does on the choices we make. To rejuvenate the ethic of sufficiency, a critical mass of individuals committed to living by it must emerge. But Durning argues that if we are to succeed, we must balance our efforts to change ourselves with a bold agenda to challenge the laws, institutions, and interests that promote unsustainable consumption.

15. Simplicity, Community, and Private Land

Eric T. Freyfogle

Simple living involves the quest for calm, balanced lives, with less clutter, less artificiality, and lessened impact on nature. It involves the elevation of quality over quantity, time over money, and community over competition. What does all this mean, though, at the community or landscape level, particularly with respect to the ways we dwell upon the land? How might simple living affect our patterns of living on land, individually and collectively? And what would this mean in terms of private property rights, the functions of government, and the ways we think about democracy and self-rule? In Chapter Fifteen, Eric Freyfogle delves into these important questions, making particularly astute observations about the nature of private property: that it is a human creation which can take any number of forms, that we must define it collectively, that it can and should evolve as society changes. His point is that 'free market' capitalism as we know it is *not* the only alternative to communism. Freyfogle argues that for a society of simple livers to emerge, people as individuals need to take stock of who they are and how they live, and imagine better ways. Many steps, he notes, can be taken in daily life to shift toward greater simplicity, and they should be taken. But Freyfogle concludes that ultimately some form of collective action will also be needed to change the governing structures within which we act out our daily lives.

16. The New Politics of Consumption

Juliet Schor

However much we might want to live simply, it is a fact that western society (and increasingly global society) is structurally opposed to voluntary simplicity. That is, our political and economic institutions make living simply much more difficult than it needs to be, as was outlined in the previous two chapters. This has lead simplicity theorist, Juliet Schor, to call for a 'politics of consumption.' In Chapter Sixteen, Schor sketches an outline of a 'politics of consumption' by considering what institutional reforms could facilitate the emergence of a society of simple livers. Importantly, she also exposes ways that the conceptual framework usually used to think about consumption is defective – how it blinds us to possibilities and poses the wrong questions. By fixing those defects, Schor opens up a whole new set of problems, but she also points to a new and hopeful set of solutions.

17. Political Prescriptions

John de Graaf

John de Graaf does not believe that the world's social and environmental problems associated with overconsumption can be cured by personal action alone. Like Durning, Freyfogle, Schor, and many others, he is convinced that political action will be a necessary part of any adequate solution. In Chapter Seventeen, de Graaf discusses what political action he believes is required to move our society in a better direction, including reducing working hours, restructuring tax and earning systems, investing in sustainable infrastructure, redirecting state subsidies, protecting children from advertising, and developing new ideas about economic growth. Anticipating that many will look upon his proposals with skepticism, he everywhere cites examples of where European nations have *already* implemented them – and implemented them successfully. So it seems the choice is ours, if only we choose it, a point which suggests that the relationship between 'the personal' and 'the political' is so close as to be one of identity.

18. Extending the Movement

Mary Grigsby

When considered from the mutually reinforcing perspectives of personal happiness, the environment, distributive justice, spiritual awakening, opposing global capitalism, fostering human solidarity, etc., the Voluntary Simplicity Movement, though still in its infancy, is arguably the most promising social movement on the planet today. Many of the problems facing humankind seem *connected*, and voluntary simplicity offers a compelling and graceful solution to many of them. The movement, as I have noted, is sometimes described as 'the quiet revolution,' and this may indeed indicate its potential. But the problem is that currently, with the environmental clock ticking and the Third World expanding, it may be *too* quiet. In other words, if the Voluntary Simplicity Movement remains a small, unorganized, 'subculture,' it will probably fail to have enough impact on the course of history to do much good. In Chapter Eighteen Mary Grigsby considers this problem and discusses whether or in what ways the Voluntary Simplicity Movement could extend into the mainstream and become a more significant oppositional force.

19. Transcendental Simplicity

David Shi

In Chapter Nineteen, which lays the foundation for the final chapter, celebrated historian David Shi returns to 19th century America to examine the fascinating version of 'the simple life' articulated by the New England Transcendentalists, that colorful group of inspired poets, mystics, and philosophers centered in Concord. According to this group, plain living was designed to lead to high thinking of one sort or another – intellectual, moral, spiritual. William Henry Channing succinctly expressed their credo: 'To live content with small means; to seek elegance rather than luxury, and refinement rather than fashion; to be worthy, not respectable, and wealthy, not rich; to study hard, think quietly, talk gently, act frankly.' This was the symphony of Transcendentalism – the ability to live within one's means in order to afford the luxury of contemplation and creativity. As Ralph Waldo Emerson was to assert, 'It is better to go without than to have possessions at too great a cost. Let us learn the meaning of Economy.'

20. 'Economy' (from *Walden)*

Henry David Thoreau

In 1845, at age 28, Henry David Thoreau left his town of Concord and went to live alone in the woods, on the shores of Walden Pond, a mile from any neighbor. He there built himself a modest cabin, and for two years and two months earned a simple living by the labor of his own hands. 'I went to the woods because I wished to live deliberately,' wrote Thoreau, 'to front only the essential facts of life, and see if I could not learn what they had to teach, and not, when I came to die, discover that I had not lived.' While at the pond he wrote *Walden*, a book that is widely regarded as the greatest statement ever made on the subject of voluntary simplicity. The final chapter of this anthology is the famous 'Economy' chapter from that extraordinary book. While it may be the most challenging chapter – which is one reason it is placed at the end of this anthology – if it is read as deliberately as it was written, it will also be the most rewarding. The language and ideas are masterfully dense, so even the best reader will profit from a second or third reading. Be warned, however, that Thoreau intends to do nothing less than change your life.

Conclusion: Meditations on Simplicity

Samuel Alexander

Dissatisfaction with our material situations may often be the result of failing to look properly at our lives, rather than the result of any 'lack.' For that reason, this anthology concludes with a 'study guide,' of sorts, comprising of thought experiments and discussion questions. These are intended to facilitate further introspection and provoke conversation about the central themes of this anthology, in the hope that this leads to a more direct and practical understanding of voluntary simplicity *in relation to one's own life.* There are also three appendices attached to the anthology, which were constructed in the same spirit. The first appendix, 'The Manifesto,' is a collection of quotations expressing, in various ways, the philosophy of voluntary simplicity. The second appendix, 'Peaceful Acts of Opposition,' is an attempt to reduce the philosophy of voluntary simplicity to a list of broad proposals for personal action. The third appendix, 'Declaration on Degrowth,' is a short statement on the politics of simplicity. I hope that these documents may be of some use, although I should point out that they are in need of creative interpretation.

Closing Remarks

As the globalization of western consumption habits pushes our planet towards the brink of environmental collapse, as evidence mounts that consumer culture has failed to fulfill its promise of a better life, and at a time when three billion of our fellow human beings still live in the darkness of poverty amidst plenty, one may be forgiven for thinking that there is a certain inescapable logic to pursuing a way of life that is 'outwardly simple, inwardly rich.' Yet, from earliest childhood onward, first upon somebody's knee, then through lessons ratified by polite society, we are educated into a materialistic form of life that squarely contradicts that of voluntary simplicity. What is more, it seems we are forbidden to admit this.

If it is true, however, as some existentialists have argued, that we can always make something new out of what we have been made into, then it might be interesting to inquire: Did you choose your mode of living because you preferred it to any other? Or did you honestly think that it was the only way? Reading and talking about voluntary simplicity with these questions in mind can be unsettling, rather like being shaken awake from the most dogmatic slumber. But it can also be exhilarating and uplifting, in the most unexpected ways. I hope that some readers will find, or have already found, that this is so.

Despite what seems to be a strong case for voluntary simplicity, one may nearly despair of the possibility that the entrenched economics of consumerism will ever lose its authority over western minds. But as Theodore Roszak has said:

> There is one way forward: the creation of flesh-and-blood examples of low-consumption, high-quality alternatives to the mainstream pattern of life. This we can see happening already on the counter cultural fringes. And nothing – no amount of argument or research – will take the place of such living proof. What people must see is that ecologically sane, socially responsible living is *good* living; that simplicity, thrift, and reciprocity make for an existence that is free.[11]

This anthology will have served its purpose if the reader goes away with an increased curiosity about this life-affirming freedom, and an appreciation that with a little courage and some imaginative effort, the door to voluntary simplicity will swing gracefully open.

Our world can change. Thoughtful, dedicated people like you and me can change it. And if not us, then who? If not now, then when? My closing words must be that if it is not us, then it will be nobody. And if not now, then never.

'Old deeds for old people, and new deeds for new.'[12]

(Endnotes)

1 Clive Hamilton, *Growth Fetish* (2003) xi. This paragraph draws on Hamilton's discussion.

2 Many of the chapters which follow draw on this social science when discussing the correlation between wealth and wellbeing. See Chapter Two, especially.

3 Duane Elgin, *Voluntary Simplicity: Toward a Way of Life that is Outwardly Simple, Inwardly Rich* (Revised edition, 1993).

4 See, for example, the United Nations Human Development Report 2007/8.

5 Henry David Thoreau, *Walden*, in Carl Bode (ed.) *The Portable Thoreau* (1982) 286.

6 For more elaborate financial exercises, see Vicki Robin and Joe Dominguez, *Your Money or Your Life: Transforming your relationship with money and achieving financial independence* (1992) and Jim Merkel, *Radical Simplicity: Small Footprints on a Finite Planet* (2003).

7 Henry David Thoreau, *Walden*, in Carl Bode (ed.) *The Portable Thoreau* (1982) 290.

8 Duane Elgin, *Voluntary Simplicity: Toward a Way of Life that is Outwardly Simple, Inwardly Rich* (Revised edition, 1993) 150–51.

9 This argument has been made most famously by Juliet Schor, in *The Overworked American: The Unexpected Decline of Leisure* (1992) and *The Overspent American: Upscaling, Downshifting, and the New Consumer* (1998), and by John de Graaf et al, in *Take Back Your Time: Fighting Overwork and Time Poverty in America* (2003).

10 Clive Hamilton, *Growth Fetish* (2003) 2.

11 Theodore Roszak, *Where the Wasteland Ends* (1972) 422 (emphasis in original).

12 Henry David Thoreau, *Walden*, in Carl Bode (ed.) *The Portable Thoreau* (1982) 264. Also, see www.simplicitycollective.com.

Chapter One

VOLUNTARY SIMPLICITY THE 'MIDDLE WAY' TO SUSTAINABILITY

Mark A. Burch

Fashioning a New Culture

In his book *Ishmael,*[1] Daniel Quinn suggests that every society is an enactment of a story the people of that society tell themselves about the nature and purpose of their existence and of the world they live in. Quinn believes that modern societies, with all their triumphs and abuses, enact a story that claims human beings are the crown jewel of evolution and that all the world's species and resources exist to satisfy human desires. By extension, the story of our 'consumer society' tells us that the purpose of human existence is to find meaning, pleasure, and identity through consumption. In this story, the world exists for the sole purpose of satisfying human desires for things to consume. Technology is our instrument for making available new things to consume and economics measures our success in doing so. We have embraced the story of consumption, but have forgotten that 'to consume' means to eat, use up, to waste or suffer destruction, and be obsessed by.

No doubt many people will protest that this assertion is too bold a generalization; that we cherish many non-material values; that our lives embrace more than just tripping back and forth to work and then shopping at the mall. As our churches, art galleries, public libraries, and parks fall into disrepair, as homeless people crowd our streets, as species disappear from our forests and the forests themselves dwindle, our protests sound more and more like lip-service to values we may still cherish intellectually, but which we have lost sight of how to live out – how to *enact.*

While it is not widely advertised, there is much evidence to suggest that we are now writing the concluding chapters in the story of consumer society. Even as its technical advances exceed anything we have previously known, even as its business mergers surpass the scale and monetary value of the entire economies of many countries, even as its markets are jammed with more merchandise than ever before, and even as the promise of economic growth appears to be limitless, the story of our society – the myth we tell ourselves about ourselves – is everywhere vitiated with contradiction, disillusionment, and emptiness.

Many people are beginning to understand that we need to tell a new story if we are interested in sustaining civilized human societies – a story that affirms higher goals than the acquisition and consumption of material things and that better measures human progress than the yardstick of 'economics.'

Consumer culture is spent, even though it continues to amass record profits. It never was socially sustainable. Now it is proving to be environmentally unsustainable, even toxic. It has no way to account for its environmental deficits, and because of those deficits, it will perish in an ocean of its own poisonous wastes. It has few mechanisms for equitably distributing its material benefits, and because of this, it will also perish – whether in an ocean of violence or a sigh of indifference remains to be seen. The only real question is which of these will happen first.

Fashioning a new culture is an immensely creative challenge. Its first crystals have been seeded in the alembic of personal transformation. This new culture is emerging in human freedom as a voluntary choice and along a trajectory quite different from the more-is-better consumer ethic, with its Horatio Alger myth of elitist competition for positions of hierarchical privilege. It is not being foisted on people through media blitzes, nor is it being proclaimed as the inevitable direction of a global market economy.

On the contrary, a new culture is *not* inevitable. The choice to live in equitable and sustainable relationships with other people and with the ecosphere is just that: a *choice*. It is coming into existence through countless small, quiet decisions being made by individuals and small collectives, not in the grand councils of global international treaty-makers or in the boardrooms of transnational corporations.

Just as the roots of the consumer culture can be traced back to the values and decisions of people who think of themselves as 'consumers,' the roots of the new culture are found in the ethos of *voluntary simplicity*. Voluntary simplicity offers an alternative story to that told by the consumer culture. The values that underpin simple living express a different reason for living. The practices that comprise voluntary simplicity, whether the people living it call it that or not, are an alternative way of relating to other people and to the living world.

Voluntary simplicity is a social movement, a spiritual sensibility, an aesthetic, a practice of livelihood – but is decidedly *not* a life-*style*. All sorts of people practice simplicity who might not call it by that name: environmentalists hungry to live more lightly on the land; artists, musicians, and scholars who live simply for the sake of their work; spiritual pilgrims who cannot truck clutter in the work of spiritual growth; people burned out and disillusioned by the frantic pace and empty promises of consumer hype; people in retreat from the dismal dangers of urban neighborhoods seeking friendlier communities and more caring relationships; people of wealth and social standing who hold themselves to a higher purpose than simply amassing more money or power over others; people fallen sick in mind or soul or body and forced thereby to reconsider what really matters to them and then find a way to live for it.

Voluntary simplicity isn't a fad cooked up by Madison Avenue to sell a new line of clothing or kitchen gadgets (although Madison Avenue is scrambling to co-opt the language of simplicity), nor has it sprung from academe as a philosophical system or research finding. In recent research conducted by Anthony Spina, voluntary simplicity is associated with the 'successfully discontented,' the 'mainstream disillusioned,' and with the 'cultural creatives.'[2] In short, it is appearing in the lives of people who have sampled many of the rewards promised by consumerism and found them tasteless. Having gorged on food that does not satisfy, they are creating something different – something *profoundly* different – but not, paradoxically, something new.

Duane Elgin calls voluntary simplicity a 'way of life which is outwardly simple and inwardly rich.'[3] It involves directing progressively more time and energy toward pursuing non-material aspirations while providing for material needs as simply, directly, and efficiently as possible. It measures personal and social progress by increases in the qualitative richness of daily living, the cultivation of relationships, and the development of personal and spiritual potentials. Simple living does not denigrate the material aspects of life but rather, by attending to quality, it values material things more highly than a society that merely consumes them.

The term 'voluntary simplicity' was first coined by Richard Gregg, a follower of Mahatma Gandhi. Gregg described it as follows:

> Voluntary simplicity involves both inner and outer condition. It means singleness of purpose, sincerity and honesty within, as well as avoidance of exterior clutter, of many possessions irrelevant to the chief purpose of life. It means an ordering and guiding of our energy and our desires, a partial restraint in some directions in order to secure greater abundance of life in other directions. It involves a deliberate organization of life for a purpose.[4]

Gregg's description nicely captures many different aspects of voluntary simplicity: that it involves many different 'layers' of experience and that it includes stripping away whatever is extraneous to the central purposes of life. These are essentially *positive* things to do because we do so in service of things we value more than what is stripped away. Living simply is about the 'deliberate organization of life for a purpose.'

Voluntary simplicity begins in *personal action*. It has little meaning apart from how it configures individual lives. Anyone can understand it. Anyone can practice it in some way, regardless of income, cultural background, or educational attainment. Practicing simplicity requires no special training, expert advice, or official sanction.

The practice of simplicity begins with individuals and is well attuned to the humanistic outlook of modern society. It also reconnects a person with traditional values of thrift, temperance, self-reliance, responsibility, and, where appropriate, spiritual asceticism. It immediately empowers people to make realistic, creative changes in understandable areas of their lives at no additional cost and at whatever pace is comfortable. Moreover, voluntary simplicity is highly 'adjustable' since a person can simplify his or her life to any degree and in whatever way they find most congenial. It follows that how we practice simple living will change with each of life's seasons and situations.

One of the most encouraging aspects of voluntary simplicity is that there is no need to wait for one's neighbors to attain enlightenment, a federal election, an ascendance of principled politicians, a sea-change in social consciousness, new technology, global spiritual awakening, or a new political party before positive change can begin. Thus, simple living sidesteps the cynicism, delays, and dithering that come with large, complex institutions, policy discussions, government 'procedures,' or commercial ventures. For all these reasons, adopting simple living is at one time a humble, personal endeavor, and is also socially, economically, and politically radical.

While some colorful practitioners of voluntary simplicity have worked publicly to change social institutions, thousands of lovers of simplicity have practiced the art quietly and unobtrusively. They are creating patterns of livelihood that progressively free them from the obsessions and disquiet that so plague their neighbors. When asked, they happily share their discoveries. The very nature of their journey, however, shrinks their footprints on the world, making them progressively less visible to their neighbors. As this journey unfolds, one can actually fall in love with the aesthetic of minimalism, with an image of lightness of being and of the gracefulness that characterizes changing seasons, winds, and waves that leave no traces, and beings that love without thought of recognition or reward. A feeling-sense emerges about one's proper role in the world that is the very opposite of needing to 'leave one's mark' on it. In a sense, we might then say that the mature practice of voluntary simplicity is creative play leading toward practical invisibility.

Nine Characteristics Of Voluntary Simplicity

One approach to understanding voluntary simplicity is to consider some of the *values* shared by those who practice it.

In 1997, I initiated a 'delphi exercise'[5] involving some participants in an internet-based discussion group on simple living. The delphi process is a method for developing consensus on an issue or question among a group of people knowledgeable about the question. Everyone participating in the process had been practicing voluntary simplicity in their personal lives for some time, though none would claim to be an 'expert.' I asked participants what values they thought were *essential* to the meaning of voluntary simplicity. After six rounds of the delphi process, a consensus formed around the following values, or characteristics, of voluntary simplicity though no priority should be inferred from the order in which I describe them:

★ Sufficiency, minimalism; anti-consumerism; deliberate reduction of consumption, clutter, noise, social over-commitment, superfluous ornamentation, and scale.

Practitioners of voluntary simplicity value living with few material possessions. Those they do have are deliberately and selectively chosen to reduce the 'equipment' of life to its essentials without compromising aesthetic values. This 'aesthetic and functional minimalism' is also carried into the realm of social relations, the organization of daily routines, and a striving to cultivate a simplicity of outlook that is honest and unpretentious.

As implied in the definition provided by Richard Gregg, this preference for sufficiency has both an inner and outer aspect. Living simply obviously means reducing the number and variety of one's material possessions. It also implies an inner 'house cleaning' applying to attitudes, prejudices, pretensions, worries, and expectations.

Valuing minimalism has complicated roots in aesthetic preferences for spaciousness, clarity, gracefulness, streamlining, and efficiency. It also contains resonances with more traditional values like frugality, thrift, common sense, and modesty. The rejection of consumerism is partly a reaction to the intrusiveness of consumer advertising and marketing, the pervasive transfer of public properties to private ownership, the commercialization of cultural events and public education, and especially the exploitation of children.

★ Self-reliance, socially responsible autonomy, personal authenticity, and wholeness.

Practitioners of voluntary simplicity value personal integrity expressed through striving to match their actions with their values (walking their talk), which they maintain through balanced choices and the cultivation of healthy self-reliance. Healthy self-reliance implies cultivating the capacities to meet some of one's own needs within a social context of equity and cooperation rather than in disregard for the needs of one's neighbors or the ecosphere.

'Simplicity' implies a certain directness in managing the affairs of one's life, and directness, in turn, implies personal knowledge and involvement. Life is not delegated but *lived.* Meeting one's real needs through one's own activities eliminates the 'middle men' who tend to clutter our lives with agendas other than our own. For example, some practitioners of simple living learn to grow some or all of their own food; maintain personal health; create their own entertainment; and repair and maintain their homes, appliances, vehicles, etc. Of course, the degree of self-reliance is a matter of individual preference and aptitude. But there are clear links between developing self-reliance and a sense of empowerment, competence, and high self-esteem. The products and services of consumerism tend to dumb life down, remove risk, promote passivity, and create dependency.

Ideally, developing self-reliance leads to 'healthy autonomy.' Healthy autonomy does not mean living in defiance of the community (as might be the case for a survivalist or misanthrope), rather living in society as a contributing member capable of making a constructive difference to the quality of community life. It is partly through developing the skills and capacities essential to self-reliance and healthy autonomy that we also lay the foundations for well-being and self-esteem.

★ Connection, interdependence, co-operation with the Earth, other beings, nature, other people.

Practitioners of voluntary simplicity value the capacity to experience connection with the ecosphere and with other people, who obviously comprise a part of the ecosphere. They strive to express this connection through co-operative interdependence in family and community relationships, and through activities that strengthen and deepen the quality of community life. The value of connection also finds expression in concern for equality, international justice, and compassion for oppressed people. Practitioners of voluntary simplicity value social and economic equity and strive to practice compassion toward all those suffering marginalization in any way.

For some, voluntary simplicity especially represents a way of living in greater harmony with other species and natural processes. The North American consumer lifestyle is destroying the Earth. Many people sense that consumerism cannot be sustained, but rich, rewarding alternatives seldom get 'air time' in the consumer-dominated media.

Few doubt that the extraction of resources and the manufacture and consumption of material goods and services contributes to environmental damage. These activities may not be carried out with the *intention* of harming the ecosphere, but they often do cause harm. Moreover, no imaginable technology designed to serve endless craving could do otherwise, except as a matter of *degree,* because no imaginable technology can sidestep the Laws of Thermodynamics or the Law of Conservation of Matter and Energy. We cannot *create* energy on planet Earth. The final limit on what we can consume is determined by the energy the planet receives from the sun as well as energy stored in fossil fuels and fissionable elements. When fossil fuels are exhausted, even if this could be done without radically changing Earth's climate, all living things and all industrial activities would necessarily be limited to the energy available to us from the sun. Since the amount of this energy is more or less fixed, the limit that it imposes will sooner or later constrain the production and consumption activities of human beings.

At the end of the day, reducing environmental damage implies creating a richly satisfying way of life while also reducing consumption of resources and production of wastes. Advocates of cleaner production technology say resource consumption and waste production can be reduced by increasing efficiency – which is true, *to some degree.* But simpler living *halts* both resource consumption and waste production *at source, immediately,* for all those products and services that practitioners forgo. Increasing production efficiency alone cannot achieve sustainability if we continue to pursue a consumerist ideology of the good life while also failing to control human population growth. But if improving production efficiencies could be linked to effective population controls *and* a cultural ethos of simpler living, a sustainable livelihood might be in sight.

Voluntary simplicity suggests a *minimalist* emphasis as the goal for technical development rather than *growth.* In a demonstrably finite world, such a goal is inherently more sustainable in its general intent. Moreover, voluntary simplicity emphasizes attention to *true development,* which is a qualitative improvement of life rather than a quantitative expansion of consumption as the measure of a good life. As people adopt simpler living, they may initially reduce the quantity of their material consumption, but eventually they increase the sophistication and efficiency of providing for their essential needs and realizing their personal aspirations in life.

Finally, voluntary simplicity contributes directly to environmental sustainability because it engages a powerful 'reverse multiplier' effect. Every pound of 'product' we see at the retail level represents tens, or even hundreds, of pounds of resources and energy expended in the extraction, manufacturing, distribution, and retailing stages 'upstream' in the lifecycle of the product. Individuals often feel as though their choices matter little in meeting the global challenge of environmental preservation. Yet, as individuals forgo excessive consumption, each such decision avoids all the 'upstream' environmental costs incurred in bringing the product to market. Gradually we come to perceive each thing we might own as the visible 'tip' of a less visible environmental 'iceberg' lying just beneath the surface of the economy. For example, it is estimated that every American consumes about 32 pounds of resources (forest products, minerals, energy resources) per week, while over 2,000 pounds of waste are discarded to support that consumption.[6] Thus, each consumption decision matters a great deal and can have more or less dramatic effects, depending on the items purchased. For many people, this by itself is enough reason to simplify the material side of their lives.

★ Mindfulness, spirituality.

Practitioners of voluntary simplicity value a mindful, unhurried, intentional (rather than impulsive), and appreciative approach to living. Some practitioners value *mindfulness* as a personal spiritual practice in its own right. They also see applying the insights that they gain through cultivating a mindful approach to living as part of living with personal integrity. For many, this is synonymous with spiritual practice.

In order to live 'voluntarily,' to bring more consciousness about making choices into our lives, we must be awake and paying attention to our experiences here and now. Those who value simplicity also value taking responsibility for making life choices. This is the exact opposite of allowing yourself to be just another automaton at the conveyor belt of consumer culture, of being narcotized by advertising, hypnotized by marketing imagery, or manipulated by flimflam artists. Mindfulness is the means of maintaining connection with our experience – another of the values essential to simple living. By cultivating mindfulness, we also happily discover that it can become a pathway to our deepest spiritual intuitions.

You needn't be a devotee of simple living to share the values of mindfulness and spirituality. But to the degree that these values *are* shared and lived out, it seems that people who hold them gradually develop simpler ways of life as a consequence. Each of us has limited time and energy. We each decide how much we will give to nurturing relationships versus acquiring, maintaining, and protecting possessions. While the two focuses are not entirely exclusive of each other, they clearly represent different ways of being in the world. Similarly, many people find that cultivating the depth dimension of their experience calls for silence, solitude, time for reflection and appreciation, and energy for exploration and new learning. Pursuing these kinds of purposes usually takes you out of the consumer mainstream into quieter pools where the currents are slower and deeper and different forms of reflection become possible.

It would be misleading, however, to think of people who are attracted to voluntary simplicity as only fashioning a life based on practical applications of abstract values. Closer to the mark perhaps is to imagine myriad life experiments guided by a certain sensibility, an inner image of gracefulness and spaciousness that expresses itself first through a *practice* of livelihood that only later reveals its values. Values and practice become closely linked and strengthen each other. In the words of the Franciscan theologian Richard Rohr, 'We don't think our way into a new life; we live our way into a new kind of thinking.'[7]

The idea of 'practice' is especially helpful because it links simple living with other practices, such as meditation, artistic development, scholarship, crafts and trades, farming, dancing, martial arts – in short, any human endeavor that allows one to be a *perpetual student*. Those who 'practice' are always on the road, always learning, always developing and deepening their practice and understanding. This is the case no matter how skillful or adept they may become. Great pianists and dancers still practice. Practice requires openness and humility. It is the attitude of one who communicates and co-operates rather than one who dominates and controls.

★ Deliberate reduction in number of material possessions and amount of consumption, reduction of clutter and unnecessary complexity, and a conscious re-direction of consumption decisions in favor of more environmentally sustainable forms of transportation, food production, housing, and entertainment.

This characteristic of voluntary simplicity is more a cluster of practices that aim to apply the values of sufficiency and minimalism. The practices of reducing material possessions, consumables and clutter, and redirecting choices to more environmentally sustainable forms of transportation, diet, housing, and entertainment echo the 'Golden Mean' or 'Middle Way' espoused by philosophers and spiritual teachers. This cluster also entails reducing unnecessary complexity in the financial aspects of everyday living, and developing financial responsibility, frugality, freedom from debt, and financial literacy. All these help provide for a more fully humane existence that is marked neither by conspicuous excess nor by deprivation.

Clearly, what might be 'excess' to one person at one time in life may prove entirely necessary and appropriate in another situation with different personal or family responsibilities. Regardless of climate, geography, or social station, those who love simplicity are attracted to a leaner, more streamlined form or existence.

This process of 'stripping down' is not something painful. Pejorative presentations of simplicity suggesting that it is driven by a grim commitment to moral principle make it hard to appreciate how joyous the material side of simple living can be. Picture a toddler stripping off clothes as he runs for the beach! What is happening *is* loss of a sort, but what is being gained in the process is a more intense connection with daily experience. Reducing excess baggage reveals more and more clearly what are the central purposes of our lives. Since these purposes are often beautiful and frequently go unlived in a consumer-oriented society, the simplification of material possessions becomes a form of personal liberation – invigorating as a good skinny dip!

★ Practices that develop one's spiritual, intellectual, emotional, physical, interpersonal, and aesthetic potentials.

These can take a diversity of forms, including meditation, music, fine and folk arts, martial arts, various forms of physical culture such as yoga, Qi-Gong, or sports that contribute to a sense of 'flow,' such as long-distance running, cross-country skiing, and cycling. What is shared is an active commitment to holistic personal growth.

This cluster of practices is the enactment of the value of self-reliance and the cultivation of healthy autonomy. For some people, the inner aspect of voluntary simplicity serves as their starting point. The practice of inner simplicity, as we shall see later, begins with cultivating the capacity to be conscious and mindful of ourselves, our relationships, and our moment-to-moment experience. It's that 'simple.' From the cultivation of mindfulness there unfolds a whole array of other attitudes, emotions, insights, and habits that serve to express and embody a progressively clearer awareness of *who* we are, *what* we want our lives to be about, and just *how* we can express that most artfully.

From the cultivation of mindfulness, a new center for personal identity is forged that spins itself into forms and actions in the world – a new pattern of activities and commitments that define a new way of living. We cease to pursue a life*style* and instead start fashioning a *life*. In this process, the organization of one's outer life comes to reflect and help sustain what is growing in one's inner life. The reduction of material clutter finds its psychological and spiritual counterpart in increasing mindfulness, integrity, heightened attention, deliberateness, focus, and clarity. We cultivate a way of life that is free of pretense, affectation, façade; in short, a life decidedly uninterested in *image* but passionately interested in *substance*. It matters less and less what one *has*, but more and more what sort of person one *is*.

The consumer economy actively strives to divert individuals from realizing their inherent potential, unless it can be easily linked with selling goods and services. Advertising, marketing, manufacturing, a great part of the legal code, many financial enterprises, and the very physical shape of communities distracts people from the knowledge and expression of their inherent potential, or else it strives to re-interpret and re-align personal aspirations to economic goals. Vanishingly few commercial ventures are launched with the goal of helping people come home to *themselves*. Rather, consumerism seeks to bring people to the *marketplace*.

Just living in a technically complex and increasingly populous society can divert our attention and energy from the inner life and direct them instead toward the activities necessary for physical subsistence and safety in urban centers that have become so fast, noisy, mechanical, and dangerous that a moment's lapse of attention can be lethal.

Voluntary simplicity is all about realizing our inherent potential. It involves 'growth by subtraction,' or paring away whatever distracts us or is extraneous or alien to what we believe are our central purposes in life. When we begin to practice self-reliance and healthy autonomy and learn not to succumb to the distractions on which the consumer economy depends, we learn to recognize our life purposes, the quality of their depth and mystery, and how to best express and honor them in how we live.

★ Practices that build strong, intimate, non-violent, and compassionate relationships with people and with nature that contribute to the personal and common good.

Nurturing interpersonal connections is important to practitioners of voluntary simplicity, especially through co-operative activities that serve one's family or community, including the wider international and natural communities. Many North Americans say they feel oppressed by stress, hurry, bureaucracy, debt, fear of violence, or fear of abandonment – in short, they feel disconnected and unsupported; anxiety increases. The pace and direction of life in a consumer society can carry us away from connections and relationships that would nourish us and sustain our self-worth or heal our disappointments, while at the same time promising us that all its gadgets and services will give us more time to cultivate and enjoy relationships. Increasingly, we spend more time with technological devices (machines, computers, paperwork) and less time with people.

Fashioning a simpler way of life is part of fashioning a life that offers more opportunity to establish relationships and then live within them. Those who practice simple living make building and sustaining relationships a conscious part of daily activity.

★ Development of a conscious, intentional, approach to living rather than unconscious impulsiveness.

Many practitioners of simple living actively develop awareness, knowledge of issues, and intellectual and emotional skills that support making responsible life choices. These may include participating in civic affairs and making sound purchasing decisions rather than being driven by momentary impulse, appetite, or urgent necessity.

This cluster of practices grows out of the values placed on mindfulness in daily living and our capacity to exercise our freedom of choice in making life decisions. We have already seen how these are linked. The practice of cultivating and maintaining consciousness in making life choices, including purchasing decisions and being involved in issues of community concern, even in our approach to individual and work relationships, is simply seen as a mode of life appropriate to living simply. Developing a conscious, intentional approach to living affirms some of what is best about life, rather than focuses, as consumerism often does, on whatever will promote sales.

Related to this is the belief, implied by the practice of mindfulness, that our choices *matter*. They matter in how they contribute to our own quality of life, to the future we give our children, to the quality of life enjoyed by people elsewhere in the world, to the security of life enjoyed by other species, to the promotion of justice and wellness in our own communities, and in how they contribute to our spiritual growth. Since our choices and the quality of our daily experience matter, blundering through life purely on impulse, following appetite, chasing the ephemeral, accepting what amounts to lies – all these are betrayals of ourselves. In effect, they silently testify that we don't value our own lives. Practicing a conscious, deliberate, attentive approach to living directly opposes the siren song of consumerism. What consumerism prefers in its customers is that they only be awake enough to 'swipe the plastic.'

★ Practices contributing to a holistic approach to personal health.

There are many examples of how some people live out this general practice. For instance, adopting a vegetarian or vegan diet incurs lower environmental impact during food production, can (though not always) simplify food preparation, and some people feel represents a more compassionate way of meeting our nutritional needs than diets rich in animal products. A preference for organically produced foods further expresses the conviction that personal health cannot be cultivated in isolation from planetary health or secured through the use of pesticides, fertilizers, and herbicides in food production. Healthy habits of rest and exercise, commitment to health maintenance practices, and activities that relieve stress and promote wellness are seen as primary foundations for personal health rather than reliance on disease-care services in the first instance. Some practitioners of simple living also express a preference for alternative (e.g., homeopathic, nutritional, energy, massage, etc.) treatment approaches in time of illness, perhaps because many of these call for a greater level of involvement and control to be exercised by the 'patient' during illness treatment than is the case with allopathic approaches to treating disease. Taking more responsibility for our health and also our treatment in times of illness is simply another expression of the values of mindfulness and self-reliance in living.

Attention to maintaining one's health is a logical outgrowth of self-reliance and the directness implied in simpler living. Increasingly, practitioners of simple living perceive a professionalized, impersonal, medical-pharmaceutical *industry* that promotes 'consumerism' of its own products and services and is not necessarily interested in human health *per se,* despite its protestations to the contrary. Documented examples abound of the 'over-medication' of North Americans, especially vulnerable seniors and children; of the specialized and often arcane medical vocabularies that serve more to alienate than to connect people with their own bodies and wellness processes; a readiness to prescribe rather than collaborate and advise; disproportionate over-funding of disease-cure technology and services and concomitant under-funding of health and wellness promotion and education programs; a general tendency to respond to illness by treating its effects rather than attending to its causes in environmental pollution, sanitation issues, and general education.

These considerations and many others incline those practicing voluntary simplicity to the view that healthy food, knowledge of one's body and environment, wholesome exercise, and safe communities make a more direct and immediate contribution to personal health than sophisticated technology, exotic and expensive pharmaceuticals, and large medical service bureaucracies. Certainly people get sick and sometimes need invasive interventions. But the concern is one of emphasis and how priorities are established. It makes little sense to spend billions on cancer research while turning a blind eye to lifestyle and environmental factors that clearly cause cancer. Promoting wellness is far less expensive and far more pleasant than curing disease.

Perspectives from History and for Today

As David Shi illustrated in his book, *The Simple Life,*[8] simple living has a long history in American culture reaching back to the Puritan and Quaker religious movements in Europe and their subsequent settlements in North America. Perhaps because simple living has periodically gained a high profile in North American history, it has also accumulated some stereotypes and nostalgic fantasies. For this reason, another useful perspective on voluntary simplicity is to consider what it is *not.*

First, voluntary simplicity is *not new.* Those who portray it as some radically new social innovation overlook its deep roots in traditional values and virtues. Thrift, temperance, co-operative self-reliance, community interdependence, harmony with nature and the pre-eminence of spiritual and interpersonal values over material and consumer values have a far older heritage in our culture than the more recent messages to spend, consume, compete and radically isolate oneself through the 'in-your-face' behavior celebrated by consumerism. Voluntary simplicity reaffirms values that have an established track record in contributing to survival and human well-being than anything emerging from the muddy dreams of advertising agencies.

Simplicity has an ancient pedigree. The Chinese philosopher Lao Tzu left a career in the Mandarin civil service to live simply as a mountain-dwelling hermit, during which time he wrote one of the classic texts of Taoism, the *Tao-Te-Ching*. The Greek philosopher Diogenes was said to live in a tub in the agora of Athens, where he walked the streets and questioned passersby in search of one honest person. Siddhartha Gautama, himself the heir to a throne in ancient India, forsook the pleasures and power of a kingdom to search for enlightenment. Eventually attaining it as the Buddha, he taught that attachment to material things was simply one of many impediments to liberation from suffering. Jesus of Nazareth embraced simplicity in solidarity with society's outcasts and in order to set his heart first of all on his Heavenly Father's kingdom. St. Francis of Assisi, innumerable desert recluses and hermits, and thousands of people entering religious orders that include vows of religious poverty, embraced simplicity in imitation of Christ. The same is true for millions of the followers of Buddhism, Taoism, Islam, Hasidic Judaism, Sufism, and Hinduism. Thus, simplicity has drawn its enthusiasts from both the high- and low-born and has included intellectuals and spiritual leaders, as well as legions of ordinary folk.

In more recent times, the Russian literary giant Leo Tolstoy sang the praises of simple living, while North America has seen a long line of people who lived simply as part of their religious practice (Puritans, Shakers, Amish, Quakers, Mennonites, among others) or from philosophical convictions, such as Henry David Thoreau and the New England Transcendentalists.

The birth of modern India in 1948 was sparked by the forceful simplicity of one of its most charismatic leaders, Mahatma Gandhi. Partly inspired by his example, a whole generation of youth in North America and Europe, at least for a time, took their ideological leave from the materialism of the 1950s in a variety of counterculture 'back to the land' experiments during the 1960s and '70s.

While the love of simple living, and even occasional extremes of material asceticism, can claim some lofty figures among its proponents as described above, there have been periods during which very large numbers of ordinary people have adopted simplicity to some degree for a variety of reasons. Usually people embrace simplicity because it is either a pathway to or expression of values that they believe are more meaningful and rewarding than the material benefits they forgo. Sometimes, as Shi points out, people embrace simplicity to assist with a war effort or some other national crisis, only to revert again to whatever is the historical equivalent of consumerism. But in any case, the concept of simple living is certainly not an invention of the 1990s.

Given its venerable history, some people are surprised to discover that voluntary simplicity is *not about going back* to anything. There is deep nostalgia within our society for what we suppose were the 'simpler' values of North America's aboriginal or rural agrarian past. Many people (including myself) who participated in the 'back to the land' spin-off of the 1960s counterculture discovered that rural living using 19th century technology is anything but simple! For some, this experiment has been deeply satisfying. For others, it was a stepping stone that helped disentangle sentimental illusions about nature, rural living, and earlier periods of history from the realities of living a physically more demanding, direct, and rooted way of life. We have come away from these experiences with the awareness that simple living is indeed rewarding and that one can live simply in *any* century and in *both* rural and urban settings. The essence of simplicity is not about a historical period or level of technical development. It certainly is not about returning to the 'Little House on the Prairie,' or reconstructing tube-powered radios as if integrated circuits didn't represent an immense advance in quality of life with a simultaneous reduction in the intensity of its energy and resource use. While the ranks of those living simply probably includes some 'technophobes,' voluntary simplicity is a *forward-looking* cultural development aimed at higher states of focus, attention, mindfulness, awareness, and conscious purpose. Technology, however advanced it may be, must serve these values. Technology is not the enemy. It can very much be a part of living simply and not, as it is currently presented, a rationale for 'consumerism.'

Simplicity, on the other hand, is all about knowing how much consumption is *enough* and then setting aside efforts to further expand consumption in favor of pursuing other goals. Simplicity is what a healthy culture develops toward if it escapes getting caught in the *growth* trap. Our society is fixated on expanding the scale and volume of everything it does. Consumer economies, and the political interests that serve them, depend on economic growth to generate increasing profits and shareholder dividends. The practice of voluntary simplicity shifts focus onto the quality and meaning of life and away from its scale and quantity.

In his original essay on voluntary simplicity, Richard Gregg refers to the work of historian Arnold Toynbee, who argued that the essence of civilization consists in a progressive 'etherealization of culture.' That is, mature civilizations, after having sufficiently provided the necessities of life, turn their energies to other goals: spiritual development, learning, art, promoting justice and peace, cultural development. Any society that simply goes on to produce more and more of what it already has is stuck in a kind of perpetual cultural immaturity, never ripening to full maturity. Thus, on both the personal and societal levels, the movement toward voluntary simplicity is a sign of personal and cultural maturation, not merely a nostalgic indulgence, a throw-back that may have sentimental appeal but no relevance to modern life.

Voluntary simplicity is not necessarily anti-technological or anti-modern. Instead, it calls for the re-orientation of technology as a means of achieving economic growth for its own sake to being a means of developing sufficiency and equity in society. The goal is to recognize that human well-being can never be achieved solely by maximizing production and profit. In fact, the opposite is closer to the truth: That we should be striving to maximize human and ecological well-being on the *minimum of production.* This is a *post-modern* goal, not an exercise in nostalgia.

Despite its venerable history and association with many spiritual traditions, voluntary simplicity is *not a religion.* Its close relationship with spiritual practice is both instrumental and essential. There is no 'creed of simplicity' that binds all its practitioners. Simple living is trans-denominational and has its proponents in all major spiritual traditions. It has also been practiced by secular humanists, atheistic philosophers, and some followers of schools of spiritual thinking such as Henry David Thoreau, a New England Transcendentalist.[9]

There are also people who embrace simplicity for financial reasons, to find relief from stress, because the Zen-like aesthetics of simplicity appeal to them, or because it's a practical response to the demands of a particularly compelling life work, such as the completion of an art work or saving money to put a child through university.

Simple living is purely a *means.* It is not a creed but a *practice,* not a destination but a *vehicle.* Its value rests in what it helps us achieve: more time, peace, solitude, gracefulness, mindfulness, justice, ecological sustainability, equity, sufficiency, silence, gratitude, generosity, interdependence, spiritual intuition, humility. That the lovers of simplicity share certain values or configure their lives in similar ways in no sense requires that they hold the same opinions on religious matters, or that they subscribe to any religion at all.

Simplicity and Clearing Away Distractions

Simplicity by itself does not automatically improve human character. It merely 'clears the decks' so that something new can grow according to the aspirations of the person concerned. If a person happens to be narcissistic or selfish, he can live simply and still be narcissistic and selfish.

It is important to recognize that voluntary simplicity is *not poverty,* puritanical self-denial, or negative asceticism. Those advocating simplicity are *not* saying that poverty is noble, a good thing, or a way of life that should be adopted. Rather, simple living is practiced for the values it conserves, many of which are antithetical to any philosophy that espouses the denial of pleasure for the sake of denial.

Poverty often arises from uncontrollable circumstances (such as chronic or catastrophic illness, unemployment, natural disaster) or results from systemic injustice (such as discrimination, existing inequitable patterns of privilege and want that exist in many places today). Poverty is usually not voluntary. Extreme poverty can result in destitution, a condition of material, psychological, and sometimes even spiritual impoverishment in which choice and mindfulness are not options. Negative asceticism and some other self-denial philosophies view consumption and the enjoyment of material things as morally suspect. None of this has anything to do with simple living.

Today, in North America, poverty and destitution are spreading like cancers. A whole generation of young people is being cut off from education and employment opportunities while their elders are being forced into 'early retirement.' All alike are exposed to the same daily drone of messages from advertisers that promote an idea of a good life that fewer and fewer people can afford.

Both the affluent *and* the poor are enmeshed in the same destructive system. Consumerism exploits the poor and the affluent at the same time as it lies to both. While the poor suffer the pain of deprivation, the affluent suffer the pain of disillusionment when all they have to show for their affluence is a lot of 'stuff,' but spiritual emptiness. Consumerism as a way of life is destructive of people and communities as a whole, even those people who suppose they are in control of it.

Simple living speaks directly to the moral, social, spiritual, and ecological costs of affluence. It enables the freedom of choice open to the affluent to conserve their communities, the planet's ecosystems, and their own opportunity to find meaning in life. The message of simple living can heighten awareness among the affluent of the ever-increasing stresses and costs that attend the ever-diminishing rewards of an acquisitive lifestyle. Finally, voluntary simplicity can underline the truth that, beyond what is needed for sufficiency, looking for meaning in life through consumption is futile.

Advocates of simplicity have never idealized destitution. Death by starvation is agony. Homelessness, illness, inadequate clothing, loneliness – all these are not only personal calamities, they are socially degrading. The fact that our social systems don't remedy or prevent them offends our principles of decency. The only appropriate response to conditions such as these is to do what many of the great philosophers and spiritual teachers of history have always taught: Feed the hungry, clothe the naked, house the homeless, care for the sick, educate the ignorant, visit the lonely, welcome the stranger, look after the orphan, comfort the afflicted – in a word – *love* each other.

Yet when we have *enough,* and there are very many of us who do, what then? Could it be that some of the discontent associated with a modest income is caused by the ceaseless din of advertising messages that one can be happier by earning or owning more? And could it be that if we were less open to these messages, our minds and hearts would be more open to those aspects of living that cannot be bought and sold? Could it be that some of the pain of unemployment (apart from the very real and legitimate fear of starvation and homelessness) comes from the loss of a sense of personal identity that consumer societies find only in working and earning and owning? In truth, is this an appropriate basis for personal identity in any case? If the answer to any of these questions is 'yes,' then simplicity has something to say to nearly everyone.

Closely related to the misconception that simple living celebrates poverty is the idea that it celebrates *cheapness.* Practicing simplicity doesn't mean surrounding oneself with junk, regardless of its price. Neither does it require always purchasing used items, such as clothing or cars, or always riding a bicycle for transportation.

On the contrary, there is a strong aesthetic element in simple living. More, it seems to imply a love and stewardship of material things, which in turn implies that they be beautiful and well-crafted. Consumer society, for all its supposed emphasis on 'materialism,' is often deeply hostile to the material world, to the senses, and to the care and love of material things. It expresses this hostility by converting almost everything it touches to *waste* that can neither be cherished nor used for long, nor passed along as a heritage. Consumerism hurries its worshipers through life with little time to linger or enjoy or feel anything.

Simplicity, by contrast, seeks reduction of the material items used to provide for life's basic needs, but insists that they be beautiful, sturdy, and functional celebrations of the Earth and the human intelligence that fashioned them. There is certainly scope within simple living for works of art that celebrate creativity and beauty as values in their own right. In her book *Frugal Luxuries,*[10] Tracy McBride nicely expresses this sensibility, which is capable of experiencing great reward in simple pleasures.

Should voluntary simplicity become the cultural mainstream in North America, I imagine people living not cheaply or meanly or with any sort of barren austerity. Rather, homes and communities would reflect elegant design (in the sense of intelligent design, not Parisian fashion!) and a deep respect for the laws of physical and biological nature. Our inventions would work with efficiency and directness. 'Quality' would encompass beauty as well as durability, utility, and price. I imagine people living in smaller homes, less cluttered with 'technology,' but each one of unique design and each one a jewel expressing the taste and life of its owner. Our homes and communities would communicate the sense that people living there actually intended to have grandchildren, to be around for a while, to sustain their culture, and to leave behind things to be admired and enjoyed for a long time.

Simplicity involves centering thinking and action upon what is most essential and central to our humanity. Precisely because of this, simplicity also inclines toward a healthy kind of 'materialism.' By this I mean a deep respect for the material, or physical, world for the resources it provides us, for the responsibility and power we have to be the co-creators either of beauty, utility, and lasting value, or of ugliness, futility, and waste. Doing this may involve living inexpensively, although not always. It will certainly involve applying human ingenuity to existing materials and wastes to bring out of them something better than we have now. But in both cases, the goal is not just to minimise spending or maximise recycling. The goal is to build our lives around *different values.*

Simplicity and Financial Freedom

Frugality concerns economics, whereas simplicity relates to one's outlook on the whole of life. In his classic book, *Small Is Beautiful,*[11] the economist E.F. Schumacher wrote that the goal of any sane economy should not be to maximize wealth measured in money, but to meet real human needs ever more efficiently with less and less investment of labor, time, and resources. The goal of a sane economy is to *free* people to do more important things than make more money or consume more goods. A humane economy certainly would not place people on a treadmill of frustration or avarice by manufacturing and marketing an ever-changing and expanding menu of distractions and unfulfillable desires.

Amazingly, in its most recent incarnation, voluntary simplicity has been confused with being independently wealthy! Voluntary simplicity is not essentially a financial management system for the wealthy, nor is it the rigorous practice of living cheaply.[12]

Those who live simply must manage their finances well and make thoughtful purchasing decisions. The simplest, most environmentally sustainable and socially responsible way of meeting one's needs may not always be achieved by purchasing the cheapest items available. In addition, simple living encourages people to focus attention on those life goals and activities that bring them lasting reward. These will be different for different people, and for some activities may imply significant expense.

A popular book in the United States, *Your Money or Your Life,* by Joe Dominguez and Vicki Robin,[13] has been described as the 'bible' of the recent renaissance in simple living. The book contains a great deal of valuable information and insightful analysis, much of which is directly pertinent to simpler living, especially when it helps readers develop more mindfulness (awareness and choicefulness) regarding their use of money. Calling it a 'bible' was unfortunate, however, because I don't think Dominguez and Robin ever set out to write scripture, and certainly not to become the focus of quasi-religious commentary. The popularity of the book has helped contribute to the idea that voluntary simplicity is mainly for those affluent enough to need financial planning assistance and fortunate enough to contemplate a day when they might receive an income without working for it. Linking the practice of simple living to financial independence inclines to the misleading conclusion that the latter is somehow the prerequisite of the former – a notion that Jesus, Gandhi, St. Francis, Gautama, and Thoreau would have found utterly laughable. Voluntary simplicity can be practiced *immediately*, by *anyone*, in any area of life wherever there is room for choice. It has little to do with money and a person certainly doesn't have to be financially independent (or even interested in becoming so) before they can take up simple living.

Again, while I don't believe it was the intent of Dominguez and Robin, the popularity of their message fits logically with the dominance of the pecuniary spirit in North America. Money is seen as prerequisite to almost everything else, the axis around which the North American mind turns. This may be partly due to our deep-seated delusion that possessing money confers freedom. It's not money that many people say they want, so much as the 'freedom' they think money will give them to do as they like, when they wish, wherever they want – as if any imaginable constraint in any of these directions somehow negates our capacity for happiness or meaning.

Freedom gained through money, just like beauty, love, sexual attractiveness or power gained through buying the 'right stuff,' is a 'supply-side' approach to living: To increase freedom, increase the supply of money. But it's an insecure freedom since it depends upon the security and constancy of the supply of money. Interrupt or take away the money and you also take away the freedom. Moreover, the focus is on 'freedom to' (the freedom *to* indulge one's impulses and appetites without thought for, or much involvement with, others, etc.), with little attention to 'freedom from' (freedom *from* loneliness, violence, insecurity, distraction, injustice, a polluted environment).

Since the 'freedom' offered by consumerism depends on wealth, from this single contingency flows a great deal of uproar and unpleasantness. People compete with each other for new supplies of wealth or are tempted to exploit others to increase their wealth. They may build defences and amass hoards to keep their wealth secure. Paradoxically, as the hoard of money increases, so can the anxiety about losing it and the frenzy to conserve and protect it. As the financial capacity to consume grows, decisions on how, when, and what to consume gradually come to occupy more and more time and attention. Since monetary wealth, and hence consumerism's understanding of freedom, depends on the continuation of the existing order of things that supplies the wealth, radical conservatism is inevitable. How can we permit change when change may reduce the supply of money that we think assures our freedom?

Another feature of 'supply-side' freedom is that it emphasises scarcity rather than abundance. It simply won't do for everyone to print his own supply of money, although this is a natural spin-off from supply-side freedom. Indeed, promising business ventures are sometimes referred to as 'a licence to print money.' But when people actually do this, we call it counterfeiting and prosecute them. Only governments can print money, which means that they also control the supply. But if the supply is limited, it is also likely to be scarce, and unless very special social and economic arrangements are put in place, some people will have more and others less of it.

When the measure of freedom is monetary, and someone else controls the supply of money, then someone else controls our freedom. This can never be a secure freedom.

Another way of thinking about freedom grows from the practice of simplicity. Simplicity is a 'demand-side' pathway to freedom. It is freedom gained through reducing and redirecting *desires*. It grows from the insight that *satisfying desire does not produce happiness or contentment.* In fact, seeking happiness through the satisfaction of desires leads to suffering and conflict. To construct an entire social and economic system on the cyclical and deliberate generation of *artificial* desires, their temporary satisfaction and then re-stimulation is, in a word, lunacy. Yet this is the 'miracle' of consumerism.

To increase freedom, contentment, and happiness, we must instead *reduce* artificial wants and desires. This approach to securing freedom is within the reach of everyone at no charge. There is no way to make money from this recommendation, corner the market on it, or really convince other people who understand the idea that you have it and they can't unless they buy something from you. It's not about scarcity.

Unlike the steps taken to become wealthier, each step into simplicity *increases* security rather than reduces it. Simplicity is always secure since it doesn't depend on anything outside ourselves and divine providence. Nothing has to be hoarded (or can be). Nothing has to be defended because the freedom conferred by simplicity doesn't require a secure or expanded supply of anything except mindfulness. Once a small measure of simplicity is attempted, the door is opened a crack to provide time to develop deeper mindfulness. Mindfulness is delightful. This can cause people to search for additional ways to simplify their lives so that they can feel more secure and have more time to grow in mindfulness and the delight in living that it brings. A self-stoking cycle is set in motion that runs entirely opposite to received wisdom about where freedom comes from, how it can be 'secured' and enlarged, and what exactly contributes to feelings of reward and contentment in life.

Yet another aspect of thinking of freedom in terms of financial wealth is that having conspicuously more than our neighbours can undermine relationships.

Indeed, it *must,* since the false freedom and false security promised by money tends to become an enclosed, isolated, defiant, and self-absorbed condition. Often wealth can elicit jealousy, envy, suspicion, distrust, and sometimes even violence from other people. The 'freedom' brought by consumerism comes at the price of continually looking over one's shoulder and living in 'private compounds' and 'exclusive' clubs that witness as much to fear as they do to privilege. What sort of freedom is that? Why would anyone aspire to it?

The freedom of simplicity is found in *relationship* and *social solidarity.* For those who live simply, freedom of choice and action grow up through social influence and community connections. Pleasure and security in living are enlarged not through consumption but through social co-operation, sharing, and interdependence. Rather than the 'security' offered by bank accounts and alarm systems, the security of simplicity is achieved by embedding our lives in the affections and shared debts of love that make up community. The 'price' we pay for this sort of life, access to this variety of freedom, is reduced 'freedom' to consume. It remains for each person to decide how important is the freedom to consume without restraint compared to other kinds of freedom. Simple living is most joyful for people who have discovered something they love more than 'stuff.'

Despite the rangy tone in Thoreau's *Walden,* voluntary simplicity is *not necessarily about rugged individualism* or a survivalist brand of self-reliance. As Duane Elgin has described it,[14] simpler living is usually about living more *directly* and with greater depth of *personal involvement* in the daily tasks of meeting one's needs, but this isn't the same thing as antisocial individualism. Simple living seeks a healthy integration of self-reliance (doing what one can and appropriately should do for oneself) and community interdependence (sharing goods, resources, and time toward a common goal of healthy community). Achieving this integration is, of course, an endlessly creative process.

People who interpret simple living as *autonomous* living have found that meeting all of their personal and family needs on a strictly self-sufficient basis is not simple! Historically, those lifestyles that optimize the personal practice of simplicity are usually *communitarian,* e.g., tribal villages, monastic communities practicing vows of poverty, fraternities and sororities, kibbutzim, co-housing co-operatives, etc. When applied to an appropriate degree, the specialization and division of labor that is possible in communities can contribute to the common welfare and reduce the complexity of life for individual members, at least as this concerns the meeting of basic material needs. By sharing those tools, appliances, and other material possessions that can be shared, individuals can transfer 'ownership' of such things to the community and hence be free of them. It is a matter of historical record that the growth of individualism in society has paralleled the growth of commercially driven consumerism. And from a commercial perspective, the most profitable society imaginable would be one of fully 'cocooned' individuals, terrified of their neighbors and deeply possessive of their 'things.' In such a society, every person must have his or her 'own' collection of possessions to support their life, numb their boredom and, of course, protect themselves from all the other intensely lonely and envious individuals who might steal what is 'theirs' rather than simply borrow things from a shared inventory, use them, and return them! By contrast, simpler living has more to do with 'going it together' than with 'going it alone.'

It is often for sake of family and community that individuals choose simpler living in the first place. It may be through re-establishing relationships of community interdependence that individuals find ways for developing their own practice of simplicity.

For example, by consciously reducing the material complexity of their lives, practitioners of voluntary simplicity liberate time, money, and emotional energy for deeper involvement with others. To the degree that simpler living brings with it a greater measure of inner peace, financial security, and relief from the stresses associated with the competitive pursuit of consumerism, it helps people become more emotionally and psychologically available to others. It also frees up resources for creative contributions to one's household and community as well as time and energy for creative efforts to build up the cultural richness of one's neighbourhood or town. Survey after survey of the determinates of life satisfaction reveal that people find spending time with each other consistently more rewarding than spending time with things.

Conversely, it is through deepening interpersonal bonds that people develop mutual commitments to shared values. Strengthening relationships also helps develop a sense of connection and interdependence within one's community. A person with time *for* others finds that bonds begin to develop that place one in solidarity *with* others. This in turn makes it emotionally possible to substitute collective sharing for personal ownership. Thus at one and the same moment a much wider range of material 'riches' becomes available to the individual at no additional personal burden of ownership. For example, communities whose members can muster strong collective support for parks reduce everyone's individual need to maintain a private yard at great savings of land, environmental impact, and personal cost. Moreover, the shared space of a park provides another opportunity to nurture community rather than isolation. In this way, community can be both a value that is strengthened through the practice of simplicity and also a *means* to a simpler life.

Voluntary simplicity is *not about 'dumbing down' our lives*. Voluntary simplicity is built on paradox – the paradox that less can be more, that growth can be deadly, that affluence destroys happiness, that making life more 'difficult' can make it easier, and that simplicity enfolds complexity. The practice of simplicity consists in the voluntary removal of *extraneous complexity* so that more mental, emotional, and physical energy is available to engage *meaningful complexity.*

For example, meditation is an outwardly simple but inwardly extremely complex and active process. Music consists of simple, straightforward conventions, yet musical compositions can be very rich and intricate. The individual movements included in T'ai-chi are very simple, but the choreography of their linkages and the mental and physical effects they produce are anything but simple. Simplifying life in service of pursuing some of these other activities is the exact opposite of dumbing down. It is consumerism, in fact, that dumbs life down in search of the lowest common denominator in the marketplace. Simplicity, by contrast, requires that we smarten up.

★ ★ ★

Finally, there is a great hunger in the media for the next new 'miracle' development that will solve all the world's problems – the silver bullet that kills all bad guys. Unfortunately, voluntary simplicity is *not a panacea.* As mentioned above, simple living is purely a *means* that is especially accessible by individuals. It clears the way for some fresh thinking, perhaps for some alternative institutional innovations, and certainly for higher levels of cultural and political involvement by ordinary people. Voluntary simplicity is not an automatic antidote to all of the systemic and structural problems of society. This, however, in no way detracts from its value.

Voluntary simplicity points in a constructive direction toward the evolution of an environmentally sustainable and socially equitable society. Because it is an individual practice, it circumvents the delays and rigidities we encounter in organizing larger scale social reform movements; the directness of simpler living achieves immediate 'results.' It is not a preparation for something else that will achieve results, nor does it displace responsibility for action onto someone or something else. To conserve energy, governments write new legislation, business awaits new technology, economists fiddle with monetary policy, academics do research projects – but voluntary simplicity just steps up and turns off the lights.

Voluntary simplicity doesn't necessarily demand instant, radical changes in our lives. Of course, there may be some people who are ready to attempt major changes, but many people come to simplicity as a *practice* that they develop over a long period of time and through many shifting seasons and experiments. Simple living can be adopted at any pace, rapidly if desired, but normally in an organic and gradual way. In my view, slowly diffusing simplicity into one's life grounds it more solidly in daily routines than does giving way to impulsiveness, as if simplicity were just another fad. The practice of simplicity takes different forms in the lives of young people, the newly married, young families, more mature families, 'empty nesters,' and among elders. In the words of a Chinese proverb: 'Be not afraid of growing slowly; be afraid only of standing still.'

The Question of Values

Proposing voluntary simplicity as a more sustainable way to live is no more, nor any less, value-laden than traditional technological or economic recipes for the good life. It is most definitely *not* about indoctrinating people to a particular set of values. The values we mentioned above, as interesting as they are for discussion purposes, don't form a creed to which a person must subscribe in order to practice simplicity. They merely reflect a consensus among a small group of people currently doing so.

In fact, it is *consumerism* that attempts to systematically configure North American values to its own ends through the incessant efforts of its multi-billion dollar marketing and advertising industries.

It can be *observed* that as people develop a conscious awareness and recollection of their personal experiences of value in life, most of these experiences are not associated particularly strongly with consumption, ownership, or possession of material things. From this perspective, the consumer culture of North America is actually an organized *distraction system* that attempts to superimpose the values and imagery of consumerism onto those of the individual.

One of the key findings of a study done by the Merck Family Foundation[15] of American of US-American views on consumption, materialism, and environment revealed what its authors described as a deep 'ambivalence' about modern culture. On the one hand, Americans enjoy material things. They can be *induced* to purchase them and have been *taught* to associate material affluence with security and personal well-being. They believe what they have been taught – almost. On the other hand, they feel they have lost touch with time for, and energy to pursue, other more important and fundamental values associated with family, community, and personal well-being. They are also deeply concerned about how their consumption affects the environment.

The Merck study described these findings in terms of 'ambivalence.' But another interpretation that can be offered for the data is that they reflect a society in deep *value conflict,* specifically between what respondents know they value, e.g., identity and affiliation values, versus what they have been *taught to want* through the culturally pervasive activities of commercial advertisers. Had the Merck study included questions that asked people to rank their values, or to identify values that they believed were more or less authentically their own, ambivalence might have been more readily identifiable as conflict. Readiness to entertain voluntary simplicity as a life choice increases as this conflict becomes more acute.

Anthony Spina has conducted research on people practicing simple living and likens their life changes to 'tuning' a radio so that static (noise) is reduced and signal (music, meaningful words) is increased. He attributes 'noise' in modern society to the clatter and clutter of 'system' messages, i.e., 'data smog' representing the views of governments, commercial retailers, and organized institutions. The 'signal' that most people find rewarding in their lives is connections with their 'Lifeworld' – a sense of personal meaning, goodness, and vitality that is contained in ordinary human relationships, sensuous contact with the world of nature, and in experiences of face-to-face community. As 'signal' from the Lifeworld becomes increasingly lost in the data smog generated by large corporate and government systems, we become increasingly lost, disoriented, and feel cut off from our sources of meaning and reward in life. People practicing voluntary simplicity do so, Spina argues, because it has proven to be an effective means for them to reconnect with the 'signals' coming from their Lifeworld.[16]

Simpler living begins when people become conscious of their values and live congruently with them, *whatever they may be*. This is itself a value. It is the approach we are suggesting that is significantly different from that of the consumer culture.

Practitioners of voluntary simplicity begin from *questions* such as: What do I value in life? How can I align my practice of daily living so that it brings me more into the presence of my values or expresses them more clearly? What in my life distracts me from this task or clutters my expression of these values, and how can I rid myself of it?

Consumerism asks no questions; it *advertises imperatives*. If you want to be happy, sexy, socially influential, odor-free, a nice person, a financial success, etc., *buy this*.

The challenge of sustainability cannot be met without addressing the relationship between consumption and values. This subject is no less 'realistic,' 'objective,' or 'practical' than are technical and economic matters. Some spokespeople for science and economics seem to believe that their pronouncements emanate from an 'objective' realm that has irrefutable validity and stands above, or outside, more 'subjective' matters like human values. But contemporary science, particularly physics and mathematics, have long since departed from such a view.[17] Every assertion of 'fact' and every act of 'observation' is also at the same time necessarily an assertion of value and an act of subjective creativity. No system of thinking, including economics, can claim to stand outside a relativistic universe. Therefore, discussion of values is just as essential to the future of society as discussion of observational methods is essential to the progress of science. And many of the most important things in life cannot be measured or observed at all.

From the perspective of a consumer-dominated culture, the idea that simple living might be widely adopted can seem far-fetched. But there are already signs of movement toward simpler living.

The factors that will push the societies of developed countries toward simpler living have already been mentioned above as the challenges to environmental and social sustainability. Simpler living will be a key characteristic of any imaginable *civilized* future for the mass of humanity. The critical decision before us is whether we voluntarily embrace the practice of simplicity now or see it involuntarily imposed by circumstances which, through neglect or denial, become self-stoking transnational emergencies that no longer allow for choice, for conservation of civil and political liberties, or perhaps even for the survival of democracy. Despite the scoffing ridicule directed toward simpler living by the captains of commerce, an inescapable challenge must be addressed: If voluntary simplicity were adopted by all the world's people, it is at least plausible to foresee a sustainable, healthy, and reasonably peaceable future for all humanity. If everyone on Earth adopted the North American 'standard' of consumerism, can we honestly foresee a similar future?

There are also increasing indications that traditional values surrounding work and compensation for work through material reward are buckling under the strains of exploitation inherent in a consumer, growth-oriented economy. Studies conducted in 1997 by the Angus Reid polling organization and Statistics Canada clearly reveal the increasing strain on individuals and families from the need to work more hours and often multiple jobs in order to maintain the same or oftentimes diminishing material benefits. Two million Canadians (about 20 percent of the workforce) now work 25 percent or more overtime hours per week, much of it unpaid. Use of employee assistance counseling programs to help workers cope with personal and family stress has nearly doubled since 1995, and enrolments in 'time management' classes are exploding.[18] People are coming increasingly to understand that the system doesn't deliver what it promises. Diligence and hard work are not delivering a better life. The consumer system is delivering a less secure, more stressful and driven life. For increasing numbers, it's time for a change.

By now one of the central paradoxes of voluntary simplicity should be clear. The meaning of simplicity is simple – finding a 'middle way' in life that minimizes material and non-material clutter except what is essential to our chief purposes in living – but as this chapter and those which follow make clear, the implications and connections arising from this way of living are complex and numerous.

(ENDNOTES)

1 Daniel Quinn, *Ishmael* (New York: Bantam Books, 1992).
2 Anthony Spina, 'Research shows new aspects of voluntary simplicity,' www.sln.net (1999).
3 Duane Elgin, *Voluntary Simplicity*, (New York: William Morrow, 1993), p3.
4 Richard Gregg, 'The Value of Voluntary Simplicity,' *Visva-Bharati Quarterly* (August 1936).
5 The 'delphi method' was invented in the 1970s by social researchers to provide a vehicle for large numbers of people knowledgeable about certain subjects, but having different opinions on it, to arrive at a consensus. A delphi process begins with a standard set of questions to which all participants respond. The responses are collated in various ways and then fed back to participants. The participants read the summaries of all the responses and then answer the same of similar questions again. Through successive rounds of this process, a consensus of views tends to emerge, not necessarily reflecting complete agreement on all points but clearly identifying 'core' areas of agreement on the subject at hand.

In 1997, I invited participants in an Internet discussion group on voluntary simplicity to take part in such a delphi process. It was opened with three questions: (1) What do you think are the essential values of voluntary simplicity? (2) What do you think are the essential practices comprising voluntary simplicity? (3) What do you think are the key benefits of voluntary simplicity? Among those participating in the process, a significant degree of consensus was reached after six delphi 'rounds.' While the results of this process certainly do no purport to be representative of the North American population as a whole (the whole process was not conducted with the rigor required for truly reliable social research), they were nonetheless interesting.
6 Paul Hawken, *The Ecology of Commerce: A Declaration of Sustainability* (New York: Harper Collins, 1993), p37.
7 Richard Rohr, *Simplicity: The Art of Living* (New York: Crossroad Publishing Company, 1991) p59.
8 David Shi, *The Simple Life: Plain Living and High Thinking in American Culture*, (New York: Oxford University Press, 1985).
9 Henry David Thoreau, *Walden and Other Writings* (New York: Bantam, 1989).
10 Tracy McBride, *Frugal Luxuries: Simple Pleasures to Enhance Your Life and Comfort Your Soul* (New York: Bantam, 1997).
11 E.F. Schumacher, *Small is Beautiful: A Study of Economics as if People Mattered* (London: Vintage, 1993).
12 Ernest Callenbach, *Living Cheaply With Style* (Berkeley: Ronin Publications, 1992). See also Amy Dacyczyn, *The Tightwad Gazette: Promising Thrift As a Viable Alternative Lifestyle* (New York: Villard Books, 1993).
13 Joe Dominguez and Vicki Robin, *Your Money or Your Life: Transforming Your Relationship With Money and Achieving Financial Independence* (New York: Penguin, 1992).
14 Elgin, above, p113.
15 The Harwood Group, *Yearning For Balance: Views of Americans on Consumption, Materialism, and the Environment* (Takoma Park: Merck Family Fund, 1995), p12.
16 Anthony Spina, 'Research shows new aspects of voluntary simplicity,' www.sln.net (1999).
17 Fritjof Capra, *The Turning Point: Science, Society, and the Rising Culture* (New York: Bantam Books, 1982). See also James Glieck, *Chaos: Making a New Science* (New York: Penguin, 1987) and Margaret J. Wheatley, *Leadership and the New Science: Learning About Organization from an Orderly Universe* (San Francisco: Berrett-Koehler Publishers, 1994).
18 Alanna Mitchell, Karen Unland, and Chad Skelton, 'Canadians pay for busy lives' *Globe and Mail*, July 19, 1997, p7.

Chapter Two

A NEW SOCIAL MOVEMENT?

Amatai Etzioni

The idea that achieving ever-higher levels of consumption of products and services is a vacuous goal has been with us from the onset of industrialization. These ideas often have taken the form of comparing the attractive life of the much poorer, preindustrial artisan to that of the more endowed industrial assembly-line worker. Many alternative approaches to life within a capitalist system have been proposed since the advent of capitalism, some more successful than others. One such approach, referred to by its adherents as voluntary simplicity, has been steadily gaining in popularity. This chapter examines this living strategy with regard to its sociological significance as a possible counterbalance to mainstream capitalist society.

Since the 1960s, criticism of consumerism has been common among the followers of counterculture movements, voiced largely in reaction to the postwar boom in consumer spending. These counterculture adherents sought a lifestyle that consumed and produced little, at least in terms of marketable objects, and sought to derive satisfaction, meaning, and a sense of purpose from contemplation, communion with nature, bonding, mood -altering substances, sex, and inexpensive products.[1] Over the years, many members of Western societies embraced an attenuated version of the values and mores of the counterculture. In fact, one survey suggests that North American attitudes to materialism are changing. For example, '83 percent of those surveyed believe that the United States consumes too much, and 88 percent believe that protecting the environment will require major changes in the way we live.'[2]

Some scholars postulate that a shift in values in relation to the material aspects of life emerges as societies move from a modern to a postmodern era. Under this paradigm:

> [m]odernized nations become postmodern as diminishing returns from economic growth, bureaucratization, and state intervention and unprecedented levels of affluence and welfare state security give rise to new constellations of values: postmaterialist emphases on the quality of life, self-expression, participation, and continued declines in traditional social norms.[3]

This change is effected through 'intergenerational value replacement' in which individuals born into the high levels of material security of developed democratic capitalism emphasize (nonmaterial) subjective well-being: socialization during formative years produces deeply ingrained postmaterialist value orientations.[4]

In a survey conducted by researchers Ronald Inglehart and Paul Abramson, the percentage of respondents with clear postmaterialist values doubled from 9 percent in 1972 to 18 percent in 1991, while those with clear materialist values dropped by more than half, from 35 percent to 16 percent. (Those with mixed commitments moved more slowly, from 55 percent to 65 percent.)[5] Trends were similar for most Western European countries.[6]

Personal consumption, however, continued to grow, most dramatically during the 1980s. Consumer debt rose from approximately $350 billion in 1980 to $1,231 trillion in 1997,[7] and personal consumption expenditures jumped from $3,009.7 to $4,471.1 trillion (real dollars) between 1980 and 1994.[8] Meanwhile, the personal savings rate of Americans fell from 7.9 percent in 1980 to 4.2 percent in 1990 and has remained near this level ever since.[9] As one commentator notes, during the 1980s:

> Laissez-faire economic policies and newly internationalized stock and bond markets created an easy-money euphoria among the well to do, which translated into a 'get it while you can' binge in the middle echelons of the consumer society.... not since the Roaring Twenties had conspicuous consumption been so lauded. Over the decade, personal debt matched national debt in soaring to new heights, as consumers filled their houses and garages with third cars, motor boats, home entertainment centers, and whirlpool baths.[10]

Still, the search for alternatives to a consumerist-oriented lifestyle has survived such periods of intensive conspicuous consumption and continues to attract people, such as those involved in the voluntary simplicity approach. Voluntary simplicity refers to the decision to limit expenditures on consumer goods and services and to cultivate nonmaterialistic sources of satisfaction and meaning, out of free will rather than out of coercion by poverty, government austerity programs, or imprisonment. It has been described by one of its main proponents, author Duane Elgin, as 'a manner of living that is outwardly more simple and inwardly more rich.... a deliberate choice to live with less in the belief that more of life will be returned to us in the process.'[11]

As I already have suggested, criticism of consumerism and the quest for alternatives is as old as capitalism itself. However, the issue is increasingly relevant to our lives. The collapse of non-capitalist economic systems has led many to assume that capitalism is the superior system and therefore to refrain from critically examining its goals, even though capitalism does harbor serious defects. Recent developments in former communist countries as they grapple with the free market raise numerous concerns. Many in the East and West find that capitalism does not address spiritual concerns – the quest for transcendental connections and meanings – they believe are important to all.[12] Furthermore, as many societies with rapidly rising populations now seek affluence as their primary domestic goal, they face environmental, psychological, and other issues raised by consumerism on a scale not previously considered. For instance, the undesirable side effects of intensive consumerism that used to be of concern chiefly to highly industrialized societies now are faced by hundreds of millions of people in Asian countries and in other places where rapid economic development has occurred recently. Finally, the transition from consumption based on the satisfaction of perceived basic needs (secure shelter, food, clothing) to consumerism (the preoccupation with gaining ever higher levels of consumption, including a considerable measure of conspicuous consumption of status goods) seems to be more pronounced as societies become wealthier. Hence, a reexamination of this aspect of mature capitalism is particularly timely. Indeed, the current environment of increasing and expansive affluence might be particularly hospitable to moderate forms of voluntary simplicity.

This examination proceeds first by providing a description of voluntary simplicity, exploring its different manifestations and its relationship to competitiveness as the need and urge to gain higher levels of income is curbed. It then considers whether higher income, and the greater consumption it enables, produces higher contentment. This is a crucial issue because it makes a world of difference to the sustainability of voluntary simplicity if it is perceived as generating deprivations and hence requires strong motivational forces in order to spread and persevere, or if consumerism is found to be an obsessive and possibly addictive habit, in which case voluntary simplicity would be liberating and much more self-propelling and sustaining. An application of eminent psychologist Abraham Maslow's theory of human needs is particularly relevant here in answering the question and in determining the future of voluntary simplicity as a major cultural factor. This theory is further reinforced by examining the 'consumption' of a subcategory of goods whose supply and demand are not governed by the condition of scarcity in the postmodern era. The chapter closes with a discussion of the societal consequences of voluntary simplicity.

One rather moderate form of voluntary simplicity is practiced by economically well-off people who voluntarily give up some consumer goods they could readily afford but basically maintain their consumption-oriented lifestyle. For example, they 'dress down' in one way or another, or drive old cars.

These trends are reflected in the stylistic return during the 1990s to classic, 'simple' design and natural looks, which, while they may appear simpler, often are just as costly, as Pilar Viladas writes: 'In architecture and design today, less is more again. Houses, rooms and furnishings are less ornate, less complicated and less ostentatious than they were 10 years ago. Rather than putting their money on display, people seem to be investing in a quieter brand of luxury, based on comfort and quality?'[13]

While this tendency, referred to as 'downshifting,' is moderate in scope, and perhaps because it is moderate, it is not limited to the very wealthy. Some professionals and other members of the middle class are replacing elaborate dinner parties with simple meals, pot-luck dinners, take-out food, or social events built around desserts only. Some lawyers are reported to have cut back on the billing-hours race that drives many of their colleagues to work late hours and on weekends to gain increased income and a higher year-end bonus and to incur the favor of the firms for which they work.[14] Some businesses have encouraged limited degrees of voluntary simplicity. For instance, many workplaces have established 'casual dress' Fridays. In some workplaces, especially on the West coast, employees may dress down any workday.

It has been estimated that 'by 2000, about 15 percent of Americans will have scaled back their lives in one way or another.'[15] The most common recent changes have included reducing work hours, switching to lower-paying jobs, and quitting work to stay at home,[16] changes that may, but do not necessarily correlate with downshifting. In fact, as one 1996 poll found, '48 percent of Americans [had] done at least one of the following [between 1991 and 1996]: cut back their hours at work, declined or didn't seek a promotion, lowered their expectations for what they need out of life, reduced their commitments or moved to a community with a less hectic way of life?'[17] Another survey reports that 'one in three adults say they would accept a smaller paycheck in exchange for having a simpler lifestyle.'[18]

In addition, there are people who have given up high-paying, high-stress jobs to live on less – often much less – income. In one case, a couple quit their jobs as high-paid executives in the telecommunications industry and now live on their savings, expending about $25,000 per year and using their time writing and performing volunteer work.[19]

Ideas associated with voluntary simplicity are widely held, although not necessarily reflected in actual behavior. In 1989 a majority of working Americans rated 'a happy family life' as a much more important indicator of success than 'earning a lot of money' – by a notably wide margin of 62 percent to 10 percent.[20]

In addition, numerous women and some men prefer part-time jobs or jobs that allow them to work at home, even if better-paying full-time jobs are open to them, because they are willing to reconcile themselves with earning a lower income in order to dedicate more time to their children and be at home when their children are there.[21] People who switch to new careers that are more personally meaningful but less lucrative also fall into this category. For instance, a 1997 source reports that 'a growing wave of engineers, military officers, lawyers, and business people ... are switching careers and becoming teachers.'[22] Such career changers have significantly redefined their attitudes toward work. They ask themselves, as psychologist Barry Schwartz has put it, a crucial question: 'Why have so many of us allowed ourselves to be put in a position where we spend half our waking lives doing what we don't want to do in a place we don't want to be?'[23]

People who voluntarily and significantly curtail their income tend to be stronger simplifiers than those who only moderate their lifestyle, because a significant reduction of income often leads to a much more encompassing 'simplification' of lifestyle than selective downshifting. While it is possible for an affluent person to cease working; altogether and still lead an affluent lifestyle, *and* for someone who does not reduce his or her income to cut spending drastically, it is expected that those who significantly curtail their income will simplify more than those who only moderate their consumption. Once people reduce their income, unless they have large savings, a new inheritance, or some other such non-work-related income, they must adjust their consumption.

People who adjust their lifestyles only or mainly because of economic pressures (having lost their main or second job, or for any other reason) do *not* qualify as voluntary simplifiers on the grounds that their shift is not voluntary. It can be argued that some poor people freely choose not to earn more and keep their consumption level meager. Many advocates of voluntary simplicity, however, take great pains to distinguish this way of life from one of poverty, stressing that while poverty is the life of the powerless, voluntary simplicity is empowering. As Elgin states, 'Poverty is involuntary whereas simplicity is consciously chosen. Poverty is repressive; simplicity is liberating. Poverty generates a sense of helplessness, passivity, and despair; simplicity fosters personal empowerment, creativity, and a sense of ever present opportunity.'[24]

The discussion here, however, focuses on people who had an affluent lifestyle and chose to give it up, for reasons that will become evident toward the end of the discussion.

Finally, holistic simplifiers adjust their whole life patterns according to the ethos of voluntary simplicity. Often many move from affluent suburbs or gentrified parts of major cities to smaller towns, the countryside, farms, and less affluent or less urbanized parts of the country – the Pacific Northwest is especially popular – with the explicit goal of leading a 'simpler' life, although proponents of the voluntary simplicity philosophy are quick to point out that it is a viable living strategy in any environment. A small, loosely connected social movement, sometimes called the 'simple living movement,' has developed – complete with its own how-to books, multiple-step programs, and newsletters, although many have embarked on a life of voluntary simplicity independently, and some reports suggest that many who 'experiment with simplicity of living said they did not view themselves as part of a social movement.'[25]

The true simplifiers differ from the downshifters and even strong simplifiers not only in the scope of change in their conduct but also in that it is motivated by a coherently articulated philosophy. Elgin's 1981 book *Voluntary Simplicity* which draws on the traditions of the Quakers, the Puritans, transcendentalists such as Ralph Waldo Emerson and Henry David Thoreau, and various world religions to provide a philosophical basis for living a simple life continues to be a major source of inspiration among voluntary simplicity's proponents.[26] Indeed, many note that the simplicity movement as a whole is much in debt to many of the world's major religions and philosophical traditions. As social historian David Shi has noted:

> The great spiritual teachers of the East Zarathustra, Buddha, Lao-tse, and Confucius – all stressed that material self-control was essential to the good life.... By far, however, the most important historical influence on American simplicity has been the combined heritage of Greco-Roman culture and Judeo-Christian ethics. Most Greek and Roman philosophers were emphatic in their praise of simple living, as were the Hebrew prophets and Jesus.[27]

These simplicity-oriented philosophies often are explicitly anticonsumerist. Elgin, for example, calls for 'dramatic changes in the overall levels and patterns of consumption in developed nations,' adding that 'this will require dramatic changes in the consumerist messages we give ourselves through the mass media.'[28] In 1997 the Public Broadcasting Corporation broadcast a special called *Affluenza*. Voluntary simplicity was said to provide a treatment for an 'epidemic' whose symptoms are 'shopping fever, a rash of personal debt, chronic stress, overwork and exhaustion of natural resources.' It promised a follow-up on 'better living for less.' The Center for a New American Dream publishes a quarterly report on the same issues simply called *Enough!* The message that reducing wasteful consumerist practices is essential has been voiced on an international level as well, as witnessed by statements such as the following issued at the United Nations' 1992 Rio Conference on the Environment: 'To achieve sustainable development and a higher quality of life for all people, states should reduce and eliminate unsustainable patterns of production and consumption.'[29]

While one can readily profile the various kinds of simplifiers, there are no reliable measurements that enable us to establish the number of each of the three kinds of simplifiers or to determine whether their ranks are growing. One recent publication, though, estimates that nearly one out of four adult Americans, for a total of 44 million, is a 'Cultural Creative,' who ranks voluntary simplicity high among his or her values.[30]

Social Implications of Voluntary Simplicity

The question of whether voluntary simplicity can greatly expand its reach depends to a significant extent on the question of whether voluntary simplicity constitutes a sacrifice that people must be constantly motivated to make or is in itself a major source of satisfaction, and hence self-motivating.

Consumerism is justified largely in terms of the notion that the more goods and services a person uses, the more satisfied a person will be. Early economists thought that people had a fixed set of needs, and they worried what would motivate people to work and save once their income allowed them to satisfy those needs. Subsequently, however, it was widely agreed that people's needs can be enhanced artificially through advertising and social pressures, and hence they are said to have if not unlimited, at least very expandable consumer needs.

In contrast, critics argue that the cult of consumer goods (of objects) stands between people and contentment, and prevents people from experiencing authentic expressions of affection and appreciation by others. Western popular culture is replete with narratives about fathers (in earlier days), and recently of mothers as well, who slaved to bring home consumer goods – but, far from being appreciated by their children and spouses, found often only late in life, that their families would have preferred if the breadwinners had spent more time with them and showed them affection and appreciation (or expressed their feelings directly, through attention and attendance, hugs and pats on the back, rather than mediate that expression by working hard and long to buy things). Playwright Arthur Miller's *Death of a Salesman* is a telling example of this genre. Miller's work remains relevant today, as evidenced by the popular response to Neil Simon's *Proposals*, a remake of his story.

Social science findings (which admittedly may have many well-known limitations and do not all correlate on this topic) in *toto* seem to support the notion that income does not significantly affect contentment, with the important exception of the poor. For instance, Frank M. Andrews and Stephen B. Withey found that the level of one's socioeconomic status had meager effects on one's 'sense of well-being' and no significant effect on 'satisfaction with life-as-a-whole.'[31] And Jonathan Freedman discovered that levels of reported happiness did not vary greatly among the members of different economic classes, with the exception of the very poor, who tended to be less happy than others.[32]

Researchers David G. Myers and Ed Diener find that among the poor in poor countries – those who cannot afford life's necessities – satisfaction with income 'is a moderate predictor' of subjective well-being.[33] They also report, though, that 'once people are able to afford life's necessities, increasing levels of affluence matter surprisingly little.'[34] Diener and R. J. Larsen found 'a mere +.12 correlation between income and happiness' and uncovered no long-term effect of increases or decreases in income on happiness.[35]

A survey of the people on *Forbes's* wealthiest Americans list finds that those individuals were not significantly happier than other Americans and that, in fact, 37 percent reported being less happy than the average American, a statistic Myers and Diener also report.[36] Even as personal income in the United States has climbed from roughly $4,000 (in 1990 dollars) in 1930 to approximately $16,000 (in 1990 dollars) in the early 1990s, the percentage of people describing themselves as 'very happy' generally has hovered in the low- to mid-30s.[37]

Researcher Angus Campbell reports that in 20 years' surveys 'the proportion of 'very happy' people is higher as we move from low- to high-income levels,' but he is careful to note that this is a 'very stable relationship, but by no means an exclusive one. Even among the most affluent, there are a large majority who describe themselves as less than very happy and a sizable minority of the least affluent claim that they are very happy.'[38] As he summarizes, 'Happiness is far from the exclusive domain of the well-to-do.'[39]

Studies of the country's well-being show that economic growth does not significantly affect happiness (though at *any* given time the people of poor countries are generally less happy than those of wealthy ones). As Worldwatch Institute researcher Alan Durning states, 'People living in the nineties are on average four-and-a-half times richer than their great-grandparents were at the turn of the century, but they are not four-and-a-half times happier. Psychological evidence shows that the relationship between consumption and personal happiness is weak.'[40] In addition, it has been reported that while per-capita disposable (after-tax) income in inflation-adjusted dollars almost exactly doubled between 1960 and 1990, 32 percent of Americans reported that they were 'very happy' in 1993, almost the same proportion as did in 1957 (35 percent). Although economic growth slowed since the mid-1970s, Americans' reported happiness was remarkably stable (nearly always between 30 and 35 percent) across both high-growth and low-growth periods. Moreover, in the same period, from the late 1950 to the early 1990s, rates of depression, violent crime, divorce, and teen suicide have all risen dramatically.[41]

Recent psychological studies have made even stronger claims: that the *more* concerned people are with their financial well-being, the *less* likely they are to be happy. One group of researchers found that '[h]ighly central financial success aspirations ... were associated with less self-actualization, less vitality, more depression, and more anxiety.'[42] Another scholar, Robert Lane, pointed out that:

> ...most studies agree that a satisfying family life is the most important contributor to well-being.... [T]he joys of friendship often rank second. Indeed, according to one study, an individual's number of friends is a better predictor of his well-being than is the size of his income. Satisfying work and leisure often rank third or fourth but, strangely, neither is closely related to actual income.[43]

Increases in individual income briefly boost happiness, but the additional happiness is not sustainable because the higher income level becomes the standard against which people measure their future achievements.[44]

These and other such findings raise the following question: If higher levels of income do not buy happiness, why do people work hard to gain higher income? The answer is complex. High income in consumer-based capitalist societies 'buys' prestige; others find purpose and meaning and contentment in the income-producing work *per se*. There is, however, also good reason to suggest that the combination of artificial fanning of needs and other cultural pressures, manifest through such vehicles as the aggressive American marketing industry, maintains people in consumer-based roles when these are not truly or deeply satisfying. As social historian Robert Bellah has stated, '[t]hat happiness is to be attained through limitless material acquisition is denied by every religion and philosophy known to man but is preached incessantly by every American television set.'[45]

Voluntary simplicity works because consuming less, once one's basic creature-comfort needs are taken care of, is not a source of deprivation, so long as one is freed from the culture of consumerism and the artificial 'needs' it induces. Voluntary simplicity represents a new culture, one that respects work (even if it generates only low or moderate income) and appreciates conservation and modest rather than conspicuous or lavish consumption, but does not advocate a life of sacrifice or service (and in this sense is rather different from ascetic religious orders or some socialist expressions, as in kibbutzim). Voluntary simplicity suggests that there is a declining marginal satisfaction in the pursuit of ever-higher levels of consumption. And it points to sources of satisfaction in deliberately and voluntarily avoiding the quest for ever-growing levels of affluence and consumption and making one's personal and social project the pursuit of other purposes. These purposes are not specifically defined other than that they are not materialistic. Indeed, just as some people intrinsically find satisfaction in work and savings rather than in purchasing power, so some voluntary simplicity followers find satisfaction in the very fact that they choose (and have not been forced to choose) a simpler lifestyle and are proud of their choice. Moreover, as they learn to cultivate other pursuits, simplifiers gain more satisfaction out of lifelong learning, public life, volunteering, community participation, sports, cultural activities, and observing or communing with nature.

In each of these areas, some simplifiers slip back into consumerism, promoted by marketers. Thus, those engaged in sports may feel they 'need' a large variety of expensive, ever-changing, fashionable clothing and equipment to enjoy their sport of choice. But a considerable number of members of the affluent classes in affluent societies – especially, it seems, societies that have been well off for a while – find that they can keep consumerism under control and truly learn to cultivate lower-cost sources of contentment and meaning. They enjoy touch football, a well-worn pair of sneakers, doing their own home repairs and cooking, or take pride in their beat-up car.

The obsessive nature of some consumerism is evident in that people who seek to curb it often find doing so difficult. Many people purchase things they later realize they neither need nor desire, or stop shopping only after they have exhausted all their sources of credit. (This reference is not to the poor but to those who have several credit cards and who constantly 'max' them out.) In short, the *conversion* of a large number of people to voluntary simplicity requires taking into account the fact that constant consumption cannot simply be stopped, that transitional help may be required, and that conversion is best achieved when consumerism is replaced with other sources of satisfaction and meaning.

Abraham Maslow, The Haves and The Have-Nots, and Simplicity

We have seen that there is reason to suggest that the continued psychological investment in ever-higher levels of consumption has an unpleasant addictive quality. People seek to purchase and amass ever more goods whether they need them (in any sense of the term) or not. It follows that voluntary simplicity, far from being a source of stress, is a source of a more profound satisfaction. This point is further supported by examining the implications of Maslow's theory to these points.

The rise of voluntary simplicity in advanced stages of capitalism, and for the privileged members of these societies, can be assessed in light of a psychological theory of Abraham Maslow, detailed especially in his work *Towards a Psychology of Being*. There he suggested that 'the basic motivations supply ready-made an hierarchy of values which are related to each other as higher needs and lower needs, stronger and weaker, more vital and more dispensable,' and ordered 'in an integrated hierarchy ... that is, they rest one upon another.'[46] At the base of the hierarchy are basic creature comforts, such as the need for food, shelter, and clothing. Higher up are the need for love and esteem. Self-expression crowns the hierarchy. Although there are some connections; these needs are disassociated from the classical Freudian concept of 'instincts.'

Maslow theorized that people seek to satisfy lower needs before they turn to higher ones, and that:

> healthy people have sufficiently gratified their basic needs for safety, belongingness, love, respect and self-esteem so that they are motivated primarily by trends to self-actualization (defined as ongoing actualization of potentials, capacities and talents, as fulfillment of mission [or call, fate, destiny, or vocation], as a fuller knowledge of, and acceptance of, the person's own intrinsic nature, as an unceasing trend toward unity, integration or synergy within the person).[47]

Maslow's theory does not, however, postulate that basic needs are superseded by higher pursuits. As he states, '[g]rowth is seen then not only as progressive gratification of basic needs to the point where they 'disappear,' but also in the specific growth motivations over and above these basic needs.... We are thereby helped also to realize that basic needs and self-actualization do not contradict each other any more than do childhood and maturity?'[48] The primary issue relevant here is whether or not people continue to invest themselves heavily in the quest for 'creature comforts' long after they are quite richly endowed in such goods, and if in the process other needs, such as emotional interaction and care for others, are ignored or undervalued.

Maslow's thesis is compatible with the suggestion that voluntary simplicity may appeal to people after their basic needs are well satisfied. Once they feel secure that these needs will be attended to in the future, they are objectively ready to focus on their higher, 'self-actualizing' needs – even if their consumeristic tendencies blind them to the fact that they are read to shift upward, so to speak. Voluntary simplicity is thus a choice a successful corporate lawyer, not a homeless person, faces; Singapore, not Rwanda. Indeed, to urge the poor or near poor to draw satisfaction from consuming less is to ignore the profound connection between the hierarchy of human needs and consumption. Consumption becomes an obsession that can be overcome only after basic creature-comfort needs are sated.

Consumerism has one often-observed feature that is particularly relevant here. Consumerism sustains itself, in part because it is visible. People who are 'successful' in traditional capitalist terms need to signal their achievements in ways that are readily visible to others in order to gain their appreciation, approval, and respect. They do so by displaying their income by buying expensive status goods, as social critic Vance Packard demonstrated several decades ago.[49]

People who are well socialized into the capitalist system often believe that they need income to buy things they 'need' (or that without additional income they 'cannot make ends meet'). But examinations of the purchases of those who are not poor or near poor shows that they buy numerous items not needed for survival but needed to meet status needs. This is the sociological role of Nike sneakers, leather jackets, fur coats, jewelry, fancy watches, expensive cars, and numerous other such goods, all items that are highly visible to people who are not members of one's community, who do not know one personally. These goods allow people to display the size of their income and wealth without attaching their accountant's statement to their lapels.

In such a culture, if people *choose* a job or career pattern that is not income-maximizing but is voluntarily simplistic, they have no established means of signaling that they choose such a course rather than having been forced into it and that they have not failed by the mores of the capitalist society. There are no lapel pins stating 'I could have but preferred not to.' Voluntary simplicity responds to this need for status recognition without expensive conspicuous consumption by choosing lower-cost but visible consumer goods that enable one to signal that one has chosen, rather than been coerced into, a less affluent lifestyle.

Voluntary simplicity achieves this by using select consumer goods that are clearly associated with a simpler life pattern and are as visible as the traditional status symbols *and/or* cannot be afforded by those who reduced consumption merely because their income fell. Which specific consumption items signal voluntary simplicity vs. coerced simplicity change over time and from one sub-culture to another. Some refer to this practice as 'conspicuous non-consumption.'[50] In this way, voluntary simplifiers can satisfy what Maslow considers another basic human need, that of gaining the appreciation of others; without using a high – and ever escalating – level of consumption as their principle means of gaining positive feedback.

This idea is of considerable import when voluntary simplicity is examined not merely as an empirical phenomenon, as a pattern for social science to observe and dissect, but also as a set of values that has advocates and that may be judged in terms of the moral appropriateness of those values. As I see it, voluntary simplicity advocates addressing those who are in the higher reaches of income, those who are privileged but who are fixated on the creature-comfort level; it may help them free themselves from the artificial fanning of these basic needs and assist them in moving to higher levels of satisfaction. The same advocacy addressed to the poor or near poor (or disadvantaged groups or the 'have-not' countries) might correctly be seen as an attempt to deny them the satisfaction of basic human needs. Consumerism, not consumption, is the target for voluntary simplicity.

Oddly, a major development brought about by technological innovations makes it more likely that voluntary simplicity may be expanded and that the less privileged and have-nots may gain in the process. In considering this development, I first discuss the nature of non-scarce objects and then turn to their implications for the reallocation of wealth.

Voluntary Simplicity in the Cyber Age

Developed societies, it has been argued for decades, are moving from economies that rely heavily on the industrial sector to economies that increasingly draw on the information industry.[51] The scope of this transition and its implications are often compared to those societies that experienced as they moved from farming to manufacturing. It should be noted that there is a measure of overblown rhetoric in such generalizations. Computers are, for instance, classified as a major item of the rising knowledge industry rather than of traditional manufacturing. However, once a specific computer is programmed and designed, a prototype tested and debugged, the routine fastening of millions of chip boards into millions of boxes to make personal computers is not significantly different from, say, the manufacturing of toasters. And while publishers of books are now often classified as part of the knowledge industry and computers are widely used to manufacture books, books are still objects that are made, shipped, and sold like other non-knowledge industry products. Acknowledging these examples of overblown claims is not to deny that a major transformation is taking place, only that its growth and scope are much slower and less dramatic than was originally expected. Indeed, given this slower rate of change, societies are able to face the ramifications in a more orderly manner.

The main significance of the rise of the cyber-age is that the resulting shrinking of scarcity enhances the possibility for the expansion of voluntary simplicity. This important point is surprisingly rarely noted. Unlike the consumer objects that dominated the manufacturing age – cars, washers, bikes, televisions, houses (and computers) – many knowledge 'objects' can be consumed, possessed, and still be had by numerous others – that is shared at minimal loss or cost. Hence, in this basic sense, *knowledge defies scarcity* thus reducing scarcity, a major driving principle behind industrial capitalist economies. Compare, for instance, a Porsche to Beethoven's Ninth Symphony (or a minivan to a folk song). If an affluent citizen buys a particular Porsche (or any other of the billions of traditional consumer objects), this Porsche – and the resources that were invested in making it – is unavailable to any others (if one disregards friends and family). Once the Porsche is 'consumed,' little of value remains. By contrast, the Ninth (and a rising number of other such objects of knowledge) can be copied millions of times, enjoyed by millions at one and the same time, and is still available in its full, original glory.

Perhaps there is a measure of snobbism in showing a preference for the Ninth over a Porsche. But this is hardly the issue here; the same advantage is found when one compares an obscene rap song to a Volkswagen Beetle, or a pornographic image on the Internet to a low-income housing project. The criterion at issue is the difference between the resources that go into making each item and the extent to which it can be copied, consumed, and still be 'possessed' and shared.

True, even knowledge-related objects have some minimal costs, because they need some non-knowledge 'carrier'; they have some limited material base, a disk, a tape, or some paper, and most require an instrument – a radio, for instance – to access them. However, typically the costs of these material carriers are minimal compared to those of most consumer goods. While many perishable goods (consumer objects such as food or gasoline) are low in cost per item, one needs to buy many of them repeatedly to keep consuming them. In contrast, 'knowledge' objects such as cassette tapes or laser discs can be enjoyed numerous times and are not 'consumed' (eaten up, so to speak). In that sense, knowledge objects have the miraculous quality of the bush Moses saw at Mount Sinai: It burned but was not consumed.

What is said for music also holds for books and art. Shakespeare in a 99cent paperback edition is no less Shakespeare than in an expensive leather-bound edition, and above all, millions can read Shakespeare – his writings are still available, undiminished, for millions of others. Millions of students can read Kafka's short stories, solve geographical puzzles, and study Plato, without any diminution of these items. That is, these sources of satiation are governed by laws that are the mirror opposite of those laws of economics that govern oil, steel, and other traditional consumer objects from cellular phones to lasers.

Numerous games (although not all) are based on symbolic patterns and hence, like knowledge objects, are learned but not consumed, with minimal costs. Children play checkers (and other games) with discarded bottle caps. Chess played by inmates, using figures made of stale bread, is not less enjoyable than a game played with raze, ivory hand-carved pieces. (One may gain a secondary satisfaction from the aesthetic beauty or expense of the set, but these satisfactions have nothing to do with the game of chess per se.)

Similarly, bonding, love, intimacy, friendship, contemplation, communion with nature, certain forms of exercise (yoga, for example, as distinct from step aerobics), all can free one, to a large extent, from key laws of capitalist economies. In effect, these relationship-based sources of satisfaction are superior from this viewpoint to knowledge objects, because in the kind of relationships just enumerated, when one gives more, one often receives more, and thus both sides (or, in larger social entities such as communities, all sides) are 'enriched' by the same 'transactions.' Thus when two individuals are getting to know one another as persons and become 'invested' in one another during the ritual known as dating, often both are richer for it. (This important point is often overlooked by those who coined the term 'social capital' to claim that relations are akin to transactions.) Similarly, parents who are more involved with their children often (although by no means always) find that their children are more involved with them, and both draw more satisfaction from the relationship. Excesses are far from unknown – for example, when some parents attempt to draw most of their satisfaction from their children, or in sharply asymmetrical relations in which one side exploits the other's dedication or love. Nonetheless, mutual 'enrichment' seems much more common.

The various sources of nonmaterialist satisfaction listed here were celebrated by counterculture movements. However, voluntary simplicity differs from these counterculture movements in that voluntary simplicity, even by those highly dedicated to it, seeks to combine a reasonable level of work and consumption to attend to creature-comfort needs with satisfaction from higher sources. The counterculture movements of the past tried to minimize work and consumption, denying attention to basic needs, and hence became unsustainable. To put it more charitably, they provided an extreme, pathblazing version for the voluntary simplicity ideology that followed. While much more moderate than the lifestyle advocated by the counterculture, the voluntary simplicity approach, because it fosters satisfaction from knowledge rather than consumer objects, reduces the need to work and shop. As a result, it frees time and other scarce resources for further cultivation of nonmaterialistic sources of satisfaction, from acquiring music appreciation to visiting museums, from slowing down to enjoy nature to relearning the reading of challenging books or watching classic films.

None of the *specific* sources of nonmaterialistic satisfaction are necessarily tied to voluntary simplicity. One can engage in a voluntarily simple life without enjoying music or nature, being a loving person or a consumed chess player, an Internet buff or a domino aficionado. However, voluntary simplicity does point to the quest for *some* sources of satisfaction other than the consumption of goods and services. This statement is based on the elementary assumption that people prefer higher levels of satisfaction over lower ones; hence if higher satisfaction is not derived from ever-higher levels of consumption, their 'excess' quest, that which is not invested in the unnecessary pursuit of creature comforts, seeks to be invested elsewhere. It follows that while the specific activities that serve as the sources of nonmaterialist satisfaction will vary, some such must be cultivated or voluntary simplicity may not be sustainable.

A Voluntarily Simplistic Society

The shift to voluntary simplicity has significant consequences for society at large, above and beyond the lives of the individuals who are involved. A promising way to think about these effects is to ask what the societal consequences would be if more and more members of society, possibly an overwhelming majority, engaged in one kind or another of voluntary simplicity. These consequences are quite self-evident for environmental concerns; however, they are much less self-evident for social justice and thus warrant further attention.

The more comprehensively voluntary simplicity is embraced as a lifestyle by a given population, the greater the potential for realizing a fundamental element of social justice, that of basic socioeconomic equality. Before this claim is justified, a few words are needed on the meaning of the term 'equality,' a complex and much-contested notion.

While conservatives tend to favor limiting equality to legal and political statutes, those who are more politically left and liberal favor various degrees of redistribution of wealth in ways that would enhance socioeconomic equality. Members of the left-liberal camp differ significantly in the extent of equality they seek. Some favor far-reaching, if not total, socioeconomic equality in which all persons would share alike in whatever assets, income, and consumption are available, an idea championed by the early kibbutz movements. Others limit their quest for equality to ensuring that all members of society will at least have their basic creature comforts equally provided, a position championed by many liberals. The following discussion focuses on this quest for socioeconomic and not just legal and political equality, focusing on equality at the basic, creature-comfort level rather than comprehensive overall equality. (The debate about whether or not holistic equality is virtuous, and if it entails undercutting both liberty and the level of economic performance on which the provision of creature comforts depends, is an important subject. However, it need not be addressed until basic socioeconomic equality is achieved, and so far this has proven to be an elusive goal.)

If one seeks to advance basic socioeconomic equality, one must identify sources that will propel the desired change. Social science findings and recent historical experience leave little doubt that ideological arguments (such as pointing to the injustices of inequalities, fanning guilt, introducing various other liberal and socialist arguments that favor greater economic equality), organizing labor unions and left-leaning political parties, and introducing various items of legislation (such as estate taxes and progressive income tax) have thus far not effected the desired result namely, significant wealth redistribution – in democratic societies. The most that can said for them is that they helped prevent inequality from growing bigger.[52] Additionally, in recent years, many of the measures, arguments, and organizations that championed these limited, rather ineffectual efforts to advance equality could not be sustained, or were successful only after they had been greatly scaled back.[53] Moreover, for these and other reasons that need not be explored here, economic *in*equalities seem to have increased in many parts of the world. The former communist countries, including the Soviet Union, where once a sacrifice of liberties was associated with a minimal but usually reliable provision of subsistence needs, have moved to a socioeconomic system that tolerates, indeed is built on, a much higher level of inequality, one in which millions have no reliable source of creature comforts. Numerous other countries that had measures of socialist policies, from India to Mexico, have been moving in the same direction. And in many Western countries social safety nets are under attack, being shredded in some countries and merely lowered in others. When all is said and done, it seems clear that if basic socioeconomic equality is to be significantly advanced, it will need some new or additional force.

Voluntary simplicity, if more widely embraced, might well be the best new way to foster the societal conditions under which the limited reallocation of wealth needed to ensure the basic needs of all could become politically possible. The reason is as basic and simple as it is essential: To the extent that the privileged (those whose basic creature comforts are well sated and who are engaging in conspicuous consumption) will find value, meaning, and satisfaction in other pursuits, ones that are not labor or capital intensive, they can be expected to be more willing to give up some consumer goods and some income. These 'freed' resources, in turn, can be shifted to those whose basic needs have not been sated, without undue political resistance or backlash.

Enhancing basic equality in a society in which voluntary simplicity is spreading is rather different from doing so in a society in which the same cause is served by coercive measures. First, the economically privileged are often those who are in power, who command political skills, or who can afford to buy support. Hence, to force them to yield significant parts of their wealth often has proven impractical, whether it is just or theoretically correct or not. Second, even if the privileged can somehow be made to yield a significant part of their wealth, such forced concessions leave in their wake strong feelings of resentment that often have led the wealthy to nullify or circumvent programs such as progressive income taxes and inheritance taxes, or to support political parties or regimes that oppose wealth reallocation.

Finally, the record shows that when people are strongly and positively motivated by nonconsumerist values and sources of satisfaction, they are less inclined to exceed their basic consumption needs and more willing to share their 'excess' resources. Voluntary simplicity provides a culturally fashioned expression for such inclinations and helps enforce them, and it provides a socially approved and supported lifestyle that is both psychologically sustainable and compatible with basic socioeconomic equality.

A variety of public policies, especially in Holland but also in France and Germany, seek to transfer some wealth and income from the privileged to those who do not have the resources needed to meet their basic needs has been introduced recently. A major category of such policies are those that concern the distribution of labor, especially in countries in which unemployment is high, by curbing overtime, shortening the work week, and allowing more part-time work.

Another batch of policies seeks to ensure that all members of society will have sufficient income to satisfy at least some of their *basic* needs, approaching the matter from the income rather than the work side. These include increases in the minimum wage, the introduction of the earned income tax credit, attempts at establishing universal health insurance, and housing allowances for the deserving poor.

In short, if voluntary simplicity is more and more extensively embraced as a combined result of changes in culture and public policies by those whose basic creature comforts have been sated, it might provide the foundations for a society that accommodates basic socioeconomic equality much more readily than societies in which conspicuous consumption is rampant.

(Endnotes)

1 See Frank Musgrove, *Ecstasy and Holiness: Counter Culture and the Open Society* (Bloomington: Indiana University Press, 1974), pp. 17–18, 40–41, 198. Musgrove notes the paradox that although the counterculture is 'marked by frugality and low consumption,' it arises specifically in wealthy societies, p17.

2 United Nations Environment Programme, *Global Environmental Outlook-1*; *Chapter 2: Regional Perspectives*. http://unep.unep.org/unep/eia/geol/ch/ch2_12.htm

3 Duane Swank, 'Modernization and Postmodernization: Cultural, Economic, and Political Change in 43 Societies,' *Comparative Political Studies* (April 1998), p247.

4 Ibid.

5 Paul R. Abramson and Ronald Inglehart, *Value Change in Global Perspective* (Ann Arbor: University of Michigan Press, 1995), p19. Similar shifts occurred in most developed nations, pp. 12–15.

6 Ibid., 12–15.

7 *Public Agenda*, 'Consumer Debt Rising in Recent Years,' 1998. Available: http://www.publicagenda.org:80/CGI/getdoc ... 168994x0y64&pg=economy _factf les l3.htm1.

8 U.S. Bureau of the Census, *Statistical Abstract of the United States*, 1996(116th ed.) (Washington, D.C.: U.S. Bureau of the Census, 1996), table 695.

9 U.S. Bureau of the Census, *Statistical Abstract of the United States*, 1994 (114th ed.) (Washington, D.C.: U.S. Bureau of the Census, 1996), table 695.

10 Alan Durning, *How Much Is Enough? The Consumer Society and the Future of the Earth* (New York Worldwatch Institute, 1992), p33.

11 Duane Elgin, *Voluntary Simplicity: Toward a Way of Life That is Outwardly Simple, Inwardly Rich* (New York: William Morrow, 1981).

12 See, for instance, Charles Handy, *The Hungry Spirit: Beyond Capitalism: A Quest for Purpose in the Modern World* (New York Broadway Books, 1998).

13 Pilar Viladas, 'Inconspicuous Consumption,' *New York Times Magazine*, April 13, 1997, p25.

14 Rita Henley Jensen, 'Recycling the American Dream,' *ABA Journal* (April 1996), pp. 68–72.

15 Trends Research Institute, cited in Stephanie Zimmerman, 'Living Frugal and Free,' *Chicago Sun-Times*, April 20, 1997, p6.

16 'Choosing the Joys of a Simplified Life,' *New York Times*, September 21, 1995, Cl; Merck Family Fund, *Yearning for a Balance: Views of Americans on Consumption, Materialism, and the Environment, Executive Summary* (The Harwood Group, 1995).

17 John Martellaro, 'More People Opting for a Simpler Lifestyle,' *The Plain Dealer* (Kansas City), February 10, 1996, 1E.

18 'Boomers Would Pay To Simplify' *USA Today*, November 7, 1997, 1A.

19 'Voluntary Simplicity,' *NPR Morning Edition*, February 26, 1997.

20 'Is Greed Dead?' *Fortune*, August 14, 1989, p41.

21 'More Mothers Staying at Home,' *Boston Globe*, December 18, 1994, NW1.

22 'More Career-Switchers Declare, "Those Who Can, Teach,"' *Wall Street Journal*, April 8, 1997, B1.

23 Barry Schwartz, *The Costs of Living: How Market Freedom Erodes the Best Things in Life* (New York: W.W. Norton and Company, 1994), pp.235–36.

24 Elgin, *Voluntary Simplicity*, p34.

25 Ibid., 51.

26 Ibid., esp. pp.27–28.

27 David E. Shi, *The Simple Life: Plain Living and High Thinking in American Culture* (New York: Oxford University Press, 1985), p4.

28 Duane Elgin, *Voluntary Simplicity*, 201.

29 United Nations, *The Rio Declaration on Environment and Development*, 1992, Principle 8.

30 Paul H. Ray, 'The Emerging Culture,' *American Demographics* (February 1997), pp. 29, 31.

31 Frank M. Andrews and Stephen B. Withey, *Social Indicators of Well-Being: Americans' Perceptions of Life Quality* (New York Plenum Press, 1976), pp.254–55.

32 Jonathan Freedman, *Happy People: What Happiness Is, Who Has It, and Why* (New York: Harcourt Brace Jovanovich, 1978).
33 David G. Myers and Ed Diener, 'Who Is Happy?' *Psychological Science* 6 (1995), p13.
34 Ibid.
35 Ed Diener and R. J. Larsen, 'The Experience of Emotional Well-Being,' in M. Lewis and J. M. Haviland, eds., *Handbook of Emotions* (New York: Guilford Press, 1993): 404–415. Cited in Myers and Diener, 'Who Is Happy?'
36 Myers and Diener, 'Who Is Happy?,' p13.
37 Data culled by Myers and Diener, ibid., from various sources.
38 Angus Campbell, *The Sense of Well-Being in America: Recent Patterns and Trends* (New York McGraw-Hill, 1981), pp. 56–57.
39 Ibid.
40 Durning, *How Much Is Enough?*, p23.
41 Myers and Diener, 'Who Is Happy?,' pp.12–13; see also Ed Diener, E. Sandvik, L. Sedulity, and M. Diener, 'The Relationship Between Income and Subjective Well-Being: Relative or Absolute?' *Social Indicators Research* 28 (1993), p208.
42 Tim Kasser and Richard M. Ryan, 'A Dark Side of the American Dream: Correlates of Financial Success as a Central Life Aspiration,' *Journal of Personality and Social Psychology* 65 (1993), p420.
43 Robert E. Lane, 'Does Money Buy Happiness?' *Public Interest* (Fall 1993), p58.
44 Ibid., 56–65.
45 Robert Bellah, The Broken Covenant: American Civil Religion in Time of Trial (New York Seabury Press, 1975), 134.
46 Abraham H. Maslow, *Toward A Psychology of Being* (Princeton: Von Nostrand, 1968), p172.
47 Ibid., p25.
48 Ibid., 26–27.
49 Vance Packard, *The Status Seekers: An Exploration of Class Behavior in America and the Hidden Barriers That Affect You, Your Community, Your Future* (New York: D. McKay Co., 1959).
50 David Brooks, 'The Liberal Gentry,' *The Weekly Standard*, December 30, 1996, January 6, 1997, p25.
51 Alvin Toffler, *Future Shock* (New York: Random House, 1970). Daniel Bell, *The Coming of Post-Industrial Society: A Venture in Social Forecasting* (New York: Basic Books, 1973).
52 Joseph A. Pechman, *Federal Tax Policy* (Washington, D.C.: The Brookings Institution, 1987), p6.
53 For instance, note the changes in the Labour Party in the United Kingdom and the Democratic Party in United States in the mid-1990s.

Chapter Three

TWO WAYS OF THINKING ABOUT MONEY

Jerome Segal

In popular imagery, especially when seen from afar, America is often portrayed as singing a single song, as if there were only one meaning to the American Dream. This is not so. The ambivalent response that many in the world have toward American life is mirrored in an ambivalence that many Americans have toward their own life, and this is an essential part of the American tradition, even when people are 'making it' in America. There is always that nagging question, 'Is this really the way to live?'

Long before there was an America, there were two American Dreams, and they reflect two ways of thinking about money. In Western thought, from the very beginning to the present day, people had doubts about the real value of riches and the things money can buy. There has always been a conflict between the view that 'more is better' and the view that 'just enough is plenty.'

This divide is reflected in two very different visions of the good life. The underlying thesis of what follows is that the Alternative Dream, the dream that rests upon the attainment of a simple life, is the sounder vision.

Aristotle's Challenge to Our Way of Life

This chapter is about contemporary life, but I want to start with Aristotle for two reasons. First, because his challenge to a money-oriented form of life remains as powerful today as it was 2,300 years ago. Second, because, for all his wisdom, Aristotle never had to wrestle with the problems we face. So many of the contemporary problems that prevent people in the middle class from enjoying the good life emerge from three forms of genuine moral and social progress that Aristotle never envisioned: the elimination of slavery, the liberation of women, and the affirmation of the right of ordinary working people to self-fulfillment. Seeing both the strengths and weaknesses in Aristotle gives us a clearer perspective on our own situation.

Aristotle's *Politics* is surprising in that it opens with a discussion of the household. But this is exactly the right touchstone for both politics and economics. The household is a central ground of the good life, and all economic arrangements must be judged by whether they enable the household to perform its function as locus and support for the human good. This is one of the central messages of my book *Graceful Simplicity* (from which this chapter is drawn): we must put the proper functioning of the household at the center of the way we think about economic life.

The core issue, as Aristotle puts it, is property and 'the art of acquisition' – that is, how people make a living. He starts with the observation that there are a variety of different modes of subsistence, and that this gives rise to a variety of different ways of life. This is as true among animals as it is of humans. Some animals live in herds, and others live in isolation. Some eat plants and others meat. Among human beings, Aristotle identifies five 'natural' ways of life: pastoral, farming, fishing, hunting, and, interestingly, piracy. What he calls 'true wealth' is acquired through these activities and consists of the amount of household property that suffices for the good life. This he regards as a limited amount. We can call this the perspective that 'just enough is plenty.'

In distinction to these modes of acquisition that supply the household with its needs, there is a second form of the art of acquisition, which Aristotle believes to be 'unnatural':

> The other form is a matter only of retail trade, and it is concerned only with getting a fund of money, and that only by the method of conducting the exchange of commodities.
>
> The acquisition of wealth by the art of household management [as contrasted with the art of acquisition in its retail form] has a limit; and the object of that art is not an unlimited amount of wealth.[1]

The difference is between an approach to acquisition that views it as functional to the life of the household and one in which it takes on a life of its own, such that it reproduces unchecked without regard to the larger life of the organism, and ultimately undermines that life – the very description of what we now understand as cancer.

What Aristotle presents in these lines isn't just an academic distinction, but a clash between two different ways of life, each captured by a way of thinking about money. In the first, money and the things one can buy with it play an important but limited role. Life is not about money. It is not about getting rich. It is about something higher, whether it is philosophy, or art, or the pursuit of knowledge, or participation with one's fellow citizens in the ever-absorbing process of governing the democratic polis. Every person lives within a household, and the household has its economic needs–but the point is to attain only what is sufficient to enable one to turn away from money-getting and undertake the real activities of life.

In this first vision of life, only some ways of making a living are viewed by Aristotle as acceptable. His list of farmer, hunter, fisherman, herdsman, or pirate has an arbitrary quality to it. What is important is what these choices are intended to rule out. The one thing you cannot do is spend your life grubbing for money. You do not become a businessman, a retail trader, a man of commerce. These all represent a kind of slavishness to money. Nor (one would hope) do you find yourself so destitute that you must work for someone else, for that, too, is a form of slavery. The good life requires some degree of good fortune. Ideally for Aristotle, you are born financially independent.

But how do people manage to go so wrong about money? How does it gain such control over their lives? Aristotle suggests that this emerges from a deep misconception about the nature of human happiness; it is this that leads to the focus on the pursuit of higher and higher levels of consumption and of the higher income necessary to sustain them.

Aristotle identifies what he terms 'external goods'; these externals include wealth, property, power, and reputation. These are the elements that make up the standard vision of success both then and now. To these, Aristotle contrasts elements of character, what he terms the 'goods of the soul,' fortitude, temperance, justice, and wisdom.[2] This is a familiar distinction, between inner and outer, between matters of worldliness and matters of virtue. We continue to make these distinctions when we are reflective, not so much about our own lives, but when we think about what we want for our children – are we more concerned that our children be rich and successful or that they develop into good human beings? We tell them that these 'externals' are not what is really important in life, and we hope that they will listen.

Aristotle tells us that happiness 'belongs more to those who have cultivated their character and mind to the uttermost, and kept acquisition of external goods within moderate limits.'[3] Those who lose in life are those 'who have managed to acquire more external goods than they can possibly use, and are lacking in the goods of the soul.'[4] (For 'soul' we might substitute 'character' or 'mental health.')

Of course, one might say, 'Why the either/or? Why not have both?' But Aristotle, and many others, have thought that we really do have to choose. In explaining the relationship between externals and the good life, Aristotle tells us: 'External goods, like all other instruments, have a necessary limit of size ... any excessive amount of such things must either cause its possessor some injury, or at any rate, bring him no benefit.'[5]

This passage, which has been overlooked by many historians of economics, implicitly is the first statement of the principle of diminishing marginal utility. We might remember from introductory economics that marginal utility is the extra utility (or happiness, satisfaction, pleasure, fulfillment) that someone gets from each successive unit of something. Marginal utility generally declines; the pleasure from the first ice-cream cone is greater than from the second, and most of us can hardly eat a third.

Aristotle is saying that with all external goods, we find that the more we have, the less utility we receive from each additional amount, and that at some point 'any excessive amount' does us no good and may even harm us.

Actually, Aristotle's view of what nineteenth-century economists would identify as the 'utility curve' is quite radical. As we acquire more and more things, not only does the total utility (i.e., happiness, satisfaction) level fail to rise beyond an upper bound (as in classical presentations of the diminishing character of marginal utility), but the total utility level may actually diminish, implying that the marginal benefit attached to excessive amounts of external goods diminishes beyond the zero level and actually becomes harmful. Translated into a thesis about money, Aristotle's formulation tells us that beyond a given level, additional increments of money are not only useless, but negative in their effect. Translated into a thesis about the society at large, it suggests that economic growth beyond a given point is actually harmful to human happiness. It is a straightforward rejection of the idea that 'more is better.'

Aristotle goes further in his account. The problem is not merely of the sort that John Kenneth Galbraith described (twenty-three centuries later) in *The Affluent Society*, where economic life is compared to life on a squirrel wheel, each of us fruitlessly expending time and resources but not getting anywhere as the wheel just spins faster and faster. For Galbraith the indictment is that we are wasting our time and energy, and thus wasting our lives.

For Aristotle the issue is even more serious than a life of wasted pursuit. The pursuit of higher and higher levels of income results in a distortion of the personality, such that we never come to be the persons that we most truly are; we are divorced from our truest selves. Instead people are 'led to occupy themselves wholly in the making of money ... using each and every capacity in a way not consonant with its nature.'[6]

When Aristotle says 'the lower form of the art of acquisition has come into vogue,' he is quietly telling us that he sees his own civilization threatened by a new and troubling vision of the place of money in the good life. He is giving voice to concerns that, centuries later, in religious form and in America, will be repeated in the form of fiery jeremiads issued from the pulpit.

Though he might have, Aristotle doesn't use phrases such as 'we have lost our souls' – instead he speaks of a distortion of human capacities. He offers an example:

> The proper function of courage, for example, is not to produce money but to give confidence. The same is true of military and medical ability: neither has the function of producing money: the one has the function

> of producing victory, and the other that of producing health. But those of whom we are speaking turn all such capacities into forms of the art of acquisition, as though to make money were the one aim and everything else must contribute to that aim.[7]

Consider this comment about 'medical ability' – Aristotle is talking about what it is to be a doctor. What we once expected to encounter when we went to the doctor was someone whose motivation centered around the inherent value of medicine – the health of the patient. What we did not expect, and once would have been repelled by, was to have encountered a businessman in a white coat or an entrepreneur with aides who are specialists in billing practices. When this happens across the board, when everything is about money, a civilization is cracking apart. It should be clear that Aristotle's critique is not merely about certain specific economic activities (e.g., retail sales as opposed to production). It is an indictment of a general outlook and form of life. When these become dominant in society, the object of criticism is then the entire form of social life or civilization.

Such a civilization, and I believe Aristotle would include much of the modern world in this category, is to be condemned as representing a distortion of human nature and a general thwarting of the possibility of human fulfillment.

When every human capacity gets placed at the service of obtaining money, *we ourselves are transformed and distorted.*[8] That's why you can't have it all – why there is conflict between the two American Dreams – who 'you' are changes through the choices you (and your household) make toward matters of acquisition, careers, 'success.' Within the Aristotelian framework, to say that our capacities, that is, our selves, are separated from their proper function, is to say that we are thus denied self-actualization or human fulfillment. It is also to say that we are thus denied the possibility of living well; for to live well for Aristotle is to express one's richest potentials at high levels of excellence.

It is easy to miss the full significance of this, as the Aristotelian vocabulary is not our own. But we can shift the language a bit. Perhaps we would speak of a life so absorbed in moment-to-moment gain and careerism that one loses or never deeply develops a sense of oneself and never lives the life he or she intended to. In the end, one is left with a sense of emptiness and waste. It's captured in the bumper sticker that reads: 'No one ever died wishing they had spent more time at the office.'

These matters largely fall by the wayside in contemporary thinking about the economic realm. Instead we hear a very different story, one in which we come to the economic realm as well-formed consumers. We have multiple wants and desires. There are limited resources. Producers compete for our spending money by creating the products that best satisfy our desires. In an efficient system, the companies that serve people's desires most adequately and efficiently make profits; the others disappear. The result is more and more consumer satisfaction. As consumers we are said to be sovereign. But to participate in the process, we must sell our labor services to those who can make best use of them. Thus, we take jobs that pay more, and we are enabled to buy more. When the system is working well, some of what is earned is reinvested, and the economy grows, gaining greater capacity to produce. Incomes rise and the level of consumption rises within, making us even better off than we were before.

In contrast we can identify an approach that might be termed Aristotelian:

- ★ There is no distinct economic realm.
- ★ Economic institutions and policy must be judged in terms of how they affect the good life and the healthy personality.
- ★ The central institution to be supported by economic life is the household (which in turn supports worthwhile activity in the larger world).
- ★ The good life is not one of consumption, but of the flourishing of our deepest selves.
- ★ Absorption in a life-of acquisitiveness distorts the personality out of all recognition.
- ★ What we need for our well-being is only a moderate supply of material goods. As we acquire more, material possessions are of diminishing value.

Ultimately the additional contribution to the good life of having more money reaches zero, and even becomes negative.

Aristotle, in his analysis of the limited place of money in the good life, and in his emphasis on how absorption in acquisition undermines both the healthy personality and the good life, can be seen as the intellectual father of a philosophy of simple living.

But before leaving Aristotle, we must recognize the other side of the picture. Aristotle was not a believer in the general equality of all men and women. Though he did not hold a racial theory, he believed that there were some people who were 'natural slaves' in that they lacked the capability of governing themselves. Of course, at some point in life – when we are children – we all lack this capability. But Aristotle believed that a significant class of adult males, and women generally, lacked the capability to govern themselves.

These views about the naturalness of slavery and the subservience of women turn out to have an intimate relationship to the question of simple living, and to graceful living in particular. Later, I will consider the question 'What is real wealth?' Ultimately I want to argue that most wealth resides in the ability to draw on the services of other people, and this is especially true of that wealth which contributes to graceful living. We normally think of such wealth as residing in financial assets (e.g., money, stocks, bonds, real estate), but it can equally reside in relationships (e.g., friendship, parent-child relationships, marriage). It can also reside in institutionalized relations of unequal power such as slavery, rigid class distinctions, and the domination of women. When one has access to the services of others through such institutional structures, it is indeed easier to live well, even gracefully, with less money; one has found nonmonetized ways of accessing valued services. The great challenge is to find a way to live simply, gracefully, and well, not only without excessive dependence upon money, but without reliance on unjust social institutions.

For Aristotle, this never realty clicked into place. While he recognized that not all who were in fact slaves were of a 'slavish nature,' he did not challenge slavery itself. It is similar when he considers the situation of artisans; that is, skilled craftsmen employed in making the artifacts of everyday life. He speaks of the mechanical type of artisan as being subject to a 'limited servitude,' by which he means that the artisan is in parts of his life subject to the will of his master. But then, in contrast to the situation with slaves, Aristotle tells us that while 'the slave belongs to the class of those who are naturally what they are; ... no shoemaker or any other artisan, belongs to that class.'[9]

Here Aristotle makes two points of great importance. First, artisans – and, we can say, most working people – are subject to a limited servitude; their lives bear some significant resemblance to slavery. (Twenty-three centuries later people would speak of 'wage slavery.') Second, Aristotle says that no artisan is 'naturally' what he is. That is, such limited slavery is unnatural.

Aristotle should have concluded from this that there is something unnatural, or at least inadequate, about the polis, understood as the sum of the socioeconomic processes and structures within which Greek life occurred. He fails to do so. In his discussion of the limited slavery of workers, there is no proposal for an alternative social arrangement, despite the fact that he sees the way the institution is incompatible with the fulfillment of the deeper potentials of those who labor within it. This, I believe, emerged from an unexamined assumption that such must necessarily be the case if we are to have a social order in which there are at least some people who are fully developed and living a free and flourishing existence. There is a passage in Aristotle in which he considers the possibility of a world in which it would not be necessary for people to work in partial or full enslavement. But he offers this speculation not as a future that might someday be, but as a fantasy that cannot be. Thus, it shows why things must be as they are:

> There is only one condition in which we can imagine managers not needing subordinates, and masters not needing slaves. This condition would be that each (inanimate) instrument could do its own work, at the word of command or by intelligent anticipation ... as a shuttle should weave of itself and a plectrum should do its own harp playing.[10]

It is revealing that he speaks here of the 'needs' of managers and masters, rather than of the needs of slaves and people who work for a living. In part this merely shows the partial blindness of even the greatest minds, but it also reflects his inability to foresee the actual occurrence of major sustained technological progress. It is too much to expect that he could have truly foreseen full automation – where the machines operate on their own. But he might have had a vision of the continued increase in the productivity of labor.

Given that Aristotle was clear about the limited value of acquiring more and more, he would have been led to the alternative use of productivity increases: not to have more and more, but to allow the ordinary person to work less and less in order to produce that limited output that is required for the good and free life. In short, through productivity growth there is a potential that can be put in the service of self-actualization for the ordinary person. It is such productivity growth that allowed us to go from the twelve-hour day to the eight-hour day, and opens the possibility of the six-hour day, or the three-day weekend. For a hundred years this was part of how we used productivity growth; we stopped doing this sixty years ago. Had he seen the deeper potentials of all people, Aristotle would have seen the polis of his day not as a model for humankind, but as modeling only in the life of its free male citizens, a life that someday might be available to all, provided that we used that productivity growth, not for ever-increasing amounts of unnecessary goods, but for the elimination of slavish forms of activity.

Put in other terms, for Aristotle the existence of mass poverty does not emerge as a problem. With his acceptance of the naturalness of slavery and the subservience of women, and his acquiescence to the limited servitude of workers, the socioeconomic framework of the polis fits neatly into a theory of human development. The polis is the environment with which human fulfillment occurs. The situation of the vast majority of persons simply falls by the wayside, as not raising any pressing problems. Having limited potential, they reach their full development within subservient roles. Indeed, it is really not until the eighteenth century that the equality of ordinary people in their entitlement and potential for achieving the highest levels of human development are embedded within the structures of political ideology and action. And it is not until the twentieth century that equality begins to be substantially extended to women.

What Aristotle did do, however, remains of enormous importance. He challenged the idea that acquiring more and more things was good for the individual. He set his critique of commercial and acquisitive forms of life within a theory of human development that stressed the exercise and perfection of distinctly human capacities, capacities that are distorted and stunted if we allow economic pursuits to dominate our lives.

Appreciating the virtues of Aristotle along with his limitations is particularly important for a balanced appreciation of the problem inherent in our own way of life. We live in a society that, as a result of both economic growth and social struggle, is substantially along the way to overcoming historic legacies of slavery, mass poverty, and the subjugation of women. Yet many of the problems that we face, problems that make it more difficult to achieve simple living, emerge because of these legacies and transitions. But they also endure because we have lost sight of much that Aristotle has to teach us with respect to the place of the economic within the good life: *The point of an economy, even a dynamic economy, is not to have more and more; it is to liberate us from the economic – to provide a material platform from which we may go forth to build the good life. That's the Alternative American Dream.*

Simple Living and American Dreams

We entirely mistake our own history if we think of simple living as some recent fad. The idea of simple living has always been part of the American psyche – sometimes central, sometimes only a minor theme, but always present. From the earliest days of the American experience, advocates of simple living have challenged consumerism and materialism. Simple living, especially in America, has meant many things.[11] For Christians the central inspiration for a life of simplicity has been the life of Jesus. In the hands of the Puritans, this emerged as a life of religious devotion, a lack of ostentation, and plenty of hard work. It was certainly not a leisure expansion movement as it is today. Nor was simple living a matter of individual choice; sumptuary laws invoked the power of the state to restrict consumption display, and economic life was regulated to limit the role of greed in human affairs.

In the hands of the Quakers, the concept of the simple life underwent an evolution. For the Puritans, at least part of the motivation for sumptuary laws was to prevent those in the lower classes from putting on the manners of those above them; among Quakers, the restrictions on display and consumption became more widely applicable. Most important, the pursuit of luxurious consumption was linked to a broad range of injustices and social problems, including alcoholism, poverty, slavery, and ill treatment of the Indians. Here, perhaps, are the origins of a radical politics of plain living

– the belief that if people adopted the simple life, all of society would be transformed.

The key Quaker theorist of the simple life was John Woolman. Central to Woolman's thought was the recognition that people could be 'necessitated to labour too hard.' He focused on the plight of those who did not own their own land but rented it from large estates. If the rent was too high, the amount of labor required of the poor would oppress them and draw them away from the proper affairs of life. But rent was an intermediate concern; what was really at issue was the extent to which one person would be required to labor so that another might have superfluous luxuries. Woolman wrote, 'Were all superfluities, and the desires of outward greatness laid aside,' then 'moderate labour with the blessing of Heaven would answer all good purposes ... and a sufficient number have time to attend on the proper affairs of civil society.'[12] Thus, he maintained that 'every degree of luxury of what kind soever and every demand for money inconsistent with divine order hath some connexion with unnecessary labour.' Woolman called on his listeners to follow the example of Jesus in simple food and dress. He saw their desire for luxurious consumption as the core motive that resulted in the practice 'of fetching men to help to labour from distant parts of the world, to spend the remainder of their lives in the uncomfortable conditions of slaves.' He also identified selfishness as the cause of past wars, telling us to 'look upon our treasures, and the furniture of our houses, and the garment in which we array ourselves, and try whether the seeds of war have nourishment in these our possessions, or not.' Were Woolman alive today, it is likely that he would extend his critique, arguing that excessive consumption, and the desire for it, is at the root of both the drug and environmental problems we face. Indeed, Woolman would probably have been receptive to the idea that the harsh poverty of many Third World countries emerges from the excessive consumption of the rich nations.

In the mid-1700s, in the years prior to the Revolution, the ideas of simple living and democratic government were intertwined. For many of the leaders of the Revolution, however, the ideal was not the simple life of Jesus, but the simple life of the self-governing citizens of ancient Greece and Rome. Key figures in the revolutionary period, in particular Samuel Adams, were deeply concerned about the relationship between our political health and the individual pursuit of luxury. The rebirth of democracy in the world brought with it an interest in the ancient Greek and Roman experiments, and why they disappeared. There was a concern (as there is today) with the virtue of officeholders. Genuine democracy seemed incompatible with too great an absorption in getting rich. There was great fear of the corrupting influences of unbridled commercialism. When the colonists boycotted British goods, it was not just a tactic of the independence movement; Britain was viewed as the Great Satan, exporting the corruptions of capitalism.

In their correspondence, John Adams and Thomas Jefferson assessed the prospects for building a nonmaterialist society. Jefferson emphasized civic virtue, and looked to public policy, in particular state-supported schools and values education, as the foundation of such a society. Adams viewed this as unrealistically 'undertaking to build a new universe.' He himself feared economic growth, however, and argued for preventing both extreme poverty and extravagant riches. Both men feared rather than celebrated boundless economic opportunity.

Benjamin Franklin's views on these questions are also worth noting; they, too, have a contemporary echo. In Franklin we have an unusual mixture: the espousal of frugality, hard work, and restrained consumption as the vehicles for getting ahead, the central patterns of behavior that will lead to wealth. Thus, in the preface to *Poor Richard's Almanac*, which was reprinted in fourteen languages under the title *The Way to Wealth*,[13] Franklin writes, 'But dost thou love Life, then do not squander Time; for that's the stuff Life is made of.' And 'If Time be of all Things the most precious, wasting Time must be, as Poor Richard says, the greatest Prodigality.' Franklin was concerned 'with how the average person might remain free in his own life, his own master. 'Employ thy Time well, if thou meanest to gain Leisure.' He warns of the perils of spending and in particular of borrowing. The great thing is to save. 'We must add Frugality, if we would make our Industry more certainly successful. A Man may, if he knows not how to save as he gets, keep his Nose all his Life, to the Grindstone, and die not worth a Groat at last .... If you would be wealthy ... think of Saving as well as Getting.' Note that here Franklin is advocating simple living as a means to future wealth, quite a different reason than those that animated Woolman.

Franklin warned that the dangers of excessive consumption are easily missed. And he was quite demanding in what he viewed as 'excessive.' He wrote, 'You may think perhaps, that a little Tea, or a little Punch now and then, Diet a little more costly, Clothes a little finer, and a little Entertainment now and then, may be no great Matter; but remember what Poor Richard says, Many a Little makes a Mickle ... A small Leak will sink a great Ship.'

He continued, 'The artificial Wants of Mankind thus become more numerous than the Natural. ... When you have bought one fine Thing, you must buy ten more, that your Appearance may be all of a Piece... 'Tis easier to suppress the first Desire, than to satisfy all that follows it .... What Use is this Pride of Appearance, for which so much is risked, so much is suffered? It cannot promote Health, or ease Pain; it makes no Increase of Merit in the Person, it creates Envy, it hastens Misfortune.'

Franklin rails against going into debt. Credit cards would have seemed to him the instruments of our undoing. 'What Madness must it be to run in Debt for these Superfluities! ... think what you do when you turn in Debt;

you give to another Power over your Liberty .... Preserve your Freedom; and maintain your Independency: Be Industrious and free; be frugal and free.'

While Franklin spoke to the individual, in American history, the mode of response to the dominant commercial culture has often been communal. Americans have been utopian, not in the sense of speculation on utopia, but in the actual establishment of a community wherein this dominance by the economic is overcome. Utopian thought has a long and rich history, much of it European. But it was in America, both before and after the founding of the United States, that the impulse to go ahead and just create that better world was the strongest.

Though the formation of these communities was not unique to the American experience, the abundance and constancy of utopian communities does appear to be distinctly American. Indeed there has not been a single year in the history of the United States without communes. One recent study of American communes concluded: 'The extent and continuity of the communal phenomenon had no equal outside the United States .... In modern times the United States is the only place where voluntary communes have existed continuously for 250 years.'[14]

Two features of these utopian communities are particularly noteworthy. First, with few exceptions, they were communes. Property was typically held in common, and sometimes income was pooled. And second, they were typically not merely residential sites, but work sites as well. The community collectively owned land and capital, and the community both provided for itself and collectively produced for the outside world. Thus, virtually all of these communities challenge the boundaries between household and work place that had begun to emerge in the seventeenth century. In doing so as a community, through the holding of the common property of the unified home/work site, they were reestablishing the extended establishment – family. In a sense, these communities could be seen as large establishment – households.

The uninterrupted history of utopian communes throughout American history speaks of an ongoing practical discourse that seeks through actual life experiments to break the boundaries between home and economy, and to replace the harsh marketplace relations of worker/master, of owner/ employer, with a simpler life within a 'circle of affection.' In the mid-1800s such communes flourished. In some ways this period prefigured the communes, vegetarianism, nudism, and animal rights efforts of the 1960s.

Filled with a sense of adventure and experiment, but of a more individualist bent, was Henry David Thoreau. In *Walden* he looked about him and saw mostly foolishness – people not knowing how to grab hold of the gift of life. He reveled in the energy of youth and in its ability to find out what older generations had never seen.

> Practically, the old have no very important advice to give the young, their own experience has been so partial, and their lives have been such miserable failures.... Here is life, an experiment to a great extent untried by me.... If I have any experience which I think valuable, I am sure to reflect that this my Mentors, said nothing about.[15]

With words that had echoes of Aristotle, he told Americans that our necessities are few, yet we subject ourselves to endless labor. He described a world that had taken the wrong turn. 'The twelve labors of Hercules were trifling in comparison with those which my neighbors have undertaken; for they were only twelve and had an end.'[16] Wealth itself is a curse because it enslaves us. 'I see young men, my townsmen, whose misfortune it is to have inherited farms, houses, barns, cattle and farming tools; for these are more easily acquired than got rid of.' Of most men Thoreau says, 'they begin digging their graves as soon as they are born .... Men labor under a mistake. The better part of the man is soon ploughed into the soil for compost.' We must take better care of ourselves, of our potentials. 'The finest qualities of our nature, like the bloom on fruits, can be preserved only by the most delicate handling. Yet we do not treat ourselves nor one another thus tenderly.' We miss that which is best in life. 'Most men, even in this comparatively free country, through mere ignorance and mistake, are so occupied with the factitious cares and superfluously coarse labors of life that its finer fruits cannot be plucked by them.'[17]

Yes, the necessities must be met, 'for not till we have secured these are we prepared to entertain the true problems of life with freedom and a prospect of success.'[18] But 'most of the luxuries, and many of the so called comforts of life are not only not indispensable, but positive hindrances to the elevation of mankind. With respect to luxuries and comforts, the wisest have ever lived a more simple and meager life than the poor.'[19] He tells us that 'none can be an impartial or wise observer of human life but from the vantage ground of what we should call voluntary poverty.'[20] The dictates of wisdom call for 'a life of simplicity, independence, magnanimity and trust.'

For Thoreau it is not necessity that enslaves us. Rather we have become the 'slave-drivers' of ourselves, 'the slave and prisoner of [our] own opinion of [ourselves].' Once we have satisfied our necessities, rather than laboring for superfluities, it is time to 'adventure on life.' But few undertake this adventure. Instead, 'the mass of men lead lives of quiet desperation.' It is from a disease of the spirit that Thoreau recoils, one that people may not even be aware of. 'A stereotyped but unconscious despair is concealed even under what are called the games and amusements of mankind. There is no play in them ....'[21]

Thus Thoreau called Americans away from their overabsorption with economic life, from their self-subjugation to a life of toil. Unlike earlier advocates of simple living, he was not calling people to religion or to civic engagement; rather he was calling us as individuals to find our own nature, to define ourselves at a higher level of experience. He called for simple living in order to enable the life of the mind; of art, literature, poetry, philosophy, and an almost reverential engagement with Nature.

Interest in simple living was harder to find in the post-Civil War period, but it reemerged powerfully toward the turn of the century. There was a reaction against materialism and the hectic pace of urban life. In those days it was *The Ladies' Home Journal* (of all things) that led the charge against the dominant materialist ethos. Under a crusading editor, Edward Bok, it served as a guide for those in the middle class seeking simplicity. By 1910, the *Journal* had a circulation of close to 2 million, making it the largest-selling magazine in the world. This period also witnessed a movement of aesthetic simplicity. It was influenced by the English thinkers John Ruskin and William Morris, and recognized that only in a world which appreciated fine crafts would there be jobs for fine craftsmen. It is from this mileau that we have the 'mission' furniture, much sought by antique dealers today.

One dimension of the renewed interest in simple living was a 'country life' movement that sought to use modern technology to improve country life for the small farmer and to keep young people on the farm. Lately, in 1933, the Department of 'the Interior created a Division of Subsistence Homesteads to resettle the urban and rural poor in planned communities based on 'handicrafts, community activities, closer relationships, and cooperative enterprises.' About one hundred such communities were established, most of them failing in their grand design to replace individualism with 'mutualism.'

After World War II, as after World War I, the Civil War, and the American Revolution, there was a surge in consumption, and simple living receded into the background. But again in the 1960s there was a critique of the affluent lifestyle and a renewed interest in plain living. In the 1970s, with the energy crisis, this merged with a broad environmentalism. Many saw the energy crisis not as an economic or political problem to be overcome, but as an occasion for a spiritual renewal that would turn us away from the rampant materialism of modern life. One of these was President Jimmy Carter.

'We worship self-indulgence and consumption,' Carter declared, taking his place in a great American tradition of social criticism. 'Human identity is no longer defined by what one does but by what one owns.' And like earlier critics, Carter lamented the emptiness of such an existence. 'We've discovered that owning things and consuming things does not satisfy our longing for meaning.'

Carter saw the problem as residing in what he termed 'a mistaken idea of freedom' – one in which we advocate 'the right to grasp for ourselves some advantage over others.' He called on Americans to unite together in a crusade of energy conservation:

> We often think of conservation only in terms of sacrifice ... solutions to our energy crisis can also help us to conquer the crisis of spirit in our country. It can rekindle a sense of unity, our confidence in the future, and give our nation and all of us individually a new sense of purpose.[22]

This was his so-called 'malaise' speech, and while it failed as an effort to transform the national spirit, and certainly failed Carter politically, it did capture well the link between environmental concerns and simple living that many Americans continue to feel today. Carter was followed by the Reagan and Bush administrations, during which no similar critique was heard. But now, at the turn of the millennium, there is renewed interest in simple living, if not in the White House, then at least in the heartland.

This quick historical survey reveals that 'simple living' has meant many things. There is an anticonsumptionist core in much American thinking on this subject, but great diversity with respect to the human good and the place of work, religion, civic engagement, nature, literature, and the arts. Concern with simple living has been largely apolitical at some times, and at others the heart of a general political and social vision.

Today, when there is once again a great interest in simple living in America, it is mainly an apolitical enthusiasm. Most, though not all, of the literature is of a 'how to' variety, offering advice on how to live more rewardingly with less money. The attainment of a simpler, more meaningful life is seen as an individual project, not as a matter of collective politics.

Simple Living and Poverty

The question sometimes arises, 'What is the difference between simple living and poverty?' Several responses are possible. One calls attention to the difference between voluntarily choosing to live in a certain way and having to. This is certainly of great importance. Often enough, people who adopt simple living have the ability to earn more income if they choose. Thus, there is an actual and psychological freedom that attends their life. This freedom is not part of the life experience of those trapped in poverty. It is true that not all of the poor are 'trapped'; some people do manage to escape from poverty. On the other hand, a person is not truly poor if the exit is readily available.

Yet this emphasis on freedom can go only so far. First, there are situations in which the choice to live a simple life is not reversible, situations in which an exit to higher levels of consumption may not be readily at hand. Second, the core of the distinction cannot rest on whether the condition is chosen. We can imagine situations in which for one reason or another (e.g., as a penance) someone chooses to live in irreversible poverty. Alternatively, there are people who have been born into a community or culture based on a tradition of simple living. Simple living is consistent with there being no choice, no awareness of alternatives, and, under some conditions, with no opportunity for opulent living.

The essential matter is not how people come to simple living as opposed to poverty, but a difference that resides in the life itself. Even with no knowledge of how someone got there, it should be possible to distinguish poverty from simple living, just by examining the life people do live.

One approach might be to say that it is a matter of degree, that simple living occupies a place between poverty and middle-class life. Thus, as government agencies sometimes do, we can define poverty arbitrarily in terms of a certain level of income (e.g., the poverty line for a family can be set at 60 percent of median family income). And proceeding in this way, we can also define simple living in terms of income, as a tier that exists between poverty and middle-class status.

While this has the virtue of clarity and precision, it offers little insight. Moreover, there are many variants of simple living, and while some operate above the income levels used to define poverty, others may be below.

Let me offer a different answer. The touchstone here is to ask, 'What is it for a life itself to be impoverished?' As soon as the issue is put in this way, one must ask, 'Impoverished in what dimensions?' The human good is too diverse to try to capture either its richness or its poverty in a single dimension. For instance, we can identify five forms of impoverishment:

★ *Material impoverishment*, meaning inadequacies of goods and services such that the individual experiences (or is exposed to) disease, hunger, starvation. This could be caused by inadequacies of monetary income, inadequacies of public investment, inadequacies of human support systems, or even simply by bad luck.
★ *Intellectual impoverishment*, meaning an inadequacy of education and/or absence of interactions with others so that the individual does not partake in a life of the mind. This can be brought about through lack of schooling leading to illiteracy, or more commonly a culture of intellectual isolation.
★ *Spiritual impoverishment*, meaning the absence of any transcendent meaning in the experiences or activities of the individual. This might include, but certainly should not be limited to or defined in terms of, religious experience.
★ *Aesthetic impoverishment*, meaning the absence of beauty within the person's life, whether it be the beauty of material possessions, the natural environment, the urban world, or the absence of ceremony.

★ *Social impoverishment*, meaning an absence of central relationships, of friends and loved ones.

Who are 'the poor'? There is no single answer. The term covers a wide diversity of people and circumstances. In material terms, it may refer to the average person in a poor African country. There the central facts may be a persistent inadequacy of food and clean water, yet at the same time there may be a vibrant communal, family, and religious life. Alternatively, we may be speaking about the poor in the United States; yet this, too, may refer to highly varied circumstances. There is a great difference between hardworking sharecropper families in Mississippi, with limited income and education, on the one hand, and young inner-city street hustlers, without fathers, in a drug culture, amid gangs and prostitution. Both may face low levels of life expectancy, the sharecropping family from malnutrition, the inner-city drug users from a high probability of either getting shot or acquiring AIDS from shared needles.

When simple living is advocated, it is generally implicit that material needs are met. Today's popular simple living literature focuses strongly on how we can meet our material needs with limited financial means. This, however, must be thought of as a precondition for simple living – by achieving relative independence from material need, one is freed to create a life that is rich in some nonmaterial sense. The central distinction is not between simple living and material poverty (indeed, these can overlap) but between simple living and a life that is impoverished in one or more of its multiple nonmaterial dimensions.

Thus understood, the richness of simple living rests upon the material and non material wealth we both possess and successfully actualize, wealth that may be public or private, cultural or natural, aesthetic, religious, intellectual, interpersonal, or psychological. It may reside in the capabilities of our families and communities, in our relationships with others, or more narrowly within ourselves, as our human capital, psychological and physical.

From this it follows that simple living is not merely a matter of downsizing, of living on less, or of working less. It's possible to do that, and have the result be nothing more than a general impoverishment. Simple living is not the residue that emerges when one consumes less; it is an achievement. It is what can emerge when as a result of subjecting the material dimension to a larger vision, one succeeds in creating a life that is rich and exciting in its aesthetic, intellectual, spiritual, and social dimensions.

(Endnotes)

1 Aristotle, *Politics*, trans. Ernest Barker (New York: Oxford University Press, 1961), p26.

2 Ibid., p26.

3 Ibid., p280.

4 Ibid., p280.

5 Ibid., p280.

6 Ibid., p26.

7 Ibid., p27.

8 Contemporary economic thought, taken in formal terms, can accommodate almost anything. Thus, the distortion of personality can be viewed as 'an externality' generated by market transactions, adding to the costs of every market interaction. But virtually no economists have expanded the idea of externalities to include distortions of personality. It remains a formal possibility, but consideration of such impacts, central to earlier eras, is largely outside of the way we think of the economic realm.

9 Aristotle, *Politics*, p37.

10 Ibid., p10.

11 This is wonderfully explicated in David Shi's study *The Simple Life: Plain Living and High Thinking in American Culture* (Oxford: Oxford University Press, 1985), and I have drawn heavily upon Shi's account for this summary.

12 John Woolman, 'A Word of Remembrance and Caution to the Rich,' in *Words That Made American History*, ed. Richard N. Current and John A Garroty (Boston: Little, Brown and Co., 1965).

13 'The Way to Wealth,' in *Benjamin Franklin, Autobiography and Other Writings* (Cambridge, Mass.: The Riverside Press), 1958).

14 Yaacov Oved, *Two Hundred Years of American Communes* (New Brunswick: Transaction Books, 1988), pp. xiii–xiv.

15 Henry David Thoreau, *Walden* (Princeton: Princeton University Press, 1973) p9.

16 Ibid., p4.

17 Ibid., p6.

18 Ibid., p11.

19 Ibid., p14.

20 Ibid. p14.

21 Ibid., p8.

22 Jimmy Carter, 'Energy Problems: The Erosion of Confidence,' *Vital Speeches* XLV (15 August 1979): 642, 643 as excerpted in David E. Shi, *In Search of the Simple Life* (Salt Lake City: Gibbs M. Smith, 1986).

Chapter Four

WHAT IS AFFLUENZA?

Clive Hamilton and Richard Denniss

Af-flu-en-za n. 1. The bloated, sluggish and unfulfilled feeling that results from efforts to keep up with the Joneses. 2. An epidemic of stress, overwork, waste and indebtedness caused by dogged pursuit of the Australian dream. 3. An unsustainable addiction to economic growth.[1]

Wanting

In 2004 the Australian economy grew by over $25 billion, yet the tenor of public debate suggests that the country is in a dire situation. We are repeatedly told of funding shortages for hospitals, schools, universities and public transport, and politicians constantly appeal to that icon of Australian spirit, the 'Aussie battler.' Political rhetoric and social commentary continue to emphasise deprivation – as if we are living in the nineteenth century and the problems facing the country have arisen because we are not rich enough.

When the Labour Party lost the federal election in 2004 it declared that, like the conservatives, it must pay more attention to growth and the economy. It would seem that achieving an economic growth rate of 4 percent is the magic potion to cure all our ills. But how rich do we have to be before we are no longer a nation of battlers? Australia's GDP has doubled since 1980; at a growth rate of 3 percent, it will double again in 23 years and quadruple 23 years after that. Will our problems be solved then? Or will the relentless emphasis on economic growth and higher incomes simply make us feel more dissatisfied?

In the private domain, Australia is beset by a constant rumble of complaint – as if we are experiencing hard times. When asked whether they can afford to buy everything they really need, nearly two-thirds of Australians say 'no'. If we remember that Australia is one of the world's richest countries and that Australians today have real incomes three times higher than in 1950, it is remarkable that such a high proportion feel so deprived. Average earnings exceed $50,000 a year, yet a substantial majority of Australians who experience no real hardship – and indeed live lives of abundance – believe that they have difficulty making ends meet and that they qualify as battlers.

In the coming decade most of our income growth will be spent on consumer products the craving for which has yet to be created by advertisers. Our public concerns might be about health and the environment, but our private spending patterns show that the majority of Australians feel they suffer from a chronic lack of 'stuff.' The problem is that after we have renewed our stuff yet again, there is not enough money left to fund investments in hospitals and schools. We want better public services but seem unwilling to forgo more income in the form of taxes to pay for those services. Australia does not have a public health funding crisis: it has a flat-screen TV crisis.

It wasn't meant to be this way. Nineteenth century economists predicted that the abundance made possible by technological advance and the modern organisation of work would result in the emergence of 'post-materialist' humans – people existing on a higher plane, where their cultural, intellectual and spiritual powers are refined. In such a world the importance of economic considerations would naturally diminish. The 1960s and 1970s saw a flood of literature predicting a future in which technological progress would allow for us to work only a few hours a week and our main problem would be how best to enjoy our leisure. Futurists saw a society transformed by the fruits of sustained growth – a society in which humankind, freed of the chore of making a living, would devote itself to activities that are truly fulfilling.

But, instead of witnessing the end of economics, we live in a time when economics and its concerns are more dominant than ever before. Instead of our growing wealth freeing us of our materialist preoccupations, it seems to have had the opposite effect. People in affluent countries are now even more obsessed with money and material acquisition, and the richer they are the more this seems to be the case.

As a rule, no matter how much money people have they feel they need more. Why else would people in rich countries such as Australia keep striving to become richer, often at the expense of their own happiness and that of their families? Even the mega-rich seem unable to accept that they have all they need, always comparing themselves unfavourably with their neighbours. Most people cling to the belief that more money means more happiness. Yet when they reach the financial goals they have set they find they do not feel happier – except perhaps fleetingly. Rather than question the whole project, they engage in an internal dialogue that goes like this:

> I hoped that getting to this income level would make me feel contented. I do have more stuff, but it doesn't seem to have done the trick. I obviously need to set my goals higher. I'm sure I'll be happy when I'm earning an extra $10 000 because then I'll be able to buy the other things I want.

Of course, raising the threshold of desire in this way creates an endless cycle of self-deception: like the horizon, our desires always seem to stay ahead of where we are. This cycle of hope and disappointment lies at the heart of consumer capitalism.

Our own achievements are never enough in a society like this. As Gore Vidal said, 'Whenever a friend succeeds, a little something in me dies.' Even if we do come out in front of our peers, the chances are we will start to compare ourselves with those on the next rung of the ladder. Our new discontent causes us to set our goals higher still. In a world dominated by money hunger, if our expectations continue to rise in advance of our incomes we will never achieve a level of income that satisfies. Richard Easterlin, who did much of the early work in this field, described this phenomenon as a 'hedonic treadmill,' where people have to keep running in order to keep up with the others but never advance. The only way to win is to stop playing the game.

Rich societies such as Australia seem to be in the grip of a collective psychological disorder. We react with alarm and sympathy when we come across an anorexic who is convinced she is fat, whose view of reality is so obviously distorted. Yet, as a society surrounded by affluence, we indulge in the illusion that we are deprived. Despite the obvious failure of the continued accumulation of material things to make us happy, we appear unable to change our behaviour. We have grown fat but we persist in the belief that we are thin and must consume more. Perhaps we blind ourselves to the facts; perhaps the cure seems more frightening than the disease; or perhaps we just don't know there is an alternative. For these reasons the epidemic of overconsumption that pervades rich societies has been dubbed 'affluenza.'[2] Psychotherapist and 'affluenza authority' Jessie H. O'Neill has provided a 'clinical definition' of the condition:

> The collective addictions, character flaws, psychological wounds, neuroses, and behavioral disorders caused or exacerbated by the presence of, or desire for money/wealth... In individuals, it takes the form of a dysfunctional or unhealthy relationship with money, regardless of one's socio-economic level. It manifests as behaviors resulting from a preoccupation with – or imbalance around – the money in our lives.

Affluenza describes a condition in which we are confused about what it takes to live a worthwhile life. Part of this confusion is a failure to distinguish between what we want and what we need. In 1973, 20 percent of Americans said a second car was a 'necessity'; by 1996 the figure had risen to 37 percent.[3] Among other items that have become necessities in most Australian homes in recent years are plasma-screen TVs, air conditioning, personal computers, second bathrooms, mobile phones and, increasingly, private health insurance and private schooling for children.

Neoliberal economic policies have set out to promote higher consumption as the road to a better society. All the market-based reforms in the last two decades have been predicated on the belief that the best way to advance Australia's interests is to maximise the growth of income and consumption. No one has dared to criticise this. But the rapid expansion of consumption has imposed high costs, on the overconsumers themselves, on society and on the natural environment, as discussed in the following chapters. In addition to the rapid increase in consumer debt, higher levels of consumption are driving many Australians to work themselves sick. Yet our desire for various commodities (larger houses, sophisticated home appliances, expensive personal items, and so on) is continually recreated – an illness that entered a particularly virulent phase in the 1990s with the trend described as 'luxury fever.'

Luxury Fever

Popular folklore has always held a fascination with the profligate lifestyles of the monied classes. Sociologists have analysed how extravagance serves as a device whereby the rich differentiate themselves from the mass of the population. One of the earliest commentators on this was Thorstein Veblen, who coined the phrase 'conspicuous consumption' in his 1899 book *The Theory of the Leisure Class*. For their part, the masses watch the behaviour of the rich with a mixture of awe, envy and scorn. This attraction is the reason for the continuing popularity of magazines, newspapers and, more recently, television shows that expose the lifestyles of the rich and famous.

The sustained growth of the Australian economy in the postwar period elevated the bulk of the working class to income levels that were typical of the middle class of a previous generation. The boundaries between the consumption patterns of the middle and working classes began to blur, and it became increasingly difficult to separate their financial, educational and social aspirations. Surveys in which respondents were asked to define their social position have shown fewer and fewer people willing to identify themselves as working class. Indeed, 93 percent of Australians believe they are in the middle-income bracket (that is, the middle 60 percent) and only 6.4 percent see themselves in the bottom 20 percent and 0.7 percent in the top 20 percent.[4] The consequence of this merging of classes and the confusion about the incomes of others is that emulation of the spending and consumption habits of the wealthy, which was once confined to the upper levels of the middle class, now characterises Australian society.

The collapse of the demarcation between the rich, the middle class and the poor is associated with the scaling-up of desire for prestige brands and luxury styles of particular goods. Even people on modest incomes aspire to Luis Vuitton – if not the handbag, at least the T-shirt. We have witnessed an across-the-board escalation of lifestyle expectations. The typical household's desired standard of living is now so far above the actual standard afforded by the average income that people feel deprived of the 'good life.' Television and magazines play a crucial role in this racheting-up process, not so much through advertising but more through presenting opulence as normal and attainable.

So, although ordinary citizens have always eyed and envied the rich, in affluent countries in the past two decades a qualitative change has occurred in the relationship. In *Luxury Fever* Robert Frank noted that spending on luxury goods in the United States had been growing four times faster than spending overall.[5] The 'new luxury' market is said to be increasing by 10–15 percent a year, far outpacing the growth of the economy in general.[6] This is reflected in booming sales of luxury travel, luxury cars, pleasure craft, cosmetic surgery, trophy homes, holiday homes and professional-quality home appliances. The 'democratisation of luxury' has undermined the positional signalling of many goods previously reserved for the very rich – a trend due partly to rising incomes and partly to the marketing strategies of the makers of luxury brands, which include the introduction of entry-level products in order to increase market share.[7] The argument is made pithily in a 2004 advertisement for a car. Next to the bold declaration 'LUXURY HAS ITS PRICE. (How does $39 990 sound?)', it states, 'There was a time when luxury was a different thing, stuffy, old and unaffordable. That time has gone....'[8]

This suggests a new distinction between the specialised luxury consumption that is confined to the mega-rich and the forms of luxury consumption characteristic of the bulk of the population. Of course, the luxury spending of the mega-rich sets a benchmark for the general populace, a benchmark that must, by its nature, keep rising in order to remain out of reach of all but the few. This requires continued creativity on the part of the mega-rich and on the part of those who supply them. The boom in sales of luxury cars – sales have more than doubled since 1993[9] – is depriving the mega-rich of their exclusivity. In response, the prestige car makers are now offering vehicles made to order and costing up to $1 million, thereby excluding the ordinary rich and the middle class.

The changing symbolism of credit cards plots the path of luxury fever. Ten years ago the gold credit card was a mark of distinction, a sign that you had made it – or at least that was the message the credit card companies put out. But too many people began to qualify for the gold card and its symbolic value became diluted. So the credit card companies invented the platinum card, designed to be accessible only to those at the very top of the pile. Crucially, the platinum card was kept out of the hands of the general public: you could get one only if your bank wrote to you and offered it, and for that you needed, at a minimum, an income stretching to six figures. The mystery surrounding the platinum card added to its allure. This was a quiet symbol of superiority. It is a strange test of status: extraordinary talent won't get you one; a superior education means nothing; decades of service to the community or exceptional moral character are of no account. All you need to qualify for this status symbol is a bucket of money, acquired by fair means or foul.

And what does the owner of a platinum credit card get, apart from a very high credit limit? One bank tells its clientele that its Platinum Visa card 'is the ultimate choice for those who demand benefits and rewards that match their lifestyle. Powerful credit limits, prestige services and distinctive privileges combine to deliver exceptional levels of personal recognition.'[10] The owners of this card can luxuriate in access to a personal concierge service available 24 hours a day. The American Express Platinum card comes with a dedicated team of service professionals:

> For those times when you need assistance with life's little demands, Platinum Concierge is there for you, whenever and wherever you need it. There are times a birthday is mentioned to you a moment before it's belated. Or perhaps your anniversary is just around the corner. Simply call upon your Concierge to organise a speedy bouquet and a reservation at the finest restaurant.[11]

The card appears to be for people who neglect their families: 'No more milling about in queues, let us do the running around for you so you have more time to do the things that matter most.' Naturally, the things that matter most are concerned with making more money, rather than returning the love and care of those close to you. One commentator missed the point when he observed, 'Whether people really need some of the services is questionable... It's not that hard to make your own reservation or order flowers.'[12]

In 2004 the Commonwealth Bank spoilt the party by lowering the bar for a platinum card and allowing anyone to apply for one. Imagine that – 'platinum for the people'. Determined to stay ahead of the game, American Express has now introduced a black credit card known as the Centurion. This card promises a 'six-star life experience' and 'access to the inaccessible'. One Centurion card owner called on the concierge service in Australia to return an Armani suit for alterations to the shop in Milan where he had bought it; another sent the concierge off to Taiwan to buy some out-of-print books.[13] An envious platinum card holder breathlessly emailed:

> Regarding the AMEX Centurion, I was at a friend's place on Saturday night and he received the card Friday. It comes in the most unbelievable package – solid wood (maybe cedar) box lined with velvet. He didn't request the card, just a letter from Auspost saying that he had a package to pick up.[14]

There is a pathos about this desire for the symbols of status, one that seems to reflect a need to be loved and admired.[15] This is what the luxury fever gripping Australia reveals us to be – a nation of consumers desperately seeking acknowledgment and admiration. Having discarded the verities of a previous era, standards that, for all their faults, at least gave us a sense of who we were and how we fitted into society, we now float in a sea of ambiguity and insecurity.

Buying an Identity

Some psychologists argue that our actions are driven by a desire for 'self-completion', the theory being that we seek to bring our actual self into accord with our ideal self, or who we wish to be.[16] Today, almost all buying is to some degree an attempt to create or renew a concept of self. We complete ourselves symbolically by acquiring things that compensate for our perceived shortcomings. A vast marketing infrastructure has developed to help us manufacture ideal selves and to supply the goods to fill the gap between the actual and the ideal. The marketers understand much better than we do how we want to create an ideal self. As the CEO of Gucci says, 'Luxury brands are more than the goods. The goods are secondary because first of all you buy into a brand, then you buy the products. They give people the opportunity to live a dream.'[17] It is fair to assume that this dream is not the same as the one had by Martin Luther King.

Because it acts as the interface between the self and the world, clothing is perfect for providing the bridge between who we actually are and who we want to be seen to be. Cars and houses do the same, because people look at us 'through' our cars and houses.

In modern Australia the gap between our actual and ideal selves is widening. We are urged to aspire to a better, slimmer, richer, more sophisticated ideal self, and that ideal self is increasingly an exterior one. More than at any other time we feel the eyes of the world on us. This is the source of a longing to be something other than we are – something other than we can be. Perhaps this is why the increasing level of materialism that characterises affluent societies has been shown to be associated with declining wellbeing and a rise in pathological behaviours. American psychologist Tim Kasser summarises a decade of research into the relationship between materialistic values and our sense of security, our feelings of self-worth and the quality of our relationships:

> Materialistic values are both a symptom of an underlying insecurity and a coping strategy taken on in an attempt to alleviate problems and satisfy needs.... The arguments and data ... show that successfully pursuing materialistic goals fails to increase one's happiness. When people and nations make progress in their materialistic ambitions, they may experience some temporary improvement of mood, but it is likely to be short-lived and superficial.
>
> Materialistic values of wealth, status and image work against close interpersonal relationships and connection to others, two hallmarks of psychological health and high quality of life.[18]

These research results, which serve only to confirm centuries of folk wisdom, have begun to be replicated in Australian studies.[19] The evidence points to the conclusion that the more materialistic we become the more we try to cope with our insecurities through consuming, and the less contented we are. It also suggests that more materialism means poorer relationships.

Despite the barrage of advertising that tries to tell us otherwise, the more materialistic we are the less free we are. Why? Because we must commit more of our lives to working to pay for our material desires. And the more acquisitive we are the more our desires and the means of satisfying them are determined by others. Acquisitive people derive their sense of identity and their imagined place in society from the things they own, yet the symbols that confer that self-worth and status are at the whim of external forces – of fashion. Materialism thus robs us of autonomy.[20]

We have no trouble recognising that excessive alcohol consumption and excessive gambling harm the people concerned as well as those around them. Yet shopping can also be a response to obsessive or addictive behaviour. Psychologists have recently identified a pathological condition known as 'oniomania', or 'compulsive shopping', defined in the American Psychiatric Association's Diagnostic and Statistical Manual of Mental Disorders as an obsessive-compulsive disorder. People with oniomania find their shopping is out of control; they buy more than they need, often setting out to buy one or two items but coming home with bags full of things they could not resist. They often spend more than they can afford and rack up debts that build until a crisis occurs. After shopping binges they are visited by feelings of regret. If this sounds like the experience of almost everyone, then that is no more than a central theme of this book, and the psychiatrists have merely identified the more extreme form of a widespread social condition.

Compulsive shopping has been called the 'smiled upon' addiction because it is socially sanctioned. But its consequences can be far-reaching. It often results in financial hardship, distress and family difficulties. Psychologists have also noticed some interesting patterns of co-morbidity, that is, the simultaneous presence of other disorders. Individuals afflicted by oniomania often suffer from eating disorders, drug dependence, and other impulse-control disorders such as anorexia among women and gambling among men.[21] The research shows that most compulsive buyers have histories of depression, anxiety disorders and substance abuse. Yet 'shopping til you drop' is seen as the sign of a happy-go-lucky disposition rather than a meaningless life.

Like alcohol, shopping has become both an expression of our discontent and an apparent cure for it. Indeed, it has recently been shown that oniomania can be treated effectively with particular antidepressant drugs,[22] suggesting that the condition is not in itself a psychological disorder but rather a manifestation of something more pervasive – entrenched depression and anxiety for which shopping is a form of self-medication, a phenomenon widely acknowledged in the expression 'retail therapy.'

Must We Wear Hairshirts?

Some readers might accuse us of being too harsh, too judgmental, perhaps a touch Calvinistic. Why shouldn't Australians enjoy the fruits of their labour? What's wrong with a bit of luxury? Isn't it reasonable to want to build some financial security? The answer to these questions is of course 'yes.' We are not arguing that we should build humpies and live in self-satisfied deprivation. That would be to completely misconstrue the argument of this chapter. It is not money and material possessions that are the root of the problem: it is our attachment to them and the way they condition our thinking, give us our self-definition and rule our lives.

The problem is not that people own things: the problem is that things own people. It is not consuming but consumerism we criticise; not affluence but affluenza. The signs are easy to see in others – the subtle and not-so-subtle displays of wealth, the oneupmanship, the self-doubt – and most Australians acknowledge that our society is too materialistic and money driven. But it is much harder to recognise and admit to the signs in ourselves because that can be confronting. So our claim that the answer lies in detachment rather than denial has more in common with Buddhism than with Calvinism. We argue that the obsessive pursuit of more and more fails to make us happy and that in pursuit people often sacrifice the things that really can make them happier.

There is, of course, a trap in the distinction between having money and being attached to money: it is easy to convince ourselves that, apart from a few special things, we can take or leave our possessions. Many wealthy people grow tired of being defined by their wealth and convince themselves they could do perfectly well without it. And most of us, at times, fantasise about living a simpler life, unencumbered by 'stuff'. Until we test ourselves, though, these are just comforting stories. This is why the emerging group of downshifters – people who have voluntarily reduced their income – is so important. Each downshifter has, so to speak, put their money where their mouth is.

The defenders of consumerism – the advertisers and the neoliberal commentators, think-tankers and politicians – repeat the comforting stories. It's good to aspire to own your own home, surround yourself with nice things, look after the needs of your children, and save for your retirement. Yes, we are lucky that in a rich country such as Australia many of us can do these things, but most people reach a point in their lives, some at eighteen and some at 88, when they ask, 'Work, buy, consume, die: is that all there is?' Each time someone asks such a question the market shudders, because if there is more to life than earning and consuming the odds are that when people realise it they will devote less time to paid work and consume less.

In writing about affluenza in Australia we do not deny that poverty remains. We are, however, saying that material deprivation is not the dominant feature of life in Australia. Affluence is. It helps no one to exaggerate the extent of poverty: that simply reinforces the curious but widespread belief that most people are struggling. If the majority of people can't afford to buy everything they really need, why should we be particularly concerned with the poor? And the bigger the problem seems the less likely the populace is willing to believe that something can be done about it.

We argue that, to tackle the problem of poverty, we must first tackle the problem of affluence. And the problem with affluence is that once people become affluent they continue to believe that more money is the key to a happier life when the evidence suggests that it makes no difference beyond a certain threshold. This belief has powerful personal and social ramifications, not the least being that the affluent become more preoccupied with themselves. That is why Australians are richer than ever but less inclined to sympathise with the dispossessed. So conservative politicians and radio shock jocks vilify the poor. Consumerism and growth fetishism have become the enemies of a fairer Australia.

(ENDNOTES)

1 *Affluenza*, www.affluenza.org [23 December 2004]. Definition modified.

2 The term was popularised in the United States by KCTS/Seattle and Oregon Public Broadcasting documentary, *Affluenza* (1997, http://www.pbs.org/kcts/affluenza/show/about.html [12 January 2005]). One of the producers, John de Graaf, subsequently wrote a book using the term as its title – see John de Graaf, David Wann and Thomas H. Naylor, *Affluenza: the all-consuming epidemic*, (Berrett-Koehler Publishers Inc., San Francisco, 2001).

3 Juliet Schor, *The Overspent American* (Harper Collins, New York, 1998) Table 1.4.

4 P. Saunders, C. Thomson and C. Evans, *Social Change and Social Policy: results from a national survey of public opinion*, Discussion paper no. 106, Social Policy Research Centre, University of New South Wales, Sydney, 2000, p19.

5 Robert Frank, *Luxury Fever: money and happiness in an era of excess* (Princeton University Press, New Jersey, 1999), p18.

6 Kate Betts, 'Luxury Fever: how long will it last?', *Time Magazine*, 'Style and design supplement,' Fall, 2004, p44.

7 Economists have developed the concept of 'prestige goods' – also known as 'positional goods' – the possession of which signals status. Such goods serve their function only as long as they are unavailable to others.

8 *Good Weekend*, 30–31 October 2004.

9 'Perspective,' *Australian Financial Review*, 20–21 November 2004, p20.

10 HSBC website, www.hsbc.com.au/personal/cards/platinum [11 January 2005].

11 American Express Website: www.americanexpress.com/australia/personal/cards/benefits/platinum_lifestyle.shtml

12 Denis Orrock, cited in B. Brown, 'Credit cards with bells and whistles to allow consumers to tap into a wealth of opportunity,' *The Australian*, 30 June 2004.

13 Brown, op. cit.

14 www.frequentflyer.com.au/discuss/viewtopic.php?p=2651 [11 January 2005]

15 See Alain de Botton, *Status Anxiety* (London: Penguin, 2004).

16 See especially Helga Dittmar, 'The role of self-image in excessive buying' in April Lane Benson (ed.) *I Shop, Therefore I am: compulsive buying and the search for self,* (Lanham: Rowan & Littlefield, 2000) pp. 105–32.

17 Quoted by Betts, op. cit., p.30.

18 Tim Kasser, *The High Price of Materialism* (Cambridge: MIT Press, 2002) pp. 42, 59, 72.

19 See Richard Eckersley, *Well and Good: how we feel and why it matters* (Melbourne: Text Publishing, 2004) p86.

20 For a deeper discussion, see Clive Hamilton, *The Disappointment of Liberalism and the Quest for Inner Freedom*, Discussion paper no. 7, The Australian Institute, Canberra, 2004.

21 See April Lane Benson, op. cit.; Morris Holbrook, Review of *I Shop, Therefore I Am,* in *Psychology and Marketing*, vol. 18, no. 9, September 2001.

22 L. Koran, K. Outlock, J. Hartson, M. Elliot and V. D'Andrea, 'Citalopram treatment of compulsive shopping: an open-label study,' *Journal of Clinical Psychiatry, The Primary Care Companion,* vol. 63, 2002, pp. 704–8.

Chapter Five

THE CONUNDRUM OF CONSUMPTION

Alan Durning

For Sidney Quarrier of Essex, Connecticut, Earth Day 1990 was Judgment Day – the day of ecological reckoning. While tens of millions of people around the world were marching and celebrating in the streets, Sidney was sitting at his kitchen table with a yellow legal pad and a pocket calculator. The task he set himself was to tally up the burden he and his family had placed on the planet since Earth Day 1970.[1]

Early that spring morning he began tabulating everything that had gone into their house – oil for heating, nuclear-generated electricity, water for showers and watering the lawn, cans of paint, appliances, square footage of carpet, furniture, clothes, food, and thousands of other things – and everything that had come out – garbage pails of junk mail and packaging, newspapers and magazines by the cubic meter, polluted water, and smoke from the furnace. He listed the resources they had tapped to move them around by car and airplane, from fuel and lubricants to tires and replacement parts. 'I worked on that list most of the day,' Sid remembers. 'I dug out wads of old receipts, weighed trash cans and the daily mail, excavated the basement and shed, and used triangulation techniques I hadn't practiced since graduate school to estimate the materials we used in the roofing job.'[2]

Manufacturing and delivering each of the objects on his list, Sid knew, had required additional resources he was unable to count. National statistics suggested, for example, that he should double the energy he used in his house and car to allow for what businesses and government used to provide him with goods and services. He visualized a global industrial network of factories making things for him, freighters and trucks transporting them, stores selling them, and office buildings supervising the process. He wondered how much steel and concrete his state needed for the roads, bridges, and parking garages he used. He wondered about resources used by the hospital that cared for him, the air force jets and police cars that protected him, the television stations that entertained him, and the veterinary office that cured his dog.

As his list grew, Sid was haunted by an imaginary mountain of discarded televisions, car parts, and barrels of oil – all piling up toward the sky on his lot. 'It was a sober revisiting of that period.... It's only when you put together all the years of incremental consumption that you realize the totality.' That totality hit him like the ton of paper packaging he had hauled out with the trash over the years: 'The question is,' Sid said, 'Can the earth survive the impact of Sid, and can the Sids of the future change?'[3]

That *is* the question. Sidney Quarrier and his family are no gluttons. 'During those years, we lived in a three bedroom house on two-and-a-half acres in the country, about 35 miles from my job in Hartford,' Sidney recounts. 'But we have never been rich,' he insists. 'What frightened me was that our consumption was typical of the people here in Connecticut.'[4]

Sid's class – the American middle class – is the group that, more than any other, defines and embodies the contemporary international vision of the good life. Yet the way the Quarriers lived for those 20 years is among the world's premier environmental problems, and may be the most difficult to solve.

Only population growth rivals high consumption as a cause of ecological decline, and at least population growth is now viewed as a problem by many governments and citizens of the world. Consumption, in contrast, is almost universally seen as good – indeed, increasing it is the primary goal of national economic policy. The consumption levels exemplified in the two decades Sid Quarrier reviewed are the highest achieved by any civilization in human history. They manifest the full flowering of a new form of human society: the consumer society.

This new manner of living was born in the United States, and the words of an American best capture its spirit. In the age of U.S. affluence that began after World War II, retailing analyst Victor Lebow declared: 'Our enormously productive economy ... demands that we make consumption our way of life, that we convert the buying and use of goods into rituals, that we make consumption our way of life, that we convert the buying and use of goods into rituals, that we seek our spiritual satisfaction, our ego satisfaction, in consumption.... We need things consumed, burned up, worn out, replaced, and discarded at an ever increasing rate.' Most citizens of western nations have responded to Lebow's call, and the rest of the world appears intent on following.[5]

In industrial lands, consumption now permeates social values: Opinion surveys in the world's two largest economies – Japan and the United States – show that people increasingly measure success by the amount they consume. The Japanese speak of the 'new three sacred treasures': color television, air conditioning, and the automobile. One fourth of Poles deem 'Dynasty,' which portrays the life-style of the richest Americans, their favorite television program, and villagers in the heart of Africa follow 'Dallas,' the television series that portrays American oil tycoons. In Taiwan, a billboard demands 'Why Aren't You a Millionaire Yet?' A *Business Week* correspondent beams: 'The American Dream is alive and well ... in Mexico.' Indeed, the words 'consumer' and 'person' have become virtual synonyms.[6]

The life-style made in the United States is emulated by those who can afford it around the world, but many cannot. The economic fault lines that fracture the globe defy comprehension. The world has 202 billionaires and more than 3 million millionaires. It also has 100 million homeless people who live on roadsides, in garbage dumps, and under bridges. The value of luxury goods sales worldwide – high-fashion clothing, top-of-the-line autos, and the other trappings of wealth – exceeds the gross national products of two thirds of the world's countries. Indeed, the world's average income, about $5,000 a year, is below the U.S. poverty line.[7]

The gaping divide in material consumption between the fortunate and unfortunate stands out starkly in their impacts on the natural world. The soaring consumption lines that track the rise of the consumer society are, from another perspective, surging indicators of environmental harm. The consumer society's exploitation of resources threatens to exhaust, poison, or unalterably disfigure forests, soils, water, and air. We, its members, are responsible for a disproportionate share of all the global environmental challenges facing humanity.

Ironically, high consumption is a mixed blessing in human terms too. People living in the nineties are on average four-and-a-half times richer than their great-grandparents were at the turn of the century, but they are not four-and-a-half times happier. Psychological evidence shows that the relationship between consumption and personal happiness is weak. Worse, two primary sources of human fulfillment – social relations and leisure – appear to have withered or stagnated in the rush to riches. Thus many of us in the consumer society have a sense that our world of plenty is somehow hollow that, hoodwinked by a consumerist culture, we have been fruitlessly attempting to satisfy with material things what are essentially social, psychological, and spiritual needs.[8]

Of course, the opposite of overconsumption – destitution – is no solution to either environmental or human problems. It is infinitely worse for people and bad for the natural world too. Dispossessed peasants slash-and -burn their way into the rain forests of Latin America, hungry nomads turn their herds out onto fragile African rangeland, reducing it, to desert, and small farmers in India and the Philippines cultivate steep slopes, exposing them to the erosive powers of rain. Perhaps half the world's billion-plus absolute poor are caught in a downward spiral of ecological and economic impoverishment. In desperation, they knowingly abuse the land, salvaging the present by savaging the future.[9]

If environmental destruction results when people have either too little or too much, we are left to wonder, How much is enough? What level of consumption can the earth support? When does having more cease to add appreciably to human satisfaction? Is it possible for all the world's people to live comfortably without bringing on the decline of the planet's natural health? Is there a level of living above poverty and subsistence but below the consumer life-style – a level of sufficiency? Could all the world's people have central heating? Refrigerators? Clothes dryers? Automobiles? Air conditioning? Heated swimming pools? Airplanes? Second homes?

Many of these questions cannot be answered definitively, but for each of us in the consumer society, asking is essential nonetheless. Unless we see that more is not always better, our efforts to forestall ecological decline will be overwhelmed by our appetites. Unless we ask, we will likely fail to see the forces around us that stimulate those appetites, such as relentless advertising, proliferating shopping centers, and social pressures to 'keep up with the Joneses.' We may overlook forces that make consumption more destructive than it need be, such as subsidies to mines, paper mills, and other industries with high environmental impacts. And we may not act on opportunities to improve our lives while consuming less, such as working fewer hours to spend more time with family and friends.

Still, the difficulty of transforming the consumer society into a sustainable one can scarcely be overestimated. We consumers enjoy a life-style that almost everybody else aspires to, and why shouldn't they? Who would just as soon *not* have an automobile, a big house on a big lot, and complete control over indoor temperature throughout the year? The momentum of centuries of economic history and the material cravings of 6 billion people lie on the side of increasing consumption.

We may be, therefore, in a conundrum – a problem admitting of no satisfactory solution. Limiting the consumer life-style to those who have already attained it is not politically possible, morally defensible, or ecologically sufficient. And extending that life-style to all would simply hasten the ruin of the biosphere. The global environment cannot support 1.1 billion of us living like American consumers, much less 6 billion people, or a future population of at least 8 billion. On the other hand, reducing the consumption levels of the consumer society, and tempering material aspirations elsewhere, though morally acceptable, is a quixotic proposal. It bucks the trend of centuries. Yet it may be the only option.

If the life-supporting ecosystems of the planet are to survive for future generations, the consumer society will have to dramatically curtail its use of resources – partly by shifting to high-quality, low-input durable goods and partly by seeking fulfillment through leisure, human relationships, and other nonmaterial avenues. We in the consumer society will have to live a technologically sophisticated version of the life-style currently practiced lower on the economic ladder. Scientific advances, better laws, restructured industries, new treaties, environmental taxes, grassroots campaigns – all can help us get there. But ultimately, sustaining the environment that sustains humanity will require that we change our values.

(Endnotes)

1 Sidney Quarrier, geologist, Connecticut Geological & Natural History Survey, Hartford, Conn., private communication, February 25, 1992.

2 Ibid.

3 Ibid.

4 Ibid.

5 Lebow in *Journal of Retailing*, quoted in Vance Packard, *The Waster Makers* (New York: David Mckay, 1960).

6 Sepp Linhart, 'From Industrial to Postindustrial Society: Changes in Japanese Leisure-Related Values and Behavior," *Journal of Japanese Studies*, Summer 1988; Richard A. Easterlin and Eileen M. Crimmins, "Recent Social Trends: Changes in Personal Aspirations of American Youth," *Sociology and Social Research*, July 1988; 'Dynasty' from 'Harper's Index,' *Harper's*, December 1990; 'Dallas' from Jerry Mander, *In the Absence of the Sacred* (San Francisco: Sierra Club Books, 1991); Taiwan from 'Asian Century,' *Newsweek*, February 22, 1988; Stephen Baker and S Lynne Walker, 'The American Dream is Alive and Well – in Mexico,' *Business Week*, September 30, 1991.

7 Billionaires from Jennifer Reese, 'The Billionaires: More Than Ever in 1991,' *Fortune*, September 9, 1991; millionaires estimated from Kevin R. Phillips, 'Reagan's America: A Capital Offense,' *New York Times Magazine*, June 18, 1990; homelessness from U.N. Centre for Human Settlements, New York, private communication, November 1, 1989; luxury goods from 'The Lapse of Luxury,' *Economist*, January 5, 1991; gross national product from United Nations Development Programme, *Human Development Report 1991* (New York: Oxford University Press, 1991); member countries in United Nations from U.N. Information Center, Washington, D.C., private communication, January 14, 1992; world average income from 1987, in 1987 U.S. dollars adjusted for international variations in purchasing power, from Ronald V.A. Sprout and James H. Weaver, 'International Distribution of Income: 1960–1987,' Working Paper No. 159, Department of Economics, American University, Washington, D.C., May 1991; U.S. 1987 poverty line for an individual from U.S. Bureau of the Census, *Statistical Abstract of the United States: 1990* (Washington, D.C.: U.S. Government Printing Office, 1990).

8 Four-and-half-times richer from Angus Maddison, *The World Economy in the 20th Century* (Paris: Organization for Economic Co-operation and Development, 1989).

9 Alan Durning, *Poverty and the Environment: Revising the Downward Spiral*, Worldwatch Paper 92 (Washington, D.C.: Worldwatch Institute, November 1989).

Chapter Six

THE VALUE OF VOLUNTARY SIMPLICITY

Richard B. Gregg

Introduction and Definition

Voluntary simplicity of living has been advocated and practiced by the founders of most of the great religions: Buddha, Lao Tse, Moses and Mohammed, – also by many saints and wise men such as St. Francis, John Woolman, the Hindu *rishis*, the Hebrew prophets, the Moslem *sufis*; by many artists and scientists; and by such great modern leaders as Lenin and Gandhi. It has been followed also by members of military armies and monastic orders, – organizations which have had great and prolonged influence on the world. Simplicity has always been one of the testimonies of the Mennonites and of the Society of Friends.

Clearly, then, there is or has been some vitally important element in this observance. But the vast quantities of things given to us by modern mass production and commerce, the developments of science and the complexities of existence in modern industrialized countries have raised widespread doubts as to the validity of this practice and principle. Our present 'mental climate' is not favorable either to a clear understanding of the value of simplicity or to its practice. Simplicity seems to be a foible of saints and occasional geniuses, but not something for the rest of us.

What about it?

Before going further, let us get a somewhat clearer idea of what we are discussing. We are not here considering asceticism in the sense of a suppression of instincts. What we mean by voluntary simplicity is not so austere and rigid. Simplicity is a relative matter, depending on climate, customs, culture, the character of the individual. For example, in India, except for those who are trying to imitate Westerners, everyone, wealthy as well as poor, sits on the floor, and there are no chairs. A large number of Americans, poor as well as rich, think they have to own a motor car, and many others consider a telephone exceedingly important. A person in a certain rank of society considers it necessary to have several kinds of shoes, of hats or other articles of clothing for purposes other than cleanliness or comfortable temperature. What is simplicity for an American would be far from simple to a Chinese peasant.

Voluntary simplicity involves both inner and outer condition. It means singleness of purpose, sincerity and honesty within, as well as avoidance of exterior clutter, of many possessions irrelevant to the chief purpose of life.

It means an ordering and guiding of our energy and our desires, a partial restraint in some directions in order to secure greater abundance of life in other directions. It involves a deliberate organization of life for a purpose. For example, the men who tried to climb Mount Everest concentrated their thoughts and energies on the planning of that expedition for several years, and in the actual attempt discarded every ounce of equipment not surely needed for that one purpose.

Of course, as different people have different purposes in life, what is relevant to the purpose of one person might not be relevant to the purpose of another. Yet it is easy to see that our individual lives and community life would be much changed if every one organized and graded and simplified his purposes so that one purpose would easily dominate all the others, and if each person then reorganized his outer life in accordance with this new arrangement of purposes, – discarding possessions and activities irrelevant to the main purpose. The degree of simplification is a matter for each individual to settle for himself, but the meaning of the principle is now perhaps clear enough for discussion, even though the applications of it may differ. I will not attempt more exact definition at this point, trusting to the discussion to clarify further the meaning of the topic.

Doubts

Since an emphasis on simplicity seems nowadays to many people a mistake, let us consider their doubts before we go further.

First of all, modern machine production seems to have solved the age-old condition of scarcity of the material things needed for life. Science and invention, industrialism, commerce and transportation have made it possible to produce and distribute more and better food, clothing, housing materials, tools and equipment, comforts, and luxuries than mankind has ever had hitherto. For an American, a stroll through a ten-cent store, a chain-grocery store and a department store, followed by a perusal of a catalogue of some of the large mail-order stores, is convincing on that score, to say nothing of what meets our eye on every street. Henry Ford's idea that civilization progresses by the increase in the number of people's desires and their satisfaction looks sensible. The vast quantities of paper and ink devoted to advertisements add emphasis to that belief. The financial and social stability of every industrialized country seems to be founded on the expectation of an ever-expanding market for mass production. Russia, as well as capitalistic nations, has this aim. The whole world appears to be geared to this concept. Isn't it an anachronism to talk of simplicity in such an age? Is it not our duty to rise above and master the increasing complexity of life? Without irreverence, is not that what God has done in the creation and evolution of this universe?

Furthermore, to revert to simplicity would pretty surely mean for most people the re-assumption of a vast amount of drudgery which our modern complex appliances handle for us. Complex as our paraphernalia is, nevertheless, does it not protect us against famine, disease, and extremes of temperature? Do not our tractors, electric lights, gas stoves, water pipes, electric refrigerators, house heating, airplanes, steam and motor transport, telephones, lift us beyond the threshold of animal existence, remove from us oppressive fears, give us a sense of security and at least the possibility of leisure? We must surely have leisure if civilization is to advance.

Another doubt comes readily to the mind of every parent. We all want our children to have every advantage, to be healthier and stronger than we have been, to learn more than we did, to make fewer mistakes, to have better characters, to see more of the world, to be able to live fuller and richer lives, to have more power and beauty and joy. How can they in this day acquire the necessary training and education for this, how can they come into contact and association with many people and many beautiful and stimulating things and scenes if we, their parents, cramp our lives and theirs by resorting to simplicity? Do not even their bodies require a great variety of foods in order to be healthy? How is the mind to grow unless it is fed unceasingly from a wide variety of sources? Surely beauty is a most important element in the life of both individuals and communities, and how can we have beauty if we are limited by a drab, severe and monotonous simplicity of form, line, color, material, texture and tone?

Again, many people who doubt the validity of simplicity would say that if it were put into effect it would extend itself beyond the lives of individuals and claim application to group affairs. They would then naturally say, if many people 'go simple,' who is going to carry on the necessary complex work of the world? Governments, industries, and institutions have to be carried on and they are highly complex. Are these people who so greatly desire simplicity going to dodge their share in the complex tasks of society? In most organizations power is exercised over people. Is it right for some people to try to escape wielding that power? Who is to wield such power wisely if not those with a conscience? Is it not the duty of sensitive people to grasp power and direct its use as well as possible? Is this cry for simplicity only a camouflage for irresponsibility, for lack of courage or failure of energy?

These questions suggest that in this idea of simplicity there may be a danger to our community life. The existence of a large nation or a large city is nowadays inherently complex. To insist on simplicity and really put it into effect would seem to mean eventually destroying large organizations, and that means our present mode of community and national life.

So much for the doubts. Perhaps there are others, but these at least are weighty.

Answers to Doubts

Let us consider the first major doubt, to the effect that modern science and inventions have made possible a boundless supply of goods and foods of all sorts, so that the ages of scarcity and all the assumptions, thinking and morality based thereon are outmoded, including the idea of there being any value in simplicity.

Although, from an engineering point of view, technology has made it easily possible to supply all of mankind's material needs, this possibility is far from being an actuality. There is a very big '*if*' attached. Despite the wondrous mechanical, chemical and electrical inventions, scarcity of necessities still exists to a painful degree in every country. There are large portions of the population of the United States who do not have such comforts as water piped into the house or apartment; and furnaces to provide house warmth in winter. Yet this country is one of the wealthiest and most widely mechanized. Another failure in application of technology is shown by the vast numbers of unemployed in almost all countries, probably more than ever before in the history of the world.

Our financial price system and debt structure controls production, distribution and the wherewithal to pay for consumption. That system operates to cause wheat to be burned in the United States while millions are starving in China: tons of oranges to be left to rot in California while children in our city slums are subject to rickets, bad teeth and other forms of ill health for the lack of vitamins in those oranges; and so on for a long chapter.[1]

The great advances in science and technology have not solved the moral problems of civilization. Those advances have altered the form of some of those problems, greatly increased others, dramatized some, and made others much more difficult of solution. The just distribution of material things is not merely a problem of technique or of organization. It is primarily a moral problem.

Quantitative measurement and the use of quantitative relationships are among the most powerful elements in science, technology and money. Because of this, the preponderating stimuli exerted by science, technology and money are on the quantitative rather than the qualitative aspects of life. The qualitative elements are cramped. But the essence of man's social life lies in qualitative rather than quantitative relationships: it is moral, not technological.

In volume III of Arnold J. Toynbee's great *Study of History*[2] he discusses the growth of civilizations. For some sixty pages he considers what constitutes growth of civilization, including in that term growth in wisdom as well as in stature. With immense learning he traces the developments of many civilizations, – Egyptian, Sumeric, Minoan, Hellenic, Syriac; Indic, Iranian, Chinese, Babylonic, Mayan, Japanese, etc. After spreading out the evidence, he comes to the conclusion that real growth of a civilization does not consist of increasing command over the physical environment, nor of increasing command over the human environment (i.e., over other nations or civilizations), but that it lies in what he calls 'etherealization'; a development of intangible relationships. He points out that this process involves both a simplification of the apparatus of life and also a transfer of interest and energy from material things to a higher sphere. He follows Bergson in equating complexity with Matter and simplicity with Life.[3]

If this be so, it is time to call a halt on endless gageteering. We had better turn our attention to cultivating qualitative relationships and the ways of life which promote them. Our technology is overdeveloped. It rests on a moral foundation which had developed in a simpler world and was intended for simpler conditions. Our civilization is like a huge engine resting on too small and weak a foundation. Its vibrations are tearing the whole thing to pieces. In order to carry the load and strain we need to develop stronger self-control and group and individual morality.

To those who say that machinery and the apparatus of living are merely instruments and devices which are without moral nature in themselves, but which can be used for either good or evil, I would point out that we are all influenced by the tools and means which we use. Again and again in the lives of individuals and of nations we see that when certain means are used vigorously, thoroughly and for a long time, those means assume the character and influence of an end in themselves.[4] We become obsessed by our tools. The strong quantitative elements in science, machinery and money, and in their products, tend to make the thinking and life of those who use them mechanistic and divided. The relationships which science, machinery and money create are mechanical rather than organic. Machinery and money give us more energy outwardly but they live upon and take away from us our inner energy.[5]

We think that our machinery and technology will save us time and give us more leisure, but really they make life more crowded and hurried.[6] When I install in my house a telephone, I think it will save me all the time and energy of going to market every day, and much going about for making petty inquiries and minor errands to those with whom I have dealings. True, I do use it for those purposes, but I also immediately expand the circle of my frequent contacts, and that anticipated leisure time rapidly is filled by telephone calls to me or with engagements I make by the use of it. The motor car has the same effect upon our domestic life. We are all covering much bigger territory than formerly, but the expected access of leisure is conspicuous by its absence. Indeed, where the motor cars are very numerous, as on Fifth Avenue, New York, you can now, at many times during the day, walk faster than you can go in a taxi or bus.

The mechanized countries are not the countries noted for their leisure. Any traveller to the Orient can testify that the tempo of life there is far more leisurely than it is in the industrialized West. To a lesser degree, the place to find relative leisure in the United States is not in the highly mechanized cities, but in the country.

Moreover, we continually overlook the fact that our obsession with machinery spoils our inner poise and sense of values, without which the time spared from necessitous toil ceases to be leisure and becomes time without meaning, or with sinister meaning, – time to be 'killed' by movies, radio or watching baseball games, or unemployment with its degradation of morale and personality.

Those who think that complexities of transportation, communication and finance have relieved the world from underfeeding and famine are mistaken. Probably their error comes from the fact that they belong to the comfortable and well-to-do groups among the powerful nations of the world. They have not understood, if indeed they have read, the statistics and reports of social and relief workers in regard to the extent of undernourishment in their own populations and in the rest of the world. They forget about the recurrent Chinese famines, so vast in extent. They have not examined the evidence indicating that famines in India in modern times probably have greatly exceeded in extent and perhaps in frequency those of centuries ago.

Those who shudder at the appalling loss of life by the Black Death in mediaeval Europe, forget the tens of millions killed by influenza during the World War. Those who point with pride at the statistics of the lowering incidence of contagious diseases often fail to mention the rising amount of degenerative organic diseases such as cancer, diabetes, kidney, heart and circulatory failures, and of insanity. So distinguished a physiologist as Alexis Carrel in his recent book, *Man the Unknown*, has given evidence sufficient to startle and humble our pride in respect to the alleged 'conquest of disease.'[7] He states that merely increasing the age to which people live tends to add to the number of aged people whom the young must support, and does not necessarily spell progress. He even believes that our modern techniques for comfort are doing our peoples grave biological harm by atrophying our adaptive mechanisms, to say nothing of the social evils created by industrialism.[8]

No, – the way to master the increasing complexity of life is not through more complexity. The way is to turn inward to that which unifies all, – not the intellect but the spirit, and then to devise and put into operation new forms and modes of economic and social life that will truly and vigorously express that spirit. As an aid to that and as a corrective to our feverish over-mechanization, simplicity is not outmoded but greatly needed.

Let me postpone for the time being the relation of simplicity to the education of children, for it is organically related to a subsequent part of the discussion and is better treated there.

Having discussed some of the major doubts, let us turn to the reasons for simplicity.

Economic Reasons for Simplicity

There are a number of reasons for voluntary simplicity of living, a considerable number, but perhaps not so many as to make the discussion of simplicity itself complex. If it seems complex, it is because so much intellectual clutter and underbrush has to be removed in order to see clearly.

Since our thinking today runs predominantly to economics, suppose we consider first the economic aspects of our subject.

Economics has at least three divisions: production, distribution and consumption. Of material goods we are not all producers or distributors, but we are all consumers. Simplicity of living affects primarily consumption. It sets a standard of consumption. Consumption is the area within which each individual can affect the economic life of the community. Small as his own share may be, that is the area within which every person can exercise his control over the forces of economic production and distribution. If he regards himself as responsible for our joint economic welfare, he has a duty to think out and decide upon and adhere to a standard of consumption for himself and his family. Shall he have only one hat or three, one or four pairs of shoes, a house with a separate dining room or have the meals either in the kitchen or sitting room? And so on. In this pamphlet I not attempt to set a standard for any one, for that is a matter which each must settle for himself. I am discussing only general principles, not specific applications.

The economic system in which we find ourselves is gravely defective in operation. Greed and competition are two of its harmful elements. Competitive ostentation, – 'keeping up with the Joneses,' – is a prominent feature of modern social life.[9] Simplicity of living acts as a deterrent to such ostentation and hence to both greed and competition. Therefore, all those who desire to reform the existing economic system can take an effective part by living simply and urging and encouraging others to do likewise. This thing comes close to all of us. Capitalism is no mere exterior organization of bankers and industrialists. It consists of a spirit and attitude and habitual actions in and among all of us. Even those who desire to reform or end it usually have within themselves certain of its attitudes and habits of mind and desire. If capitalism is to be reformed or ended, that change will alter the lives and thoughts and feelings of every one of us. Conversely, if I wish actively to participate in this transformation, I myself must begin to alter my own life in the desired direction. If I share too heavily in the regime I want to change, it becomes too difficult for me to disentangle myself, and I cease to become effective as a reformer. Those who live on income from investments will not dare to advocate deep economic changes, unless they live simply enough to permit a lowering of their income without too great an upset in their mode of life. My changes must be both inner and outer, and must, I believe, be in the direction of more simplicity.

I grant that such changes in my own life will be infinitesimal in comparison with the sum total of change required in all of society. Yet I have no right to criticise evil elsewhere unless and until I begin to remove it from my own life. And let no one forget that actions count more than words, that example is more powerful than exhortation, and that many, many repetitions of any small stimulus, such as one person's example, for a long period of time, create growth among all the people who receive the stimulus. One of the American Friends' Service Committee representatives in a brokendown coal mining town reports, for example, that his daily manual work in his little garden seemed to do more to create confidence in him among the suspicious and bitter unemployed people of the town than all his talk or other actions. If such simple action by me seems too tiny and insignificant to make it worth while to attempt, I should remember that it is not really insignificant, because it is an organic part of the great spirit of millions throughout the ages who have voluntarily lived simple lives. The meaning of my part in such a movement does not lie in the size of my accomplishment so far as I am aware of it, but in the quality of the principle and the quality of my participation.

Exploitation of human beings is an ancient evil, older than capitalism. It existed under European feudalism, and probably in most of the older forms of economic and social organization in every continent. It goes on today all around us, and practically everyone of us shares in it at least indirectly. The first step I can take to cut down my share in exploitation is to live simply. All luxuries require unnecessary labour, as John Woolman so clearly showed.[10] The production and consumption of luxuries divert labor and capital from tasks which are socially more productive and beneficial; they often take land away from wise use; and they waste raw materials which might be used to better advantage. This tends to increase the prices of necessities and thereby lowers real wages and makes the struggle of the poor harder.

We are told that there is a close relationship between economic and political factors in society. With that in mind, suppose we consider the possible political implications of simplicity.

Simplicity and Political Influence

It is interesting that three moderns with immense political influence, Lenin, Gandhi, and Kagawa, have led lives of extreme simplicity. Their simplicity has been a factor in their political power. Political power is based on the trust of the masses in the leader. By a life of great simplicity over a long period of time the leader demonstrates his unselfishness and sincerity, – two elements which tend to generate and maintain trust. The masses feel that such a leader will not 'sell them out.' By sharing to that extent in the circumstances of the great majority of people the leader keeps aware of their problems and keeps en rapport with them. By so acting he identifies them with himself, as well as himself with them, thus encouraging them to feel that they too, despite small material means, may become significant in the life of the community or nation. In spirit they feel closer to him and feel themselves enabled to share in his greatness, and thus their self-respect, their courage, their endurance and morale are enhanced. If an entire ruling group or intelligentsia were always to live simply, the moral unity, self-respect and endurance of the entire nation would be enhanced. If anyone wishes strong and enduring political power for a great cause, he will be wise to simplify his life greatly.

Simplicity and Religion

Besides these considerations, there are religious implications in the matter of simplicity. We are told by St. John that 'If we love one another, God dwelleth in us, and his love is perfected in us.... He that dwelleth in love dwelleth in God, and God in him.... Let us not love in word, neither in tongue; but in deed and in truth.' (1 John 4:12, 16; 3:18.) Living simply seems to be an important element in this effort to manifest love and human unity, and hence, to live in accordance with Jesus' commands. Love is the sentiment which accompanies the realization of human unity. It expresses that unity and stimulates and helps to maintain it. We have seen in the case of St. Francis how simplicity aided in his attainment of unity with his fellow creatures. Likewise simplicity helps to express and aid love.

The greatest gulf in society is between the rich and the poor. The practice of simplicity by the well-to-do helps to bridge this gulf and may be therefore an expression of love. The rich young man was advised by Jesus to sell all his goods and give to the poor and thus simplify his life, in order to perfect his religious life. No doubt such an act would have resulted in more than simplification of the young man's life, but that would have been one of the results. Hinduism and Buddhism have also emphasized the value of simplicity.

The heart of the problem of simplicity is spiritual and lies in inner detachment. But the inner state must be expressed by an outer act, in order to have sincerity, in order to prevent self-deception, in order to strengthen the inner attitude and in order to gain further insight for the next step. Christianity needs a means of implementing its ideals of human unity into a social program. While simplicity alone is only one element, it would seem to me to be one of the necessary elements in such a program. Simplicity would constitute part of a code of moral hygiene necessary for a healthy and vigorous spiritual life.

Simplicity and Personality

It is often said that possessions are important because they enable the possessors thereby to enrich and enhance their personalities and characters. The claim is that by means of ownership the powers of self-direction and self-control inherent in personality become real. Property, they say, gives stability, security, independence, a real place in the larger life of the community, a feeling of responsibility, all of which are elements of vigorous personality.[11]

Nevertheless, the greatest characters, those who have influenced the largest numbers of people for the longest time, have been people with extremely few possessions. For example, Buddha, Jesus, Moses, Mohammed, Kagawa, Socrates, St. Francis, Confucius, Sun Yat Sen, Lenin, Gandhi, many scientists, inventors and artists. 'The higher ranges of life where personality has fullest play and is most nearly free from the tyranny of circumstance, are precisely those where it depends least on possessions.... The higher we ascend among human types and the more intense personalities become, the more the importance of possessions dwindles.'[12]

The reason for this is something that we usually fail to realize, namely that the essence of personality does not lie in its isolated individuality, its separateness from other people, its uniqueness, but in its basis of relationships with other personalities. It is a capacity for friendship, for fellowship, for intercourse, for entering imaginatively into the lives of others. At its height it is a capacity for and exercise of love.[13] Friendship and love do not require ownership of property for either their ordinary or their finest expression. Creativity does not depend on possession. Intangible relationships are more important to the individual and to society than property is. If a person by love and service wins people's trust, that trust will find expression in such forms as to preserve life and increase its happiness and beauty.

It is true that a certain kind of pleasure and satisfaction come from acquiring mastery over material things, – for example, learning to drive a motor car, – or from displaying ownership of things as a proof of power.'[14] But that sort of power and that sort of satisfaction are not so secure, so permanent, so deep, so characteristic of mental and moral maturity as are some others.

The most permanent, most secure and most satisfying sort of possession of things other than the materials needed for bodily life, lies not in physical control and power of exclusion but in intellectual, emotional and spiritual understanding and appreciation. This is especially clear in regard to beauty. He who appreciates and understands a song, a symphony, a painting, some sculpture or architecture gets more satisfaction than he who owns musical instruments or works of art. The world of nature and the museums afford ample scope for such spiritual possession. Such appreciation is what some economists call 'psychic goods.' Entering into the spirit which lies at the heart of things is what enriches and enlarges personality.

There is the simplicity of the fool and the simplicity of the wise man. The fool is simple because his mind and will are incapable of dealing with many things. The wise man is simple not for that reason but because he knows that all life, both individual and group, has a certain few essential strands or elements and outside of those are a vast multiplicity of other things. If the few essential strands are kept healthy and vigorous, the rest of the details develop almost automatically, like the bark and twigs and leaves of a tree. So the wise man confines most of his attention to the few essentials of life, and that constitutes his simplicity.

We cannot have deep and enduring satisfaction, happiness or joy unless we have self-respect. There is good reason to believe that self-respect is the basis for all higher morality.[15] We cannot have self-respect unless our lives are an earnest attempt to express the finest and most enduring values which we are able to appreciate. That is to say, unless we come into close and right relationships with our fellow-men, with nature and with Truth (or God), we cannot achieve full self-respect.

Simplicity of living is, as we have seen, one of the conditions of reaching and maintaining these right relationships. Therefore simplicity is an important condition for permanent satisfaction with life. And inasmuch as national self-respect is a necessary condition for the maintenance of a nation or a civilization[16] it would seem that widespread simplicity, as a cultural habit of an entire nation, would in the long run be essential for its civilization to endure. At any rate, in the two civilizations which have endured the longest, the Chinese and the East Indian, simplicity of living has been a marked characteristic. The wealthy Indian rajahs, often considered so prominent a feature of India, are, most of them, not greatly respected in India. With but few exceptions they are not moral or intellectual leaders, and in politics they are all creatures of an alien government. True, the simplicity of living of the Indian masses has been largely the enforced simplicity of poverty. Nevertheless, among the real intellectual and moral leaders of India, the Brahmans and social reformers like Gandhi, voluntary simplicity has been and still is a definite and widely observed element of their code and custom. This is true also, I believe, of the leaders of China, the scholars.

Those by whom simplicity is dreaded because it spells lack of comfort, may be reminded that some voluntary suffering or discomfort is an inherent and necessary part of all creation, so that to avoid all voluntary suffering means the end of creative-ness. Refusal to create may result in loss of self-respect.

Simplicity is clearly a sign of a pure heart, i.e., a single purpose. Also, because environment has an undeniable influence on character, simplicity of living would help to stimulate and maintain such singleness of purpose.

Simplicity: A Kind of Psychological Hygiene

There is one further value to simplicity. It may be regarded as a mode of psychological hygiene. Just as eating too much is harmful to the body, even though the quality of all the food eaten is excellent, so it seems that there may be a limit to the number of things or the amount of property which a person may own and yet keep himself psychologically healthy. The possession of many things and of great wealth creates so many possible choices and decisions to be made every day that it becomes a nervous strain.

Furthermore, if a person lives among great possessions, they constitute an environment which influences him. His sensitiveness to certain important human relations is apt to become clogged and dulled, his imagination in regard to the subtle but important elements of personal relationships or in regard to lives in circumstances less fortunate than his own is apt to become less active and less keen. This is not always the result, but the exception is rare. When enlarged to inter-group relationships this tends to create social misunderstandings and friction.

The athlete, in order to win his contest, strips off the non-essentials of clothing, is careful of what he eats, simplifies his life in a number of ways. Great achievements of the mind, of the imagination, and of the will also require similar discriminations and disciplines.

Observance of simplicity is a recognition of the fact that everyone is greatly influenced by his surroundings and all their subtle implications. The power of environment modifies all living organisms. Therefore each person will be wise to select and create deliberately such an immediate environment of home things as will influence his character in the direction which he deems most important and such as will make it easier for him to live in the way that he believes wisest. Simplicity gives him a certain kind of freedom and clearness of vision.

Simplicity and Beauty

The foregoing discussion has answered, I think, much of the second strong doubt which we mentioned near the beginning, the doubt that parents have as to the harm that simplicity might do to the minds and general cultural development of their children. In regard to aesthetics, simplicity should not connote ugliness. The most beautiful and restful room I ever entered was in a Japanese country inn, without any furniture or pictures or applied ornaments. Its beauty lay in its wonderful proportions and the soft colors of unpainted wood beams, paper walls and straw matting. There can be beauty in complexity but complexity is not the essence of beauty. Harmony of line, proportion and color are much more important. In a sense, simplicity is an important element in all great art, for it means the removal of all details that are irrelevant to a given purpose. It is one of the arts within the great art of life. And perhaps the mind can be guided best if its activities are always kept organically related to the most important purposes in life. Mahatma Gandhi believes that the great need of young people is not so much education of the head as education of the heart.

A Caution

If simplicity of living is a valid principle, there is one important precaution and condition of its application. I can explain it best by something which Mahatma Gandhi said to me. We were talking about simple living and I said that it was easy for me to give up most things but that I had a greedy mind and wanted to keep my many books. He said, 'Then don't give them up. As long as you derive inner help and comfort from anything, you should keep it. If you were to give it up in a mood of self-sacrifice or out of a stern sense of duty, you would continue to want it back, and that unsatisfied want would make trouble for you. Only give up a thing when you want some other condition so much that the thing no longer has any attraction for you, or when it seems to interfere with that which is more greatly desired.' It is interesting to note that this advice agrees with modern Western psychology of wishes and suppressed desires. This also substantiates what we said near the beginning of our discussion, that the application of the principle of simplicity is for each person or each family to work out sincerely for themselves.

Cultivation Of Simplicity

Inasmuch as the essence of the matter does not lie in externals but in inner attitude, let us discuss certain ways by which that attitude can be cultivated. Since simplicity means the supplanting of certain kinds of desires by other desires, the best aid in that process is directing the imagination toward the new desires. We must try, of course, to understand intellectually all the implications of the new desires, but further than that, make the imagination dwell upon them in spare moments, and just before going to sleep and just after awakening. Read books or articles dealing with them. Associate with people who have ideas similar to those which you wish to cultivate. Exercise your discrimination in the relative values of different modes of living, and in the little details that compose them. Practice the desired simplicity in small ways as well as the large. Provide as many small stimuli as possible for this line of thought and conduct. Inasmuch as competition and emulation, especially the variety known as 'keeping up with the Joneses,' lead to complexity of living, and inasmuch as competition is encouraged by a sense of diversity and exaggerated individualism, we will help ourselves toward simplicity by cultivating a strong and constant feeling of human unity. Try to cultivate the ability to work without attachment to the fruit of works.[17] If you realize that the purpose of advertising is to stimulate your desires for material things, you will be wise to avoid reading many advertisements. At least exercise selection in so doing.

Other elements of character which will be desirable to cultivate for this purpose are: strength to resist the pressure of group opinion; ability to withstand misunderstanding, unfavorable comment, or ridicule; sensitiveness to intangible values and relationships more than to sense impressions; greater sensitiveness to moral beauty than to beauty perceptible by the physical senses; persistence, endurance and strength of will. If simplicity is a valuable thing, then to attain it we must pay a price. Estimate that price carefully against what you believe to be the value obtainable.

For people in industrialized countries, discrimination will be needed in the selection of machinery for personal and home use. The amount of drudgery in household and other tasks depends partly upon the kinds and extent of complexity of living. Some machinery is truly labor saving with a minimum of harmful byproducts or remote effects. In our American mechanized environment it will take intelligence to change successfully from living a complex life to a simple life.

Involuntary Simplicity

All that we have considered has to do with voluntary simplicity, for those who have enough resources to live in more or less complex fashion if they wish. What about the involuntary simplicity of the poor? Is that a good thing? Its compulsion creates frustration, a sense of inferiority, resentment and desire for the things denied to them. In so far as involuntary simplicity conduces to closeness with the healthy forces of Nature and to unity with fellow men, it would seem not wholly evil. The lives of the poor in cities, however, are not natural, but dependent on a highly artificial and complex environment which deprives them of sunshine, fresh air and food in its natural state. That environment also very frequently deprives them of normal human relationships and activities. The more voluntary simplicity is practiced by the privileged, the more will the advantages of simplicity become available to the underprivileged, for their enforced simplicity will to that extent feel to them less invidious, and their poverty perhaps may then be on the way to remedy.

Simplicity Alone is Not Enough

However important it may be, simplicity alone is not enough to secure a thoroughgoing and permanent advance in civilization. The relative failure of the Franciscan movement seems to be evidence in point.[18] In addition to the changes in consumption which widespread simplicity would bring about, it will be necessary also to develop great changes in the present modes of production. Decentralization of production would be one of these changes. The social effects of that would be far-reaching and profound. Many other great changes will be necessary, including a different control of large-scale production and of land, and changes in distribution and in money as an instrument and as a symbol.

Simplicity, to be more effective, must inform and be integrated with many aspects of life. It needs to become more social in purpose and method. It ought to be organically connected with a thoroughgoing program of non-violence as a method of persuasion to social change, and to be definitely a part of a constructive practical program for the economic security of the masses. That is too large a matter to be considered here. But no matter what changes take place in human affairs, the need for simplicity will always remain.

(Endnotes)

1 For other instances see 'The Tragedy of Waste,' by Stuart Chase, Macmillan; Chapter V of *Capitalism and It's Culture*, by Jermone Davis.

2 Oxford University Press, 1934.

3 H. Bergson, *Two Aspects of Morals and Religion*, H. Holt & Co.

4 *The Philosophy of "As If"*, by H. Vaihinger, pXXX, Harcourt, Brace & Co., New York, also an address by John Dewey to the American Philosophical Association, January, 1935.

5 See the essay on St. Francis in *Affirmations*, by Havelock Ellis, Houghton Mifflin, Boston. Also Samuel Butler's *Erewhon*, E.P. Dutton Co., New York, *What is European Civilization*, by Wihelm Haas, Oxford University Press, 1929.

6 *Social Decay and Regeneration*, by R. Austin Freeman, Constable, London, 1921; *Men and Machines*, By Stuart Chase, pp. 350-355, Macmillan; Chapter VIII of *Technics and Civilization*, by Lewis Mumford, Harcourt, Brace & Co., New York, 1934.

7 Alex Carrel *Man the Unknown*, Harper & Bros., pp. 114-16, 154, 155.

8 Ibid., pp.233, 303, 304.

9 Thorstein Veblen, *Theory of the Leisure Class*, Vanguard Press, New York.

10 *The Journal and Essays of John Woolman*, ed. By Amelia M. Gummere, Macmillan, London, 1932.

11 *Property: A Study in Social Psychology*, by Ernest Beaglehole, Allen & Unwin, London, 1931.

12 'The Christian Attitude Toward Private Property,' by Vida D Scudder (a pamphlet), Morehouse Pub. Co., Milwaukee, Wis.; cf. also Chapter VI of *Our Economic Morality*, by Harry F. Ward, Macmillan.

13 Essay on 'Property and Personality,' by Henry Scott Holland, in *Property, Its Duties and Rights*, edited by Charles Gore, Bishop of Oxford, Macmillan, London, 1915.

14 Thorstein Veblen, *Theory of the Leisure Class*, Vanguard Press, New York.

15 See the psychologists, Wm. McDougal and A. G. Tansley, also R. V. Feldman's book, cited below. The loss of self-respect is one of the greatest harms wrought by unemployment.

16 *The Domain of Selfhood*, by R.V. Feldman, p95, Allen & Unwin, London, 1934.

17 See *The Bhagavad-Gita*.

18 See *The Franciscan Adventure*, by Vida D. Scudder, E.P Dutton Co., New York, 1931; *The Romanticism of St. Francis*,' by Father Cuthbert, Longmans, Green, 1915.

Chapter Seven

LESS IS MORE

Philip Cafaro

When it comes to economic activity, less is more. Not always, and not beyond a certain minimum level. Sometimes more really is more, and less really is less. But often, less is more. If all this piece does is open up the question of whether less is more – if all it does is remind the reader that this is a question, and that our answers to it have important repercussions – then it will have served its purpose.

Many ethicists in the ancient tradition argued that human lives could be improved through decreasing our economic activity: consuming less food, avoiding ostentatious building or entertaining, thinking less about money. For Aristotle, Seneca and Epicurus the good life was equally a life devoted to right thinking and a life *not* devoted to wealth-getting.[1] These two aspects supported each other. They were held to be key to *eudaimonia*, that complex term variously translated as 'happiness,' 'excellence,' or 'human flourishing.'

A key issue in ancient ethics was whether the pursuit of the good life entailed limiting and harshly disciplining our natural desires and acquisitiveness, or providing for their moderate fulfillment. This question in turn was related to the role that pleasure and physical satisfaction were thought to play in a good life: whether defining of it, irrelevant to it, or a more or less important part of it. A wide variety of positions were staked out on these issues which I will not attempt to summarize here. The key point is that almost all of the ancient writers argued for limiting material acquisition and our attempts to satisfy our physical desires. This was true for those who thought pleasure the greatest human good and for those who declared physical pleasure irrelevant to questions of how humans should live their lives. It was true for those who argued that people should set moderate goals and accept moderate successes in life and for those who advocated the pursuit of perfection.

The ancient ethicists argued that limiting our economic activities and disciplining our appetites was necessary in order to live good lives. I agree. But another powerful motivation for reviving these arguments is environmental concern. I believe that societies focused on fulfilling their true needs and individuals focused on developing their better selves would demand less of Nature, particularly in the wealthy countries of the world, where we already have a surfeit of money and material goods, and more of the same will not improve our lives.

Environmental degradation and the transformation of wild nature into managed natural resources are overwhelmingly the result of human economic activities. More benign forms of production and lower levels of consumption are therefore typical goals of environmentalists, in addition to the direct preservation of wild places and species. These goals reinforce each other. For example, less paper consumption allows for less wood-pulp production. This in turn lessens the pressure to log heretofore unlogged lands, or to convert low-productivity, natural forests into high-productivity, managed tree farms.

I am convinced that greater attention to our true happiness would do as much to protect wild nature as the greater acceptance of nature's intrinsic value for which so many environmental ethicists have rightly argued.[2] Both positions, if thought through and acted upon, would result in less consumption and a more conscious production, and hence in less environmental damage.

Consider as an example our consumption of food. This is among our most necessary and pleasurable economic acts. It is also one of the most important ways we affect the environment. For example, 'eating lower on the food chain' by switching to a meatless diet uses considerably less resources, whether calculated in land needed to grow food or energy used to produce it. As *The State of the Environment Atlas* notes: 'in cycling our grain through livestock, we waste 90 percent of its protein and 96 percent of its calories. An acre of cereal can produce five times more protein than an acre devoted to meat production; and legumes (beans, lentils, peas) can produce ten times as much.'[3]

Eating locally grown foods also limits resource use, by cutting out the energy needed to transport food long distances. Buying food from organic growers discourages pesticide and herbicide use. And whatever diet we choose, the less we consume, the less we take from the earth.

So *if* we value environmental protection, we have a strong *prima facie* argument for eating less, for eating less meat, and for being conscious generally about what we do eat. But my main point here is that 'selfish' interests also argue for many of these changes. This is true whether we consider our health or our purse, and whether we define our well-being in terms of pleasure or personal excellence.

All our pleasures and achievements rest on staying healthy, and from a health perspective westerners eat too many calories and too much meat. Studies commonly suggest Americans consume 20–30% more calories than is advisable.[4] Regarding meat, according to one massive study involving 26,000 respondents in California 'meat eating is strongly related to deaths from heart diseases and diabetes. The more meat consumed, the greater the risk.'[5] This same study found that respondents who practiced vegetarianism and abstained from coffee and cigarettes lived 12 years longer than the national average. Israeli, Finnish and Australian studies have found that vegetarians have low incidences of high blood pressure, and American vegetarians are also less than half as likely to be obese as meat-eaters.[6] While debate continues over whether we should cut back or cut out meat from our diets, authorities seem to agree that consuming less fat and less calories is a key to living into a healthy old age.[7] At a minimum it seems clear that health may be preserved with a wholly vegetarian diet, so that health considerations do not stand in the way of our acting on our environmental principles (acting on the basis of deontological considerations grounded on the intrinsic value of nature).[8]

Objective, scientific studies are perhaps less definitive than suggestive to individuals, who must decide for themselves how and how much to eat. Here every reader must consult his or her own experience, and perhaps enlarge it through experiment and greater attentiveness. Personally I have found that removing meat from my diet hasn't harmed my health or limited my vitality. My backsliding has been caused not by health problems but as a concession to taste and convenience. Indeed during those sad times when I find myself working all day at a desk a small, meatless lunch leaves me feeling better and more able to work than a larger, heavier meal.

Simple meatless diets are also less costly than more elaborate ones. Eating simply thus frees up money for other uses. And it frees up time: the time devoted to earning the money for elaborate meals; the time devoted to preparing them. One of the benefits of living in a wealthy country is that one *can* spend less on food, comparatively: in the United States people spend an average of 10% of their earnings on food, while in African countries the average is 50% and above.[9] Our wealth provides the opportunity to concentrate on other things besides food. But it is also possible to use up this potential savings by eating more expensively and constantly dining out. And a rich man may be just as obsessed with food as a poor man, obsessed not with whether or how he will obtain food, but with its quality.

Here though a meat-eating gourmand might reply: 'I *like* my current diet! I enjoy the taste of meat and sampling varied and rich foods. I don't want to eat what's good for me or for the planet, but what I find most pleasurable. That is what makes life enjoyable. Further, I am wealthy enough to afford it!'

The proper response to this depends, first, on the resources commanded by this person and their own definition of the good life; second, on whether we wish to contest this definition, or merely suggest its more efficient pursuit. Let us assume that we are talking to a wealthy person who believes that increased pleasure is life's great desideratum, and let us further accept this definition of the good life for the purpose of argument. Even in this case, reason and the nature of our physical bodies argue for moderation in eating.

First, there is a natural limit to the amount of food our bodies can handle. Beyond that point we endanger our health and hence our ability to feel pleasure. If our interlocutor says that he values current, certain pleasures over future, uncertain pains, the reply must be that rationality demands probable reasoning and the disciplining of current actions in the service of future happiness. Anyone who has been seriously ill, to the point where life itself became a burden, will be more likely to calculate rightly here.

Second, there is a natural limit to the pleasure we can obtain by eating and drinking. While a fat sirloin steak might give one great pleasure at the dinner table, two steaks aren't likely to double the pleasure. A beer at the end of the day tastes wonderful and two beers sends me into a pleasurable state, but four do not make me feel better and eight are disastrous. If I want to maximize pleasure, my best means are to remember the maxim that 'hunger is the best spice' and go for an all-day hike. That is when my food tastes best, and many a glutted gourmand has failed to enjoy his dinner for lack of this spice. (This points to an important limitation concerning the *passive* gratification of desires.) At the very least, the hungry hiker and the satisfied gourmand are on a level in terms of enjoying their dinner at the end of the day. Thus a person may enjoy food while partaking of it modestly, if her environmental principles so incline her.

This leads to a third point: that we find a variety of sensual pleasures in the active use of our healthy bodies, and overeating can lessen or make impossible these pleasures. It is a pleasure to hike along a mountain ridge or bicycle for 50 kilometers through a green countryside. It feels good to use our muscles. It even feels good to push these to the point of exhaustion (and it feels good when we stop!). There is no lack of physical, sensuous pleasures to be found in a walk through the woods: the dawn chorus of newly-arrived birds in spring, the taste of ripe huckleberries in autumn. For many people greater sensuous pleasure could be found in devoting less time to passive types of consumption and more to the active use of their bodies.[10]

I have been arguing as if with a wealthy person who defined the good life solely in terms of maximal pleasure. But many of us are *not* wealthy, and must cook the majority of our own dinners and pay for the rest out of a finite paycheck. It is something of a comfort then to think that with no more than a vigorous morning hike I can come to my lunch with as keen an appetite as Donald Trump to his. I do not need fancy dishes. As diverting and enjoyable as these may be, I can enjoy simpler meals just as well. And therefore I need not worry about earning the money to purchase these fancy things, or envy Mr. Trump.

Further, most of us judge our well-being not merely in terms of pleasure but also in terms of character and personal achievement. From this fuller and (to use an archaic but necessary word) less ignoble perspective, it is very much to the point that we *may* limit our consumption of food to what will gratify a healthy appetite and sustain our higher aspirations. This, I assert, is the real benefit of living in a wealthy, free society – not the opportunity to dine largely or elaborately.

In *Walden*, Henry Thoreau likens the provision of economic necessities to stoking a furnace. He goes on to ask his readers:

> When a man is warmed by the several modes which I have described, what does he want next? Surely not more warmth of the same kind, as more and richer food, larger and more splendid houses, finer and more abundant clothing, more numerous incessant and hotter fires, and the like. When he has obtained those things which are necessary to life, there is another alternative than to obtain the superfluities; and that is, to adventure on life now, his vacation from humbler toil having commenced. The soil, it appears, is suited to the seed, for it has sent its radicle downward, and it may now send its shoot upward also with confidence. Why has man rooted himself thus firmly in the earth, but that he may rise in the same proportion into the heavens above?[11]

This may sound grandiose but the question is: do you believe it? And if not: what do you believe instead? All our other judgments upon our economic lives depend on our answer here: all our calculations of profit and loss, of lives well or ill-spent.

We need not follow Thoreau so far as to see merely an instrumental value in 'stoking the furnace.' We may believe that pleasure is a necessary part of a good human life, and still agree that achievements besides maximizing pleasure are also important. First in importance is the creation of ourselves: that is, the development of personal character and lives of which we can be proud. But also such achievements as raising happy children, publishing a novel, or saving a free-flowing river for posterity. These are the things for which we strive, and on which serious people judge the success of their lives. Such self-development and personal achievement depend not on the greatest or most refined gratification of our appetites, for food or anything else. On the contrary, they demand some knowledge of when less is more, and the discipline to act on that knowledge. The healthy side to all asceticism and self-denial is its fostering of this necessary discipline and its recognition of higher goals.

The relative value of pleasure, self-development and personal achievement in a good human life, is one of the most vexed questions in ethics.[12] We may strive to live lives which further all of these, while recognizing that sometimes we must choose between them. Each of us answers this question within our own lives. Whatever our answer, our economic lives should support it. This is not necessarily to put on a hair shirt. To the extent that wealth, or possessions, or physical pleasure further our true goals, they should be pursued – but no further. For 'there is no more fatal blunderer than he who consumes the greater part of his life getting his living,'[13] unless it is he who consumes the greater part of his life consuming.

The most important thing wealth can buy us is the freedom to live according to our principles. We have a selfish interest in acting from principle, if only because self-esteem demands it. Thoreau writes: 'It is hard to provide and cook so simple and clean a diet as will not offend the imagination; but this, I think, is to be fed when we feed the body; they should both sit down at the same table.'[14] Both environmental and animal rights concerns argue strongly for a simple, meatless diet.[15] If these concerns are our concerns, a new diet may prove easier to stomach in more ways than one. Here is yet another way in which duty and happiness may coincide, and less may be more.

It is easy in a matter as mundane as food consumption to simply do as we have always done. And certain features of the modern economy conspire to keep us from facing up to the ethical implications of our economic choices, including an intricate division of labor and sterile modern food packaging. Little is left to overtly remind us that land is plowed and animals killed in order to sustain us. But they are. A closer attention to our experience as consumers and to what truly brings us pleasure, combined with a closer attention to our principles and what they demand, will point us towards a better way here.

★ ★ ★

What holds true for food holds true for consumption and use in general: whether pleasure or self-development is our goal, it is an intelligent and moderate consumption which makes for happiness, not the endless pursuit of ever more of these. The ancient moralists understood this; more and more, contemporary economic thinkers are echoing the theme.

Amartya Sen asks that we replace overall Gross National Product or per capita GNP as measurements of third-world development, with measurements that more carefully track improvements in the lives and 'capabilities' of citizens. Robert Lane argues that advanced economies should be judged by the happiness of their participants and the opportunities for self-development they provide, rather than solely by their capacity to create wealth. Herman Daly and John Cobb, Jr. go further, and argue that an economy which undermines local communities and environmental health is a failure, regardless of 'the bottom line.'[16]

Sen, Lane and Daly write as political economists, while I have primarily discussed individuals' personal economies. Yet our arguments run parallel. They, too, remind us that there are alternatives to viewing the purpose of economic activity as the maximization of wealth or production/consumption, and that ignoring this slights our human nature. They too, along with most environmentalists, see clear limits to the benefits of economic growth. Recognizing this puts economic activities in the proper, wider context of our attempts to live good lives and create good societies.

From this perspective, we will often find that less is more. Less consumption equals greater health and happiness. Less resource use equals more wild nature and wider human horizons. The choices are ours to make.

(Endnotes)

1 For Aristotle see *Nicomachean Ethics* bk. 1 chpt. 5, and *Politics* bk. 1, chpts. 2, 8–10. For Stoics and Epicureans see Martha Nussbaum, *The Therapy of Desire* (Princeton: 1994), 103–4, 360–2, 501–2.

2 On the intrinsic value of wild nature see Holmes Rolston, III, *Environmental Ethics* (Philadelphia: Temple University Press, 1988) and Paul Taylor, *Respect for Nature* (Princeton: 1986).

3 Joni Seager, *The State of the Environment Atlas* (London: Penguin Books, 1995) 103.

4 *The New York Times*, May 10, 1995, 'Personal Health: Common Sense and Conflicting Health Studies,' by Jane Brody, section C, page 12.

5 *The New York Times*, November 11, 1986, 'Adventists are Gold Mine for Research on Disease,' by Jane Brody, section C, page 1, column 1.

6 *The New York Times*, October 12, 1983, 'Personal Health: New Research on the Vegetarian Diet,' by Jane Brody, section C, page 1, column 1.

7 Brody, 1995.

8 Brody, 1983.

9 Seager, 14.

10 Arne Naess makes this point convincingly in *Ecology, community and lifestyle: outline of an ecosophy* (Cambridge: Cambridge University Press, 1990), 51.

11 Henry David Thoreau, *Walden and Resistance to Civil Government*, 2nd ed., (New York: W.W. Norton, 1992), 10. Note the passage's transition from a mechanical to an organic metaphor.

12 See Amartya Sen, *On Ethics and Economics* (Oxford: 1987), 43–46, and Sen, 'Capability and Well-Being,' in Sen and Nussbaum, *The Quality of Life* (Oxford: 1993). Sen argues that general disagreements concerning what constitutes the good life need not preclude agreement on specific measures for economic and social reform. Similarly I believe that hedonists and ascetics can sometimes agree to limit their economic activity in order to support their very different life goals.

13 Thoreau, *Reform Papers* (Princeton: 1973), 160.

14 *Walden*, 144.

15 Standard arguments for animal rights and against meat-eating are found in Peter Singer, *Animal Liberation* (New York: Avon Books, 1975) and Tom Regan, *All That Dwell Therein: Animal Rights and Environmental Ethics* (Berkeley: 1982).

16 Amartya Sen, *The Standard of Living* (Cambridge: 1987); Robert Lane, *The Market Experience* (Cambridge: 1991); Herman Daly and John Cobb, Jr., *For the Common Good* (Boston: Beacon Press, 1989). Before these works there was E.F. Schumacher, *Small is Beautiful: A Study of Economics as if People Mattered* (London: Blond and Briggs, 1973).

Chapter Eight

BUILDING THE CASE FOR GLOBAL LIVING

Jim Merkel

Imagine you are at a potluck buffet and see that you are the first in line. How do you know how much to take? Imagine that this potluck spread includes not just food and water, but also the materials needed for shelter, clothing, healthcare and education. It all looks and smells so good and you are hungry. What will you heap on your plate? How much is enough to leave for your neighbors behind you in the line? Now extend this cornucopia to today's global economy, where the necessities for life come from around the world. Six billion people, shoulder to shoulder, form a line that circles around the globe to Cairo, onto Hawaii over ocean bridges, then back, and around the globe again, 180 times more. With plates in hand, they too wait in line, hearty appetites in place. And along with them are giraffes and klipspringers, manatees and spiders, untold millions of species, millions of billions of unique beings, all with the same lusty appetites. And behind them, the soon-to-be-born children, cubs, and larvae.

A harmonious feast just might be possible. But it requires a bit of restraint, or shall we say, a tamed appetite, as our plate becomes a shopping cart, becomes a pickup truck – filling our home, attic, basement, garage, and maybe even a rented storage unit with nature transformed into things. As we sit down for a good hearty meal with new friends and creatures from around the world, what is the level of equity that we would feel great about? At what level of inequity would we say, 'Wait a minute, that's not fair?'

The Global Living Project was founded back in 1995 with a mission to discover how to live sustainably in North America. 'Global living' was defined as an equitable and harmonious lifestyle among not only the entire human population, but also among the estimated 7–25 million other species,[1] and the countless unborn generations. When one practices global living, each of our daily actions improves the health of the whole – locally and globally. The ecological, social, political, and spiritual systems at all levels are then able to regenerate and flourish.

★ ★ ★

So there you are, plate in hand, first in that mega-line. You are determined to be fair as you look over the wonderful buffet, which looks limitless. You glance over your shoulder at the line – its length is too hard for you to fathom. If you had landed on an island paradise with three friends, the answer of how much to take would be intuitive enough, similar to sitting around a large pizza on Friday night – a no-brainer. But the scale of the buffet is too big to wrap your mind around. As you contemplate your real-world life, a soft voice whispers one or more of the following in your ear:

- ★ There is abundance in the universe, plenty for everyone, isn't there.
- ★ If I don't take it, someone else will.
- ★ It's the corporate elite who take too much.
- ★ We all do the best we can.
- ★ Everything is this way for a reason.
- ★ I've really worked hard for my money.
- ★ When I get my next raise, I know I'll do some good with it.
- ★ If I didn't do my part as a consumer, everyone would be out of work.
- ★ Until everyone else takes less, it's futile.
- ★ You could almost say we are biologically programmed to consume – survival of the fittest.
- ★ Come to think of it, in some ways, I'm an exception. I need my (fill in the blank) because (fill in the blank).
- ★ Who knows? It might even be my karma to have so much – otherwise there would be no have-nots.
- ★ What's with all this guilt tripping? Dig in and eat!

You see a burger sizzling on the barbecue that smells really good. 'That will get me started.' Just as you are ready to put it on your bun, you remember reading *Diet for a New America*.[2] Eating high on the food chain uses much more land, up to fifty times more than a vegetarian diet. The line is long. You remember staring at corn stalks for days on end on a cross-country trip – corn grown only to feed to cattle. You remember the cleared forests and prairies, the manure and soil running off into streams, lakes, and coastal waters, and that 43 percent of the US is grazed or grows feed for livestock. Meat's impact on the environment is second only to automobiles.[3]

'All right, all right,' you say as you look for a tofu burger. Both burgers will require processing facilities, packaging and shipping. Each will leave a trail of waste and pollution. You've heard that soybeans are lower on the food chain – they produce an equal amount of protein on one-sixteenth the land needed for beef. The tofu burger is not perfect. The thought of genetically modified beans grown on monoculture fields sprayed with pesticides leaves you a bit queasy. But it's a substantial reduction in cost to the Earth. And it's tasty.

With appetite abated, your mind wanders to dream getaways. This grand buffet has it all. Two tickets to Bali and in just 22 hours you could be released from the icy grip of the coming winter. 'I can taste those mangos, feel the hot sand. The plane is going anyway....' You think it through further. Well... not exactly. You do a quick calculation and discover you'd need four acres of forests working year round to absorb the jet emissions for your seat on this once-a-year 44-hour roundtrip flight.[4] You realize that the non-renewable jet fuel once burned will push atmospheric CO2 levels higher. A second consciousness-raising thought enters: the $1,280 tab for this flight is equal to the annual wages of five typical Balinese.[5] 'I'll stay home then,' you conclude. Then you think, 'To pass those long cold days, I could use a faster computer. With the latest information, I could do some great activism.' But wait. You remember reading that a computer uses 1,000 substances, including 350 different hazardous chemicals in its manufacturing processes.[6] Computers' designed obsolescence earned 20 million machines an early retirement in 1998. You also remember reading about the rural rice-growing town of Guiyu, China, which has become an electronic waste (e-waste) processing center. Women and children earn $1.50 per day to strip computers down to components. Soil and water tests there have revealed lead levels 2,400 times greater than those allowed by the World Health Organizations guidelines. Several other heavy metals tested far exceeded the Environmental Protection Agency standards: barium by 10 times; tin by 152 times; and chromium by 1,338 times. A year after the operation started, the village had to truck in water. Many of the substances are known carcinogens or cause birth defects and skin and lung irritation.[7]

Let's face it: in North America and other wealthy regions of the world it can be challenging to find products that don't have a large negative environmental impact. And just as challenging is to say no to what is so easy for us to have... to say no to what just seems *normal* to have. As we look more deeply into the products and services we use, one question we can ask ourselves is: 'Am I in control of what I choose to put on my plate?' If not, then who is? Why do we feel such a knee-jerk resistance to taming our appetites? This is a spiritual, social, psychological, and emotional question. Does it come from internal fears of not having enough? Or is it the product of pathological pressures generated externally?

Inside Ourselves

More desperate whispering in the ear: 'If I decided to attempt radical simplicity, might I wind up without adequate food and shelter? Will I be able to pay for new clothes and healthcare? How will I finish my education, or pay for my children's? Who will hire me? How can I afford to just kick back and have a good time now and then? Will I lose status, respect, and friends? How will I ever get to travel, and do all those other things I've dreamed of? My children will hate me, my partner will never understand. Mom and Dad might not ever say it, but somehow, I just know they'll be disappointed. And then, someday I'll be old, and who will take care of me? Who will pay the bills?'

Global living: A nice concept, but pretty scary.

Outside Ourselves

Have you ever wondered where the pressure to consume comes from? Does the rush of modern culture keep you plunging forward on the same unquestioned path day after day? Have you become resigned to the realization that there is no longer enough clean water available, no longer a way to avoid the catastrophic consequences of global warming? All of society – our government (we elected them), our employers (we went to work for them), and the church and schools we have chosen to attend, all seem to support economic growth and unsustainable behavior from A to Z. Mainstream media and corporate advertisers seem to control the bulk of information, and influence who gets elected, so much so that millions of people don't even vote. With the corporate dream machine cranking away, it's easy to see why. In the US:[8]

- ★ 99.5 percent of households have televisions.
- ★ 95 percent of the population watches TV every day.
- ★ The average home has a TV on for eight hours a day. The average adult watches for five hours; children between ages two and five watch for three and a half hours; and adults over 55 for nearly six hours.
- ★ Aside from sleep and work, watching TV is America's primary activity.

If you grew up like other North Americans, you have watched 40,000 TV commercials a year.[9] Add to that the bombardment of sales pitches from radio, print media, billboards, and signs and logos, and your internal landscape may very well be etched with a lust and desire for things. Once we are able to satisfy the hunger for this or that, we are still tempted into more exotic vacations, more trips to the hair salon or meditation center, and more gas-guzzling experiences skiing or snowmobiling. Advertisers know how to get to the money in your pockets. They are trained to have you seek fulfillment outside yourself, for your dreams to include their products, their view of life – for their dream to become your dream.

If you received 12, 16, or 20 years of institutional education, you'll have other influences to overcome. In *Dumbing Us Down*,[10] John T. Gatto, a New York State Teacher of the Year, shows how public schools have mostly taught young people to follow orders. Some schools might be excellent, but often our intrinsic creativity, spark, curiosity, and ability to self-motivate are dampened during our most dynamic and open years. All this time spent indoors, sitting in rows, with someone else calling the shots while the natural world beckons, is a sad injustice. To initiate a lifestyle of our own design, in alignment with our personal values, is a skill we just haven't been taught unless we were lucky enough to have family, adult friends, or an inspiring teacher who modeled the behaviors that make dreams come true.

Most cities and towns have been redesigned for cars, while bus systems and bike lanes are few and far between. Neighborhoods with services accessible by foot, the corner store where you chat with neighbors and carry home some provisions, are mostly things of the past. Our homes may be ten to eighty miles from work, with groceries in a strip mall in the opposite direction. Our favorite park might be clear across town; our best friend, across the state; and our family spread across the continent. Many towns have laws that make it illegal to have a home business, a composting toilet, or a greywater system. Building codes often make a simply-built home illegal. Making a small outside fire at night to sing around is often illegal, even on your own property.

Yes, at the start, reinventing our own slice of life can look pretty much impossible. The more deeply we search for the causes of our world's drastic imbalances, the more we realize the full extent of the violence we have unknowingly supported. Who would have thought that children in China would get sick from our e-waste? Or that a meat-based diet destroys habitats in Brazil? That the sea level could rise and aquatic habitats in Polynesia become contaminated with toxins because of our fossil fuel dependence? And that, with the flick of a light switch, we may contribute to the genocide of indigenous peoples in Arizona?

By participating in the economics of globalization and the politics of corporate-government rule, backed up by the military-industrial complex, we are actively involved, day to day, in the greatest exploitation of people and nature that the Earth has ever witnessed. Consider these statistics:

- ★ Currently the world's wealthiest one billion people alone consume the equivalent of the Earth's entire sustainable yield. All six billion people are consuming at a level that is 20 percent over sustainable yield.[11]
- ★ Human numbers are predicted to reach nine billion by the year 2050 and peak at 11 billion.[12]
- ★ Private consumption in high-income countries rose from $4,752 billion in 1980 to $14,054 billion in 1998.[13]
- ★ Scientists estimate that between 1,000 and 100,000 species of life become extinct every 24 hours, a rate 100 to 1,000 times faster than the natural rate.[14]
- ★ More than half of all accessible surface fresh water is used by humanity.[15]
- ★ The concentration of atmospheric CO2 has increased from 280 parts per million (ppm) before the Industrial Revolution to 360 ppm today, and is

predicted to reach 560 ppm by 2050. A panel of 1,500 scientists warned that average global temperatures might rise between 3.6 and 6.3 degrees Fahrenheit by 2100.[16]

★ Over 70 percent of remaining oil reserves lie under the soil of Islamic nations of Asia, from the Red Sea to Indonesia.[17] The US imports $19 billion in oil annually and spends another $55 billion annually safeguarding these oil supplies. The Gulf War of the 1990s killed between 160,000 and 220,000 Iraqi people while 19 Americans died.[18]

★ Over the last century, wars have claimed 175 million lives. Worldwide, $780 billion is spent annually on military, $380 billion in the US.[19]

With all these forces, inside and out, conspiring against us, it is understandable that we might ask whether global living is simply impossible.

We Have No Other Choice

We must know first that our acts are useless, and yet we must proceed as if we didn't know it. That is a sorcerer's controlled folly.[20]

– Don Juan

If we want a sustainable future, sharing Earth with all is humanity's only compassionate, long-term choice. Our intellect, backed by the best of science concludes that economic growth on a finite planet is suicide. The intuitive self knows this, and might even have the solution. Our ethical and spiritual selves yearn to secure the future for all life. To avert the ecological catastrophe already in full swing, we have no choice but to radically reduce consumption, immediately stabilize population growth, and rapidly make better use of technology. If we make these changes now, the damage can be minimized. If we delay, a crash is inevitable, with the holders of the most weapons dominating until the bitter end. We have no choice but to stop damaging the Earth's life support systems.

The Dalai Lama, when talking about how to solve world problems, said, 'But first we must change within ourselves.... If there were another method that was easier and more practical, it would be better, but there is none.'[21] As long as we ourselves contribute to the crisis, happiness will be elusive – in the shape of a melancholic surrender, or a party-till-the-cows-come-home abandon. If we live like there is no tomorrow, we will create just that – no tomorrow. It comes down to, 'If not me, then who? If not now, then when?' At some point, we will have no other choice but to make our stand.

Global living is a modern-day journey to reclaim our connections to the Earth, however ancient, and to fall in love with the land again, wherever we decide to call home.

(ENDNOTES)
1 Pimm, Stuart L., *The World According to Pimm: A Scientist Audits the Earth* (New York: McGraw Hill Professional, 2001).
2 Robbins, John, *Diet for a New America: How Your Food Choices Affect Your Health, Happiness and the Future of Life on Earth* (Tiburon, H.J. Kramer, 1987).
3 Brower, Michael and Warren Leon, *The Consumer's Guide to Effective Environmental Choices: Practical Advice from the Union of Concerned Scientists* (New York: Three Rivers Press, 1999).
4 Merkel, Jim, *The Global Living Handbook* (Winlaw: The Global Living Project, 2000).
5 World Bank, *2000 World Development Indicators CD-ROM* (Washington, DC: World Bank, 2000).
6 Puckett, Jim and Ted Smith (editors), *Exporting Harm: The High-Tech Trashing of Asia* (Seattle: Basal Action Network, 2002. A joint report issued with the Silicon Valley Toxics Coalition.)
7 Puckett, Jim and Ted Smith (editors), *Exporting Harm: The High-Tech Trashing of Asia* (Seattle: Basal Action Network, 2002. A joint report issued with the Silicon Valley Toxics Coalition.)
8 Mander, Jerry, *In the Absence of the Sacred* (San Francisco: Sierra Club Books, 1991).
9 New Road Map Foundation, *All Consuming Passion: Waking up from the American Dream* (Seattle: New Road Map Foundation, 1998. In partnership with Northwest Environmental Watch.)
10 Gatto, John T., *Dumbing Us Down: The Hidden Curricula of Compulsory Schooling* (Gabriola Island: New Society Publishers, 1991).
11 World Wide Fund for Nature (WWF), *Living Planet Report 2002* (Gland: WWF, 2002).
12 World Bank, *2000 World Development Indicators CD-ROM* (Washington, DC: World Bank, 2000).
13 World Bank, *2000 World Development Indicators CD-ROM* (Washington, DC: World Bank, 2000).
14 Pimm, Stuart L., *The World According to Pimm: A Scientist Audits the Earth* (New York: McGraw Hill Professional, 2001).
15 Vitousek, Peter M., Harold A. Mooney, Jane Lubchenco, and Jerry M. Melillo, "Human Domination of Earth's Ecosystems." *Science* 277 (1997), pp. 494–499.
16 McKibbon, Bill, *Maybe One: An Environmental and Personal Argument for Single-child Families* (New York: Simon & Schuster, 1998).
17 The Energy Information Administration, Table 8.1 "World Crude Oil and Natural Gas Reserves," *International Energy Annual,* (2001).
18 Ludwig, Art, "U.S. Terrorism?" *Hopedance*, Special Issue, (October 2001).
19 Bell, Dick and Michael Renner, "A New Marshal Plan? Advancing Human Security and Controlling Terrorism." World Watch Institute Press Release (October 9, 2001).
20 Castaneda Carlos, *A Separate Reality* (New York: Washington Square Press, 1991).
21 Pitburn, Sydney (editor), *A Policy of Kindness: An Anthology of Writings by and about the Dalai Lama, Winner of the Nobel Peace Prize* (Ithaca: Snow Lion Publications, 1993).

Chapter Nine

VOLUNTARY SIMPLICITY

Duane Elgin and Arnold Mitchell

Introduction

For the past several years the popular press has paid occasional attention to stories of people returning to the simple life – of people moving back to the country or making their own bread or building their own solar-heated home, and so on. Beneath this popular image of simple living we think there is a major social movement afoot which has the potential of touching the Unites States and other developed nations to their cores. This is the movement towards 'voluntary simplicity' – a phrase we have borrowed from Richard Gregg who, in 1936, was describing a way of life marked by a new balance between inner and outer growth. Further, we think that voluntary simplicity may prove an increasingly powerful economic, social, and political force over the coming decade and beyond if large numbers of people of diverse backgrounds come to see it as a workable and purposeful response to many of the critical problems that we face. The emergence of voluntary simplicity could represent a major transformation of traditional Western values. In this context, it may be a harbinger of multifold shifts, not only in values, but in consumption patterns, institutional operations, social movements, national policies, and so on.

Although there are many precursors and contributing streams to this social flow (environmentalism, consumerism, consciousness movement, etc.), there is little direct evidence to measure the magnitude of this way of life. This discussion then is not intended to be predictive or definitive; rather, as social conjecture and pattern recognition, it is inherently speculative and intended to provoke further thought and comment regarding voluntary simplicity.

What Is Voluntary Simplicity?

The essence of voluntary simplicity is living in a way what is outwardly simple and inwardly rich. This way of life embraces frugality of consumption, a strong sense of environmental urgency, a desire to return to living and working environments which are of a more human scale, and an intention to realize our higher human potential – both psychological and spiritual – in community with others. The driving forces behind voluntary simplicity range from acutely personal concerns to critical national problems. The appeal of simple living appears to be extraordinarily widespread, even gathering sympathy from among those who are not presently attempting to simplify their own life patterns. Voluntary simplicity is important because it may foreshadow a major transformation in the goals and values of developed nations in the coming decades. Although a social movement still in its early stages, its practical and ethical positions seem well enough developed to permit useful analysis of this way of life.

Voluntary simplicity is not new. Nonetheless, the conditions and trends which appear to be driving its contemporary emergence do seem new in their magnitude and intensity. Historically, voluntary simplicity has its roots in the legendary frugality and self-reliance of the Puritans; in Thoreau's naturalistic vision at Walden Pond; in Emerson's spiritual and practical plea for 'plain living and high thinking'; in the teachings and social philosophy of a number of spiritual leaders such as Jesus and Gandhi.

A uniquely modern aspect of voluntary simplicity is that this way of life seems to be driven by a sense of urgency and social responsibility that scarcely existed ten or fifteen years ago. This sense of urgency appears to derive from many serious societal problems, including: the prospects of a chronic energy shortage; growing terrorist activities at the same time that developed nations seem increasingly vulnerable to disruption; growing demands of the less developed nations for a more equitable share of the world's resources; the prospect that before we run out of resources on any absolute basis we may poison ourselves to death with environmental contaminants; a growing social malaise and purposelessness which causes us to drift in our social evolution; and so on. These are but a few of the more modern elements which converge to make voluntary simplicity a seemingly rational response to a pressing situation.

Values Central To Voluntary Simplicity

Voluntary simplicity is a name which denotes a social movement of great diversity and richness. Not surprisingly, there are many values congruent with voluntary simplicity – that radiate out, so to speak, touching global as well as close-to-home issues, idealistic as well as practical matters, and worldly along with personal concerns. Yet, there seems to be an underlying coherence to the rich diversity of expression of this way of life. Consequently, we have selected a skeletal list of those values, which seem to us to lie at the heart of this emerging way of life. These five values are the following:

★ Material Simplicity
★ Human Scale
★ Self-Determination
★ Ecological Awareness
★ Personal Growth

These are considered in detail below.

1. Material Simplicity

Simplification of the material aspects of life is one of the core values of voluntary simplicity. The American Friends Service Committee, long a leader in exploring a way of life of creative simplicity, defines simple living as a 'non-consumerist life-style based upon being and becoming, not having.' The Friends have identified four consumption criteria which evoke the essence of voluntary material simplicity:

★ Does what I own or buy promote activity, self-reliance, and involvement, or does it induce passivity and dependence?
★ Are my consumption patters basically satisfying, or do I buy much that serves no real need?
★ How tied are my present job and lifestyle to installment payments, maintenance and repair costs, and the expectations of others?
★ Do I consider the impact of my consumption patterns on other people and on the earth?

These consumption criteria imply an intention to 'reduce frills and luxuries in our present lifestyle but at the same time emphasize the beauty and joy of living.' They are designed to (1) help people lead lives of creative simplicity, freed from excessive attachment to material goods; (2) aid the nation release more of its wealth to share with those who presently do not have even the basic necessities of life; (3) help individuals become more self-sufficient and less dependent upon large, complex institutions, whether public or private; and (4) restore to life a sense of proportion and balance between the material and non-material aspects of living.

Although living simply implies consuming quantitatively less (particularly items that are energy inefficient, nonbiodegradable, nonessential luxuries, etc.), this does not mean that the overall cost of consumption will go down drastically. Living simply need not be equated with living cheaply. The hand crafted, durable, esthetically enduring products that appeal to frugal consumers are oftentimes purchased at a considerable premium over mass-produced items. Therefore, although the quantity of consumption may decrease and the environmental costs of consumption may be considerably moderated, the overall cost of consumption may remain relatively high since our economy is not oriented to producing the kinds of products which fit these criteria. Material simplicity will thus likely be manifest in consumption styles that are less ascetic (of strictly enforced austerity) and more aesthetic (where each person will consider whether his or her level and pattern of consumption fits, with grace and integrity, into the practical art of daily living). In this view, material possessions are supportive of rather than central to, the process of human growth. Since the ways of expressing that growth are diverse, it seems likely that the degree and nature of material simplification will be a matter for each individual to settle largely for him or herself.

2. Human Scale

A preference for human-sized living and working environments is a central feature of the values constellation embraced by voluntary simplicity. Adherents to voluntary simplicity tend to equate the gigantic scale of institutions and living environments with anonymity, incomprehensibility, and artificiality.

In contrast, as E.F. Schumacher has so powerfully stated, 'Small is Beautiful.' The smallness theme touches on many facets of living. It implies that living and working environments as well as supportive institutions (which have grown to enormous levels of scale and complexity) should, whenever possible, be decentralized into more comprehensible and manageable entities. This further implies that people's endeavors should be of such dimensions that each knows what he/she contributes to the whole and, hence, has a sense of shared rewards and shared responsibility. Reduction of scale is seen as a means of getting back to basics by restoring to life a more human sense of proportion and perspective.

3. Self-Determination

Voluntary simplicity embraces an intention to be more self-determining and less dependent upon large, complex institutions whether in the private sector (the economy) or public sector (the political processes). Self-determination manifests itself in consumption as a desire to assume greater control over one's personal destiny and not lead a life so tied to 'installment payments, maintenance costs and the expectations of others.' To counterbalance the trend towards increasing material dependency a person may seek to become more materially self-sufficient – to grow one's own, to make one's own, to do without, and to exercise self-discipline in his pattern and level of consumption so that the degree of dependency (both physical and psychological) is reduced.

Self-determination shows up in production as a counterbalancing force to combat excessive division of labor. Therefore, instead of embracing specialization the adherent to voluntary simplicity may seek greater work integration and synthesis so that the relationship between one's work and its contribution to the whole is more evident.

In the public sector, the drive for greater self-determination is revealed by a growing distrust of and sense of alienation from large and complex social bureaucracies. The individual – particularly the adherent to voluntary simplicity – seems to want to take charge of his/her life more fully and to manage his/her own affairs without the undue or unnecessary intrusion of a remote bureaucracy. This dimension of voluntary simplicity may explain some of the unusual political coalitions that seem to be emerging between the right and left – where neither support the further intrusion of big institutions into their lives, but rather wish for greater local self-determination and grass roots political action. This aversion to being controlled by increasingly distant bureaucracies is reminiscent of the stubborn independence out of which was born the American Revolution.

4. Ecological Awareness

A sense of ecological awareness which acknowledges the interconnectedness and interdependence of people and resources is central to voluntary simplicity. There emerges from this awareness a number of themes that are hallmarks of this way of life. For example, ecological awareness prompts recognition that our earth is indeed limited, with all that implies for conservation of physical resources, reduction of environmental pollution, and maintenance of the beauty and integrity of the natural environment. Importantly, this awareness often seems to extend beyond a concern for purely physical resources to include other human beings as well. The philosophy of 'welfare' espoused by Gandhi (sarvodaya – not wanting what the least of the inhabitants of this earth cannot have) seems to bring, in substantial part, from this intimate sense of felt connection with those who are less fortunate than we. From this awareness there may arise a sense of compassion and caring that extends beyond the boundaries of the nation-state to include all of humankind. In acknowledging the underlying unity of the human race, the growth of an ecological awareness expands the vision of voluntary simplicity outward and brings with it a strong sense of social responsibility and worldly involvement to what otherwise could be a relatively isolated and self-centered way of life.

Some of the more concrete expressions of this awareness might include: a willingness to share resources with those who are disadvantaged; a sense of global citizenship with commensurate adjustments in lifestyle, social vision, and political commitments; a preference for living where there is ready access to nature; and a desire to foster human and institutional diversity at a grass roots level.

5. Personal Growth

For many persons taking up a materially simple way of life, the primary reason is to clear away external clutter so as to be freer to explore the 'inner life.' The themes of material simplicity, self-sufficiency, a more human scale to living and working, and an ecological awareness are, in a way, devices to sweep away impediments to inner growth. The goal, then, is to free oneself of the overwhelming externals so as to provide the space in which to grow – both psychologically and spiritually. Simone de Beauvoir succinctly stated the rationale for this desire for self-realization when she said: 'Life is occupied in both perpetuating itself and in surpassing itself; if all it does is maintain itself, then living is only not dying.' From the vantage point of many adherents to voluntary simplicity, contemporary American society is primarily occupied in perpetuating itself – and living has become 'only not dying.' As the workability and meaning of traditional values and goals becomes less compelling, a small but rapidly growing number of Americans have become intensively engaged in the attempt to surpass themselves. Although personal growth often includes a distinctly spiritual aspect, involvement with the inner/nonmaterial dimension of life should not be associated with any particular philosophy or religion – its scope embraces activities ranging from biofeedback, humanistic psychology, transpersonal psychology, Eastern philosophy, fundamentalist Christianity, and more.

A concern for the subjective aspect of experience and for the quality of human relationships has been reflected in a steady current of evolving social trends over the past 15 years. Developments have included the emergence and proliferation of the 'human potential movement'; the emergence of 'transpersonal psychology' coupled with a rapid increase of interest and involvement in many Eastern meditative traditions; the growth of feminism; a cultural fascination with psychic phenomena; developments in brain research that confirm a biological basis for both the rational and the intuitive side to human nature; a growing interest in sports as both a physical and spiritual process (e.g., the 'inner game' of tennis); and more.

Without the compelling goal of exploring inner potentials, it seems unlikely that there will be sufficient motivation to adopt voluntarily a way of life of material simplicity. Without greater simplicity, it seems unlikely that we will be able to cope successfully with the problems engendered, for example, by scarcity. Finally, unless inner learning expands, it seems unlikely there will develop the degree of internal maturation necessary for the human species to act as wise trustees of conscious evolution on this earth.

Still, this analysis does not penetrate to the roots of the connection between personal growth and voluntary simplicity. To explain adequately, we must look to a deeper underlying vision. It is an old vision – perhaps as old as civilized man – but an enduring one that seems destined to be rediscovered again and again. The nature of this vision is succinctly summed up by the eminent historian, Arnold Toynbee:

These religious founders (Jesus, Buddha, Lao Tse, St. Francis of Assisi) disagreed with each other in their pictures of what is the nature of the universe, the nature of spiritual life, the nature of ultimate spiritual reality. But they all agreed in their ethical precepts. They all agreed that the pursuit of material wealth is a wrong aim. We should aim only at the minimum wealth needed to maintain life; and our main aim should be spiritual. They all said with one voice that if we made material wealth our paramount aim, this would lead to disaster. They all spoke in favor of unselfishness and of love for other people as the key to happiness and to success in human affairs.

The foregoing five themes do not exhaust the range of basic values that may emerge as hallmarks of the way of life termed voluntary simplicity. Moreover, these values will surely be held to differing degrees in differing combinations by different people. Nonetheless, these values possess an underlying coherence which suggests that they have not arisen randomly but rather as a strongly reinforcing set or pattern. Just a few moments of reflection reveals how powerfully reinforcing these values are: for example, personal growth may foster an ecological awareness which may prompt greater material simplicity and thereby allow greater opportunity for living and working at a smaller, more human scale which, in turn, may allow greater opportunity for local self-determination. No one value theme alone could create the vitality and coherence that emerges from the synergistic interaction of these values. To the extent that these values provide people with a realistic basis for both maintaining and surpassing themselves, they then constitute a practical 'world view' – a coherent pattern of perception, belief, and behavior which could provide an important bridge between the traditional industrial world view and an uncertain and difficult social future.

What Voluntary Simplicity Is Not

We have been trying to define what voluntary simplicity is. We can also get a sense of voluntary simplicity by suggesting what it is not.

Voluntary simplicity should not be equated with a back-to-nature movement. Although an historic shift in net population migration towards small towns and rural places is underway, the large majority of people continue to reside in urban environments. Voluntary simplicity seems perhaps as compelling for this urban majority as it does for the rural minority. An urban existence need not be incompatible with voluntary simplicity; indeed, many of the experiments with appropriate technology, intensive gardening, and such have been conducted in urban contexts.

Although voluntary simplicity surely traces some of its contemporary heritage and vitality to the counterculture movement of the 1960s, its present constituency is certainly not limited to that group. Many of its adherents are of an age and background far removed from the proponents of the so-called 'new values' a decade ago.

Voluntary simplicity should not be equated with living in poverty. Indeed, impoverishment is in many ways the opposite of simple living in that poverty tends to make life a struggle to maintain oneself and provides little opportunity to surpass oneself.

Voluntary simplicity is not a social panacea. It does imply social evolution towards what its adherents view as the minimal requirements for long term global survival but that does not itself cure the problems we confront; rather, voluntary simplicity may provide a basis from which societal responses with some long term hope for success can emerge.

It is not a movement with heart but without the skills necessary to bring it to fruition. Among those who adhere to many of the tenets of voluntary simplicity are, in our estimation, some of the most creative and capable intellects, artists, and humanistic capitalists in the United States. Voluntary simplicity draws its ranks substantially from the well-educated, and, as such, has access to a rich pool of talent.

Voluntary simplicity is not a social movement confined to the United States. Virtually all of the developed Western nations seem to be moving in a somewhat similar direction (although its expression may be altered by the cultural context and social experience). Many European nations, with more limited land and resources, have been learning how to cope with scarcity for far longer than the United States has. And there is evidence that other nations may be opting for voluntary simplicity rather than endure the stress of striving for affluence. For example, a recent poll in Norway found that '74 percent of the total sample claimed they would prefer a simple life with no more than essentials (these were, however, not defined) to a high income and many material benefits if these have to be obtained through increased stress.'

Voluntary simplicity is not a fad. Its roots reach far too deeply into the needs and ideals of people everywhere to be regarded as a transitory response to a passing societal condition.

The Push Toward Voluntary Simplicity

We have suggested that there is a strong pull towards voluntary simplicity. It seems to offer a practical, workable, and meaningful way of life for a small but significant segment of the population. Yet, despite the strength of this pull to voluntary simplicity, there is little reason to think that this way of life will grow to embrace substantial proportions of the population unless the pull is matched by substantial pushes. These twin elements of push and pull need to be considered if we are to assess the likelihood that voluntary simplicity will gather social momentum in the future. We turn, then, to consideration of whether society problems will push us in a direction similar to that exerted by the pull toward voluntary simplicity.

The range and diversity of contemporary societal problems is enormous. Space does not allow more than a cursory glance at some of the more prominent problems which may, in their eventual resolution, push us towards a simple way of life. These problems include:

- ★ The prospect of running out of cheaply available, critical, industrial raw materials.
- ★ The prospect of chronic energy shortages and a difficult transition to a much more energy-efficient economy.
- ★ The growing threat that before we run out of material resources in any absolute sense we will pollute ourselves to death with the intrusion of many thousands of hazardous substances into our living environments and food chains.
- ★ Rising material demands of the third and fourth world, coupled with climatic changes which may induce periodic but massive famine in certain areas, coupled with the growing threat of terrorism (conventional, nuclear, biological), coupled with the growing vulnerability of the highly complex and interdependent technology (e.g., communications, energy, and transportation systems) common to developed nations.
- ★ The changing balance of global power, given rapid nuclear proliferation.
- ★ The poverty of abundance – growing dissatisfaction with the output of our industrial society as the sole or even primary reward and reason for our individual existences.
- ★ Challenge to the legitimacy of leaders in nearly all major institutions – both public and private.
- ★ Apparent loss of social purpose and direction coupled with rising levels of individual alienation.
- ★ Chronic and pervasive fiscal crises of many of our largest cities, coupled with an historic and unexpected turnaround in migration patterns (the net flow is now to small towns and rural areas).

- ★ Decline in the expected number of meaningful work roles, coupled with growing levels of automation, coupled with chronic underemployment and unemployment.
- ★ The prospect that we have created social bureaucracies (at the federal, state, and local levels) of such extreme levels of scale, complexity, and interdependence that they now exceed our capacity to comprehend and, therefore, to manage them; coupled with growing protests that we are becoming an excessively overregulated society, coupled with growing demands upon government at all levels.
- ★ Growing demands that domestic economic inequities be moderated, coupled with the prospect of a little- or no-growth economy in the foreseeable future, yielding the spectre of intense competition for a fixed or slowly growing pie.

Resolution of problems such as these will likely push our society in a direction which is more ecologically conscious, more frugal in its consumption, more globally oriented, more decentralized, more allowing of local self-determination, and so on. To some considerable extent, it appears that resolution of these increasingly serious problems will push in a direction at least similar to that implied by the pull toward voluntary simplicity.

Conclusions

The phenomenon we have called voluntary simplicity appears to be of deep social significance for three fundamental reasons. First, it is a concept and a way of life whose time seems at last to be arriving. The idea of voluntary simplicity has been discussed for millennia. However, our present era of relative abundance contrasts sharply with the material poverty of the past. The voluntary assumption of a life materially simple and nonmaterially rich, therefore, is not only increasingly psychologically acceptable but physically feasible for perhaps the first time in history for large numbers of people.

Second, it specifically addresses the critical issues of our times – the problems of ecosystem overload, alienation, unmanageable scale and complexity of institutions, worldwide antagonism, and so on. Voluntary simplicity is a creative, comprehensive, and holistic approach to a host of problems customarily considered to be separate. By coping simultaneously with scores of interrelated specifics, voluntary simplicity seems to provide a solution that could not be achieved via the one-by-one route.

Third, it meshes with the eternal needs of individuals to continue to grow. The emphasis on the inner life inherent in voluntary simplicity permits people to grow psychologically even if material growth may be denied by events beyond their control. Further, there is reason to think that the kind of growth fostered by voluntary simplicity is especially appropriate to our times and circumstances. In brief, the need of the individual uniquely matches the need of the society.

Of what other emergent life patterns can these things be said?

Chapter Ten

THOREAU'S ALTERNATIVE ECONOMICS

Philip Cafaro

'My purpose in going to Walden Pond,' Henry Thoreau writes early in *Walden*, 'was not to live cheaply nor to live dearly there, but to transact some private business with the fewest possible obstacles' (19). The 'business' referred to includes living a good life, 'private' not because it is best pursued alone, but because no one can do it for us.

Whatever his original intentions, an important part of Thoreau's experiment at the pond turned out to involve answering basic economic questions. What is the best way to earn a living? How much time should I spend at it? How much food and what kind of shelter are necessary to live, or to live well? Thoreau believed that these questions were best posed and answered by individuals attending carefully to their own lives, rather than by reformers attending to institutions. He argued that the real importance of our economic lives lies not in how much wealth they create, but what sorts of people they make us, and how they relate us to others.[1]

In effect, Thoreau saw economics as a branch of applied virtue ethics, as it was for Aristotle and St. Thomas Aquinas. He argued the primacy of ethical over economic considerations, principles over pleasure, final or higher ends over proximate ends or mere means. But Thoreau did not rest content with a screed against materialism. Instead, he extended his arguments for subordinating economic activity to self-development, into an analysis of all aspects of economic life: consumption and production, spending and saving, enterprise and leisure. Always the goal was to specify the best life he could live and how these activities might move him toward that life, whether as means or as constituent ends.

While virtue ethics arguably provides the proper framework for considering our economic lives, the complexity of modern economic life works to obscure it. In response, Thoreau structured his personal economy so as to clarify this framework, primarily through simple living and a rejection of the division of labor – 'a principle,' he wrote, 'which should never be followed but with circumspection' (50). As far as possible he secured his own food, in the bean-field and the pond. He built his own shack, using local materials. Thoreau lingered over these experiments, and then over their interpretation. He saw the effects of his economic actions, because he was looking and because they were written directly into the land around him.

In the end, Thoreau concluded that a good life involved both limiting his economic activities and carefully attending to them. Thus, they became means to know himself and his world, and a springboard for higher achievements. 'Economy is a subject which admits of being treated with levity,' he wrote, 'but it cannot so be disposed of' (20).

First Things First

In *Walden*, 'Economy' comes first. It is the first and longest of eighteen chapters. Before serious 'Reading' or entertaining 'Visitors,' before considering 'Higher Laws' or visiting 'The Ponds,' Thoreau treats 'Economy.'

Economy must come first, for two reasons. First, insofar as 'economy' is defined as that personal economy which consists in a correct matching of means to ends, an 'industrious' and 'enterprising' temperament and a keen desire to 'improve one's opportunities,' such economy is the key to all practical effectiveness. 'I have always endeavored to acquire strict business habits,' Thoreau writes, 'they are indispensable to every man' – but especially to one pursuing difficult goals which are neither well regarded nor well rewarded by society (20).

Second, we are all tasked, transcendentalists no less than tradesmen, to support ourselves. Economic activity will thus be a part of our lives: how large a part is a key question. No matter what our overall goals in life, we must ask whether our economic activities further these directly, or provide the means to engage in other activities which do so. Such questions demand answers, because 'The Economy' has its own logic and its own answers, which can easily become ours by default. We also have a tendency to lose ourselves in our proximate economic purposes. Our economic forethought, valuable and necessary, can end by narrowing our lives.

Within the first half-dozen pages of this first chapter, Thoreau sets up a framework which will allow a careful analysis of his own and his neighbors' economic lives. His first words concerning these are meant to jolt us and stir our imaginations, preparatory to re-seeing:

> I have travelled a good deal in Concord; and every where, in shops, and offices, and fields, the inhabitants have appeared to me to be doing penance in a thousand remarkable ways. What I have heard of Brahmins sitting exposed to four fires and looking in the face of the sun; or hanging suspended, with their heads downward, over flames; or looking at the heavens over their shoulders 'until it becomes impossible for them to resume their natural position, while from the twist of the neck nothing but liquids can pass into the stomach;' or dwelling, chained for life at the foot of a tree; or measuring with their bodies, like caterpillars, the breadth of vast empires; or

> standing on one leg on the tops of pillars,-even these forms of conscious penance are hardly more incredible and astonishing than the scenes which I daily witness. (4)

The rhetoric here is sly and well-considered. To his largely Protestant audience in mid-1850's America, the religious form of 'penance' would have seemed outlandish enough – another odd and wrong custom brought in by the Irish Catholics streaming into their midst – doubly odd when presented in connection with Indian Brahmins. Yet in the standard Biblical account work is a penance: God's punishment for humanity's sin and disobedience at the Fall. For many Christians this hard, work-filled life is itself something to be endured, in hope of a better life to come. Perhaps these ideas, too, are outlandish. In fact, Thoreau believes life-denying Christian otherworldliness is a main obstacle to philosophical discussion of the nature of the good life and to its practical pursuit (72–80, 314–316). The passage invites readers to deny Thoreau's charge, challenging each of us to specify the point of our economic lives – thus opening up discussion.

Taken most simply, this hyperbolic description claims that most of the work performed by Thoreau's neighbors is experienced by them as unpleasant, unfulfilling drudgery. Thoreau's reader must ask himself or herself: is this my experience? Crucially, there is no mention here of money, implying that the enjoyment we get out of work and its effect on us – not pay – should be the primary factors in our deciding where, whether and how much to work. When Thoreau later describes his own work (farming, building, surveying, teaching, reading, writing) he repeatedly returns to this point (42, 162).

The passage also suggests that his neighbors' work deforms their characters and lives rather than improving them. This is most clearly implied by the Brahmins' twisted, paralyzed necks, and emphasized by the images of immobility and stasis ('hanging suspended,' 'chained for life,' 'standing ...on the tops of pillars'). Thoreau writes near the beginning of New England's industrialization, with first-hand knowledge of the sorts of ailments and deformities to which factory life could lead: limbs lost to machines, lungs ruined from stoking furnaces in unventilated rooms. These are the extreme cases. But *Walden* focuses on those who are comparatively luckier and hence perhaps less aware of their peril: people whose work lives fail to allow them to develop as human beings. 'Most men,' Thoreau writes, 'are so occupied with the factitious cares and superfluously course labors of life that its finer fruits cannot be plucked by them. Their fingers, from excessive toil, are too clumsy and tremble too much for that' (6).

Thoreau means, in these general and metaphorical remarks, to get us to feel or admit dissatisfaction. He thus pushes us in the direction of asking more from our economic lives. Thoreau's views show strong affinities with Nobel prize-winning economist Amartya Sen's 'capabilities-based' conception of human well-being, particularly in their shared emphasis on the active nature of the good life. According to Sen, we have capacities or capabilities whose use and development constitute human well-being.[2] According to Thoreau, our work should be an occasion for such development, because for most of us it takes up the best part of our day. The office worker sitting immobile in a chair for forty or fifty hours a week will likely become soft and flabby. The same is true for someone who, by choice or chance, is stuck in a monotonous, repetitive job which does not engage her mental capabilities.

The invocation of nature and the natural will be a part of any ethics based on capabilities: recall the Brahmins' necks twisted out of their natural position and the inhuman, worm-like wriggling of some of the other 'penitents.' But their use is problematic. We can speak of both capabilities and their development as natural, meaning simply that most people in our society and others like it have these capabilities and develop them to a certain extent. But the mere existence of some capability cannot justify its positive evaluation: 'natural' is not a synonym for 'good.' Nor does its typical use fully specify how a capability is best developed. The higher and more rarefied the use to which a capability is put, the less natural, in the sense of normal, it becomes.

The best the ethicist can do is point out that people typically have certain capabilities that can be developed in different ways, and argue further that certain ways are better than others. The word 'natural' here does no direct justificatory work, but rather represents the claim that the capability or the potential for its higher development are widely present. So, for example, young children have the capacity to learn about wild nature and a boundless curiosity about it. Most adults lose this curiosity as they get older, but some, scientists and naturalists, keep it, improving their capacity to learn and increasing their knowledge. This can be seen as nurturing a natural capability and putting it to a better use than normal. But that this use is better must still be argued.

According to Thoreau, then, we should judge our work and economic activities generally by whether they are enjoyable and whether they further our self-development. Instead, we often pursue money or possessions, and neglect those further ends which they may support. Even worse, we sometimes just run in the ruts and act for no conscious purpose. The Brahmins' efforts as Thoreau presents them hang in the air, unexplained, standing for the undirected economic lives of his neighbors. He continues: 'The twelve labors of Hercules were trifling in comparison with those which my neighbors have undertaken; for they were only twelve, and had an end; but I could never see that these men slew or captured any monster or finished any labor.' (4) If we cannot identify their purpose, then we cannot know when our efforts have succeeded. We cannot have the satisfaction of saying 'this is a job well done.' Or 'that job is finished, I can rest now.' Or 'I have enough of what I was pursuing,' either money or the things that money can buy. To be able to do so, we must consider our economic efforts as they relate to more-than-economic ends. Even the prodigious drudgery of Hercules compares favorably with the labors of those who cannot do so.

Means/ends analysis – economy – is thus essential to virtue ethics, as Aristotle recognized long ago.[3] Not surprisingly, such analysis is central to ethical discussion in *Walden*. Virtually every page comments on the goodness of some putative ends or the suitedness of particular means to attain them.

Thoreau's analysis of means and ends is extremely complex. It occurs at various levels of generality, includes both detailed discussions and short, seemingly off-hand remarks, and shifts from earnestness to irony and back again. But the main analytic moves are (somewhat schematically) the following:

★ point out pointless action (4, 104–105, 164).
★ challenge overwrought means to fairly simple ends (33–36, 65, 91–93).
★ deny the goodness of certain widely pursued ends (65–66, 74–75, 195–196).
★ suggest new means to accepted ends (53, 131–132).
★ contest or more fully specify the meaning of accepted ends (97–101).
★ argue for greater emphasis on our higher ends (21, 89–90, 323–324).
★ define our 'chief end' (16–18, 90–91, 328–329).

I present these in no particular order, as Thoreau shifts freely from one to the other in *Walden*. Such a procedure accurately portrays our ordinary ethical reasoning. I believe it also reflects the true situation of the ethical theorist, who cannot settle questions at the most general level and then read off the particulars of how individuals should live, but must continually revisit general assumptions and particular judgments, revising both as he goes along.[4] Thoreau's attention to the full spectrum of means/ends reasoning and his attempts to tie general principles to particular ethical judgments are strengths of his ethical philosophy. Ironically, however, this comprehensiveness and specificity make it harder for most academic philosophers to recognize *Walden* as a genuine work in ethical philosophy, since contemporary ethical philosophy usually remains at a high level of generality and theoretical abstractness.

Key to Thoreau pursuing a comprehensive means/ends analysis is his rejection of two basic postulates of modern economic theory. First, that our ultimate goals in life are arbitrary, mere 'preferences' beyond the range of rational debate. Second, that human beings have infinite desires for wealth, ownership and consumption whose pursuit is limited only by scarcity of resources. We must reject these views, Thoreau believes, in favor of the classical beliefs that some goals are ignoble and childish, and that reason may convince us that we have consumed enough or garnered enough material wealth. These are old, simple and very necessary ethical themes.

Thoreau asserts that economic anxiety is a common affliction in his busy, commercial society. Both the wealthy speculator monitoring his investments and the poor laborer who cannot get out of debt can find themselves obsessed with money, possessions and the status they provide (11). But is such anxiety widespread, and is Thoreau propounding a reasonable alternative to this anxious life? Critics often note that Thoreau did not need to worry about supporting a wife and children, and that his superior abilities and education made it relatively easy for him to support himself. These factors certainly increased his economic choices and helped alleviate the anxiety he might have felt in undertaking his economic experiment at the pond. Still, Thoreau's situation was probably not essentially different from many of his readers today, both young, single ones and older ones with families but with relatively secure, well-paid jobs. Indeed, the immense increase in per capita wealth in the United States between Thoreau's time and our own should have made an easy economic sufficiency more widely available. Perhaps it is more widely available and Americans remain chained to high consumption, high anxiety lifestyles less by choice than through inertia.

Interestingly, empirical studies have repeatedly shown that most people value security of income more highly than increases in income. Studies in the U.S. show that beyond the poorest 10% to 15% of the population, happiness and contentment do not correlate with some absolute level of wealth, or some particular level relative to one's neighbors. Rather, the evidence is clear that for most people, happiness depends on their assurance that they will have enough.[5] A dynamic capitalist economy offers natural risk-takers great scope for testing their luck and abilities: a few succeed spectacularly, and many more enjoy the game. But most of us are not entrepreneurs or speculators and would rather have a sufficiency. To this majority, Thoreau says we can have enough, but most easily and certainly by scaling back our material wants and finding inexpensive paths to personal fulfillment.[6]

One half of saying 'enough' involves recognizing happiness and such higher goals as self-development, an enriched experience, or increased knowledge, as the ultimate purposes of our economic activities. The other half is to recognize the limited value of money or possessions for achieving these goals. Thoreau continues his introductory remarks: 'I see young men, my townsmen, whose misfortune it is to have inherited farms, houses, barns, cattle, and farming tools; for these are more easily acquired than got rid of' (5). From a common-sense perspective it could hardly be a 'misfortune' to be given the start on an economically productive life, which inheriting a farm still meant throughout mid-nineteenth century America. Nor, from the perspective of the market, can it ever be disadvantageous to be given something for free which has substantial market value. Such a thing can be translated into money, which can then buy something that we do want.

But the abstraction of the market is no defense against an over concern with money, while possessions may cause great harm without their disciplined use. If they are too numerous, we are forced to attend to them; if too valuable, we worry about theft and loss. The pursuit of money and possessions can lead us into careers that do not support our higher aspirations. This possibility, that men and women may become 'the tools of their tools,' that 'when the farmer has got his house, he may not be the richer but the poorer for it, and it be the house that has got him,' is a recurring theme in *Walden* (33, 37, 65–66).

Our inheritance, which includes old things and old ways of looking at things, may not be the start of our fortune, but rather a misfortune. Often, Thoreau believes:

> men labor under a mistake. The better part of the man is soon ploughed into the soil for compost. By a seeming fate, commonly called necessity, they are employed, as it says in an old book, laying up treasures which moth and rust will corrupt and thieves break through and steal. It is a fool's life, as they will find when they get to the end of it, if not before. (5)

That there is a 'better part' of ourselves, which it is our duty to cultivate and not 'plough into the soil' to fertilize the projects of others or our own unthinking, vegetable life, must be a basic tenet of any virtue ethics. So must be the denial of 'fate,' opening up the possibility that through increased self-knowledge, we may recognize that we 'labor under a mistake' and change our lives accordingly.

This toil is not fated. We may organize our lives in new ways, ones more consonant with our ideals and happiness. Our present lives only seem fated, because the grooves have worn so deep. We must try new ways and just as important, imagine new ways of living. For 'what a man thinks of himself, that it is which determines, or rather indicates, his fate' (7). Earlier, Thoreau had invoked the naturalistic, foundational side of virtue ethics. Here he expresses its romantic, idealistic side, which recognizes that while no account of human nature can unshakably ground or fully specify our ethics, the freedom this opens up for self-creation and enacting our ideals is valuable recompense. The key to exploring these possibilities, Thoreau believes, is economy, defined now as 'simplicity of life and elevation of purpose' (92).

Thoreau needs one more set of categories to support his economic/ethical analysis: necessities, comforts and luxuries. Of the many things that our money can buy, we want to ask whether they are indispensable (necessities), superfluous (luxuries) or truly serve to make our lives more pleasurable (comforts). Thoreau's definitions of these are straightforward, the key term being the first: 'By the words, necessary of life, I mean whatever, of all that man obtains by his own exertions, has been from the first, or from long use has become, so important to human life that few, if any, whether from savageness, or poverty, or philosophy, ever attempt to do without it.' (12) Although history and anthropology give us hints, the true necessities of life can only be found in experience. This is one reason Thoreau went to the pond. As for the rest, 'most of the luxuries, and many of the so called comforts of life, are not only not indispensable, but positive hindrances to the elevation of mankind' (14). Indulging in them might please but rarely improves us, Thoreau believes.

Thoreau's position here is too simplistic, however, perhaps because he sees Americans so sunk in materialism that he does not want to confuse the issue. To note one important complication: he divides possessions into necessities, luxuries and the intermediate term 'comforts.' But given his own ethical position, he needs a fourth intermediate category, 'aids': things which genuinely further self-development, just as comforts genuinely further pleasure. Judging by Thoreau's own life, he would have included books, musical instruments, hand lenses and field glasses within this category. What we include within it remains to be seen, and we must remember that aids may no longer aid and comforts may no longer bring pleasure when used unwisely or excessively. Complicating Thoreau's position in this way only strengthens it, I believe.

Likening the provision of economic necessities to stoking a furnace, Thoreau asks his readers:

> When a man is warmed by the several modes which I have described, what does he want next? Surely not more warmth of the same kind, as more and richer food, larger and more splendid houses, finer and more abundant clothing, more numerous incessant and hotter fires, and the like. When he has obtained those things which are necessary to life, there is another alternative than to obtain the superfluities; and that is, to adventure on life now, his vacation from humbler toil having commenced. The soil, it appears, is suited to the seed, for it has sent its radicle downward, and it may now send its shoot upward also with confidence. Why has man rooted himself thus firmly in the earth, but that he may rise in the same proportion into the heavens above? (115)

This may sound grandiose, but the question is: do you believe it? And if not: what do you believe instead? All our other judgments upon our economic lives depend on our answers here: all our calculations of profit and loss, of lives well or ill-spent.

We need not follow Thoreau so far as to see merely an instrumental value in 'stoking the furnace.' We may believe that pleasure is a necessary part of a good human life and still agree that achievements besides maximizing pleasure are also important. First in importance is the creation of ourselves: that is, the development of personal characters and lives of which we can be proud. But also such achievements as raising happy children, learning about the world, building professional careers which support us and are genuinely useful to society. These are the things for which we strive and on which serious people judge the success of their lives. The healthy side to all asceticism is its recognition of higher goals and its fostering the discipline necessary to achieve them.

The relative value of pleasure, self-development and personal achievement in a good human life is perhaps the most vexing question in virtue ethics. We may strive to further all these, while recognizing that sometimes we must choose between them. Each of us answers this question within his or her own life. Whatever our answers, our economic lives should support them. This is not necessarily to put on a hair shirt. To the extent that wealth or possessions further our true goals, they should be pursued. But no further. For 'there is no more fatal blunderer than he who consumes the greater part of his life getting his living.'[7]

Economy As Method And Metaphor

For Thoreau 'economy' is both a key method and a key metaphor for ethics. Thoreau's method may be quickly summarized. First, he attempted to simplify his life. From his furniture to the number of dishes he cooked for dinner, the refrain is 'simplicity, simplicity, simplicity!' (91). Second, he carefully attended to his economic experience: the quantifiable and the non-quantifiable aspects; the money earned and the economic processes themselves; the effects on him and the effects radiating out from him. Third, he frequently returned to the question of the final or true ends of his efforts and whether in fact his economic activities were furthering them. These three moves – simplification, attentiveness, preserving the full means/ends spectrum – supported one another. Thoreau applies them to numerous activities in *Walden*, from eating huckleberries to building his house.

Several points should be made about this method. For one thing, it personalizes ethics. The focus is on my economy and on what I should do in particular instances, not on The Economy and on what, ideally, we all should be doing. For another, it is flexible, clarifying the purposes and relative success of different people's actions, who may have quite varied goals. Finally, the method works. Follow it and you will live more consciously, successfully, happily.

Despite this last, crucial fact – that the method works, that it worked for Thoreau and can work for you or me – it has its limitations. Economy is not a substitute for effort, but makes our efforts more effective. Thoreau's method, like Aristotle's practical reason (phronesis), combines thought and action, and the thinking part is worthless by itself. In fact, ethical thought leads to pointless hair-splitting, bootless system-building, aimless fantasizing and plain hypocrisy, if not vitalized by action.

Furthermore, the method recognizes the limits of rationality, as both comprehensiveness and certainty elude our economic judgments. Thoreau has several nice ways of indicating this: for example, the mix of seriousness and whimsy with which he treats figures for income and expenditures at the pond (49, 55, 59–60). Thoreau keeps a complete list of the materials used to make his shack and their cost, telling us: 'I give the details because very few are able to tell exactly what their houses cost, and fewer still, if any, the separate cost of the various materials which compose them' (48–49). Thus we know that he paid two dollars and forty three cents for 'two second hand windows with glass,' thirty one cents for horsehair to mix with his plaster, and ten cents for a latch for his door. We learn exactly what he paid the town grocers for his food over the course of a year and exactly what the produce from his fields earned. 'These statistics,' he concludes, 'however accidental and therefore uninstructive they may appear, as they have a certain completeness, have a certain value also. Nothing was given me of which I have not rendered some account.' (60)

What is this 'certain value'? Well, if you can specify income and expenditures clearly, you can limit your use of resources and direct them to where they will do the most good. The price of horsehair or second-hand windows varies 'accidentally,' with supply and demand, but we must track these accidents and act accordingly, if we wish to build and live economically. Still, such monetary metrics cannot capture the higher value of our activities or achievements. During his own lifetime, Thoreau earned more for his bushels of beans, little as that was, than for *A Week on the Concord and Merrimack Rivers*, the wonderful book he wrote while living at Walden Pond. Even if the public had paid more, much more, for the book, that would not have shown its true worth relative to the beans. It would not have captured the relative worth of hoeing beans and writing the book for Thoreau. Nor can the figures express or explain the value of Thoreau's faithfulness to the moral, artistic and spiritual imperatives suggested by the notion of 'rendering some account' of all we are given.

This suggests that if we follow the figures too slavishly, we will make mistakes. It may be a false economy, for example, to pay someone to plant your garden while you work overtime at the office, even though you earn more money than the gardener costs. 'Where is this division of labor to end?' Thoreau asks, 'and what object does it finally serve? No doubt another *may* also think for me; but it is not therefore desirable that he should do so to the exclusion of my thinking for myself' (46). Some essential faculties cannot be exercised by proxy. Some valuable experiences are more enjoyable than profitable.

Careful accounting helps Thoreau construct a sturdy, comfortable house for under $30 and feed himself on 'about twenty-seven cents a week' (60–61). More important, it helps him devote time to other things besides food and shelter. For the purpose of life is to live well, and 'the cost of a thing is the amount of what I will call life which is required to be exchanged for it, immediately or in the long run' (31). This suggests that the part of our valuing that we can express in a monetary metric must be folded in to a larger ethical reasoning, and that this in turn must be folded in to a life where we make choices and deal with the 'accidental' truths of our particular lives. Close figuring has tremendous value within this context, but it is badly misleading beyond it.

Thoreau also reminds us that efficient reasoning and efficient action can be carried too far. We do not want our lives completely organized. *Walden* contains plenty of fishing, loafing and woolgathering. Appealing characters such as Alek Therien, the careless French Canadian wood chopper, make a nice contrast to the striving Thoreau and suggest other ethical options. Once again, the method should not be allowed to take over. It is valuable solely in service to a rich life. Maximal efficiency in not a legitimate goal, even though philosophical speculation, moralistic hectoring, or market pressures might push us in that direction.

But if method and order have their limits, so do genius and idealism. Without discipline and calculation, without specific skills and abilities, we cannot instantiate our ideals. We fail just as surely as those without ideals, or with base ideals.

Thoreau repeatedly uses the word 'economy' as a synonym for right living, and *Walden* employs economy as one of its main ethical metaphors. Stanley Cavell, in his influential study *The Senses of Walden,* notes the centrality of economic terms in the book's first chapter:

> 'Economy' turns into a nightmare maze of terms about money and possessions and work, each turning toward and joining the others. No summary of this chapter will capture the number of economic terms the writers sets in motion in it. There is profit and loss, rich and poor, cost and expense, borrow and pay, owe and own, business, commerce, enterprises, ventures, affairs, capital, price, amount, improvement, bargain, employment, inheritance, bankruptcy, work, trade, labor, idle, spend, waste, allowance, fortune, gain, earn, afford, possession, change, settling, living, interest, prospects, means, terms.[8]

By 'setting these terms in motion,' Thoreau forces us to think about them. In place of our previously settled judgments about our enterprises, we now have question marks and unsettling comparisons. Thoreau will deliver a chesty maxim which appropriates the hard, no nonsense language of business – but with a catch. For example, the bland 'I have always endeavored to acquire strict business habits; they are indispensable to every man,' followed by the fantastically extended metaphor of 'trading with the Celestial Empire,' which clearly calls us to higher ventures (20). Or again: 'Who would not be early to rise, and rise earlier and earlier every successive day of his life, till he became unspeakably healthy, wealthy, and wise?' (127). This little bit of literary larceny simultaneously advocates and pokes fun at 'method,' provides an utterly practical piece of advice, and suggests higher goals and endless, heroic striving.

I think Cavell takes too negative a view of this 'unsettling' of our economic terms. 'What we call the Protestant Ethic, the use of worldly loss and gain to symbolize heavenly standing,' he writes, 'appears in *Walden* as some last suffocation of the soul. America and its Christianity have become perfect, dreamlike literalizations or parodies of themselves.'[9] But using monetary or commercial metaphors to express higher values is not necessarily wrong, or perverse. Like using physical metaphors to 'picture' the mental or spiritual realms, it is useful and deeply ingrained in our thinking.[10] Just as physical metaphors can suggest the reality of the spiritual realm, so economic metaphors can suggest the possibility of instantiating higher values. The prevailing tone of *Walden* is one of hope, not suffocating despair, largely because Thoreau believes in the practical possibility of self-improvement. Rather than picturing a 'nightmare,' 'Economy' moves on from his despairing neighbors and the immobile Brahmins to discuss the concrete ways Thoreau improved his life at the pond. By implication, such improvements are also open to his neighbors and his readers.

Thoreau's appropriation of business discourse, like his appropriation of Christian ethical categories and rhetoric, involves both earnestness and irony. Modern commentators, who tend to be intellectuals and English professors, not businessmen, are apt to catch the irony and miss the earnestness. But Thoreau really does believe that strict business habits are indispensable. He really does think people have a responsibility to get their own living, rather than sponging off their neighbors. Thoreau challenges the business culture's aims, but also hopes to harness its drive. He tries to meet people where they live, ethically, and for many in Thoreau's time as in ours, that meant the worlds of business and commerce.

In effect, Thoreau's playfulness with economic terms – his use of irony, his multiple meanings, his straightforward denials of conventional economic judgments alongside examples of them – invites the reader to reconsider his economic life and his life in general. Just as the cut-and-dried nature of economic calculation can be used to serve this greater good, so too can the inherent ambiguity and uncertainty of language. For the upshot is a rich, flexible language of means and ends, profit and loss, which allows us to make decisions and choices, but also forces us to question them. We can never rest in our judgments because we can never rest in our language. Just as idealists cannot escape economic realities, so economic 'realists' cannot ignore the reality that they are making moral choices in their economic lives. Both must reckon with a larger view of freedom.

Thoreau's words in *Walden* provoked ever more readers over the next hundred and fifty years as he questioned their success or dared them to pursue their true vocations. Those words still irk and inspire students today, as anyone who teaches *Walden* can attest. Not just because Thoreau continues to speak our language, and undermine it, but because there is a life behind the words. It is Thoreau's reflective practice, the combination of earnest living and clear thinking, that continues to move readers. 'Economy' works as a metaphor because it is also a method.

The Train to Fitchburg

Thoreau wasn't the most systematic or influential economic thinker of the nineteenth century, but he might have been the funniest. Putting down a breathless account of the latest construction on the information super-highway, I pick up *Walden* and read the following: 'We are in great haste to construct a magnetic telegraph from Maine to Texas [Thoreau writes in 1854]; but Maine and Texas, it may be, have nothing important to communicate ... As if the main object were to talk fast and not to talk sensibly. We are eager to tunnel under the Atlantic and bring the old world some weeks nearer to the new; but perchance the first news that will leak through into the broad, flapping American ear will be that the Princess Adelaide has the whooping cough.' (52) Or, that the Duchess of York has a new boyfriend.

This passage is funny, but it also expresses the attitudes and makes the distinctions on which any useful theory of 'appropriate technology' must rest. These are a broad skepticism concerning progress; a focus on the point of the technology in question and whether it in fact fosters its intended goals; a consideration of possible unintended side-effects; and a recognition that technology helps to form us, its makers. What sets Thoreau apart from most of today's writers on appropriate technology is his insistence on analyzing technology at the individual, not the social, level, and the high, almost rarefied goals he posits of individuals. The point of communication technology, the passage says, is mutual enlightenment. Not diversion, profit, or the spread of ever more information. Thoreau asks his readers to consider the proper ends of communication technology and to use it – or not use it – accordingly. He discusses the telegraph and the penny press, innovations of the day, but his ideas apply just as well to television and the internet.

Writing at a time of great technological innovation, Thoreau is skeptical of new technologies and consumer products: 'Our inventions are wont to be pretty toys, which distract our attention from serious things. They are but improved means to an unimproved end, an end which it was already but too easy to arrive at; as railroads lead to Boston or New York.' (52) Still, such skepticism does not preclude the recognition that technologies may improve people's lives.[11] The point is to evaluate new technologies consciously and use them selectively, rather than blindly praising or rejecting 'the latest thing.' Thoreau himself developed a new pencil making process which revived his father's flagging business. He also attached little leather booties to Mrs. Emerson's chickens, when she asked him to stop their digging in her garden. Clearly the search for appropriate technology involves ingenuity and a sense of humor (as well as limits to our attempts to change, control, or 'booty-fy' nature).

One danger of technological improvements is that they tend to distance us from wild nature and from our immediate environment. This theme is explored in one of *Walden's* most famous passages. Though it focuses on transportation, its argument has wide applicability to our technology and consumer decisions:

> One says to me, 'I wonder that you do not lay up money; you love to travel; you might take the cars and go to Fitchburg today and see the country.' But I am wiser than that. I have learned that the swiftest traveller is he that goes afoot. I say to my friend, Suppose we try who will get there first. The distance is thirty miles; the fare ninety cents. That is almost a day's wages. I remember when wages were sixty cents a day for laborers on this very road. Well, I start now on foot, and get there before night; I have travelled at that rate by the week together. You will in the mean while have earned your fare, and arrive there some time tomorrow, or possibly this evening, if you are lucky enough to get a job in season. Instead of going to Fitchburg, you will be working here the greater part of the day. And so, if the railroad reached round the world, I think that I should keep ahead of you; and as for seeing the country and getting experience of that kind, I should have to cut your acquaintance altogether. (53)

The original suggestion, reasonable on its face, is that Thoreau or indeed anyone would be better off using the most modern, efficient means of transportation available. Thoreau denies this by making explicit his true purposes, and by considering the full costs of the various means that might be used to achieve them.

The suggested goals are 'to travel' and 'to see the country,' broadened slightly at the end of the passage to 'seeing the country and getting experience.' But the fastest and most efficient means of transportation are not the best ones for these purposes. For there is a world of sights worth seeing along the country roads to Fitchburg. Thoreau wants to look closely, find new plants, sample the huckleberries, note the colors shining in a pond at dusk, compare the ways people talk or farm in different townships. He wants not merely to see, but to see/hear/smell/taste/touch. He wants not merely to see, but to understand. This takes time. For this sort of seeing, covering less ground more slowly is better.

Thoreau the traveler wants to 'get experience,' but the experiences of walking the roads and riding the rails to Fitchburg are completely different. In walking, you experience changes in the weather (not always pleasant!) and hear birds calling and people working. You feel changes in the topography in your bones and muscles, while the train's bed has been graded and smoothed. You might have to walk up to a farmhouse and ask for directions, food and lodging–and who knows whether they will be forthcoming? On the train, these matters are largely settled beforehand, and the people you interact with are being paid to serve you. This has its positive side, but also its limits. People usually disclose more of themselves when encountered in situ and sometimes offer genuine hospitality, one of life's greatest gifts. If it is chiefly these experiences which we value in travel, then slower means are better. If we simply want to get to Fitchburg as quickly as possible and we have the fare in our pocket, then perhaps the train is better. But then we must recognize that we are giving up 'experiencing' or more deeply 'seeing' the countryside. There is a trade-off.

The other major factor to consider along with the purpose of any purchase is its cost. We must pay for these things, both in money and in the time needed to earn the money. This is a truism, but how we judge the price of things is crucial. The professional economist notes, correctly, that greater wealth gives one prima facie the ability to utilize more goods and services. Thoreau notes, correctly, that our time is limited and that out of that time most of us must both earn whatever money we feel is sufficient and live and enjoy life. The Fitchburg example reminds us that we may maximize money-earning or free time. Depending on our overall goals, the one or the other will more likely help us achieve them, and live more satisfying lives.

Now Thoreau certainly took advantage of the railroad. He rode it to Boston, New York, and yes, Fitchburg, to give lectures, and to Maine, New Hampshire and Cape Cod for longer trips to wilder landscapes. But he could take it or leave it as this suited his needs and interests. Given technology's importance in our lives, such a wary, conscious use is well worth emulating.

How many of us, for example, might benefit from riding a bicycle to work rather than driving a car? Bicycling can help keep us active and fit. Some amount of physical exertion is necessary for our health and comfort, and incorporating daily exercise into our schedules keeps us at it on days when we might shirk a trip to the health club. Bicycling can also save us money, provide new experiences and increase our knowledge of the places we live. None of this proves that most people should bicycle to work, much less that everyone should. There is no one right answer here for all of us. Still, there are better or worse answers for each of us, which we are free to pursue. Often, mere inertia and lack of imagination keep us from doing so.

Thoreau reminds us that our economic actions affect us in complex ways. Transportation does not just take us from point A to point B, more or less efficiently. It also relates us to everything in between – or it can do so. Transportation changes us: helps make us flabby or fit, for example. Transportation changes the landscape itself, and in the modern world that too often means choking it on pollution or destroying it by paving it over. It isn't clear that this is in our best interests, comprehensively defined, for this world we are rushing through is also the world we must live in. Here, of course, the discussion must be broadened to evaluate the effects of different transportation systems on whole societies. When we do so, these new considerations may well argue for communal action and mutual restraint.

Thoreau, though, would remind us that as individuals we cannot wait for society to choose wisely. We must choose 'appropriate technology' in our own lives. Society's choices may constrain ours, but they do not determine them. In fact, we have much greater choice concerning how, when and whether to use various technologies than we commonly believe. If we allow ourselves, in Emerson's words, to 'become the tools of our tools,' we have no one to blame but ourselves.

Similar points may be made about 'appropriate consumption.' Many writers in the ancient virtue ethics tradition argued that human lives could be improved through decreasing consumption and indeed through decreasing economic activity generally: consuming less food, avoiding ostentatious building or entertaining, thinking less about money. For Plato and Aristotle, Epicurus and Seneca, the good life was equally a life devoted to right thinking and a life not devoted to wealth-getting or sybaritism. These two positions supported each other and were held to be key to achieving happiness.[12]

A leading issue in ancient ethical debate was whether the pursuit of the good life entailed limiting consumption and harshly disciplining our natural desires, or providing for their moderate fulfillment. This question in turn was related to the role that pleasure and physical satisfaction were thought to play in a good life: whether defining of it, irrelevant to it, or a more or less important part of it. A wide variety of positions were staked out on these issues, which I will not attempt to summarize here. The main point is that almost all of the ancient writers argued for limiting material acquisition and limiting our attempts to satisfy our physical desires through consumption. This was true for those who thought pleasure the greatest human good, and for those who declared physical pleasure irrelevant to questions of how people should live their lives. It was true for those who argued that individuals should set moderate goals and accept moderate successes in life, and for those who advocated the pursuit of perfection. The major philosophical schools all accepted the idea that proper levels of consumption depended on the role of consumption in a good human life.

Walden recapitulates this ancient, inconclusive debate. Early in the book, Thoreau strikes a strong ascetic note, writing: 'The ancient philosophers, Chinese, Hindoo, Persian, and Greek, were a class than which none has been poorer in outward riches, none so rich in inward ...None can be an impartial or wise observer of human life but from the vantage ground of what we should call voluntary poverty.' (14) This asserts more than that 'voluntary poverty' is a necessary effect of the wise man's concentrating on higher things. There is a further, positive value to such freely chosen poverty. Money, things and their pursuit distract us from what is truly important. They warp our sense of justice (our 'impartiality'). Their possession makes us soft. Wealth and the things that wealth can buy are positive hindrances to wisdom and a good life. Often, particularly in *Walden's* first chapter, Thoreau suggests an absolute correlation: the more wealth and consumption, the less virtue, wisdom and striving for higher things.

Elsewhere, though, Thoreau takes a more moderate, reformist tone. *Walden* portrays many simple, graceful acts of consumption: Thoreau eating bread that he has baked himself, or burning wood that he has cut and split. These are pleasant, enjoyable acts. They manifest nature's bounty, which, he says, we should enjoy to the fullest. In his late manuscript *Wild Fruits*, Thoreau gives free rein to such enjoyable consumption. For example, he mentions a variety of huckleberries – 'large, often pear-shaped, sweet blue ones' – which tend to sprout in cut-over woods: 'They have not borne there before for a century, being over-shadowed and stinted by the forest, but they have the more concentrated their juices, and profited by the new recipes which Nature has given them, and now they offer to you fruit of the very finest flavor, like wine of the oldest vintage.'[13] Thoreau as gourmand! But reading *Wild Fruits*, we see that making distinctions through a discriminating palate helps Thoreau know nature's variety. Not just different kinds of berries, but also variations in habitat, rainfall and season, all affect the quality of this wild produce.

Thoreau's emphasis on moral principle, his natural genius for asceticism, and his belief that we often fail to do right due to greed and gluttony, all lead him to denigrate sensuality and the consumption that it occasions. But his keen senses, his naturalist's interest in the world around him, and his joy at connecting to nature, all lead him back to his senses and to praising a reasonable consumption. *Walden* is clearly the work of a sensualist as well as an ascetic. A reasonable consumption, kept within bounds by principles and higher goals, adds to Thoreau's sensual delight in nature.

Whether he is strictly limiting or tastefully refining his consumption, Thoreau takes a strong stand against thoughtless gluttony. In 'Higher Laws,' a chapter of *Walden* largely devoted to discussing food consumption, he bluntly restates this position: 'The abdomen under the wings of the butterfly still represents the larva. This is the tid-bit which tempts his insectivorous fate. The gross feeder is a man in the larva state; and there are whole nations in that condition, nations without fancy or imagination, whose vast abdomens betray them.' (215) Here we find the idea, familiar in ancient ethics, that a life devoted to physical consumption is ignoble or infantile. The reference to larvae neatly combines these two thoughts, for a larva is both the infant butterfly and metaphorically less noble than the adult, grubbing along the ground where the adult flies freely through the air. The grub chews indiscriminately and voraciously, while the butterfly sips the nectar of a few, select plants. Both consume, but the grub only takes, while the butterfly also pollinates plants, manifesting a creative role. Just so, Thoreau believes physical consumption should be subordinate to self-development and artistic creation. When 'gross feeding' replaces personal development, our 'vast abdomens' then become both the cause and the sign of our downfall.

Clearly and emphatically, Thoreau argues against overconsumption. Our consumption should further our lives. To the extent that it does so without harming others, it is good. To the extent that it substitutes for living well or actually impedes it, consumption is bad. Whether discussing food, furniture, or numerous other possessions and consumables, *Walden* repeats that there is a limit to their usefulness. We should make particular consumption decisions accordingly. More generally, we must ask: 'Shall we always study to obtain more of these things, and not sometimes to be content with less?' (36).

The Bean-Field

As with consumption, so with production: our work should improve our lives and the lives of those around us. This, not some fanciful attempt at full economic autarky, lies behind Thoreau's self-bestowed commission as a 'jack of all trades.' It underlies all his 'work' at the pond – physical, intellectual and spiritual – and his repeated criticisms of our modern division of labor. Thoreau's chief quarrel with economic specialization is that it robs people of experience. In building his shack, for example, he is by turns architect, carpenter and bricklayer. There is a pleasure in this variety, Thoreau believes. It keeps our work from becoming boring, and our thought agile and engaged (40–45). Thoreau adds that work may also further knowledge of the natural world. His chimney taught him which clays made the best bricks, and whether shells or limestone made the best mortar. He learned the feel of these materials and where they could be found locally (240–246).

Just as important, in making a chimney or a table, we attend to its purpose. Thus to how it can best fulfill its purpose and to whether it is necessary at all. In this way, Thoreau discovered that he didn't need yeast to leaven his bread and never again bothered with it. In this way, he discovered that he only needed a one-room shack, and was saved the trouble and expense of building something more grand.

Of course there are losses to balance against the gains of such autarky. First, losses in efficiency and productivity. Second, for those who aren't as handy as Thoreau, a loss in the quality of the products of our labor. Is the knowledge and experience gained worth the trade-off? For Thoreau it often was, if only to get closer to certain elemental aspects of human life.

One important example of this is recounted in the chapter titled 'The Bean-Field': 'Before I finished my house, wishing to earn ten or twelve dollars by some honest and agreeable method, in order to meet my unusual expenses, I planted about two acres and a half of light and sandy soil near it chiefly with beans ...Removing the weeds, putting fresh soil about the bean stems, and encouraging this weed which I had sown, making the yellow soil express its summer thought in bean leaves and blossoms rather than in wormwood and piper and millet grass, making the earth say beans instead of grass, – this was my daily work.' (54, 156–157) Despite his pursuit of a limited autarky, the need to function within a market society dictates that Thoreau earn some money. But in deciding to earn it in this particular way, through farming, Thoreau doubly resists allowing market forces supremacy. First, he could have earned the money with less effort by surveying or working as a day-laborer, as he well knew. Such work paid a dollar or two a day, while his total profits for a season of relatively hard work added up to less than ten dollars (55). Still, he chose to farm. Second, unlike the 'gentlemen farmers' and agricultural reformers to whom he compares his efforts, his innovations aim neither at a greater crop yield or a greater monetary profit. He makes a point of doing most of the work himself, rather than contracting it out to more productive specialists with more elaborate tools. He does not, he tells us, bother with 'imported' fertilizers. These moves would increase his productivity, but he refuses to allow that to dictate how he will farm.

What did Thoreau's determination to farm, and to farm in his own way, teach him? 'As I had little aid from horses or cattle,' he writes, 'or hired men or boys, or improved implements of husbandry, I was much slower, and became much more intimate with my beans than usual. But labor of the hands, even when pursued to the verge of drudgery, is perhaps never the worst form of idleness. It has a constant and imperishable moral, and to the scholar it yields a classic result.' (157) All was not pastoral bliss in the bean-field. Thoreau was up most days at dawn and worked long forenoons tending his beans. True, he did hear brown thrashers as he worked his rows and saw nighthawks circling overhead as he rested on his hoe. Not being in a hurry, he had plenty of time to watch the wildlife at the margins of his field, strengthening his ties to his 'brute neighbors' and adding to his knowledge of the landscape. To a poet-naturalist, the opportunity for such encounters, even the opportunity to feel changes in the weather and mark the natural course of the day, are strengthening and vivifying. Thoreau contrasts this work with factory and office work, suggesting again that the experience lost is not made up in increased pay or productivity.

Still, he tells us that the genial sun blistered his feet, and his account makes it clear that he sometimes pursued this work not merely to the verge of drudgery, but beyond it. Summing up the experience, he writes that 'it was on the whole a rare amusement, which, continued too long, might have become a dissipation' (162) The dissipation, that is, of which Thoreau accuses his fellow townsmen – a surrender to drudgery.

But negative results are as valuable as positive ones; they also convey information. What is the 'constant and imperishable moral,' the 'classic result' of which Thoreau speaks? First, I think, a real appreciation of the value of leisure, such as a wealthy or pampered person cannot know. Also, confirmation that some human activities really are 'higher,' through direct comparison with drudgery. Also, the valuable knowledge that some work fails to allow him to develop his capacities, that it is deadening – and this irrespective of how well that work pays. But these lessons are only yielded to 'scholars,' those who bring a questioning attitude to bear on their work. And only if they pursue such labor to the verge of drudgery, not if they continue it indefinitely. For to do so risks allowing our higher capacities to atrophy, so that we cease feeling their lack of fulfillment. Drudgery can turn us into drudges.

The scholar – taking the word now in a different sense, as one like Thoreau who belongs to the learned class – also learns that this drudge-work exists and that someone must do it. This opens up further questions concerning the division of labor. One is whether we will let the more clever among us avoid all this dirty and unpleasant work and monopolize the most fulfilling employment. Another question is how the scholar is to justify, or truly earn, his privileged position. Is it through performing his share of the necessary drudge work of society? Or through a commitment to teaching his fellow citizens? Or through the indirect effects of his knowledge, filtering down to the general public through the popular media and technological change (a sort of academic trickle-down effect)?

Such questions hardly make sense within our standard economic models. One does not justify one's economic position, one competes for it. One need not earn a place in society, one earns the money which shows that some people value one's contributions enough to pay for them.[14] Under the spell of this economic view, these questions are easily forgotten as we intellectuals type away in our offices and someone else empties the wastebaskets. But this attitude and this economy, with its great disparities in wealth and status, tend to undermine democratic government and the democratic spirit. No matter what our eventual answers here, the questions are important. We may resurrect them by attending to those experiences which call them forth.

In the end, Thoreau's very lack of productivity helped clarify the results of his experiment at the pond. Because as unremunerative as his farming was, it proved sufficient to his needs. After summarizing his first year's expenses and income, and toting up his profits – $8.71 1/2 – he remarks: 'The next year I did better still, for I spaded up all the land which I required [rather than hiring a team and plowman], about a third of an acre, and I learned from the experience of both years ...that if one would live simply and eat only the crop which he raised, and raise no more than he ate, and not exchange it for an insufficient quantity of more luxurious and expensive things, he would need to cultivate only a few rods of ground ...and he could do all his necessary farm work as it were with his left hand at odd hours in the summer.' (55–56) The most important question that Thoreau asked concerning both production and consumption was how little of these he could get by with, the goal being to dispose of his economic necessities as efficiently as possible. In latter years he preferred to earn what little money he required primarily by land surveying, which like farming kept him out in the open air, and paid better. But either way, the main point was proved. And because so many of his fellow townsmen were farmers, Thoreau's experiment allowed him to speak directly to their lives.

The move beyond pay and profit to the experience of work is necessary, then, to order our own personal economy most efficiently. We must move beyond economic abstractions to further our true goals: happiness, self-development and flourishing. But such attentiveness also opens us to deep economic issues concerning the meaning of work and the proper relation between our human economy and the economy of nature. Already in the second sentence of 'The Bean-field,' Thoreau writes: 'What was the meaning of this so steady and self-respecting, this small Herculean labor, I knew not. I came to love my rows, my beans, though so many more than I wanted. They attached me to the earth, and so I got strength like Antaeus. But why should I raise them? Only Heaven knows. This was my curious labor all summer.' (155) What is the meaning of work? 'The Market' gives one answer: 'your work is worth eight dollars and seventy-one and one half cents, or its equivalent in goods and services.' Thoreau believes that through his personal economy, he has earned the right to see this answer as unimportant.

The remark 'only Heaven knows' refers obliquely to another answer, given in the Bible's story of humanity's fall from grace. In this view, you will recall, work is a misfortune, a punishment for disobeying God and eating of the tree of knowledge:

> And the LORD God said unto Adam ...Because thou hast hearkened unto the voice of thy wife, and hast eaten of the tree, of which I commanded thee, saying, Thou shalt not eat of it: cursed is the ground for thy sake; in sorrow shalt thou eat of it all the days of thy life; Thorns also and thistles shall it bring forth to thee; and thou shalt eat the herb of the field; In the sweat of thy face shalt thou eat bread, till thou return unto the ground.[15]

'In sorrow shalt thou eat' – work is bad. 'Cursed is the ground' – nature is no longer supremely bountiful, supplying a surfeit of fruit, but now brings forth 'thorns and thistles.' The harmony between man and nature is broken and nature provides for us only through our own efforts. These misfortunes have come about through the desire to understand the world and obtain the divine power that comes with knowledge.

The only part of the Biblical account that Thoreau accepts is the connection between knowledge and divinity. For Thoreau believes that the search for knowledge, rightly undertaken, manifests not human disobedience, but a true reverence. Nor need it be the occasion for a rift between humanity and nature. The pursuit of knowledge is rather the best hope for our reconciliation. In a practical inversion of the Biblical attitude toward work, Thoreau seeks to use his work, as we have seen, as a means to better know nature. And he denies the Fall, as applied to nature or humanity. For nature is still bountiful, he insists: 'Nature does her best to feed her children.'[16] He believes his experiment has proven that 'it is not necessary that a man should earn his living by the sweat of his brow, unless he sweats easier than I do' (71).

Modern societies have in one sense turned away from the Bible's fatalistic attitude toward work, pursuing scientific knowledge of nature and applying it to increase economic productivity. Yet this alone, Thoreau insists, cannot remove the curse of work. It cannot dry the sweating brow of humanity, nor alleviate the 'anxiety and strain' that blight our lives, nor end the struggle against nature which our economy has become. But a different sort of knowledge – self-knowledge concerning the limits of our material needs – can allow us to turn our work into 'a pastime.' If there is some limit to the yields that we demand, then farming may appear as a cooperation between a bountiful nature and a resourceful humanity (absent this, it can be nothing but struggle). This, in turn, may give us the time needed to explore the Garden, from which we are barred by our own greed and inattentiveness, not by divine decree.

Against the Biblical account, Thoreau juxtaposes the legend of Antaeus. According to Greek myth, Antaeus was the son of a mortal consort and Demeter, the goddess of the earth. He wrestled with Hercules (himself of mixed human and divine parentage). Hercules found that every time he pinned him to the ground, Antaeus' strength was renewed and he sprang up stronger than ever. Hercules eventually defeated Antaeus by holding him above the earth, thus completing one of the twelve tasks necessary to gain his place in Heaven.

Thoreau here likens himself to Antaeus, who got strength from touching his mother the Earth. How? Above all, through the physical sustenance he obtained. Here again, we see the value of simplicity in forcing us to reckon with the obvious. For most of us work at least part of the time to provide basic sustenance for ourselves and our loved ones. But we forget this. Our work can then seem pointless, and we may forget our dependence on the good earth in achieving this basic goal.

Thoreau found strength, too, he suggests, through the discipline demanded by his 'steady' and 'self-respecting' labor. Work develops discipline, which may then be put in the service of whatever goals we choose. Disciplined, useful work also gives the average citizen a legitimate claim to the respect of his fellow citizens. Thoreau as transcendentalist believes he is stronger for wrestling with the problem of how to sustain himself. For he associates himself both with Antaeus, the son of the earth and Hercules, the son of the sky-god Zeus: recall his reference to 'this small Herculean labor' of tending beans, and the earlier juxtaposition of the pointless labors of the Indian Brahmins with the labors of Hercules. Thoreau sees himself and all human beings as partly divine. Like Hercules, we perform our feats on earth in order to gain a place in heaven (or, to find a heaven right here). The implication is that our economic strivings should lead us toward something more, but also that they make this 'something more' possible, and are not to be sneered at or avoided. Like Antaeus, when we no longer touch the earth, we weaken. All our efforts depend on regular sustenance and the good earth. Our abstract thought must be regularly fertilized by experience. Our ethical ideals must be tried in life.

There is still more, although it is difficult to describe: a feeling of gratitude for the earth's gifts; a belief in the rightness of nature's cycles of work and rest, growth and harvest. Finally, there is happiness and even joy at playing one's part within these cycles:

> Husbandry was once a sacred art; but it is pursued with irreverent haste and heedlessness by us, our object being to have large farms and large crops merely ...We are wont to forget that the sun looks on our cultivated fields and on the prairies and forests without distinction. They all reflect and absorb his rays alike, and the former make but a small part of the glorious picture which he beholds in his daily course. In his view the earth is all equally cultivated like a garden. Therefore we should receive the benefit of his light and heat with a corresponding trust and magnanimity. What though I value the seed of these beans, and harvest that in the fall of the year? ...These beans have results which are not harvested by me. Do they not grow for

> woodchucks partly? . . Shall I not rejoice also at the abundance of the weeds whose seeds are the granary of the birds? (165–166)

Such acceptance and rejoicing are rare in modern societies. Most of us are too busy about our beans. The places and practices where such words resonate are fast disappearing.

Yet the hope remains that agriculture and all our works may be pious undertakings, tying us closer to our native earth. A genuine gratitude for our lives and sustenance can only occur, though, in the pause from grasping, calculating and desiring. It occurs when we look up from our toil and notice a hawk cutting the air, or in a simple prayer of thanks before a meal. In such acts Thanksgiving becomes, not a once-a-year formality, but a remembrance of the goodness and fecundity of our place. We then accept our portion both of work and of the fruits of nature's bounty, without striving to alter or engross more than our share. Once we realize our proper place within nature, we can then appreciate not just our own good fortune, but the blessings given to all nature's creatures.

Within the western ethical tradition, lives of greed have generally been condemned. Still, they have remained live options, and succeeding moralists have felt obliged to repeat the introductory lessons. It is not just that our economic lives provide occasions which tempt us away from doing good. There is something about economic life which causes us to set it up as an independent realm, beyond or beneath ethics. For one thing, this is convenient. For another, economic activities themselves naturally focus our attention on the efficient use of means and away from the sharp questioning of ends.

Twentieth century ethicists' near exclusive focus on rights and duties and their neglect of human excellence have unwittingly played into this tendency to exempt our economic lives from ethical scrutiny. For while many of our economic decisions do escape the narrow compass of strict obligation, only the truly trivial ones fail to make us better or worse people, if only marginally so. I do not have a duty to quit my dead-end job, perhaps, but it may be making me stupider with each passing day. I do not have a duty to stop eating fried food, but it may be clogging my arteries and making me fatter. And if less intelligent and less healthy, then a worse person. Still a person, of course, with all the rights and responsibilities annexed thereto, but a worse person. Once again: 'Our whole life is startlingly moral. There is never an instant's truce between virtue and vice' (218). This holds true as much for our strictly economic decisions as for any others.

Ethics thus provides the proper framework for considering our economic lives, and this is one area where we moderns should move beyond the ancients. Ancient virtue ethicists often took a supercilious view of common economic activities. This was only to be expected from members of aristocratic, slave-holding societies, where the flourishing of the few was the primary concern. Modern ethicists should not take such a dismissive attitude, recognizing the substantial possibilities economic life holds for furthering happiness and self-development, and committed as we should be to promoting the excellence of all members of society. We should also remember that self-improvement and social reform are hard work, and that discipline and 'economy' are necessary in order to achieve them.

Despite a certain amount of romantic moonshine, Thoreau attempted to live a life at Walden Pond and write a story in *Walden* which explored these possibilities and shared them with others. As is typically the case with heroic exemplars in the virtue ethics tradition, his account provides material for both perfectionist and reformist arguments. True believers sharing his ultimate goals may deepen their insight into those ideals and find practical strategies for attaining them. Those attached to more conventional lives or holding less rigorous views of the good life may nevertheless be reminded of the many benefits to be found in living consciously and methodically, avoiding the pitfalls of greed and consumerism, and furthering our ties to nature.

Walden provides both practical suggestions and parables. In either case, it takes imagination and effort to apply Thoreau's message in our various situations. He hopes he is enlarging our sphere of alternatives, but exasperated undergraduates have been known to complain: 'Does he really expect us all to move to a pond and grow beans?' Not exactly. But Thoreau obviously expects a lot from his neighbors and readers, as he does from himself. He is right to do so. And regardless of the correctness or replicability of his answers, he leaves us struggling with the right questions, and provides an economic method which will help us answer them.

(ENDNOTES)

1 The best scholarly treatment of Thoreau's economic views is Leonard Neufeldt, *The Economist: Henry Thoreau and Enterprise* (Oxford: Oxford University Press, 1989). See also Leo Stoller, *After Walden: Thoreau's Changing Views of Economic Man* (Stanford: Stanford University Press, 1957) and Harold Hellenbrand, "'A True Integrity Day by Day': Thoreau's Organic Economy in *Walden*," Emerson Society Quarterly 25 (1979): 71–78.

2 See Amartya Sen, *Commodities and Capabilities* (Amsterdam: North-Holland, 1985).

3 Aristotle, *Nicomachean Ethics*, book I, chapter 1.

4 See Martha Nussbaum, *The Fragility of Goodness: Luck and Ethics in Greek Tragedy and Philosophy* (Cambridge: Cambridge University Press, 1986), 290–305.

5 These studies are summarized in Robert Lane, *The Market Experience* (Cambridge: Cambridge University Press, 1991), 524-547. They show that overall income usually bears a statistically insignificant relationship to feelings of overall satisfaction or happiness. Whether a person is satisfied with his or her income, contrarily, has a strong correlation (451–452).

6 The claim is that a "philosophical poverty" can benefit both rich and poor. To evaluate it, we must temporarily set aside issues of economic justice. This neither denies such issues nor presupposes particular answers to them. Justice and the pursuit of personal excellence are both necessary for a complete ethics.

7 Thoreau, "Life Without Principle," *Reform Papers*, 160.

8 Stanley Cavell, *The Senses of Walden* (Chicago: University of Chicago Press, 1981), 88–89.

9 Ibid., 89.

10 See George Lakoff and Mark Johnson, *Metaphors We Live By* (Chicago: University of Chicago Press, 1980).

11 Thoreau is no Luddite and various journal passages applaud useful, appropriate technology. See for example his praise of glass (*Journal* 5, 183–184 (7/5/52)).

12 For Plato see *Republic* book II, 369b–374a; book IX, 580d–588a. For Aristotle see *Nicomachean Ethics*, book I, chapter 5, and *Politics* book I, chapters 2, 8–10. For the Epicureans see extracts from Epicurus' "Letter to Menoeceus" and from Lucretius, "On the Nature of Things," in A.A. Long and D.N. Sedley, *The Hellenistic Philosophers* (Cambridge: Cambridge University Press, 1987), volume 1, 113–114, 119–120. For the Stoics see Seneca, "On the Happy Life," epistle 92, in *The Epistles of Seneca* (Cambridge: Harvard University Press, 1970), 447–455.

13 Henry David Thoreau, *Wild Fruits*, ed. Bradley Dean (New York: WW Norton, 2000), 38.

14 Compare Thoreau: "if the civilized man's pursuits are no worthier than the savage's, if he is employed the greater part of his life in obtaining gross necessaries and comforts merely, why should he have a better dwelling than the former?" (34).

15 *Bible*, Genesis 3, King James version.

16 Thoreau, *Wild Fruits*, 52.

Chapter Eleven

WHY SIMPLIFY?

Mark A. Burch

Why would anyone want to adopt voluntary simplicity? Many answers have been offered over the years to this question. It deserves attention now no less than in the past.

Today we hear a lengthening litany of environmental, social, economic, political and spiritual threats to the future of humanity. For most people likely to read this book, reviewing the details of this situation will present nothing new. But an important point of departure for voluntary simplicity can be found in the idea that many problems facing humankind are connected. Environmental degradation, militarism, economic injustice, political unrest, social decay and a host of other issues seem to keep looping back on themselves in a single tangled mass. One develops the perspective not of a basically healthy people afflicted here and there by localized difficulties, but rather a people in basic difficulty blessed here and there with pockets of nearly unaccountable sanity and love.

People of goodwill are urged to confront this ball of maladies one affliction at a time, since the limitations of human intellect and energy seemingly preclude 'solving' the whole mess at one go. We pick our issues in the hope that, together with others doing the same, we will somehow grope our way to a solution of the whole.

Intuitively, however, we wish for a more elegant way. The same intuition of the connections among problems hints at an equally holistic response to dealing with them. Nature doesn't make new flowers by gluing a leaf here, a petal there; it produces seeds, which carry within themselves a principle of potentiality that can unfold into a complete new flower. If we cannot live with the harvest of our present way of making a living, we shall have to search for new seeds – values and perspectives so basic that they promise large pattern changes. The question then is what lies within the power of individuals to do to resolve this predicament?

So, to answer the question of why anyone would adopt voluntary simplicity, I offer some of my own thoughts as well as suggestions made by others, which I think fall into four broad groups: personal, social, environmental and transpersonal (spiritual) reasons.

Living Simply For Yourself

'A clay bowl as my only wealth, a robe that does not tempt the robbers,
Thus I dwell exempt from fear...' [1]

It's paradoxical that, on the one hand, Canada is one of the most desirable places in the world to live, and on the other hand, there is very considerable evidence of personal stress and discontent. Several surveys of job satisfaction in Canada have shown that a large number of people are unhappy with their work. Divorce rates, crime rates, substance abuse rates, assaults of all kinds, increasing child poverty, chronic problems with unemployment, prejudice and social unrest all suggest that in spite of living in an economically privileged country, many of us suffer dislocation and personal turmoil.

Voluntary simplicity is not a panacea for all of these problems. Nevertheless, a very large number of people are beginning to feel overwhelmed by the pace of life in North America as well as its complexity. North American society has been built on the assumption that more, bigger, and faster defines better, healthier and happier. Yet many of us have come to question this view. If achieving worthwhile goals requires that we must live at a manic pace, is it any wonder that we yearn for holidays when we then give ourselves permission to live according to the rhythms of our bodies and the cycles of the Earth?

Some years ago I went to an island in Lake of the Woods, northern Ontario, to attend a summer institute in bioenergetic therapy. About 30 people were left on the island for two weeks of intensive group therapy. Each of us, of course, had our personal issues to attend to, but what impressed me most was how healthy it was to be on the island. Intensive group work sessions as demanding as any work I had ever done were interspersed with music, sitting, massage, group housework chores, walking along the rocky shoreline of the island, listening to the lake lap at the dock, watching the loons and cormorants clamor about in the water, listening to each other's histories, dreams and nightmares. As the days passed, I began to slow down. Layer after layer of something burdensome was peeled back leaving me feeling open, sensitive, vibrant and energized. This process required nothing more than our presence in nature and our shared desire to attend to each other rather than to grand designs for changing the world or making a fortune.

I remember wondering why I couldn't just keep on living this way. We were not idle. There was ample time for productive work of some kind, yet it could be suffused with this same spirit of measured, attentive enjoyment of the moment. All that I had lived prior to the island experience seemed artificial and oppressive. I imagined that it may have been this quality that pervaded the lives of aboriginal people before their encounter with Europeans, a dream-like quality of union with nature and with each other, with one's people. How was it that we Europeans were so obsessed, so driven, so violent? What was it that so disturbed us that we felt driven to create a civilization (if it could be called that) such as now dominated North America?

I have lived for years very close to the Earth while homesteading in northern Ontario. I don't romanticize nature and I don't entertain any illusions about the hardships that aboriginal people must have endured. But I wonder if true wellness might lie somewhere between the rigors of a hunting and gathering lifestyle and breathing the canned air in the glass-walled cells of our high-rise urban prisons.

To restate the question, it was not actually a matter of why life 'couldn't' have more of an 'island quality' about it. Beyond the broad archetypal patterns that define human nature, there is nothing in life which requires that it take a particular form. Rather, I realized, it was a matter of the choices we make that determine how much vitality and wellness we experience in the daily round. Changing these choices is within the power of individuals.

In a publication entitled *Personal Lifestyle Response to Social Injustice*,[2] Jorgen Lissner offered ten reasons for choosing simplicity. Some of his arguments address personal reasons why we might adopt simple living. Lissner calls voluntary simplicity an *act of self-defence* against the mind-polluting effects of over-consumption. To live in North American society is to be, in one way or another, under attack. We are flooded every day with countless 'messages,' 'offers,' and 'demands,' most of which have to do with consuming things or services. The language of our economic system is the language of discontent. Its monotonous message is that this or that gewgaw is what we *do* need, or *will* need, or *ought* to have in order to be better, happier and more contented than we are now.

One of the clearest prophets of the Age of Consumerism was Victor Lebow writing in the *Journal of Retailing* in the mid-1950s:

> Our enormously productive economy ... demands that we make consumption our way of life, that we convert the buying and use of goods into rituals, that we seek our spiritual satisfaction, our ego satisfaction, in consumption.... We need things consumed, burned up, worn out, replaced, and discarded at an ever increasing rate.[3]

In the ensuing five decades, North Americans have taken Mr. Lebow's advice with a vengeance. Little has changed in the 1990s except for a few qualms about the environmental decay such a lifestyle has delivered.

Added to this voice of attraction is also a voice of warning: If we do not compete, purchase and accumulate, then our welfare will be undermined by other people trying to take it away from us (e.g., the Japanese, the Chinese, the Koreans, etc.), or by circumstances (e.g., economic recession, personal unemployment, debt, uncompetitiveness). So, if our hyperactivity cannot be stoked through manufactured discontent, we are threatened with manufactured images of loss and personal disaster.

This is not an emotionally or physically healthy climate for people. At the personal level, voluntary simplicity begins with the decision to take time to re-evaluate our activities and goals.

One of the definitions of stress is any form of excessive demand. We must experience some level of demand in our lives if we are to develop to our full potential. But each of us has a 'comfort zone' where life's demands feel challenging rather than threatening. If this personal comfort level is exceeded then both emotional and physical symptoms can develop.

There are many kinds of demands. They can include physical demands such as unsatisfactory living conditions, hazardous work conditions, excessively laborious work, exposure to disease, shock, violence, threats of violence, and climatic extremes. We can also face emotional demands in relationships, at work, in our communities, families and friendships. Intellectual demands arise from the complexity of modern life, work requirements and the sheer quantity and muddle of information and decision-making we face each day. Financial demands arise as we try to match incomes with expenditures, finance college educations for our children, save for retirement, and reconcile the differing needs of family members. Finally, stresses from all of these sources can accumulate and reinforce each other.

All of this stress might be worth it if we could see clearly that it leads to higher quality of life and greater personal satisfaction. This is not the case, however. Surveys conducted ever since the 1950s have shown that while there has been a great increase in the pace and complexity of life, especially in urban centres, there has been no significant increase in perceived well-being. Personal consumption has approximately doubled since 1957,[4] but the same proportion of people (about 30%) report being 'very happy' with their lot in life now as in 1957. Other research has shown that once incomes rise above the poverty level, there is little or no correlation between income level and well-being and that people from both rich, developed countries and 'poor,' developing countries often report comparable levels of personal well-being.[5] In some cases, people report being less satisfied with their lives now than in the past.

Voluntary simplicity offers a personal way of reducing stresses arising from lifestyles that have become too complex to be healthy or fulfilling.

By living more simply we can increase financial security because less money is required and consequently a wider range of employment possibilities can provide an adequate income. By becoming more selective and conscious of our activities, we free time for family, friends and learning, which enhances our joy in life.

One of the ways that people who choose simplicity reduce demands in their lives is to apply energy selectively to those activities which make a direct contribution to livelihood and to do this, as much as possible, on a self-reliant basis or in partnership with neighbors. Meeting some of our own food needs by backyard gardening not only reduces the cash food budget, but increases self-confidence as we learn to produce and preserve our own food.

Working in partnership with friends and neighbors helps us discover our own skills and gifts as well as cementing bonds of interdependence. We rediscover that we need each other and can rely on each other. Security is then redefined not as the size of my bank balance but rather what I have to contribute to my community. Thus, simplicity finds security in relationship while consumerism seeks security in ownership.

The focus upon community that must characterize voluntary simplicity is another example of its rewards. We may be able to own and use things, but we don't have relationships with them. In many cases, the reward value claimed for the things we own comes to a focus in how they affect our relationships. The ostentatious car, the ever-changing wardrobe, the exotic cosmetics may find most of their reward value in the power we think they have to win social esteem, attention, and perhaps even love or sexual gratification. If we know how to experience social esteem, love and sexual gratification directly, why would we waste time on a flashy car?

Lissner also calls voluntary simplicity an act of withdrawal from the achievement-neurosis of our high-pressure, materialistic society. While this is true, I think we have to be clear on the meaning of 'withdrawal.' Voluntary simplicity is not a doctrine of niggardly hermithood! We don't withdraw from the existing socioeconomic treadmill simply to sit and nurse our resentment against its misguided excesses. We withdraw from one pattern of behavior in order to adopt something else that is more life-giving. Like people striving to overcome addiction, we withdraw from self-destructive habits so that we can gain health and well-being. This takes time and usually requires community support.

For a number of years I helped organize spiritual retreats for men in my church community. The practice of retreat involves spending a weekend or more at a monastery or retreat centre in very simple surroundings with a minimum of socializing. Retreatants keep silence and attend to prayer, reflection, reading and rest. Most men from our congregation would not attend retreats and many of them expressed either anxiety at the thought of spending a night and two days in silence, or else they assured me they would be driven to distraction by the boredom of 'nothing happening!' This was a real anxiety for many men and even those who attended retreats often found it impossible to sustain silence or solitude for more than a few hours.

This experience impressed me with how consistently our culture teaches us to passively focus our attention outwards rather than actively focus it inwards. The good consumer receives the world as entertainment. The more completely we are absorbed in this way of life, the less we believe in ourselves as active centres for the generation of consciousness, insight and joy. I don't believe that this is a collective inability so much as a lack of training.

On another occasion I made a solitary eight-day retreat during which my only conversation was a one-hour meeting with my retreat director once a day. One morning she said, 'Just look and see God in all things.' I thought this instruction was rather Zenish coming from a Benedictine abbess, but later that morning I sat in the monastery garden and watched a small, translucent green spider at work in a cotoneaster hedge. The days of silence before this morning helped me pay close attention to the spider. She worked methodically at spinning her web, caught an insect, paralysed it, wrapped it up in silk and fed upon it, then started repairing the web where her kill had struggled to get away. I watched all of this, deeply absorbed in it without actually thinking anything about it.

The spider simply was. And so was I. And we two were there together, absorbed together in the moment. When I was again aware of time, I realized that I had watched the spider for over an hour. I wasn't doing anything, exactly. But I felt that for a while, I had been caught up in something delicious and wonderful. Life was wonderful. Death was wonderful. The spider and the bush and the sun and I were all wonderful. Indeed, life was good and grace was everywhere. It occurred to me that I might spend several lifetimes this way considering how many flowers I could see bloom, how many webs, how many nests of birds and moulds and pond scums and leaves emerging on trees and butterflies emerging from chrysalises! Indeed. And what is human consciousness for?

We withdraw toward simplicity, then, not to become less but to become more, but in a different way from having more. What I think Jorgen Lissner means when he calls voluntary simplicity an 'act of withdrawal' from achievement-neurosis is that it is both a movement toward a way of being that is deep and active and a differently directed consciousness. The achievement orientation of our culture chronically centres our attention on ourselves, our effort, our comfort, our cravings, our fears. Furthermore, it teaches us to locate both the source and the satisfaction of these states of consciousness outside ourselves. It is 'other-centred' but only in a very special way–the way that serves the ends of the market economy. It does not allow the lingering, patient, focused and loving attention that can actually generate relationship.

A cluttered, complicated and consumption-oriented way of life leaves no time or energy for encounters with spiders, or other people for that matter. Another personal reason for adopting a simpler way of life is to dispose ourselves more often to such experiences. It is often in silence and solitude that we discover capacities for insight and joy that are intrinsic to our human nature, which cannot be bought and sold, and which preoccupation with buying and selling can actually silence.

A related aspect of all of this concerns the models of personal achievement behavior promoted by the mass media and corporate culture. The model professional is the person who can keep the most number of balls in the air at the same time: career, family, relationships, community, self-care, planetary well-being, gender issues, civil rights, healthy food, etc. He or she is wired to a computer, continually in motion, an international achiever, multilingual, always on the phone, always competent and achieving and somehow, miraculously, able to excel in all these categories. Especially for career-oriented women, the expectation seems to be to work fourteen-hour days at the same time as meeting personal and family needs and contributing to the community. This role model of the 'modern' person is clearly manic. It is utterly devoid of repose, utterly devoid of depth, and more or less devoid of direction. We assume from all of this 'busyness' that the man or woman in this picture is working hard for worthwhile goals, but we seldom know what they are. We are asked to accept that perpetual motion is its own reward, that the more one does the better, and if it can be done faster than anyone else, better still. The whole image is utterly antithetical to a measured, conscious and mindful approach to living. It is ideally suited, however, to the purposes of a corporate culture. Business wants highly mobile, image-oriented workers who can do its bidding anywhere in the world at any time.

In addition to reflecting on voluntary simplicity as an act of self-defence and an act of withdrawal, I would like to add another thought: that voluntary simplicity is an act of affirmation. Too often voluntary simplicity has the tone of puritanical renunciation, as if deprivation confers virtue. Simplicity sounds like an invitation to be cold and hungry and bored in atonement for some guilt we should feel for having been warm, fed and challenged. Little wonder that simplicity seldom appeals to many people.

Voluntary simplicity is an answer to many personal, social and environmental problems. But simplicity is not an end in itself. We may admire the clean lines of simple living just as we appreciate a Zen rock garden or an elegant mathematical proof. Yet neither of these aims to promote simplicity as such. Simplicity is a side-effect or precondition of working toward a deeper value.

The lives of people who embrace simple living display a passion for some deeper purpose from which power, possessions and the clutter of busy living represent distractions. Like freeing time to spend with a lover, lovers of simplicity free their lives of everything that might draw down their energy or obstruct the way toward their highest goals. For Jesus, it was proclaiming his Father's kingdom; for Socrates, it was the pursuit of Truth; for Thoreau, self-reliance and spiritual communion with his beloved New England; for Buddha, it was self-liberation. Though most of us keep less exalted company, we still know the pleasure of time with our children, our spouses, a craft or art form, the calling of our work or contributions we wish to make to our communities, which leave no room in our lives for excess baggage.

And here we find the evil of addictive acquisition: *that it distracts us from what is best in our lives.* Voluntary simplicity brings us nothing of its own, but it clears a space within which we can rediscover and honor our highest loves. It may be that we choose personal simplicity because of the benefits it brings to the planet and to other people. Yet these benefits must bring us personal satisfaction as well.

Thus, for many of us, the pathway to simplicity will not be found through feeling guilty about what we own. A surer route is remembering when we have felt the most profound joy and fulfilment in our humanity. These moments are still possibilities for the future. Finally, falling in love with what is truly worthy of our love, we claim the courage to dispense with whatever would cause us again to forget and go back to sleep. We simplify only partly to atone for the guilt of over-consumption. More crucial is that we shed clutter as we shed clothing to be with a lover, to be close, to join, to merge and be joyful.

Simplicity is not prerequisite to a meaningful life; it is co-requisite to it. Simplicity enables mindfulness and mindfulness enables peace and delight. The more we find our peace and delight in simplicity and mindfulness, the more completely we embrace them. Simplicity, mindfulness and peace arise gradually and together as co-requisite aspects of a self-strengthening pattern. The more they are chosen and coexist, the less room remains in our lives for unthinking hyperactivity. Voluntary simplicity is good because it makes possible attentive devotion to those experiences that define our fullest humanity rather than conferring on someone else a maximum of wealth. Only a simple life can be concentrated mindfully upon its art whatever 'art' that may be. Only a simple life is free enough from distraction to focus deeply upon its sacred goals without haste or diversion. Only a simply life can lay hold of inner riches.

Voluntary simplicity can also be an act of self-enrichment in that living simply, we realign our involvements away from things and toward self, other people and the ecosphere. One of the fruits of simple living is time. But clearly, we aren't here merely to vegetate! We naturally want to use the time for something. We meet the difference between simplicity and consumerism precisely at this point: given some time, how shall I use it? Modern society allows us to face this question only very rarely because most of our time is structured for us by the demands inherent in a wasteful, consumption-oriented way of life. Many people have trouble planning a holiday without money. In fact, we may even save money all year so that our holidays become special occasions for over-consumption!

Consciously deciding how to use time is something that is usually connected with crises in our lives such as unemployment, completing a higher education and searching for a first job, retirement, holiday planning, or some forced life change like an illness that imposes the need to radically restructure our use of time. Simple living implies making conscious decisions about how we use more and more of our time and orienting our activities around the goals we find most satisfying and meaningful. Exercises in the second part of this book are designed to assist with this process.

About a year ago I decided to begin learning T'ai-chi. I went through all the usual self-doubts, wondering if I could learn a martial art in mid-life, wondering if I could even remember all the moves in the set, wondering if I could develop the self-discipline to stay with it long enough to learn it. On the other hand, I loved watching T'ai-chi and admired anyone who could do it. To me, it embodied some of the grace and eroticism of ballet, the spirituality of Taoist meditative practice and the 'shadow' of deadliness that is one of the meanings of any martial art.

Practising T'ai-chi became wholly absorbing. It has been remarkable how something so apparently simple continues to reveal complexities and subtleties I could never have guessed by watching someone else do it. T'ai-chi has been a little like love-making. It is so intrinsically pleasurable that I want to do it over and over again. While I was learning the set, I was mentally reviewing the movements even when I wasn't practising with my body. One night, I awakened from doing the 'crane cools wings' movement in my sleep! T'ai-chi had an 'island' flavor to it and renewed the question in my mind: why are things like this, the mainstays of life, marginalized by our culture?

T'ai-chi continues to reveal benefits and levels of inner transformation as I muddle along with the practice of it. But its most important lesson for me was the realization that as I moved through the steps of the set, nothing was being consumed or owned. I was nothing, moving through nothing, shaping nothing in the fillings and emptyings, the expansions and contractions, the scoops and pushes of T'ai-chi. T'ai-chi is invisible until it enters someone's body. It does nothing to harm the ecosphere. It does nothing to oppress anyone else. You cannot own T'ai-chi. You don't need any fancy equipment or designer body suit to practise T'ai-chi. And yet doing it floods the senses and consciousness with subtle intuitions and knowings, many of which are impossible to describe in words. Now, no day feels complete without doing at least one T'ai-chi set.

Learning T'ai-chi was a form of self-enrichment. Lately I have moved along to begin teaching others what I learned and, I hope, to enrich their lives as well. My own practice of simplicity is as halting and inconsistent as anyone's. But I can see deepening that practice in my life would open time and energy for more study of T'ai-chi and disciplines like it.

To conclude, I would suggest that for many people voluntary simplicity might be an act of moral consistency.

Most people likely to read this book probably will not be directly or personally involved in the oppression of workers in developing countries, military dictatorships, unfair labor practices or massive ecological destruction. But one of the paradoxes of our century is the discontinuity between our personal moral codes and systemic evil, which arises from collective patterns of action or inaction. I may not be personally responsible for the jailing or torture or execution or exploitation of other people, yet I participate in and indirectly support economic and political systems that do these things.

While our individual responsibility to change oppressive systems is clear, our power to make a difference is largely determined by the positions of formal authority we hold in such systems. Needless to say, for those of us who have no formal position of power, the circumference of realistic personal action is measured by the choices we make in personal lifestyle issues.

I would suggest that much of the political and ecological oppression occurring in the world today is directly or indirectly linked to our economic system. This system distributes costs, benefits and wastes very unfairly. It is inherently misdirected in maintaining stark social and economic inequalities while trying to orient human consciousness toward dependency and consumerism as definitions of the 'good life.'

But personal action toward voluntary simplicity falls well within the circle of steps that fit our walk more closely to our talk. Voluntary simplicity focuses our life energies specifically on actions that have little inherent power to exploit or oppress others. The emphasis in simple living upon self-reliance and community helps assure that basic personal needs will be met close to home in solidarity with friends and neighbors. This in turn implies that *how* we meet our needs will be more closely linked to our sphere of personal action and personal responsibility wherein we *do* have the power to act with moral consistency. Furthermore, as we withhold even our indirect support and participation from the dominant economic system, we do a little bit to weaken its power to project systemic evil elsewhere in the world.

We will now turn more specifically from the personal reasons for embracing simplicity to all those reasons that relate to our lives together in society. Voluntary simplicity can be a powerful antidote to social and economic injustice.

Living Simply For Others

See us go the fool's way
gathering all about us
for a covering, a surety
a pleasure;
Opiates to fill time's hollow;
piles of things which rot away
or linger near our ankles
to stop us dancing.

Our time in history is marked by extreme differences in material well-being. One-fifth of the Earth's people consume four-fifths of its resources to support lifestyles of affluence while the least advantaged one-fifth live in rags, starvation and illness. Individual extremes of wealth and poverty are even more pronounced.

The moral unacceptability of this situation is recognized nearly everywhere, yet no society, including the most affluent, has eradicated destitution. In many cases, the affluence for the minority literally requires the involuntary impoverishment of the majority because of the centralizations, trade inequities and environmental exploitation required to deliver riches to the privileged.

Part of the reason for the persistence of such injustice can be found in the approach we have taken to redressing poverty. When one group has more and another less, there are basically two ways that greater equality can be attained. The first approach is the one that has formed the mainstay of economic thinking in northern countries. Those with less will acquire more, the theory goes, if the economy can grow. Economic growth is the proposed solution for the hardships of destitution.

In spite of enormous growth in the world economy, however, there is more poverty now than ever before. Economic growth tends to benefit those who are already in privileged positions at the expense of the poor and of the ecosphere. While growth sounds good in theory, in practice the capital needed to create growth is controlled by a minority, which in turn reaps the profits from its investment. Total wealth increases, but its distribution becomes more unequal. In addition, it is clear that there are ecospheric limits on the total scale of human economic activities.

In this context, the choice to live simply becomes an *act of sharing.* Sharing is the alternative to growth. A cynic might say that the emphasis placed on growth by economists is merely a way of trying to avoid or delay sharing. If the total economic pie can be made to grow, then I don't have to share my piece with you. We can make your piece bigger.

Sharing means that if you are to have more, I must have less. When what I think I *am* is mostly defined by what I *have,* sharing is a particularly threatening prospect. Offering to share what I own becomes 'giving up' what I *am.* Sharing one's material possessions is then a partial or total loss of identity, power, privilege and self.

Expressing it this way emphasizes what an absurd cul-de-sac we have engineered. Having does not define being, as ten seconds of introspection reveals. But market economies teach us to associate the consumption of goods and services closely with non-material states of consciousness and feeling that do define being. It takes a considerable act of self-awareness to disentangle the two. The result is that the idea of *having* less, no matter how just the cause, *feels* to us like *being* less.

Simplicity offers a way of redefining the self that confers a great freedom from this anxiety. The choice for simplicity only requires 'giving up' in order to share in the first stages of the transition from affluence to simplicity. Little is needed when we define our character and presence in the world in other ways than through material acquisition. Sharing is difficult for those who already think they have much and must relinquish what they have. For the one who has and needs little, there is always abundance of what is needed and in this abundance, a measureless sense of security.

Because simplicity is the choice to live lightly in the world, it foregoes the use of resources, which then become available to help meet the needs of others. Non-use of material things is an indirect but extremely effective way of sharing that is within the immediate power of every individual. Living in material simplicity also frees time and energy that otherwise would have been devoted to the acquisition, maintenance and disposal of possessions. One is at liberty to take pleasure in life, friendships, and in pursuing goals that are intrinsically rewarding.

Advocates of economic growth will say this argument is naive. They will point to the synergies in technological and economic development that aims at growth. They will argue that it is precisely because we have had a growth-oriented economic system that encourages individuals to increase personal gain that discoveries have been multiplied and the overall economic and social good has increased. Many of these same people will argue that growth in military production is also good because the defence industry has often been responsible for technical innovations that have eventually found their way into civilian production. As if human beings simply lose their inclination to create unless driven by threats of invasion or by the lust for nationalistic self-aggrandizement!

Whether or not a growth-oriented economy has fostered synergies that have spurred technological progress, in any case this process is now reaching ecological and social limits. It is naive in another sense to believe that because of its synergistic history, economic and technical development somehow occurs in a sealed vessel that is unaffected by the social, cultural, ecological and spiritual dimensions of livelihood. An excellent recent example of this principle is the report of the Royal Commission on Reproductive Technology, which recommended a number of constraints on the development and application of such technology based on social, psychological and moral considerations. While we may not be able to identify limiting factors within the process of technical creativity, we can certainly define some that characterize the living world as a whole. Our technical and economic system cannot continue producing ever-widening social inequities of power and privilege, or ever-widening chasms between the demand for resources and energy, without regard for the capacity of the planet to provide ecological services and resources.

Similarly, living simply can be an act of sustainable development. There has been much discussion, much of it confused, around the issue of 'sustainable development,' which is often freely interchanged with 'sustainable economic growth.'

Growth means quantitative expansion in scale, size or number. Northern, industrialized, 'developed' nations cannot stand any more growth, nor can the planet support it. If human cultures everywhere on Earth are to sustain themselves over the long term, growth must cease and the pursuit of growth as a means to riches must cease.

Development refers to qualitative or functional improvement. It is an inherently value-laden concept. It refers to changes that are desired and valued. Development is clearly possible in a steady-state, non-growing system.

The confusion of growth with development provides fertile ground for sophistry and manipulation. Those who promote growth can easily confuse and discredit people who question growth as a good means of achieving development. They make their opponents appear to be against progress and development when they question the value of growth.

One way to expand the distinction between growth and development is to note that development usually works to the good of the whole, of all species, and all participants in the development process. Growth, on the other hand, always involves 'trade offs,' finding a 'balance,' which usually means everyone loses something, and 'breaking eggs to make omelets,' which usually means degradation of ecosystems.

Growth degrades environments and communities. Development enhances and enriches them through an increase in variety, diversity, functional integration and interdependence, a deepening of relationships – but all of this without growth in scale, quantity or number.

Voluntary simplicity is all about sustainable development. That is, it is about long-term qualitative improvement in the human lot, which can be pursued indefinitely.

Simplicity is definitely not about growth for its own sake, sustainable economic growth, environmentally sustainable growth, sustainable wealth, or any other self-contradictory notion.

If reasons for living more simply include acts of sharing and sustainability, Jorgen Lissner has suggested that simplicity is an act of solidarity in community with others. Our personal choice to live simply places us in the company of those who have no choice. Acts of solidarity are expressions of both political consciousness and social affirmation. Such expressions are particularly significant when we have a real choice. To live simply because of misfortune or accident of birth is to endure one of the darker sides of fate. But to live simply as a matter of choice is to affirm the value of non-material goals in life and to bring our warmth and creativity to the world of constraints and limitations that shapes the lives of people who must live with circumstance. If life is in any way a matter of 'taking sides,' and many spiritual mentors have suggested that it is, then simplicity as an act of solidarity declares our decision to side with the mass of humanity such as it is, rather than the values and lifestyles of the privileged.

Finally, simplicity as an act of solidarity declares to those of slender means that a life of material affluence doesn't always deliver all that it promises. The most successful feature of international development projects has not been transferring technology to the developing world, eradicating disease, alleviating illiteracy or establishing social and political justice. The greatest success of international development efforts since the 1950s has been to thoroughly diffuse the North American obsession with affluence into every other culture it has touched. Now, not only do we live the unsustainable paradox of 20 percent of the world's people producing 80 percent of its ecological damage and waste, we have the remaining 80 percent of humanity clamoring to live the same way. The choice for simplicity declares by example that not everyone in North America is prepared to admire the emperor's new clothes.

I agree with Lissner that simplicity as an act of solidarity can also be *provocative* of dialogue on the values that guide the development of our societies and our families, *anticipatory* of the day when the majority of people who have been disenfranchised from affluence will make their just claims to a share of Earth's resources, and an act of *advocacy* for a cultural and economic order that is more equitable and life-giving.

Voluntary simplicity is also an *exercise of purchasing power.* Many of us live from pay cheque to pay cheque without ever attending very closely to the considerable financial power we exercise as individuals. Consider that someone employed for 40 years with a median income of perhaps $40,000 per year will be making daily decisions during that period that deploy $1.6 million. Some practitioners of simplicity will trade income for time. Others will find opportunities in their careers to make meaningful contributions in service of values they cherish, but may divert some part of their income to non-material purposes.

Whatever income is earned must eventually be spent somehow. Exactly how it is spent has a profound effect on the shape of our economy and society. For all its faults and injustices, our economy is exquisitely sensitive to market demand or the lack of it. When demand disappears for a product or service, so does the product or service. Great strides have been made in the technology of artificially creating demand for products and services that have no relation to basic human needs, or for needs that could be met much more directly in some other way. The success of the market economy and its oppressive effects on the human spirit in North America can be found in how often shopping is a substitute for a social life, *the* major antidote to boredom, a significant way to express feelings of power and control, an important opportunity to socialize and experience sensory stimulation, and the purchases resulting from it are major surrogates for self-esteem.

The choice for simplicity implies making decisions regarding how we dispose of personal income through purchasing or, as the case may be, refraining from purchasing certain goods and services. Some general principles that can help guide these decisions have been suggested by the Simple Living Collective of San Francisco. These principles essentially come down to relating our purchasing decisions directly to basic needs and activities that enhance personal independence and reduce social and international oppression.

Less obvious perhaps is the idea that voluntary simplicity is an *act of nonviolence.* Most of the time, we are not directly aware that the right to possession is maintained by violence, but it is only thinly concealed by time and distance. At the physical level, the production of any material object often requires the cutting, grinding, tearing, milking, dismembering, uprooting, crushing, heating, freezing, etc. of some living or formerly living thing. What we make is literally built of the corpses of other beings. It is not my purpose to sentimentalize this violence because it is a violence that is inherent in all living things that rely on other living things for their life. I only wish to point out that at the physical level, the decision to maximize one's possessions necessarily requires maximizing this kind of violence.

Equally important, however, is the realization that the illusion of possession implies violence between people. In fact, no one can really possess anything. We appear in the world naked and we disappear from it equally naked. During our brief tenancy here, we can attempt to claim the more or less *exclusive* right to use certain things, enjoy their properties, and dispose of them as we please, but we don't really possess them. Thus, possession, having, owning, are merely words describing a set of social arrangements that confer rights of use and disposal upon some individuals to the exclusion of other individuals. Such arrangements are not always agreeable among all parties in society and then the *enforcement* of exclusive rights of use and disposal comes to involve the coercive power – i.e. violence – of the state. The implied threat of violence or its actual application is thus the social force that supports ownership. To try to 'own' something is to participate, more or less, in this system. The more I claim to own, the more I participate.

Evidence of this is everywhere. There is a disturbingly direct relationship between increasing material wealth and security systems. The larger the house, the more expansive the grounds, the bigger the office building, the more we see surveillance cameras, fences, alarms, dogs and guns. Where very great wealth is concerned, these tools of violence and this evidence of fear is well-concealed and manicured into the landscape but a single breach, no matter how innocent, brings it into clear view.

We recognize yet a deeper meaning of 'ownership:' While it is true that the coercive power of the state enforces property 'rights,' many thoughtful people see a basis for this right that is intrinsic to human nature. That is, if I, by my effort and ingenuity, transform some trees into lumber and the lumber into a house, my right to claim exclusive possession of the house derives from my labor and my creativity. Had I not applied my talents thus, the house would not exist. Since it does exist through my constructive activity, it is said to belong to me. Some would argue that it is this relationship between a human being and the fruits of labor that constitutes ownership and that we authorize the state to protect.

But even here, the claim to 'have' something that we have made is tenuous at best. It positions the human worker on a par with Divine Being, as if we made things out of nothing. Again, what we actually do is claim temporary user rights over materials that have been loaned to us from the heart of another, truly creative mystery. Who knows, *really,* how the tree grows? Who can make it grow when it will not, or make it grow thus and not so? And from whence comes our insight, our creativity, our ability to solve problems and hatch new plans? Are we not actually *recipients* of mysterious materials, mysterious abilities and marvellous powers? Do we not, in fact, *rearrange* elements of creation we neither make nor unmake?

From this perspective, we must be more tentative in crying 'Mine!' In choosing simplicity, we further the growth of consciousness by appreciating life as gift rather than personal accomplishment. We recognize ownership as a human convention born in fear and violence, fear that we will lack something we need and violence to assure its supply, which has no cosmic basis. We then become less prone to endorse the use of violence against others to protect 'rights' that have no foundation in being.

Closely related to the capacity of the state to exercise coercive violence to maintain property rights is the extension of this violence to war-making. With the dissolution of the Soviet Union and the relaxation of East/ West tensions, much of the drive behind the post-Second World War peace movement has now dissipated. Yet war and the preparation for war continues to be a major preoccupation of many countries. The conflict in the Persian Gulf demonstrated that conventional war-making is just as destructive in both human and ecological terms as nuclear war might be. The Persian Gulf example is particularly apposite to voluntary simplicity since a major reason for North American involvement in that conflict was to assure the stability of oil prices.

While many conflicts around the world are local or regional battles related to nationalistic goals within the countries concerned, conflicts that involve North Americans have invariably been related to protecting economic interests. The lifestyle of affluence and consumption that is widely promoted in our society contributes directly to these military adventures.

Moreover, research and development activities for military purposes still largely dominate the attention of the scientific and technological establishment. Military spending still consumes a very large fraction of global wealth and resources each year while the production, use and disposal of this equipment serves no life-giving purpose.

The debate over whether or not armies are still required in today's increasingly interdependent world will likely go on for some time. What seems clear, however, is that the present level of military production and spending are unsustainable. In addition, to the extent that individuals begin to choose simple living and the overall resource and energy intensity of our economy is reduced, the motivation for military overdevelopment will be reduced as well. While military institutions may never completely disappear, it would be all gain if they could be scaled back to vestigial replicas of the monsters that are still so much with us.

Militarism is a global issue with systemic roots. The individual decision to live more simply clearly will not reverse the trend to militarization of economies and societies. But as we mentioned before, individual decisions do matter when many individuals take similar decisions. Thus, another major reason for simple living is the hope that by supporting each other in this choice we will eventually build sufficient social momentum for systemic as well as individual change.

Should this transition occur, then the opportunities for people in other regions and countries to become more autonomous in their development would greatly increase. Money and resources that are now going into arms purchases and defence would become available for local development. Savings from arms expenditures would also be available for expanding our knowledge and appreciation of the universe, for the exploration and colonization of space, and for the alleviation of much human misery.

I would now like to consider some of the reasons for simple living that relate to our place within the ecosphere.

Living Simply For The Earth

In the summer of 1989, prairie Canada sweltered in blistering drought. We had had several years of below average rainfall. The water tables had dropped substantially. The Assiniboine River, which curls its way through the community where I lived, looked like a muddy ditch with a disturbingly slender trickle of water moving slowly through its midline.

One afternoon in July, I was returning to work from my lunch break. The wind was up and the temperature around 35 Celsius. All the grass in the city had long since turned brown and the trees rustled their foliage with a serpentine hiss. The wind seemed like a blast furnace and the sun beat down, not with the friendly warmth of childhood memory, but with the ferocity of a blow torch. Everywhere dust was beginning to cloud the air, caking vehicles, buildings and people. It gave a gritty, choking quality to the air that seized me in the throat at the same time as it threatened to sand the skin from my face.

In spite of how inclement it was, I stood there absorbed in feeling the elements whirl around me. For a moment, I felt that the whole Earth had turned hostile toward me — toward us. Like a child in relation to his mother, I sometimes felt that mother was being unpleasant, yet I never questioned her basic love for me. But on this day in July, something shifted. I wondered whether this was the beginning of global warming, or if this was what it would be like when it was well under way. Like everyone else in the 20th century, I probably carried some dismal forebodings about such an event, but also like everyone else, I kept it safely suppressed beneath layers of routine, wilful ignorance and what the Trappist monk Thomas Merton once called 'sunshine and uplift.' This day, however, the weather broke through my psychological evasions. I experienced *in my body* some premonition of what it would be like for us if the planet changed in ways that rendered human life difficult or impossible to sustain.

Of course I don't personify nature and I don't believe nature can 'have it in' for human beings. When I experienced *in* that moment an ecosphere that had turned hostile rather than nurturant, what I actually experienced was a psychological projection of my own guilt for causing environmental damage. This is a very ancient sort of feeling, the feeling that the 'gods' have become angry because of human wrongdoing or greed. It was a very archetypal feeling. In a sense, my unconscious was saying, 'Look, if you keep living this way, this is what you deserve ... the wrath of nature. This is simple justice; cause and effect; the wages of sin. It's nothing personal and yet it's very personal. This is the way things are. Wise up or perish.'

Human beings can live only because we consume other creatures for food, clothing and shelter. We change the natural world, rearranging its materials, its species and landscapes, to meet our needs. This is an inescapable requirement of our being. We develop culture and technology to help us get along in the world, rather than undergoing physical change. This capacity has enabled us to inhabit nearly every bioregion on earth.

But we exploit the ecosphere not only for what we *need*, also for what we *want*. As our numbers grow, so do our needs. And as our desires increase, so does our exploitation of the ecosphere. Our economic system now manufactures not only the products to satisfy our desires, it also manufactures desires for its products. Paradoxical as it sounds, our economic system no longer operates to satisfy human craving and deliver contentment, but rather, it operates to multiply cravings and discontentment. Only unhappy and discontented people consume more than they need.

It is unlikely that any future technology will reverse these relationships: the more people and the more wants, the greater the impact on the ecosphere. The relationships are probably not linear; but they will always remain direct and positive. We have little choice in the matter.

Within the obvious requirement of our being to exploit the ecosphere to *some* degree, exactly to *what* degree is a matter of choice.

Historically, our impact on the biosphere has degraded it. When our numbers were few, technology simple, and world view animistic, we occupied certain regions for a very long time indeed. But in the case of hunter–gatherer societies, our damage to the Earth was within its capacity to heal itself. The point is that even in societies where the prevailing value is not that of personal accumulation of material goods, human activities more or less always reduce biological diversity, degrade soils, reduce forest cover and leave behind waste.

Where human numbers are large, technology powerful and world views materialistic, our impact on the ecosphere is catastrophic.

In facing the environmental emergency of the late 20th century, we have been encouraged to 'Reduce, Reuse, Recycle and Recover,' with most emphasis on recycling. Recycling is popular because it promises consumption without guilt. It allows the free market economic machine to continue operating with only minor adjustments to its input and output cycles. Recycling never requires that we cease doing a thing, only that we do the same thing differently.

But until someone discovers a way to reverse the laws of physics, recycling will reduce but never overcome our degradation of environments. It is possible, however, to minimize the degree and extent of degradation. This is accomplished by the 'first R,' the one that gets the least attention. Whenever we reduce our demand for resources and energy, pollution and consumption of resources are avoided.

This goal can be approached in two ways, both of which can be practised together. First, we can reduce demand for resources by *reducing waste*. Waste reduction stresses efficiency while leaving goals unquestioned. We live the same way, value the same things, pursue the same goals, but we use methods and technologies that reduce the wastage of energy and resources in the process. This is the conservationist approach to environmental protection and stewardship of resources. It is also essentially the approach advocated by 'sustainable development.'

Another way to reduce demand is to *reduce consumption* in an absolute sense. This involves a review of basic life goals, how we spend our time, talents and treasure, and the role accorded to material consumption as a means to pleasure, health, self–esteem or public reputation. To the extent that we live simply, we conserve the planet that is our home.

Clearly, we can both reduce waste and consumption. We can continually reassess our goals at the same time that we try to pursue them with as little waste as possible. The choice for voluntary simplicity thus becomes the most direct, personal and powerful individual *act to conserve the ecosphere and all its creatures.*

Even if we take a selfish perspective, the choice for simplicity and conservation is *an act to enhance our quality of life* in the present by enhancing the healthfulness of the natural environment. Human beings cannot flourish in degraded environments. To choose simplicity is to choose to care not only for the natural world, but in caring for it, to care for ourselves.

Thus simplicity reverses the maxim of the consumer society, that consumption defines quality of life. Rather, we assert that we are rich in proportion to the things we can afford to do without. As practitioners of simplicity, we respond to the question 'What have my grandchildren ever done for me?' with 'Caring for the world that my grandchildren inherit is another way of caring for myself.' And to the challenge 'In the long run, we're all dead' we would reply, 'No. In the long run, we're all connected.'

Naturally, we will want to assure that even those things we do choose to acquire, as well as the things we need, will be manufactured with as little degradation to the ecosphere as possible. A great challenge to human creativity will be the development of ever more efficient and benign technologies for meeting human needs and aspirations. This challenge will never end. But the choice for simplicity recognizes that only a limited part of our human potential can be realized in terms of the possession and consumption of material things.

If voluntary simplicity is ever widely adopted, it will imply a much simpler economy and a different direction for technological development. It does not necessarily imply poverty and technical primitivity. Economic activity would become more focused on meeting essential human needs directly and efficiently. Technological development would be directed not toward the generation of wealth, but toward the generation of *wisdom* and *well-being*. And there would not, of course, be any role at all for technologies intended for war, for oppression of other people, or for self-interested exploitation of the planet for personal gain.

I would suggest therefore, that voluntary simplicity is the most immediate and direct pathway for individuals to reduce waste; reduce demand for energy and resources; conserve habitats and species; assure quality of air, soil and water resources; and help maintain our planetary stocks of natural resources for future generations and the economically disadvantaged members of humanity who are already with us.

Living Simply More Deeply

We've now explored many reasons for choosing simplicity, some of which are perhaps obvious and have been mentioned by other authors in the past, and some of which may have been less obvious or less well-explored. In several places I have suggested that embracing simplicity involves a shift in attention, and often a shift in 'love interest' if such a phrase can be permitted, from preoccupation with the physical, material and consumptive aspects of life to 'other goals,' without really saying much about what these other goals might be.

Simplicity is often connected with spiritual development. This is the case because the spiritual unfolding of personality requires such singleness of purpose, clear attention, dedication of energy and unwavering intent that monastic expressions of spirituality have left little room for materialism or the complexities of a 'worldly' orientation to life. In some dualistic spiritual traditions, maintaining psychological, emotional or physical attachments to material possessions or entertaining the desire to accumulate them were associated with sin, evil, or at best, with ignorance about the nature of the world and how such attachments could become impediments to spiritual development.

While these arguments may be true and valid, they have received much more insightful and eloquent treatment by past writers than I could ever hope to bring to the discussion. I don't want to treat the spiritual dimension of simplicity purely as a call to religious asceticism or austerity, though for some it may bring them much reward.

Instead, I would suggest that the choice for simplicity can first of all be an *act of shifting attention from the quantitative aspects of things to their qualitative aspect.* Without forsaking in any way the enjoyment of our senses and our involvement with the physical and material aspects of the universe, we can yet change *how* we are present to these transactions.

A consumptive approach to existence is one that focuses attention on the outer aspects of life, on the number and quantity of things owned or consumed, and on the range or variety of possessions or property amassed. To have much is to be much. To have options, to have accumulated and controlled the largest, the most, the greatest extent or degree of whatever thing we are using at the moment, defines well-being.

Simplicity, however, *is* the choice to shift attention toward the *quality and depth of* our relationships with things rather than their number or extent. We do not eschew the getting and having of material possessions. But we do concentrate on becoming more conscious of *why* we are choosing to own something, the *extent* of its usefulness, the *fullness* of our enjoyment and use of it, and the *effects* that it has on our lives. To own the world's largest collection of guitars is one way of defining well-being. To own one guitar that we have learned to play with great sensitivity and expertise is another way of defining well-being, one which stresses the qualitative aspect of our relationship to the instrument. The choice for simple living is increasingly to attend to these qualitative aspects of our existence.

Some years ago I developed a fairly serious case of pneumonia. As my fever increased, I lost my appetite, and perhaps my judgment. I spent several days in a fevered state essentially without eating or drinking much at all. As fasting interacted with the fever, some fairly strange 'altered states' began to pervade both my waking hours and my sleep. After about six days of this, it was evident that I was very sick indeed and I finally presented myself for medical attention. One bottle of antibiotics and a stern lecture later, I was back home in bed and decided to force some fluids along with the medication.

I poured a glass of very cold apple juice and brought it to bed with me. I sipped the juice very slowly and was utterly stunned by the delicious, wine-like quality of the drink. It was the most savory and luscious delight! How had I missed this so often? Surely, this was the same juice I had always enjoyed, but what was so different this time? Clearly, it was *me*. *I* was paying attention to the juice. I had nowhere else to go, nothing else on my mind, and a clean palate from five days of fasting. But the point was that the apple juice itself must always have had these delightful qualities. I was only now paying attention to them – deep, mindful attention. The *quality* of drinking the juice was now more important than the quantitative experience of simply quenching my thirst. In that moment, sick as I was, I wondered why this sort of mindful attentiveness could not suffuse all of life's experiences.

The choice for simple living represents another shift for many people and that is the shift from attending to the outer, physical, material and objective aspects of our lives *toward the inner, psycho-emotional, non-material and subjective side of living*. This is a logical result of giving less time and attention to the clutter and complication that goes with owning many 'toys.' To the extent that I fill my life with earning, saving, buying, cleaning, maintaining, disposing, repurchasing, operating and repairing many 'things,' there is relatively less energy available for attending to subjective, intuitive, emotional, aesthetic, imaginary, social, interpersonal or cultural matters. I also have less resources at my disposal for non-material cultural and personal development.

In advocating simplicity, I am not suggesting that we become as one-sidedly inner-directed as many people have become one-sidedly outer-directed. Duane Elgin has eloquently, and I think appropriately, argued that voluntary simplicity is about an elegant *balance* between inner and outer development and activity. I would take this point a little further and say that voluntary simplicity is about *integrated and holistic* development of all aspects of our personhood, our relations with others and with the ecosphere. Modern industrial societies adopt an 'either/or' approach to development and have stressed technical and scientific mastery over the physical systems of nature in order to meet the physical needs of humans (and artificial wants based on those needs) almost to the total exclusion of the development of the depth dimension of our lives.

Predictably, this has given us a society of immense material wealth and technical power at the price of spiritual, emotional and cultural poverty. Simple living merely offers a pathway to begin bringing these two aspects of our existence into greater harmony and proportion.

Coming to some measure of this awareness is sometimes an involuntary 'accomplishment' as was the case for me. Shortly following the end of a seventeen-year marriage, I was alone with two children, my income slashed in half, one hide-a-bed, one pole lamp, a box of garage sale kitchen utensils and a total bank balance of $4.57. I remember my lawyer saying in his characteristically understated way, 'You appear to be financially exposed.' To say the least!

Life presented no immediate prospect of this situation improving or changing significantly. Concentrating on 'getting ahead' in the traditional sense of that term would only have been frustrating. But it was a fine opportunity for shifting perspective to some of the qualitative aspects of living.

One summer morning, I had just finished a five kilometre run and was strolling along to cool off. The air was mine, the sun was mine, and all the delicate colors and scents of summer seemed to be mine. It seemed to me that all the homeowners diligently working in their yards were beautifying the city specifically for me. It was like having hundreds of people working on the grounds of my own estate, cleaning it, tilling it and caring for it! Even the plants and animals that crowded everywhere in wonderful profusion seemed to give me themselves in some inalienable way that no divorce proceeding could threaten or disturb. In an objective sense, I had nothing. In a subjective sense, I felt as though I had everything and I needed nothing more. It was wonderful to realize that this plenitude of life had always been there and would always be there if only I took the time to attend to it and claim it.

Living simply also implies that the means of meeting a given human need are proportionate to and appropriate for the need in question. Understanding this concept must again take us into the realm of knowing the difference between needs and wants. But it also requires clear knowledge of how needs of different kinds are most appropriately met. Nutritious food in healthy quantities is the appropriate and proportionate means for fulfilling the human need to eat. Over-consumption of highly refined and unhealthy foods is neither a proportionate nor appropriate way to relieve anxiety or deal with depression. Computers are an appropriate and highly efficient means for handling symbolic information, solving certain problems and carrying on certain forms of communication. Virtual reality is neither a proportionate nor appropriate way of meeting social needs because the 'reality' it presents is ersatz. Simple living grows from a commitment to always grow in consciousness, awareness and mindfulness of what it is we need, what it is we want, and what are the most appropriate, proportionate and ethical means of meeting our needs and fulfilling our wants. To a very considerable extent, market economies thrive by continually confusing and blurring these distinctions and by making implicit or explicit claims for products or services that try to meet needs with inappropriate means.

Simplicity, then, is *a decision to live more deeply.* In living simply, we choose to shift our attention and effort toward a more holistic, balanced, integrated, proportionate and appropriate pattern of living. This new pattern honors both the inner, non-material, aesthetic and spiritual aspects of our lives as well as their material and physical aspects. We attend to what we wear, where we live, and how we move about in the world, but also we attend to what we say, the directness of our gaze, the singleness of our purposes in choosing our involvements and making our commitments.

(ENDNOTES)

1 Conze, Edward, *Buddhist Meditation*, (London, U.K.: George Allen and Unwin, Ltd., 1968) p 113.

2 Lissner, Jorgen, *Personal Lifestyle Response to Social Injustice.*

3 Lebow, Victor, *Journal of Retailing*, quoted in Vance Packard, *The Waste Makers* (New York: David McKay, 1960).

4 Worley, Michael, Chicago, IL: National Opinion Research Center, University of Chicago, 1990. In Lester R. Brown et al. *State of the World*, 1991 (New York: W.W. Norton & Co., 1991) p156.

5 Easterlin, R.A. 'Does economic growth improve the human lot? Some empirical evidence.' In Michael Argyle, *The Psychology of Happiness* (London: Methuen, 1987).

Chapter Twelve

SHARING THE EARTH

Jim Merkel

'Share the Earth' is an easy enough phrase to say. But as we explore more deeply this interconnected wild world, and experience the impacts of a complex global economy and then add in more variables, such as the needs of the unborn, we can soon be overwhelmed. It is not only a challenge to our scientific, spiritual, and ethical senses, but it also calls on the best of our unfettered intuition to come to grips with it responsibly. I find it helpful to remind myself: 'I am one of six billion humans. My species shares paradise with 25 million other species. Each of these species has many thousands, or even billions in their population. How do I want to share Earth with all of this life?'

Although there are infinite ways to share, the easiest is simply to take less. This will be our foundation, or first step. We take less (or share more) when we:

★ Earn less, taking less of the available work
★ Consume less
★ Make wiser choices
★ Purchase local products

You may be tempted to enthusiastically consume more than your share of available work and money and become a philanthropist, all for the joy of giving it away. But since this path is loaded with so many pitfalls, in terms of power dynamics and inner motivation, we'll keep our focus on all the possible ways of taking less. For now, imagine yourself back at that big potluck table, with all species, people, and future generations present. What is a reasonable share?

Through scientific observation, theories and experiments, we gain insights into natural phenomena and begin to ask questions such as:

★ How much Earth is there?
★ How much nature do humans use?
★ How many species are there?
★ What are the habitat needs of each species?
★ At our current rate of resource use, how much will be left for future generations?

Once we've asked these questions, we can begin to look for answers. But after years of searching for scientific answers, I've discovered that science alone can't tell us how to share – something more is needed. This is where our personal ethics come in, to navigate us through the thousands of daily choices. Quite often, our moral decisions are heavily influenced by both the rational and the irrational – we engage our hearts as well as our heads.

Our intuition doesn't need a factual basis to know what to do; it is a way of knowing without the use of our rational minds. Intuitive information is like an internal compass, guiding us in considering the well-being of the whole. Does your intuition and spirituality influence how you share the Earth? Most spiritual paths include kindness, compassion, forgiveness, and reciprocity. If our scientific mind looks deeply into natural phenomena, while our spirituality embraces all life, and we pay attention to our intuition, our personal ethics will influence how we make day to day choices. As we get out of theory and down to practice, some ethical questions might be:

★ Could Earth support all the world's people at my standard of living?
★ Do other species or people suffer because of my lifestyle?
★ Do good things come from each dollar I spend?
★ Do other species have inherent value?
★ Should my race, gender, strength, taxonomy, education, or birthplace allow me to consume more than others?
★ Are wars being fought over resources that I use?
★ Do I support corporations or industries that damage the environment or exploit workers in sweatshops?
★ Is my lifestyle in alignment with my own values?

When I first began asking these questions, I realized that the subject of how I shared the Earth was rarely part of my decision making process. Yet when I took time to explore my values, I realized that this inquiry was deeply important to me. After beating myself up one too many times, I came to accept the process of living more equitably as a life-long endeavor to enjoy.

Living Equitably

At the heart of radical simplicity is discovering how you would like to share the Earth. To help in this discovery process, we will go a level deeper and discuss three types of equity: interspecies, interhuman, and intergenerational.

Interspecies Equity

With the lightness of a butterfly Saint Francis of Assisi (1182–1226)[1] swept down to gently move an earthworm from the roadway. In prayers and canticles, he referred to Earth as mother, the wolves and birds as brothers and sisters – a non-anthropocentric communion. For Francis, mere existence granted each breeze or bug a spiritual fellowship worthy of ethical consideration. While St. Francis' spiritual and ethical treatment of all species was as radical then as it is now, nearly identical ethical and spiritual constructs have an unbroken lineage in countless indigenous cultures.

The vice president of the World Council of Indigenous peoples stated: 'The Earth ... is the seat of spirituality, the fountain from which our cultures and languages flourish. The Earth is our historian, the keeper of events and the bones of our forefathers. It is the source of our independence; it is our mother. We do not dominate Her: we must harmonize with Her.'[2] Chief Seattle, who died in 1866, forewarned of the end of living and the beginning of survival when the scent of man began to permeate the fragrant wild lands of his people.

In July of 1997, Stanford University biologist Peter M. Vitousek coauthored a paper on Human Domination of Earth's Ecosystems.[3] The report stated that:

- ★ No ecosystem is free of pervasive human influence.
- ★ Between one-third and one-half of the land surface has been transformed by human action.
- ★ Carbon dioxide concentration in the atmosphere has increased by nearly 30 percent since the industrial revolution began.
- ★ More than half of all accessible surface fresh water is put to use by humanity.
- ★ Approximately one-quarter of the bird species on Earth have been driven to extinction.

Chief Seattle's prophecy has come to be. With the current wars, ecological exploitation and poverty, one must ask what is next. The bad news is that we are not doing a very good job of sharing; in fact, the data suggests that humanity is dominating the Earth.

Ecological Overshoot of the Human Economy,[4] states that there are 28.2 billion acres of bioproductive land on Earth – the total surface area minus the deep oceans, deserts, icecaps and built-up land. When divided between six billion people, each person gets a 4.7-acre share – we'll call this area each person's 'personal planetoid.' But this assumes that humanity uses the entire planet's annual production. The question then becomes, 'How much of my 4.7-acre share do I want to use for myself and how much do I want to leave for other life forms?' You might think, 'I want to share it all.' A generous thought. But the reality is, you need to consume to survive. And what you use it not available for the deer, rabbits, or coyotes. For example, assume I am fenced into a one-acre garden with one deer and we eat the plants almost as fast as they grow, but don't deplete them. After 60 years, the land is still just as productive as it was when we entered. Generous me then invites a friend inside the fence. Now the plants can't keep pace with our appetites, and the land becomes depleted. Renewable 'resources,' or the planet's 'bioproductivity,' takes time to regenerate. They are only renewable if they're consumed at a rate slower than their annual growth or yield.

To get a scientific sense of this interspecies equity question, I cycled into the Carmanah Valley, an old growth rainforest of Vancouver Island, BC. The Western Canada Wilderness Committee (WCWC) had strapped rainforest platforms to an ancient Sitka spruce at 125', 150', 175', and 204' levels. I followed a boardwalk out of a massive clearcut into the cool wonder of cedars, hemlocks, firs, and these Sitka spruces, many of which were 200 feet tall and 20 feet around. The understory of ferns, skunk cabbage, and huckleberries, drenched in 200 inches of rain a year, was rampant and lush compared to the parched stumps of clearcut.

Here, I met up with entomologist Neville Winchester and his crew from the University of Victoria. Canada's first marbled murrelet nest had already been discovered, high in a Sitka spruce, as well as a tarantula-type spider – both old-growth dependent species. Neville described his study as assembling a biological inventory from the canopy down into the soil structure, and in the transition from forest to clearcut.

By the summer of 1993, Neville had collected 750,000 insects in five trees. Sixty new species had been tentatively identified, and he estimated there were over 200 new species to be confirmed, once they check the results with 62 identification experts. Neville said, 'Since we really have no understanding of the full range of insect species that inhabit the rainforest, and since we have absolutely no idea how the ancient temperate rainforest ecosystem works, the last thing we should be doing is liquidating our last large intact watersheds.'[5]

As I stared up through the spoked whorls, I wondered if my next photocopy run would extinct an unknown species? With a mere 1.5 million of the estimated 7 to 25 million species identified world-wide, caution is in order. And, with the current extinction rate estimated at 100 to 1,000 times faster than the natural rate,[6] humanity's current idea of sharing nature is deeply challenged.

Having looked closely at the species in just a few trees, let's approach the question of interspecies equity through conservation biology which looks at the needs of entire ecosystems. Reed F. Noss, a specialist in the field, has outlined four objectives that will maintain native biodiversity in perpetuity:[7]

★ Represent, in a system of protected areas, all native ecosystems types and serial stages across their natural range of variation.
★ Maintain viable populations of all native species in natural patterns of abundance and distribution.
★ Maintain ecological and evolutionary processes, such as distributive regimes, hydrological processes, nutrient cycles, and biotic interactions, including predation.
★ Design and manage the system to be responsive to short-term and long-term environmental change and to maintain the evolutionary potential of lineages.

How much of Earth's bioproductive space should remain wild to uphold these fundamentals? To maintain a minimum population of 1,000 animals would require 242 million acres for grizzly bears, 200 million acres for wolverines, and 100 million acres for wolves.[8] Even the six-million-acre Adirondack Park, which contains the combined areas of Yosemite, Yellowstone, Olympic, and Grand Canyon National Parks struggled to support a reintroduction of lynx.[9]

To return the wolverines, mountain lions, and timber wolves to the park-would require it to grow by thirty times. In truth, a successful reintroduction would require the cooperation of the people of New York, Vermont, New Hampshire, Massachusetts, and Maine, along with some delicate negotiations with New Brunswick and Quebec in order to meet the four fundamentals above. Reed Noss said that in order to preserve biodiversity and viability of species, between 25 and 75 percent of the total land area in most regions would need to be placed in protected reserves with buffer zones.[10] His analysis assumes that the reserves are interconnected with the larger landscape and other reserve areas of neighboring regions.

If the area outlined above was extensively restored, a 200 million acre (312,000 square mile) core area could be formed in New England and Canada. With a drastic reduction of roads and traffic, and a citizenry ready to co-exist with wildlife, these animals might make their way back down from Canada. Sound impossible? Living in British Columbia for seven years among grizzlies, cougars, and wolverines, I learned that coexisting is not rocket science, not costly, and not even difficult. But it would take a redesign of the human environment and a willingness to change habits.

Anthropocentrism, or the belief that humans are the primary measure of value, may be guiding more of our everyday decisions than we are prepared to acknowledge. A biocentric view, referred to as nonanthropocentrism or deep ecology, holds that the soil, spiders, winged and finned all have intrinsic value. When we think about interspecies equity, a more inclusive society is needed. But a society is made up of individuals, which is the place where changes begin.

Interhuman Equity

When we began defining global living, you were at a potluck buffet with six billion humans, the many life forms, and future generations all behind you in line. You had just filled your plate with that tofu burger and other low-impact delights. The grass was green and the sky blue. You found an empty seat with nine other friendly strangers; there was a girl from Uruguay, a just-married couple from Zimbabwe, a student from China, two brothers from India, a woman from the Slovak Republic, and a Mexican farmer with his son, who was in a wheelchair. You enjoyed a nice meal and got to know these interesting people.

But when the meal was over, you returned to the buffet to take what you need and want for the rest of your entire year. Now, how do you decide what is an equitable share among all the world's people? Will the student in China be able to afford tuition? Can the couple from Zimbabwe get sufficient food and shelter? What is a reasonable share that won't shortchange anyone? A strictly scientific approach might consider caloric intake, the climates of homelands, house designs, healthcare, and education – measures with a practical bottom line – to ensure all have a basic life-quality. This allocation based upon need would remove the biases of color, gender and power, and on average would provide equal shares for all people. You could assess your situation compared to the average world person. Perhaps life's been good and you could do well with less than others. Or, if you face hardships, you may decide to take some extra. So how much do you take?

The golden rule of 'do unto others' has been around a long time and has an equivalent in all major religions. It seems unlikely that with 10 of us around a friendly table, we could go too far off course. Yet we have. Why?

Let's consider two hypothetical scenarios. After your green grass and blue sky dinner, the ten people at your table get a basket of money equal to ten sustainable, equitable shares of world Gross National Product (GNP). To determine how much is in the basket, we first divide the total world GNP – $29,340 billion – by six billion people for a $4,900 share. But because the total economic activity of humanity overshoots the globe's carrying capacity by 20 percent we adjust the share to $3,900. At this level of GNP, we still have humanity consuming the entire global bioproductivity. Let's say we scale back total human impact in terms of GNP by 75 percent to make room for the millions of other species. Each person would now have an annual equitable share of world GNP equal to $980. You begin to try to imagine living on $980 a year, gulp... and you freeze. Impossible!

The basket has $9,800, or 10 times the $980 equal shares. This money is laid out in bundles of 100 one-dollar bills. Now each draws a number from a hat. You draw first, and can take what you want. Everyone watches in silence. How much do you take?

Let's consider another scenario. All six billion people draw numbers, and it's your lucky day, you draw first again. With societal pressure removed, you approach a cash machine and are free to take out up to a billion dollars – you can transfer it to your account and no one will know. You know that $980 is a sustainable equitable portion. If you know you use more, others will have to use less. When the cash machine is near depletion, the last billion will get $100 each for the year. Dinner was splendid. You met some of your world neighbors, but now you are behind the curtain. The machine will pump out a billion dollars. It is between you and the machine. Once again, how much do you take?

These are the tough questions of global living. Some claim human nature is greedy, but if that were the whole truth, how can the historic and contemporary egalitarian societies be explained? Are they an anomaly, or a reminder of the potential of human kindness?

It is difficult to speculate just how equitable earlier societies actually were, but we can glean insights from historical encounters and contemporary egalitarian communities. For example, Russell Thornton's book, *American Indian Holocaust and Survival,*[11] estimated that in 1492, 1.8 million people lived in what is now called the United States. If we divide the biologically productive area of the continent's 1.79 billion acres by 1.8 million people, each person had 1,000 acres of productive land, and we know their footprints were a fraction of ours. Anthropologist Richard Robbins wrote of native North Americans, 'Since there was little occupational specialization and little difference in individual wealth or possessions, relations were of an egalitarian nature.'[12] Other written accounts offer support for this statement.

The Spanish priest, Bartholomew de las Casas, who accompanied Columbus on his initial journey to, the new world, wrote about the Arawak of the Bahaman Islands: 'They lived in large communal bell-shaped buildings, housing up to 600 people at one time... made of very strong wood and roofed with palm leaves.... They lacked all manners of commerce, neither buying nor selling, and rely exclusively on their natural environment for maintenance. They are extremely generous with their possessions and by the same token covet the possessions of their friends and expect the same degree of liberality.... Endless testimonies... prove the mild and pacific temperament of the natives.... But our work was to exasperate, ravage, kill, mangle, and destroy.'[13]

The 1960s heralded the dawning of the Age of Aquarius, a hopeful symbol that the tides were turning – humanity was to usher in an age of harmony and understanding. Much awareness has been raised over the last 40 years, however the gap between the 20 richest and poorest percentiles has doubled. Income disparity stands at 250 to 1, measured in US dollars (74 to 1 using 'purchasing-power parity,' or 'ppp').[14] The amount of raw nature needed to provide the one billion wealthiest people with an average of $25,500 worth of income could not be found within those countries borders; in fact, it requires the entire Earth's annual yield. For the high-consumption twenty percent to take 250 times the GNP in US dollars than what lowest-consumption billion gets; no nation, no culture, no species is off limits. The World Trade Organization (WTO) and the General Agreement on Tariffs and Trade (GATT) – elite, undemocratic groups – have designed legal mechanisms to break down borders to ease raw material flows toward the industrialized world. The track record speaks for itself – a further concentration of wealth at the top.

In 1998, half of the 1.2 billion people who lived on less than $110 per year have stunted growth or mental retardation from insufficient caloric intake.[15] The poorest 3.6 billion– 60 percent of humanity – live on less than $520 per year. A third of the world's children suffer from malnutrition.[16] A Salvadoran peasant was quoted as saying, 'You will never understand violence and nonviolence until you understand the violence to the spirit that happens from watching your children die of malnutrition.'[17] Only 30 percent of the wealthiest billion report being very happy. In America, according to a poll of those earning $274 a day, 27 percent stated, 'I cannot afford to buy everything I really need.'[18] Living on $980 per year in North America might seem impossible; certainly it seems heroic.

Charles Gray, from Eugene, Oregon, author of *Toward a Nonviolent Economics*,[19] developed the concept of World Equity Wage (WEW and capped his wage at $3.14 an hour, and worked no more than 20 hours a week. His voluntary 'deprivileging' was motivated by a goal of sharing the available work and wealth with humanity and restoring the environment. When we met in 1995, he had already been living for 17 years on what he calculated to be the World Equity Budget (WEB), and averaged $1,190 in total annual living expenses from 1978 to 1993. He is a delightful, open-minded person and his book is an inspiration.

After 14 years of living on $5,000 per year (placing me amongst the wealthiest 17 percent of humanity), I know it would take a quantum redesign of my life and significantly reduced expectations of services to approach equity. I know it is hard in the context of an unsustainable culture, but every bit of societal level change, be it bike lanes, mixed zoning, or local organic markets will make the whole process easier.

★ ★ ★

As we make small steps toward better distribution of wealth, there are rewards. That girl from Uruguay might get the nutritional boost she needs and that couple from Zimbabwe might be able to set up their home. And you and I get to learn new skills and experience a life less centered upon things.

Intergenerational Equity

The year 1978 came and went. I was 20. It was a special year in both Earth's history and human history, and it passed without notice. It was the year humans claimed the entire sustainable yield of Earth. The overall system – the planet's capital if you will – would hereafter be drawn down. Before this day, if you consumed more than your average share, the wild ones paid the difference. After this day, if you consumed more, it came directly from another humans share, and at the expense of generations to come.

You and I might get to see the climax of this amazing spike of human impact; we are clearly riding a wild wave. The World Bank predicts that the doubling time to add the next billion humans might actually increase[20] – a first since we reached one billion. Population growth is slowing down. In the less industrialized world, women now have an average of four children, a clear drop from six only thirty years earlier. Demographers are uncertain as to how and why fertility levels have dropped and currently predict a peak population of between 10 and 11 billion.[21] If we assume the best, that these scientists behind their computers have a good crystal ball, then when I'm 92 in 2050, there will be 9 billion people. My $980 a year share of GNP will have shrunk to $650 and humanity will be overshooting carrying capacity by 88 percent. That is, if we don't somehow grapple with these incredibly tough issues and make some significant changes.

When my grandfather was born, in 1902, there were 1.6 billion people. On my father's birthdate in 1926, there were 2 billion. When I was born, in 1958, global population had risen to 2.9 billion. Now, 100 years after my grandfather's birth, we've added another 4.4 billion people, and the percent of fallow and wild bioproductive land has gone from 67 percent to a 20 percent overshoot. In the 150 or so years since the Industrial Revolution, we've doubled the population 4 times and doubled the size of the global economy 20 times.

A journey back 60,000 generations to the Rift Valley of what is now northeast Africa – a period of 1.5 million years representing 99 percent of the human experience – the relatively small human settlements left the bulk of Earth's bioproductive space wild.

Intergenerational equity can be summed up as simply passing the land on to the next generation with no degradation. How intensively do you want to use the Earth's bioproductivity? Do you wish to leave a buffer, as in fallow fields, so that the unborn generations will be assured a wild and bioproductive land? We know that the Earth produces a tremendous amount of life each year. Currently, humanity takes 20 percent more than is produced, thus wearing down the Earth's systems. Might it be wise to scale back our annual take to help the overworked systems rebound? We can either err on the side of caution or gamble with our children's future.

(Endnotes)

1 Almedingen, E.M., *St. Francis of Assisi: A Great Life in Brief* (New York: A.A. Knopf, 1967).

2 Report from the Frontier. *The State of the World's Indigenous Peoples* (1987).

3 Vitousek, Peter M., Harold A. Mooney, Jane Lubchenco, and Jerry M. Melillo, 'Human Domination of Earth's Ecosystems.' *Science* 277 (1997), pp. 494–499.

4 Wacker, Mathis, et al, *Tracking the Ecological Overshoot of the Human Economy.*

5 Personal communication.

6 Pimm, Stuart L., *The World According to Pimm: A Scientist Audits the Earth* (New York: McGraw Hill Professional, 2001).

7 Noss, Reed F., 'The Wildlands Project: Land Conservation Strategy,' *Wild Earth*, Special Issue (1993), pp. 10–21.

8 Thomas, C.D. 'What do real population dynamics tell us about minimum viable population sizes?' *Conservation Biology* 4 (1990), pp. 324–327.

9 Brocke, Rainer H., Kent A. Gustafson and Andrew R. Major, 'Restoration on the Lynx in New York: Biopolitical lessons,' from *Transactions of the North American Wildlife and Natural Resources Conference* (1990).

10 Noss, Reed F., and Allen Cooperrider, *Saving Nature's Legacy: Protecting and Restoring Biodiversity* (Washington, D.C.: Island Press, 1994).

11 Thornton, Russell, *American Indian Holocaust and Survival: A Population History Since 1492* (Norman: University of Oklahoma Press, 1987).

12 Robbins, Richard, *Cultural Anthropology: A Problem-Based Approach* (Itasca: F.E. Peacock Publishers, 1997).

13 Zinn, Howard, *A Peoples History of the United States* (New York: Harper Collins Publishers, 1980).

14 United Nations Development Program. *Human Development Report* (New York: Oxford University Press, 1992, 1994).

Purchasing-power parity (PPP) is a method of measuring relative purchasing power of different countries' currencies over similar goods and services. When the World Bank applies this curve to the data, the poor look three times richer, while the rich look slightly poorer. The application of PPP brings several billion people above the $1/day poverty line, an inaccurate reflection of 'wealth.' Low income countries cannot afford to be wasteful and are able to produce cheaper goods and services; high income countries *could* provide far less costly goods and services if incomes were lower and less energy and resources were embodied in their products. The Atlas method (which yields the 250 to 1 disparity) is a comparison of GNP per capita which approximates income (in US dollars). This is how much money you would find in a person's pockets and bank accounts. To reduce errors due to drastically fluctuating currencies, the average exchange rate is taken for that year and the two preceding years.

15 World Bank, *2000 World Development Indicators CD-ROM* (Washington, DC: World Bank, 2000).

16 World Bank, *2000 World Development Indicators CD-ROM* (Washington, DC: World Bank, 2000).

17 Gray, Charles, *Towards a Nonviolent Economics* (Eugene: Self-published, 1994).

18 New Road Map Foundation, *All Consuming Passion: Waking up from the American Dream* (Seattle: New Road Map Foundation, 1998. In partnership with Northwest Environmental Watch.)

19 Gray, Charles, *Towards a Nonviolent Economics* (Eugene: Self-published, 1994).

20 World Bank, *2000 World Development Indicators CD-ROM* (Washington, DC: World Bank, 2000).

21 McKibbon, Bill, *Maybe One: An Environmental and Personal Argument for Single-child Families* (New York: Simon & Schuster, 1998).

Chapter Thirteen

THE DOWNSHIFTERS

Clive Hamilton and Richard Denniss

> In the last ten years have you *voluntarily* made a long-term change in your lifestyle, other than planned retirement, which has resulted in you earning less money? For example, have you voluntarily changed to a lower paying job, reduced your work hours, or quit work to study or stay at home?
>
> – Question from Newspoll survey of downshifting

When ABC Television launched *SeaChange* in 1999 it had no idea how popular the program would become. The program appears to have captured and reflected a shared dream of city dwellers – to leave the rat race and live a slower, simpler life in which relationships and personal satisfaction take priority over material and career success.

Downshifters are people who have made a conscious decision to accept a lower income and a lower level of consumption in order to pursue other life goals. They are motivated by a desire for more balance in their lives, more personal fulfilment and more time with their families. Some qualify as 'real estate refugees', driven out of the cities by rising house prices and the pressure to work longer and harder to repay onerous mortgages. Many do not even move house; they just change the way they live their lives.

Before downshifting, there was a long history of 'voluntary simplicity', perhaps best represented in Australia by the communities in and around Nimbin in northern New South Wales. Downshifters are sometimes caricatured as new-age dreamers – hippies, greenies and vegans who have opted out. If this were ever a true picture of downshifters, it is certainly false now. For a start, there are just too many of them. At a time when market ideology and consumerism appear to have a more powerful grip than ever before, the decision to swim against the tide seems to have become a mainstream one. We are much more likely to find a downshifter living quietly next door than in a combi van.

Who are They?

In 2002 a nationwide survey found that 23 percent of adults in their 30s, 40s or 50s had downshifted during the preceding ten years:[1] that is nearly a quarter of Australians in that age range. Given the pressure to define success in terms of increasing incomes and displays of consumer goods, it is astonishing to find that such a large proportion of the population has rejected the materialist preoccupations of Australian society and chosen to emphasise other, non-material aspects of life.

The survey found that downshifters are about equally likely to be in their 30s, 40s or 50s, that men are a little more likely to downshift than women, and that households with children are just as likely to downshift as those without. Proportionally, there are more downshifters living in the cities than outside of them, although the difference is not great. This is interesting: the pressures of city living could be expected to result more often in a decision to downshift. Some downshifters, the sea-changers, do move out of the cities as a consequence of these stresses but not in numbers sufficient to exceed those who remain.

It is widely believed that the downshifting phenomenon is confined to the affluent middle class, either because they have a large enough asset base to be able to take the risk or because they are more likely to hold 'post-materialist' values. But the evidence shows this not to be the case. Downshifters are not confined to wealthy and middle-income households, and there is no appreciable difference in the prevalence of downshifting among white- and blue-collar workers. The household incomes recorded in the studies are, however, those reported by respondents after their change in lifestyle, and it is reasonable to assume the incomes had fallen as a result of the change. While the drop in income ranges from 10 percent to 100 percent, on average downshifters in Britain report a 40 percent drop;[2] the figure is probably similar in Australia.

There are four main methods of downshifting: 29 percent choose to reduce their working hours; 23 percent change to a lower paying job; 19 percent stop work; and 19 percent change careers. Why do downshifters make the change? More than a third of them say they have done so mainly because they want to spend more time with their families – an intention supported by other studies, which show that a large majority of Australians say that, instead of more income, more time with family and less stress would make them happier. The next most important motive is a healthier lifestyle (23 percent), followed by a desire for more personal fulfilment (16 percent) and a more balanced lifestyle (16 percent). The importance of a healthier lifestyle is consistent with anecdotal evidence that serious health scares, such as a heart attack or a cancer diagnosis, sometimes lead to radical life changes.

Few downshifters appear to be motivated primarily by post-materialist values: only 12 percent nominated 'a less materialistic' or 'a more environmentally friendly' lifestyle as their main reason. However, the decision to downshift usually involves a complex mix of reasons, including personal motives and matters of principle. Women are more likely to nominate more time with family and a more balanced approach to life, while men are more likely to mention a healthier lifestyle as their main reason. All income groups emphasise more time with family, although high-income downshifters are much more likely to stress personal fulfilment and those on low incomes a healthier lifestyle.

Their Stories

The statistics tell us about the extent of downshifting and some of the broad motivations, but they do not give us a feel for what the experience is really like. A more recent study examined the phenomenon through detailed interviews with twenty downshifters and discussions with three focus groups made up of some people who had downshifted and some who had not.[3]

Every downshifter's story is different, but some themes do emerge. When asked about the circumstances in their lives that led to their decision, the downshifters emphasise four main reasons: the desire to have a more balanced life; a clash between personal values and the values of their workplaces; a quest for personal fulfilment; and health concerns. Typically, they make the decision for a combination of these reasons, and for most it was a considered and gradual process.

Several factors do, however, operate to make the decision to change more difficult. Many people are preoccupied with providing for their children, giving them a head start in life in ways that can be expensive. This factor can work at a subtle level – for example, when parents want their children to be able to match their peers in living standards and access to 'stuff'. But more obvious factors also come into play. Many parents feel obliged to work long and hard in order to afford private schooling and to put their children through university without a HECS debt at the end. In some cases, shared responsibility for children from previous relationships acts as a constraint. One couple talked of the cost of maintaining three families (both had been married before) and the consequent pressure to work harder. 'My assets have been divided twice due to separation,' said the male partner. Their combined income would put them in the top 10 percent of Australian households.

The sense of responsibility to children, and sometimes to other family members, is often enough to cause potential downshifters to decide against it. Some who have not made the change describe downshifting as 'selfish'. For them, the decision is seen as one taken for one's own sake, to give oneself an easier life. But downshifters with children never see it in these terms: they see themselves as giving more to their families but measure the gift in terms of time and affection rather than money. As one downshifter said, 'A BMW won't give you a hug or draw you a picture.'

One of the dominant themes to emerge in connection with the decision not to downshift is the heightened level of financial insecurity felt by many people (especially those in their 40s and 50s), often related to perceptions about retirement. This is curious when one considers that Australians are richer than they have ever been and that we have had over a decade of sustained economic growth. When asked why they do not downshift, many people nominate 'fear' or 'anxiety.' Some admit they could downshift if they wanted to but that the prospect of such a change is too scary. As this suggests, people who do make the break frequently have to be courageous, which explains why the change often comes only after some years of deliberation and can be precipitated by a sudden, unpleasant change in circumstances, such as a new boss, ill health or a business in difficulty.

Seeking Balance

Many downshifters cite as their principal motive the difficulty of constantly juggling life's competing demands and the stresses this generates in their personal lives. Some speak of the relentless pressure to 'get it all done,' which is invariably associated with combining work and family roles. The wish to spend more time with children is another strong motive. Paul, a 44-year-old, worked long hours in television in Sydney and was often overseas for weeks at a time. When his first child was born he realized his job was incompatible with his desire to spend at least some time with his family:

> With the birth of our first child I realized there was much more to life than just working non-stop. But the job demanded being available 24 hours a day, seven days a week... I could see colleagues' marriages breaking up. I didn't want this to be me. So I made the decision not to apply for positions like these again.

Fifty-year-old Leah asked for more flexible hours at the art gallery where she worked as a curator, so that she could care for her two young children. She was refused:

> Their so-called family-friendly approach was illustrated when I had to bring my children in to a staff meeting called unexpectedly, only to be told children were not allowed in the staff room. So after eighteen years of working there I'd had enough.

While some downshifters equate a more balanced life with being able to spend more time with their families, others want more time to pursue personal interests or just to slow down and live less frenetically. For Zelda, living in a more measured way entailed leaving Sydney for a town near the north coast of New South Wales:

> It took me about six months to wind down and slow down. Now we live life more slowly; there is time to make things, grow things and savor things. It was absolutely the right decision not just because there's more time for things and each other. Luke and I would never have been able to afford a house in Sydney and didn't really want our children to grow up in such a rushed and materialistic environment.

When 35-year-old Damien changed from working long hours in the corporate sector to a job in the charity sector he was seeking more balance: 'I have time to pursue things that I believe in and that I'm passionate about as part of my day-to-day job, as opposed to being something that I had to squeeze in as part of my work life in the corporate sector, when there was never any time.'

A Clash of Values

Another important motive for downshifting is the clash between the personal values of the downshifter and those of their workplace. Changes in workplace culture and management practices, and the intensification of work in recent years, are at the heart of many decisions to change. Downsizing, outsourcing, longer work hours and the faster pace of work have all put more pressure on people and contributed to a lower quality of life. One refugee from big business observed, 'I see the corporate world as carnivorous. The pecking order is unhealthy and quite savage. I found it morally bankrupt.' Another said he got out because 'the moral structure of the business was wrong'. Other people said they could no longer tolerate the incessant demands to 'do the deals', 'bring in the business' and increase 'billable hours'. And another said, 'It is easy to lose consciousness of decisions, to lose the ability to choose. You become complicit in the culture.'

This feeling of loss of control over one's life is a theme that consistently emerges with downshifters. The more people feel they have lost control, and the more serious the personal and moral consequences, the more likely they are to move into radically different kinds of jobs – in areas such as the helping professions, the environment and charities. David, aged 59, worked in Sydney as a senior manager for a multinational corporation for many years until he downshifted at the end of 2000. He explained the circumstances of his working life at the time and the clash between his personal values and those of the corporation:

> The company was going through a horror stretch which they described as restructuring or 'right sizing,' but this actually meant massive job losses. It was not a pleasant place to be, especially as I had a key role in the process of getting rid of people. But on a personal level, I was sick of the hours (at least 12 hours a day), sick of the traffic and especially turned off by the new culture and values of the company. They brought in the 'head-kickers' from overseas.

Twenty-seven-year-old Alistair worked in a leading law firm for a number of years but left for a very different job in the non-government sector in a developing country:

> I always knew it wasn't me, not my values... You see all those people who get to the top and you're turned off. When it comes down to it, it's a business, all about you billing the client and earning money, recording every six minutes and making money for the firm. This concept is inimical to my nature.

Others just realize they are in the wrong profession: 'I remember it was at my boss's retirement party when I was just about to turn 30 and he had turned 60. I remember looking at him and thinking, "My God, I can't do this for another 30 years." The things that I was feeling – the stress, the discontentment, the disgruntlement – he was still feeling at 60.'

Affluenza induces people to put their own financial interests above everything else, and that often means moral doubts are pushed aside. For downshifters, these doubts gnaw away at them, perhaps for years, before they decide they are not willing to sell their soul any more.

Seeking Contentment

Another theme in the downshifters' narrative is the desire to make a change for what might be called existential reasons. They seek some form of inner contentment or, as one downshifter put it, 'I wanted congruence between what I do in the world and what I am in myself.' Invariably, the decision-making process is gradual and characterized by a great deal of reflection about why they feel unfulfilled in both their working and their personal lives. The journey is often difficult, sometimes causing disappointment among family members, but in each case these downshifters have found a way of living that brings greater self-acceptance and psychological wellbeing.

Franco thought a lot about the failure of material possessions to bring him any sense of fulfilment:

> Once, when I was negotiating with my boss about work, I realized I didn't want more money to motivate me. I was looking for more challenges, more responsibility, a certain type of work, and I was more than willing to sacrifice money for it. I worked this way for quite a few years and felt much better. I wasn't interested in the power politics and the money-making parts of work.

Another, a 59-year-old senior public servant, felt dissatisfied for many years in both his work and his personal life. After much searching, questioning and reflection he concluded, 'I no longer wanted to live in the milieu of high income, high expenditure, owning all sorts of things; of getting up in the morning to load yourself with the electronics and technology and getting out there and networking for whatever purpose... and the long hours.' So he quit.

Health

Many downshifters nominate health as the factor that stimulated them to make the change. In some cases it is an accumulation of stress over time. One person described the effect of long hours and pressure: 'I was losing weight, my hair was falling out, I wasn't sleeping. It was getting to the stage where it was really affecting my health and I knew I had to do something, that something had to change.' For other people, it was a case of their health suddenly breaking down. Forty-six-year-old Andrea, who ran an IT consultancy with her husband, lived a life dominated by work as 'contract after contract rolled in.' There was little time for leisure, relaxation or personal reflection. 'I dressed up in the corporate suits, went in there pretty aggressively, got the work done.' After eight years of living and working this way, Andrea suffered a breakdown: 'There were many things that caused it. Work was getting more and more stressful, but an argument with my step-daughter threw me over the edge. I had to have treatment, somehow managed to finish the current contract and then we left for a holiday.'

Fiona also experienced exhaustion and anxiety after years of supporting her partner in his own business. At the end of 2002 they decided to close down the business because they both felt they desperately needed a change: 'I felt an absolute stressed out mess, as if I'd lost my whole personality and self completely ... We both wanted to do something different. Bruce wanted to work fewer hours and have less work stress. We'd paid off our house, our kids were grown up, so we felt we were in a position to live on less.'

How Does Life Change?

People who choose to downshift usually stress that they are not dropping out of society. As one of them explained, 'We are actually creating something new, not getting out'. A change in patterns of consumption is an important step in the downshifting process. After assessing how much they consume and how much they actually need, people find it easier to change their work and consumption patterns. When asked what they do without, the downshifters' responses are remarkably uniform. All said they eat out less often and, when they do, they choose less expensive restaurants. Indeed, food features prominently in many discussions of new lifestyles. Most downshifters say they spend more time cooking and enjoy doing so. Many say they are much more careful about the food they buy, and some take pleasure in growing their own vegetables. This is partly motivated by tighter budgets, but it also reflects a new emphasis on healthy eating.

Almost all downshifters give up expensive holidays, including holidays abroad. None of those interviewed expressed regret about this; some said they just take cheaper holiday options in Australia.

On the other hand, some younger downshifters take the opportunity to use some of their new-found time to travel, especially to developing countries to experience life as it is lived by others.

Surprisingly, another frequently mentioned type of forgone consumption is spending on clothes needed for work – the corporate uniforms that are no longer needed. Downshifters often gleefully talk of discarding their suits: such clothing seems to symbolise the life they left behind.

Andrea, whose income fell dramatically after she and her husband wound up their business, summed up many of these changes: 'We feel better, we grow our own vegies, we cook more. I no longer spend $1000 on each corporate outfit. We have fewer restaurant meals now, make our own beer, don't go on overseas trips anymore. We have a better, healthier lifestyle.'

In addition to doing without these items of expenditure, many downshifters take a completely different approach to spending. Although much less preoccupied with money, they are nevertheless more careful about how they dispose of what they have. One described himself and his partner as 'aware buyers' who are rarely tempted to buy things they don't need. Others avoid shopping centres whenever possible and are not tempted to spend their leisure time window shopping or engaged in retail therapy. Some adopt a conscious strategy of avoiding exposure to affluenza sufferers; others make it clear that they will control their money rather than having it control them. They become 'conscious consumers,' rather than impulse buyers, and so put themselves beyond the reach of the marketers.

Downshifters with children often talk about how their offspring adjust to lower household incomes. Some seem to 'protect' their children from the changes, either by keeping up spending on items specific to the children or by postponing the decision to downshift until the children are well into their teens. Others say there is more discretion than is commonly believed:

> We basically set about minimizing our expenditure, and that wasn't that hard with kids. Strangely enough everyone thinks it costs a fortune... All of our friends were going to private hospitals and had private health insurance... I didn't think there was anything wrong with the public system and we had our first baby at the local public hospital.

He walks his children to school each day, avoiding travel expenses and spending that extra time with them.

Some downshifters adjust to their new financial circumstances quickly, but others have difficulty. For most, the dominant change in their lives involves taking control of their time and devoting it to more satisfying activities. This often means more time with partners and children, particularly when children are young. Many report that they spend much more time outdoors engaged in physical activity. Comments about how much healthier they feel are common; they see themselves as fitter and more invigorated. Some say the life change precipitated an instant lifting of mood and a new approach to life. Leah said she felt an enormous sense of relaxation once she downshifted: 'A lot of bullshit just disappeared. It was like being in another world, and I couldn't understand how I had been in that environment for so long. I suddenly had a clear view.'

Another downshifter who at 30 left a promising career in a big law firm to become a photographer, urged caution: 'I think it's important to make the point that downshifting is not "a one size fits all" solution.'

How Others React

Public attitudes to people who decide to make radical life changes in pursuit of greater contentment are mixed. The difference between downshifters' motives and the reactions of some of those around them reflects the fundamental feature of the downshifting phenomenon – a change in personal values, such that financial and material success is no longer the dominant motive. This spills over into everyday reactions. A young mother from Gosford told of how her friends are 'amazed' when they discover she does not own a microwave oven. There is a powerful, indeed overwhelming, assumption that everyone is committed to acquiring the best material lifestyle they reasonably can. It's just how life in Australia is, and bemusement and expressions of derision are typical responses to downshifters' decisions to flout this convention.

The spread of affluenza and market values reflects and reinforces a broader social movement towards individualism. Political leaders have promised more 'choice' and say they want to transfer responsibility from government to individuals. But it seems that only particular forms of individuality are acceptable, so that people who make the choice to reject the dominance of market values are characterized as irresponsible.

Most downshifters say the reactions of their friends and family are diverse; a few say they have received nothing but support. Many report that their friends and family are shocked when they make the change and that they are often told they must be 'nuts.' At the same time, almost all downshifters note that many of their friends and colleagues have expressed curiosity and envy. Alastair said, 'The week before I left the law firm I had a stream of people coming into the office, closing the door and going "OK, tell me how you did it? What websites did you visit, who do I call?"' Paul, who now runs his own outdoors business, said, 'A lot of my friends and colleagues have been very jealous... Everyone keeps saying "You're so lucky", they just keep saying "Don't come back".'

Negative reactions can be intensified by cultural expectations. In her early 30s, Sasha abandoned her career as a medical professional to become a counsellor. She had to withstand intense criticism from her parents, who had grown up on the Indian subcontinent and were plagued by an acute form of deferred happiness syndrome: 'They thought I was just weak and running away from my problems... Their attitude was: "Well you're not supposed to be happy. Work is work, and it pays the rent. You have all these nice things. What's wrong with you? What more do you want?"'

One consistent observation is that the decision to change causes downshifters to sort out their true friends from the ones who don't really matter to them. As Andrea said, 'I think the changes we've made to our lives have really shown who our friends are. The people who we now look on as acquaintances think we're mad, but our real friends have said "Good on you." It's been very interesting to see who in the community has been supportive.'

Downshifters often move into a new social environment. They drift away from some of their friends and work colleagues because their lives are now different and because the decision to downshift can uncover some underlying value conflicts: 'My friends changed a lot, as they no longer had the same values as me,' said one. Sometimes they also find it difficult to explain to relatives and friends what they are doing and why. This is partly because until recently in Australia downshifters have felt that their decisions were made in isolation. One said it took a long time to explain her decision to her siblings, partly because the term 'downshifting' was not used at the time.

Studies have identified a loss of status as something many downshifters must confront, particularly downshifters who make dramatic changes to their lives. Many seem to have prepared themselves for this loss of status:

after all, one of the obstacles to making the decision is the fear of losing standing among one's peers and the community, and income and associated lifestyle are perhaps the most important markers of status. Andrea summed up the feelings of some about their loss of status:

> Only in the eyes of people who don't matter. There are certainly people who now look down their noses at us, but in terms of our real friends and ourselves quite the opposite. I think we've actually gained a lot of respect from people who'd love to do the same thing but haven't got the guts. Certainly in our eyes we're prouder of ourselves because we've done what we really wanted to do, not kowtowed to society.

Difficulties and Delights

The nationwide survey of downshifters found that nearly 90 percent are happy with the change in their lifestyle, although 38 percent said they miss the extra income and 17 percent admitted that, despite being happy with the change, they have found losing the income very tough.

When asked about the difficulties they experienced as a result of downshifting, respondents usually mentioned financial concerns first. Some said they worry at times about whether they will be able to provide for their retirement. For many downshifters, at least among those who make more extensive changes, there is an early period of adjustment. Some miss the ability to indulge in certain forms of 'luxury' spending – such as, in one case, being able to buy presents for friends – or to have the occasional 'splurge.' In other words, the spontaneity that having plenty of money permits is replaced by financial discipline. Downshifters change the way they think about household finances. Andrea put it this way: 'The only real difficulty is when bills come in and you think, "How am I going to juggle this one?" I wouldn't actually say it was a difficulty, rather something that has to be managed. It's become easier and easier as I've become better at it.'

Most downshifters find they have to be more careful with their spending, to plan more effectively, and to be more disciplined in that aspect of their lives. One can say, though, that the anxiety they feel about a substantial reduction in income is remarkably mild considering the importance society attaches to financial security. Downshifting is characterized by a psychological transformation, in which money and material things are relegated to a much diminished position on the list of life's priorities. In other words, adopting a different relationship to money is an essential part of the 'contract' downshifters have with themselves.

Other changes present challenges, too. Many downshifters find instant liberation, but for some casting off an entrenched work ethic and adjusting to a different pattern of daily life is a challenge:

> Perhaps the only difficulty has been stopping the sense of guilt, because when we made the change we both felt huge guilt about sitting and having a cup of coffee at 10.30 in the morning... Allowing yourself to be who you really are took a lot of doing, shedding all that indoctrination and the social expectations, that was probably the toughest.

When asked to reflect on the benefits of the change, downshifters stress the relief and the new sense of personal freedom. Some talk of rediscovering the 'joy of living'. Fiona described the experience as 'exciting rather than frightening' and, although she sometimes feels exhausted, most of the time she feels 'exhilarated.' 'The sense of relief has just got better and better,' said another. And another simply said, 'I don't have to wear ties anymore.'

Many return to the theme of taking control of their lives, of being able to make real life choices. 'We now live by choice. What time will we get up? What shall we do today? We're not driven by external events,' said Andrea. For Paul, 'It's a more relaxed lifestyle, less stressful. In many ways, you're in charge of your own destiny.' Being in control of one's destiny is what the advertisements try to sell, but the 'choices' promised by the market are very limited. The weight of affluenza works against us making genuine choices about how we live our lives. Choosing between 49 different brands of olive oil is trivial. Downshifters often say the change has opened up their lives to opportunities that would previously have been closed off to them. A few find the responsibility that goes with the freedom difficult to cope with, although if this sense is too strong it seems to deter people from heading down the downshifting path in the first place.

Most talk of the slower pace of life: 'People don't have time to chat anymore, and we used to be like that too. But our whole pace of life has slowed down. I even drive more slowly now. I don't know how I ever had time to work. Now I can listen to the birds, smell the roses.' For others, the slower pace makes life less stimulating, although the time freed up can be devoted to creative and healthy pursuits such as sculpture, whale watching and bushwalking. A high proportion mention musical pursuits.

When the downshifters are asked if they have any regrets, there is a chorus of 'no' – except for a few who regret not doing it earlier. Downshifters talk of contentment, freedom and 'bliss.' A few say they sometimes worry about whether they will have enough savings in retirement. Some say they would recommend downshifting unreservedly, but most believe it is not for everyone. One cautioned people not to be 'under the illusion that the whole downshifting experience is euphoric.' Perhaps the last word on this should be left to Andrea: 'Anyone contemplating the change should be really honest with themselves. If people can't admit to themselves what they really want, and be absolutely honest, don't even attempt it.'

Retirement Anxiety

When Australians talk about their hopes and fears, it is apparent that for many of them, especially those in their 40s and 50s, their life plans and objectives are dominated by the prospect of retirement. They constantly return to this theme – a sign of how anxious they feel about their ability to provide for a comfortable retirement at a time when government has made it clear that people can no longer rely on the pension to meet their needs. Expectations about the amount of income needed in retirement appear to have escalated considerably, and these self-imposed benchmarks put people under great pressure. At the same time there has been a change in perceptions of retirement where baby boomers in the professions and in managerial positions are concerned. They see no clear division between their working and post-working lives and think they will be able to wind down gradually and may never retire fully. Indeed, some see the idea of working hard to save for retirement then stopping work to enjoy the fruits of their labour as pathological. As one put it, 'If you see retirement as the end then you are doing the wrong thing.'

There is a marked difference in attitudes to retirement among people who have downshifted and people who have not. It is a difference that encapsulates the psychological shift that the life change represents. Those who would not consider downshifting, or who have considered it but lack the resolve, are often preoccupied with saving for retirement to an almost obsessive degree: as one woman in her 50s said of her husband, 'He's even made a down payment on his old-person's scooter'. For people who have downshifted, though, these worries seem to become less pressing. Questions about the insecurity of retirement generate animated responses from those who have not made the change but are often met with puzzlement or unconcern by those who have. In the words of one downshifter in his 40s, 'When I worked for [a major company] I was maniacally fixated on my superannuation account. Since resigning I no longer think about it.'

There appear to be two reasons for the new attitude. The first is that concern about financial futures is inescapable in a society preoccupied with money, but downshifting involves demoting the world of material possessions and financial security so that mental energy is directed elsewhere. It is impossible to live in the present if you are obsessed with money. The second reason is that downshifters have proven themselves more willing to take risks. Many seem to be confident that things will turn out fine, instead of building walls of security around themselves – walls that they believe might be breached in any case. Perhaps a third reason can be drawn from this: in contrast with the linear path of career progress in a chosen area, downshifters generally see their lives evolving in more fluid ways, with change and unpredictability being part of their experience.

These stories provide an insight into what it means to cure oneself of affluenza. It is not always easy, and it affects all aspects of life – relationships with family and friends, attitudes to status, the approach to daily life, planning for the future and, of course, finances. It is made more difficult because it feels like an isolated act. One of the biggest questions for the future of Australia is whether the thousands of individual acts of downshifting, in which the values and goals of the market are rejected, can be turned into a political movement that challenges consumer society at its core.

Deferrers, Gratifiers, Downshifters

Most Australians fall into one of three groups: deferrers, who know their overwork is damaging their relationships but hope to make up for it later on; gratifiers, who, in the pursuit of instant satisfaction want to spend as much as they can now and are willing to borrow to get it; and downshifters. The underlying motivation of deferrers and gratifiers is the same. Gratifiers want the money and what it buys now and accumulate financial debts as a result. Deferrers want the money and the life it buys later and accumulate relationship debts as a result. Both risk bankruptcy, the difference being that in one case the bailiffs come to the front door and in the other your partner might leave through it.

Downshifters, in contrast, break the imagined link between money and happiness. While deferrers 'postpone the day' until they accumulate the resources they believe they will need to live happily, downshifters 'seize the day' in order to pursue a more fulfilling life. The deferrers tend to be motivated primarily by financial security; the downshifters place less emphasis on money and more on their relationships, their health and a sense of personal contentment. Downshifters sacrifice money for time; deferrers sacrifice time for money; and gratifiers sacrifice money later for money now.

There are roughly equal numbers of deferrers and downshifters in Australia. As noted, almost a quarter of adults aged 30 to 60 years are downshifters, while 30 percent of full-time workers have been identified as deferrers. It is not clear how many might fit into the category of gratifiers. What is clear, though, is that deferrers, gratifiers and downshifters are not concentrated in any socioeconomic group, family type or geographical area; each group comes from across the community.

Although downshifters can be thought of as people who have decided to effect a recovery from deferred happiness syndrome, it would be wrong to think that deferrers are no more than downshifters in preparation. For the most part, downshifters are not people who can 'afford to take the risk' because they have accumulated extensive assets. Risk aversion is actually a characteristic of deferrers, and it takes courage to make the leap to downshifting. So, while some deferrers might reach a point where they decide to take the risk and seize the day, many, perhaps most, will continue to defer until retirement. There is anecdotal evidence that for a substantial number of people the dream of a happy life deferred until retirement is in fact never realized.

People who choose to reject the dominance of money in their own lives are often characterized as selfish, foolish or reckless. This attitude is held by many who, while recognizing today's intense pressures, think people should be stoical and put up with the stresses for the sake of others. It is hard to avoid the conclusion, however, that much of this hostility betrays a dog-in-the-manger attitude: 'If I am stuck in a life of worries, stresses and overwork, everyone else should be too.' Growing numbers of Australians are deciding they will no longer allow such a view to determine their lives.

(Endnotes)

1 See Clive Hamilton and Elizabeth Mail, *Downshifting in Australia: a sea-change in the pursuit of happiness*, Discussion paper no. 50, The Australia Institute, Canberra, 2003. Those who 'downshifted' by refusing a promotion, stopping work to start their own businesses, going back to study or stopping work to look after a baby were excluded because their motives are unclear.

2 Clive Hamilton, *Downshifting in Britain: a sea-change in the pursuit of happiness*, Discussion paper no. 58, The Australia Institute, Canberra, 2003.

3 C. Breakspear and C. Hamilton, op. cit. The names of the people interviewed have been changed to protect their privacy.

Chapter Fourteen

A CULTURE OF PERMANENCE

Alan Durning

When Moses came down from Mount Sinai, he could count the rules of ethical behavior on the fingers of his two hands. In today's complex global economy, in which the simple act of starting an automobile engine imperceptibly changes the global climate, the rules for ecologically sound living run into the hundreds. But the basic value of a sustainable society, the ecological equivalent of the Golden Rule, is simple: each generation should meet its needs without jeopardizing the prospects for future generations to meet their own needs.[1]

Put into practice, that elementary-sounding principle translates into radical changes. It implies, for example, that we consumers have an ethical obligation to curb our consumption, since it jeopardizes the chances for future generations. Unless we climb down the consumption ladder a few rungs, our grandchildren will inherit a planetary home impoverished by our affluence – a planet whose climate has been drastically altered in mere decades, whose air and water are poisoned, whose fertile soils are worn down, whose living species are decimated in number, and whose wild habitats are shrunken and fragmentary.

Furthermore, unless we lower our consumption we will have no authority to object to the world's present middle-income and poor classes despoiling the earth. A recent cartoon captured the absurdity of the profligate preaching conservation to the poor: the driver of a luxury car idles his gas-guzzling motor and yells to a hungry peasant who is preparing to fell a tree, 'Yo! Amigo!! We need that tree to protect us from the greenhouse effect!'[2]

Ultimately, the linked fates of humanity and the natural realm depend on us, the consumers. We can curtail our use of those things that are ecologically destructive, such as fossil fuels, minerals, and paper. And we can cultivate the deeper, nonmaterial sources of fulfillment that are the main psychological determinants of happiness: family and social relationships, meaningful work, and leisure. Or we can abrogate our responsibilities and let our life-style ruin the earth.

Lowering our consumption need not deprive us of goods and services that really matter. To the contrary, life's most meaningful and pleasant activities are often paragons of environmental virtue. The preponderance of things that people name as their most rewarding pastimes – and, interestingly, the things terminally ill individuals choose to do with their remaining months – are infinitely sustainable. Religious practice, conversation, family and community gatherings, theater, music, dance, literature, sports, poetry, artistic and creative pursuits, education, and appreciation of nature all fit readily into a culture of permanence – a way of life that can endure through countless generations.[3]

The first step of reform is uncomplicated. It is to inform consumers of the damage we are causing and how we can avoid it. New values never arrive in the abstract. They come entangled in concrete situations, new realities, and new understandings of the world. Indeed, ethics exist only in practice, in the fine grain of everyday decisions. As Aristotle argued, 'In ethics, the decision lies with perception.' When most people see a large automobile and think first of the air pollution it causes rather than the social status it conveys, environmental ethics will have arrived. Likewise, when most people see excess packaging, throwaway products, or a new shopping mall and grow angry because they consider them to be crimes against their grandchildren, consumerism will be on the retreat.[4]

Sidney Quarrier, the Connecticut geographer who spent Earth Day 1990 auditing his consumption, demonstrates how information can spur change. Sid still lives far from his job, but he takes the bus to work. Now that his children have grown up and left home, he lives in a smaller house, which he has insulated and weatherized to exceptional levels of energy efficiency. He recycles meticulously, writes letters on the back of scrap paper, and conserves water wherever he can. Sid still wonders 'Will the world survive us?' and worries about the driving he does to pursue his passion for photography, but he has become an example to those around him that the culture of permanence can be built one household at a time.[5]

Informing the consumer class is a mammoth task, and in a sense is the overarching goal of most environmental organizations. Since 1989, it has vaulted ahead as literally dozens of authors, publishers, editors, and video producers have brought out guides to personal action for the earth. These volumes, packed with detailed suggestions, have spread quickly. *50 Simple Things You Can Do to Save the Earth* has sold 3.5 million copies in the United States and *The Green Consumer* was a best seller in the United Kingdom. Sometimes criticized for personalizing systemic problems, these guides nonetheless provide information most members of the consumer society had previously lacked about practical ways to slow the waste of the earth.[6]

Personal efforts to live more gently on the earth reach their logical conclusion in the quest for simpler living more generally. The attempt to live by nonmaterialistic definitions of success is not new, of course. Researcher Duane Elgin estimated in 1981 – perhaps optimistically – that 10 million adult Americans were experimenting 'wholeheartedly' with voluntary simplicity. Germany, India, the Netherlands, Norway, the United Kingdom, and many other nations all have small segments of their populations who try to adhere to a non-consuming philosophy.[7]

For these practitioners, the goal is not ascetic self-denial, but a sort of unadorned grace. Some come to feel, for example, that clotheslines, window shades, and bicycles have a functional elegance that clothes dryers, air conditioners, and automobiles lack. These modest devices are silent, manually operated, fire-proof, ozone and climate-friendly, easily repaired, and inexpensive. Because they are less 'convenient,' they breed a degree of forethought and attention to the weather that grounds life in place and time. Karen Christensen, author of *Home Ecology*, emphasizes that living simply need not be drab or tedious: 'Instead of consuming things we should cherish and value them. Instead of accepting the sobriquet "consumer," we should become not only conservers but creators.'[8]

The closest thing to an organized campaign for voluntary simplicity was started by Joe Dominguez, who made a fortune on Wall Street before realizing that getting rich was not making him one whit happier. Today, he lives contentedly on about $500 a month (which, interestingly, puts him in the earnings range of the global middle-income class), and runs the New Road Map Foundation of Seattle, Washington, which he started to disseminate the course he developed on what money can and cannot do. These seminars have helped tens of thousands of people stop fixating on money and start finding out what really makes them happy. They then draw themselves 'new road maps' for the future based on their core values. These plans typically reduce graduates' annual spending by 20 percent almost immediately, and allow them to live eventually on much less than they ever thought possible. Many 'retire' from earning an income in a matter of years, and dedicate themselves to developing their talents and struggling for causes they hold dear.[9]

Most of the people who come to low consumption, of course, find their way there on their own, not through anything like New Road Map courses. However they get there, enjoying time instead of 'spending' it seems central to their values. In 1986, Wanda Urbanska and Frank Levering left their high-paced jobs as journalists and screenwriters in southern California to run the Levering family orchard in rural Virginia. 'For us,' they write, 'simple living has come to mean spending more time attending to our lives and less time attending to our work; devoting less time to earning more money and more time to the daily doings of life.' They live more deliberately, less hurriedly. '"Time out," we've declared. Time out to write letters. Time out to sit on the porch watching the sun go down, enjoying time. Time to visit ... at midmorning or linger with the newspaper after lunch. To cook from scratch, to tend our two wood stoves, to make our beds in the mornings and clean our house on Saturdays.'[10]

Joanne Forman of Taos, New Mexico, agrees that tune is too precious to fritter away on rote consumption: 'I am one of those who voluntarily lives simply, not because I'm so virtuous, but because I am a composer and writer, and it comes with the territory; also I hate housework and am a maniacal reader and hiker. Gradually, I'm having some success with persons like the friend who is making $250 a month car payments, and sighs, "I wish I had time to read." I point out that she is working 50 hours a month – more than a week every month – to pay for her car. This is "convenience"?'[11]

Voluntary simplicity as practiced by Dominguez, by Levering and Urbanska, and by Forman is an ideal. And for most of us in the consumer class, it may be an unattainable one. Our choices are constrained by the social pressures, physical infrastructure, and institutional channels that envelop us. We feel cruel refusing to buy our children toys that their playmates all have. We would immobilize ourselves if we abandoned our cars while still living amidst mass-transit-less, antipedestrian sprawl. We do not have the option of trading extra salary for reduced working hours because our employers do not offer it, and we could not accept it quickly anyway. Mortgage and car payments, insurance premiums, college tuition, utility bills – we spend most of our disposable income on big-ticket items where the monthly outlay is determined for long stretches at a time. Thus a strategy for reducing consumption must focus as much on changing the framework in which people make choices as it does on the choices they make.

The history of Voluntary Simplicity Movements, furthermore, is not encouraging. As David Shi of North Carolina's Davidson College chronicles, the call for a simpler life has been perennial throughout the history of North America, from the Puritans of Massachusetts Bay to the back-to-the-landers of 20 years ago. None of these movements ever gained more than a slim minority of adherents. And while simplicity fads have swept the continent periodically, most have ended in consumption binges that more than made up for past atonement.[12]

Elsewhere, entire nations such as China, Kampuchea, and Vietnam have dedicated themselves to rebuilding human character in a less self-centered mold – sometimes through brutal techniques – but nowhere have they succeeded with more than a token few of their citizens. Most recently, in 1991 Cuba issued bicycles and water buffalo to its workers and farmers in a desperate attempt to survive without Soviet oil or aid. This attempt to impose frugality from on high will likely fare no better than those before it.[13]

On the other hand, potent as the allure of the consumer life-style is, it is not invulnerable. For one thing, consumerism has shallow historical roots. For members of the consumer class, to reject consumerism is not to jettison anything of lasting significance from their cultural inheritance. On the contrary, it is to reaffirm their cultures' most ancient teachings. From a historical perspective, consumerism – not moderation – is the aberrant value system. The consumer life-style is a radical departure from the conserving orientation that human cultures developed over centuries. One way or the other – either because we choose to abandon it, or because it devours its own ecological supports – consumerism is likely to be a short-lived value system as well.

The philosophy of sufficiency, by contrast, is deeply rooted in the human past. Materialism was denounced by all the sages, from Buddha to Muhammad, and every world religion is rife with warnings against the evils of excess. 'These religious founders,' observed historian Arnold Toynbee, 'disagreed with each other in the pictures of what is the nature of the universe, the nature of the spiritual life, the nature of ultimate reality. But they all agreed in their ethical precepts.... They all said with one voice that if we made material wealth our paramount aim, this would lead to disaster.'[14]

The revulsion against materialism is as strong in the teachings of the West, where the consumer society eventually took shape, as it is in the East, characterized as 'other-worldly' in the western imagination. Indeed, the first western philosopher whose words survive to the present, Thales of Miletus, said 26 centuries ago, 'If there is neither excessive wealth nor immoderate poverty in a nation, then justice may be said to prevail.'[15]

Religion or Culture	Teaching and Source
American Indian	'Miserable as we seem in thy eyes, we consider ourselves ... much happier than thou, in this that we are very content with the little that we have.' (Micmac chief)
Buddhist	'Whoever in this world overcomes his selfish cravings, his sorrows fall away from him, like drops of water from a lotus flower.' (*Dhammapada*, 336)
Christian	It is 'easier for a camel to go through the eye of a needle than for a rich man to enter into the kingdom of God.' (*Matthew* 19:23–24)
Confucian	'Excess and deficiency are equally at fault.' (Confucius, XI.15)
Ancient Greek	'Nothing in Excess.' (Inscribed at Oracle of Delphi)
Hindu	'That person who lives completely free from desires, without longing... attains peace.' (*Bhagavad-Gita*, II.71)
Islamic	'Poverty is my pride.' (Muhammad)
Jewish	'Give me neither poverty nor riches.' (*Proverbs* 30:8)
Taoist	'He who knows he has enough is rich.' (*Tao Te Ching*)

SOURCES: Compiled by Worldwatch Institute.

The Bible – especially important because a majority of the world's consumer class is Christian – echoes most of human wisdom when it asks, 'What shall it profit a man if he shall gain the whole world and lose his own soul?' Saint Francis of Assisi, Saint Thomas Aquinas, Saint Augustine, and church leaders through the ages have all held immoderate wealth a sin, and from ancient to Medieval times, monks under their vows of poverty held higher social rank than successful merchants.[16]

Less vaunted sources of wisdom counsel with equal unanimity against the incessant craving for more. In one folk tale from Poland, a fisherman who lives in a hovel by the sea catches a magic fish that grants his humble desire for a cabin and enough to eat. After a week, he is no longer satisfied and returns to the sea to catch the fish again and demand larger quarters, which again are granted. The sequence repeats itself for weeks until he lives in a castle and demands a palace. For his insolence, the fish sends him back to the hovel by the sea. In the same vein, the Roman poet Ovid's tale of the Greek King Midas is told to children throughout the West. Midas was so greedy that he wished he could turn things to gold just by touching them. To his delight, his wish came true, and he proceeded to gild everything in sight. His fate in the end was tragic, though: he killed his own beloved daughter with his magical touch.[17]

Even in the United States, now arguably the most wasteful society in human history, thrift and frugality are the buried touchstones of the national character. None other than Benjamin Franklin wrote, 'Money never made a man happy, yet nor will it. There is nothing in its nature to produce happiness. The more a man has, the more he wants. Instead of filling a vacuum, it makes one.' Only in this century did consuming rather than saving gain acceptance as a way to live. In 1907, economist Simon Nelson Patten was still considered a heretic when he declared, 'The new morality does not consist in saving but in expanding consumption.'[18]

Consumerism's roots may be shallow, and it may therefore be vulnerable, but individual action and voluntary simplicity do not appear capable of uprooting it. What must we do, then, to dig it up? The answer may lie in combining the political and the personal. To rejuvenate the ethic of sufficiency, a critical mass of individuals committed to living by it must emerge. But if they are to succeed, they must balance their efforts to change themselves with a bold agenda to challenge the laws, institutions, and interests that profit from profligacy.

Values, after all, are social creations as much as individual ones, and they effectively restrain and direct our behavior only when they are backed up by the force of social institutions. Propagating lower consumption as an ethical norm ultimately requires that we revive the nonconsuming philosophy that lies dormant in our culture – our collective memory, wisdom, and ways – and use it to mold a new culture of permanence.

A culture of permanence will not come quickly. We can expect no instant revolutions in social values, no moral awakening or 'paradigm shift.' All we can realistically hope for is painfully slow progress against consumerism, punctuated by rapid advances. The stories of cigarettes and ivory illustrate how consumption patterns change as information spreads and personal and political pressure mounts.

For four decades, U.S. health authorities and citizen advocates have warned against smoking, and accumulating scientific evidence has made their case incontrovertible. It was only in the eighties, however, that their efforts finally overcame the social cachet of cigarettes in the United States and the political clout of the tobacco lobby, and they achieved rapid legal advances against smoking. Cigarette consumption there has fallen by a third since 1980.[19]

In the case of ivory, change came more swiftly. Wildlife biologists and conservationists issued repeated pleas during the eighties for an end to the ivory poaching that was exterminating African elephants. The message spread slowly at first, slightly dulling the luster of ivory among the consumer class in North American and Europe. Late in the decade, the movement's momentum began to build, and in a matter of months in 1989 ivory became taboo for much of the global consumer society. By January 1990, public outcry had turned the informal boycott into a ban on ivory trade and backed it up with the force of international law. As with cigarettes, change came almost imperceptibly for years, before accelerating suddenly to a breakthrough.20

Given plenty of time and pressure, conspicuous consumption of all types might decline as have smoking in the United States and ivory sales worldwide. The trouble is, time is awasting for the planet, and constraining consumption of entire categories of products – fossil fuels, for example, or chemicals – is not as simple as doing it for a particular item. The challenge, then, is to generate unprecedented, organized pressure for change, and to aim that pressure where it will have the greatest effect.

Strategic targets clearly include laws and policies that favor consumption over leisure, and high-impact commodities over low-impact ones – cars over buses, for instance, or disposables over durables. They also include the excesses of advertising and retailing. The contest will be one-sided, for example, so long as commercial television is the dominant cultural force in the consumer society. As religious historian Robert Bellah wrote, 'That happiness is to be attained through limitless material acquisition is denied by every religion and philosophy known to humankind, but it is preached incessantly by every American television set.' And, of course, the wasteful consumer-society approaches to providing food, transport, and materials are excellent points to apply pressure.[21]

The best targets are the parts of our consumption that are wasted or unwanted in the first place. Germans drive 6,200 kilometers a year, mostly going places they would not need to drive to if livable neighborhoods were closer to work, a variety of local merchants closer to home, and public transit easier and faster. The Dutch would rather never see most of the 78 kilograms of packaging they have to carry out with the trash each year. Americans feel the same way about the 37 percent of the mail they receive that consists of unsolicited sales pitches. Each day, the United States turns over 23 square kilometers of rural land to new housing developments, 'industrial parks,' and commercial strips that would mostly be unnecessary if Americans insisted on well-planned land use inside city limits.[22]

Despite the ominous scale of the challenge, there could be many more people ready to begin saying 'enough' than prevailing opinion suggests. Polls in the core nations of the consumer society now show that more than half the people prefer protecting the environment if a choice must be made between environmental quality and economic growth. And, thankfully, the consumerist splurge of the eighties is over – although it was halted more by hard times than by concern for the earth. For whatever reasons, as of early 1992, public opinion in at least the United States had swung against crass materialism. The annual surveys of young Americans entering university that have showed material desires soaring since the mid-seventies began after 1987 to show slower growth and even leveling desires for certain consumer goods. And some trend watchers are starting to talk of a sea change in the making. Watts Wacker, vice president of Yankelovich Clancy Shulman, a firm that monitors consumer attitudes, says, 'We're moving away from shop-till-you-drop and moving toward dropping shopping.'[23]

In early 1992, little signs of simplifying were everywhere: American fabric stores were experiencing a revival, as more people sewed their own garments. Amy Dacyczyn of Leeds, Maine, calling herself the Frugal Zealot, started a newsletter called the *Tightwad Gazette*, which after two years and no promotional budget already had 50,000 subscribers. Of course, these trends might simply mark another rotation in the binge-and-purge cycle that moral fashion follows as the economy booms and busts, but even so they would represent an opportunity to advance the transition to a culture of permanence.[24]

The future of life on earth depends on whether we among the richest fifth of the world's people, having fully met our material needs, can turn to nonmaterial sources of fulfillment. Whether we – who have defined the tangible goals of world development – can now craft a new way of life at once simpler and more satisfying. Having invented the automobile and airplane, can we return to bicycles, buses, and trains? Having pioneered sprawl and malls, can we recreate human-scale settlements where commerce is an adjunct to civic life rather than its purpose? Having introduced the high fat, junk food diet, can we instead nourish ourselves on wholesome fare that is locally produced? Having devised disposable plastics, packaging without end, and instantaneous obsolescence, can we design objects that endure and a materials economy that takes care of things?

If our grandchildren are to inherit a planet as bounteous and beautiful as we have enjoyed, we in the consumer class must – without surrendering the quest for advanced, clean technology – eat, travel, and use energy and materials more like those on the middle rung of the world's economic ladder. If we can learn to do so, we might find ourselves happier as well, for in the consumer society, affluence has brought us to a strange pass. Who would have predicted a century ago that the richest civilizations in history would be made up of polluted tracts of suburban development dominated by the private automobile, shopping malls, and a throwaway economy? Surely, this is not the ultimate fulfillment of our destiny.

In the final analysis, accepting and living by sufficiency rather than excess offers a return to what is, culturally speaking, the human home: to the ancient order of family, community, good work, and good life; to a reverence for skill, creativity, and creation; to a daily cadence slow enough to let us watch the sunset and stroll by the water's edge; to communities worth spending a lifetime in; and to local places pregnant with the memories of generations. Perhaps Henry David Thoreau had it right when he scribbled in his notebook beside Walden Pond, 'A man is rich in proportion to the things he can afford to let alone.'[25]

(Endnotes)

1 Basic value of sustainable society from World Commission on Environment and Development, *Our Common Future* (New York: Oxford University Press, 1987).

2 Scott Willis, *The San lose Mercury News*, San Jose, Calif., 1989.

3 Paul Wachtel, *The Poverty of Affluence* (Philadelphia: New Society Publishers, 1989). The sole exception to this generalization is travel, which many people find richly rewarding but which is environmentally destructive when done by airplane or car.

4 Aristotle, *Nicomachean Ethics* 1109b23.

5 Sidney Quarrier, geologist, Connecticut Geological & Natural History Survey, Hartford, Conn., private communication, February 25, 1992.

6 EarthWorks Group, Berkeley, Calif., private communication, February 25, 1992.

7 Duane Elgin, *Voluntary Simplicity* (New York: William Morrow and Company, 1981); United Kingdom and Germany from Pierre Pradervand, independent researcher, Geneva, Switzerland, private communication, July 14, 1990, and from Groupe de Beaulieu, *Construire L'Esperance* (Lausanne: Editions de l'Aire, 1990); India from Mark Shepard, *Gandhi Today: A Report on Mahatma Gandhi's Successors* (Arcata, Calif.: Simple Productions, 1987); Netherlands and Norway from Elgin, Voluntary Simplicity.

8 Rewards of simplicity from Wendell Reny, *The Gift of Good Land* (San Francisco: North Point Press, 1981), from 'What Is Enough?' *In Context* (Bainbridge Island, Wash.), Summer 1990, and from Katy Butler, 'Pate Poverty: Downwardly Mobile Baby Boomers Lust After Luxury,' *Utne Reader*, September/October 1989; Karen Christensen, 'With the Earth in Mind: the Personal to the Political,' in Sara Parkins, ed., *Green Light on Europe* (London: Heretic Books, 1991).

9 New Road Map Foundation from Vicki Robin, president, New Road Map Foundation, Seattle, Wash., various private communications, 1990–92, and from Vicki Robin, 'How Much Is

Enough?' In Context (Bainbridge Island, Wash.), Summer 1990; number of participants from Nick Ravo, 'For the 90's, Lavish Amounts of Stinginess,' *New York Times*, January 15, 1992.
10 Frank Levering and Wanda Urbanska, *Simple Living: One Couple's Search for a Better Life* (New York: Viking Penguin, 1992).
11 Joanne Forman, Ranchos de Taos, N.M., private communication, August 28, 1991, edited slightly to shorten.
12 David Shi, *The Simple Life: Plain Living and High Thinking in American Culture* (New York: Oxford University Press, 1985).
13 Cuba from Lee Hockstader, 'Communists Press Forth—By Oxcart,' *Washington Post*, September 12, 1991.
14 Toynbee quoted in Wachtel, *Poverty of Affluence.*
15 Thales from Goldian VandenBroeck, ed., *Less Is More: The Art of Voluntary Poverty* (New York: Harper & Row, 1978).
16 Bible and Saints Augustine and Francis from VandenBroek, *Less is More*; Thomas Aquinas from Benjamin Kline Hunnicutt, *Work Without End: Abandoning Shorter Hours for the Right to Work* (Philadelphia: Temple U. Press, 1988); monks and merchants from Herman E. Daly and John B. Cobb, Jr., *For the Common Good: Redirecting the Economy Toward Community, the Environment, and a Sustainable Future* (Boston: Beacon Press, 1989).
17 Freya Littledale, adapter, *The Magic Fish* (New York: Scholastic, Inc., 1966); King Midas from Edith Hamilton, *Mythology* (Boston: Little Brown and Co., 1942).
18 Franklin quoted in Herb Goldberg and Robert T. Lewis, Money Madness: *The Psychology of Saving, Spending, Loving and Hating Money* (New York: William Morrow & Co., 1978); Patten quoted in Henry Allen, 'Bye-Bye America's Pie,' *Washington Post*, February 11, 1992.
19 Peter Weber, 'Last Gasp for U.S. Smokers,' *World Watch*, November/December 1990.
20 Michael A. O'Connell and Michael Sutton, 'The Effects of Trade Moratoria on International Commerce in African Elephant Ivory: A Preliminary Report,' World Wildlife Fund and The Conservation Foundation, Washington, D.C., June 1990.
21 Robert Bellah, *The Broken Covenant* (New York: Seabury Press, 1975).
22 Car travel is 1988 vehicle-kilometers per capita in West Germany based on International Roads Federation, *World Road Statistics* 1984-88 (Washington, D.C.: 1989); Dutch household packaging waste is Worldwatch Institute estimate based on J.M. Joosten et al., *Informative Document: Packaging Waste* (Bilthoven, Netherlands: National Institute of Public Health and Environmental Protection, 1989); mail from Blayne Cutler, 'Meet Jane Doe,' *American Demographics*, June 1989; land developed from Jim Riggle, Director of Operations, American Farmland Trust, Washington, D.C., private communication, October 17, 1990.
23 Polls in the United States found 71 percent supporting the environment versus economic growth, while in the European Community the share was 55 percent, according to Organisation for Economic Co-operation and Development, *State of the Environment, 1991* (Paris: 1991); Richard A. Easterlin and Eileen M. Crimmins, 'Private Materialism, Personal Self-Fulfillment, Family Life, and Public Interest: The Nature, Effects, and Causes of Recent Changes in the Values of American Youth,' *Public Opinion Quarterly*, Vol. 55,1991; Wacker quoted in Allen, 'Bye-Bye America's Pie.'
24 Fabric stores from Janice Castro, 'Hunkering Down,' *Time*, July 23, 1990; other signs of simplifying from Amy Saltzman, 'The New Meaning of Success,' *U.S. News & World Report*, September 17, 1990, from Joseph T. Plummer, 'Changing Values,' *The Futurist*, January/February 1989, and from Ronald Henkoff, 'Is Greed Dead?' Fortune, August 14, 1989; *Tightwad Gazette* (Leeds, Maine), various editions; subscribers from Ravo, 'For the 90's, Lavish Amounts of Stinginess.'
25 Henry David Thoreau, *Walden* (1854; reprint, Boston: Houghton Mifflin, 1957).

Chapter Fifteen

SIMPLICITY, COMMUNITY, AND PRIVATE LAND

Eric T. Freyfogle

Many people have a fair idea of what simple living looks like in daily life, or at least they know the key principles and ideals – the quest for calm, balanced, integrated lives; less clutter, less artificiality, and lessened impact on nature; and the elevation of quality over quantity, time over money, and community over competition. What does all this mean, though, at the community or landscape level, particularly with respect to the ways we dwell upon the land? How might simple living affect our patterns of living on land, individually and collectively? And what would this mean in terms of private property rights, the functions of government, and the ways we think about democracy and self-rule?

We can phrase this foundational issue in a somewhat different way: Can we achieve simple living by steps people take as individuals or instead do we need something more than that, some form of collective action to change the governing structures within which we act out our daily lives?

The basic story line today is familiar enough. We have middle-aged Joe, who lives in the suburb, drives long distances to work, and is constantly short of time and burdened by stress. Life for Joe is an endless flow of wanting, getting, and spending more, which is to say he is 'normal.' He exercises, he readily admits, much too little. He has few contacts with neighbors and he's cut off from any real engagement with nature. Too much food comes on the run, in highly processed forms. The cell phone or e-mail is the main mode of communication, not person-to-person contact. His carbon footprint is unsustainably huge; he knows this, yet without moral unease he goes with the flow, 'business as usual.'

It is easy to tell Joe to slow down, to get out of his car, to downsize, to stop and talk with people, to cultivate a garden and pay attention to his food. And perhaps Joe can do these things. But can he do them living where he does and with the job that he holds, or would he need to pack up, move to a smaller place, get another job, and join a much different community?

The problem for Joe, and for countless people like him, is that he's not in control of his life. Far from it. His life isn't just a compilation of all of the choices he has made, freely and independently. Instead, he's living to a large extent within a system that he's offered on a take-it-or-leave-it basis. He can't formulate in his own mind the world he'd like to inhabit and then, waving of a wand or with burst of smoke, bring it into being. He can't imagine a perfect arrangement of elements in his life and then push the button that says 'I choose this.'

Perhaps Joe, given a choice, would like to walk to work and to nearby shops. Perhaps he'd enjoy a large park, managed mostly as a natural area, no more than a mile or two away. Perhaps he'd prefer a neighborhood organic garden area, where he could grow food and flowers and interact meaningfully with neighbors who are doing the same. Perhaps he'd like to join with neighbors to construct a wind turbine to provide sustainable energy. And perhaps he'd enjoy some modern equivalent of the small-town square, where older people gather on shaded benches to play chess or checkers, sip coffee, share newspaper sections, and chat for hours while neighborhood life unfolds.

Among the significant points to make about this alternative vision is how dependent it is upon patterns of land use at the neighborhood and community scale. When Joe imagines his alternative life, he's not just imagining a new way to live individually. He's imagining a much different landscape in which to live. He's dreaming about a much different arrangement of buildings, roads, sidewalks, gardens, parks, shops, and gathering places.

Now, it's obvious enough that Joe on his own can't bring this new landscape into being. Perhaps his dream landscape exists somewhere. And perhaps Joe can move to it and start a new life. But what about the place where Joe now lives, and the people who'll continue living there? Are they stuck with life as it is, with no chance of improvement? And how would a soundly arranged landscape come into being in any event? Do good places just happen, or is there more to it?

The point we need to get to is that Joe's dream of living a better life in a better place challenges more than just his current way of life. It challenges more than just the earn-and-spend materialism of the modern age. It calls into question some pretty foundational elements of modern society. Indeed, it draws us into what is perhaps the most central issue in philosophy and social and political thought – the nagging issue of how the individual fits into the group or society; the never-solved question of the parts and the whole. Are people best understood as autonomous individuals who are well served by giving them maximum freedom consistent with similar freedom for others? Or is it more sensible and useful to realize that the health and happiness of a person is dependent first and foremost on relationships with others and on being part of organic structures that are themselves healthy and well-functioning?

This foundational question, about parts and wholes – about the individual and the community – is in turn linked to perhaps the core value of the modern era, exalted above all others, the value of personal liberty. For centuries now, the trajectory of modern society has been toward an expansion of individual liberty, at various paces and for various people. Liberty is the core value of modern liberalism. It is linked to democracy and supported by the vague but nonetheless useful notion of equality.

But is the meaning of liberty as clear as we might think it is? Is liberty all about having options and being free of constraints, particularly ones imposed by government, or is there something more to it?

One of the key assumptions – or confusions, we might say – of modernity is our tendency to think of liberty entirely in negative, individual terms, and to discount or ignore the broader, richer meanings that the ideal can include. Negative liberty is the freedom from constraints. Individual liberty is freedom from collective control. But liberty of this type is sufficient only for people who have goals they can achieve acting alone (rich people mostly), people who merely want to get ahead in the competitive system. Liberty of this type means Joe can buy whichever house or car he can afford, without the constraints of, say, racial discrimination. Or it means Joe can look for any job, or travel as he sees fit, or join any church or say what he likes, all as he pleases.

But let's say Joe wants to live along a river that is healthy and full of fish. How does Joe exercise this choice? What if Joe wants to breathe clean air and to live in a neighborhood that includes people of widely differing income levels? Indeed, what if Joe realizes, as many people realize, that his life is profoundly affected by the actions of other people, and that his liberty is severely limited if he has no way to get involved in these actions? The whole idea of democracy is that the sovereign governing power resides with the people collectively, the *demos*, not with a monarch or some oligarchy. But how do the people exercise this sovereign power? Are they constrained to exercise it as individuals acting alone, or can they also engage in what political writers generations ago referred to as 'self rule,' by which was meant not chiefly rule by individuals as such but rule by people coming together, as political equals, making rules and taking action to promote their collective well being?

When we dig into it, what we find is that liberty comes in many different forms. It can be individual or collective. It can be negative – freedom from – or it can be positive, the liberty to formulate goals and implement them. Joe's liberty is severely constrained if he can't get together with other citizens to take action to restore the health of their shared river or clean up their shared air. To be sure, if Joe and other citizens impose laws restricting pollution they'll be limiting the actions of many people. They'll be constraining the negative, individual liberties of many individuals, themselves included. But that is only to say that liberty comes in many forms, and that we have to make choices as to the types of liberty we want to support. We can't give individuals freedom to use their lands however they like, while at the same time empowering people collectively to craft and implement visions of how their shared landscape ought to look. We need to make choices, preferably well informed ones.

A shift to simple living is not just about doing without. It is about substituting, about moving from certain ways of living to other, better, more humane and sustainable ways. Some of those substitutions can be made by people acting individually; people of conscience, acting bravely and peacefully, can yield results. But some of the substitutions that are needed, the key ones included, really are choices people can only make collectively. They are choices that can come only when people exercise the less-exalted kinds of liberty, the positive, collective liberties that undergird democratic governance. People collectively can make bad decisions; there's no doubt about that. But many good outcomes are possible only through collective action. To oppose such collective action – to call for minimal government or maximum individual freedom – is to strip people collectively of the power to make many choices. It is to strip them of the power in tandem to shape the landscapes they inhabit, and by shaping their landscapes to help shape or reshape their own lives.

When Joe imagines a better existence – some escape from the hectic busy-ness of his daily routine – he has in mind a shift to a landscape that has distinct features to it. He imagines a community in which it is possible to walk to work and shops or otherwise convenient to travel from place to place. He imagines a world where neighbors interact, where nature is close at hand, where health is honored above wealth, and where the greatest possessions are intangible. His world would be one that protects and facilitates families that choose simple, agrarian modes of living. It would guard against ecological degradation. Land taxes would be based on current land uses, not on speculative development values. To the extent a growing community increases the market values of land parcels suitable for development, that value would go to the community that created it, not to the people who happened to own the land and who merely waited and watched while their lands increased in value. Public policies would foster the redevelopment of existing neighborhoods, not the creation of new ones on the urban fringe.

A lot of steps would need to be taken to transform our current landscapes into ones that honored simple living and helped it happen. Putting to one side questions about who wields the power, the people who do make the decisions would have to make good ones, and good decisions are not easily made. Indeed, the history of land planning is full of cautions. Grand plans by big-name designers have not often worked well, or not for long. People on the ground, people who live in a place, need to have substantial control, not just at the beginning but over time, to make changes. Overly planned communities become stifling.

That said, decisions have to be made by someone and in some manner. Someone has to lay out roads and sidewalks, either making room for pedestrians and bicycles or not. Someone has to decide how lands will be used. The power to make these decisions must reside somewhere, and there are dangers and pitfalls wherever the power goes. Better decisions don't come by chance. They emerge out of processes that enhance opportunities for study, reflection, and interaction.

Having reached this point in the story, we could turn in several directions to keep probing. We could stop to examine about the market as a mechanism for making collective decisions (it does well at some decisions, very poorly at others). Instead, we could reflect on the methods of citizen engagement and the various forms democracy can take, highlighting the profound weaknesses of voting and public opinion polls as ways of involving people in communal affairs. Or we could turn to talk, even more fundamentally, about cultural values and our tendency to understand ourselves as autonomous individuals, in charge of our lives and mostly responsible for our fates. There is truth to this conceit, but a good deal of falsity as well, not just because the playing field is never level but because so much of who we are and how happy we feel depends upon other people and the quality of relationships – which is to say upon our interactions with others, not on actions we take in isolation.

Also worth probing, and particularly relevant to Joe's fate and dream, is an element of modern society that's often taken for granted – the institution of private property rights in nature. Private property is linked with liberty. It is a bulwark of Western (and increasingly global) society and culture. Particularly in the United States private property is so honored that it stands for many people as the keystone right, the right that holds all else in place. Secure private rights make it possible for the market to move land and resources to higher valued uses. It's hard to imagine our global economy without substantial respect for private rights.

What gets overlooked in our collective rush to honor this useful social arrangement (which is, after all, what private property entails) is that private property is a distinctly human creation. It can take countless different forms, and has done so. The things that can be owned and the rights that owners possess can and do vary greatly, over time and in different cultures. To say that a person owns land is to say almost nothing, until we know what ownership means in the community to which the person belongs.

The move toward simple living cannot succeed in any full way without major changes in the ways we use nature, individually and collectively. These changes, in turn, can't take place unless and until we take time to reflect upon property as an institution, thinking about how it works, why it exists, what dangers it entails, and how we might put it to best use.

Private property is not some Platonic ideal that exists in an intangible, invisible realm, waiting for us to grab it and put it to use. It is a very-human governance arrangement that profoundly influences our landscapes and lives. A study of it should be high on the list of tasks for social reformers out to promote more simple ways of life.

A few basic points about private property can frame the issue well enough and lay the groundwork for further study. For starters, private property entails the exercise of *public* power, not private power. An owner of land or water or trees is able to control these parts of nature because laws and the state make it possible. Police, courts, and even prisons stand ready to defend the owner's claims. As property theorists have explained for over two centuries, take away the laws and property disappears. Take away the public support and we're back to a might-makes-right, king-of-the-hill game that is the antithesis of private property.

Point two: property enhances the liberty of an owner at the expense of the liberty of other people. The owner who can now control a tract of land gains that control because other people are no longer at liberty to make use of the same land. An owner who can pollute the air gains that power at the expense of others who must now put up with the pollution. A landowner whose actions are noisy gains liberty at the expense of neighboring landowners who want the neighborhood to remain quiet.

We tend to think of private property as a personal right of some sort (again, this is especially true in the United States). But when we consider how it works, particularly its moral ambiguity, we quickly realize that private property in land is justifiable only to the extent that private rights promote the common good. Private property is not good *inherently*, it is good when and to the extent it brings overall benefits in practice. And what needs justifying is not private property as a whole – as if it were a single thing that we could either embrace or not – it is each landowner right, one by one.

Why should the law give landowners the power to erode soil, to degrade ecological processes, or to build structures that diminish the lives of surrounding people? We can't avoid these questions by contending that private property inherently includes these powers because it doesn't. Landowners can have as many or as few rights as lawmakers deem wise. Every element of ownership must be justifiable by reference to the ways it contributes to the good of society generally. Only when we make these calculations – only when we've decided what private rights will enhance the common good – can we then prescribe the elements of private ownership. And only then can landowners know what rights they possess individually.

At its base, private property entails a decision by lawmakers to give to particular people (the owners) some of society's power to make decisions about parts of nature – about tracts of land, flows of water, wild species, and the like. It is a governance arrangement, involving the exercise of public power. And it is entirely appropriate, if not morally essential, for the rules of the game to shift over time, as circumstances, values, and aspirations evolve.

This brings us back to Joe and to people like him, who yearn to live more simply. It is natural, given the dominance of liberal ideals, for Joe to think first about what he can do to make changes in his personal life. It is natural for him to assume responsibility for his choices, and to accept responsibility for the life that he has crafted through his many life choices. Our assessment of things, though, shifts once we see how dependent Joe is on the landscape where he lives; once we see how his life is influenced by the accumulated decisions of the people who live around him.

Simple living is vastly easier in some landscapes than others. Fundamental changes in landscapes require collective action, which in turn means the exercise of positive, collective liberties rather than negative, individual ones. Fundamental change also requires, in many settings, a thorough rethinking of what private property is all about. What powers should owners possess, given the ways private property can both enhance and inhibit the common good? What power over land should be wielded by individual owners acting alone and what powers should remain in the hands of people collectively, to exercise through the forms of democratic self-rule?

When looking at Joe's life we can readily see how influenced he is by the cultural values of consumption and success defined in material terms. It is equally essential that we see how influenced he is by other cultural values that are every bit as influential in shaping the life that he now has. He is influenced by images of individual autonomy that discount the vital importance of relationships and communal bonds. He's influenced by the modern, chiefly Western tendency to honor individual, negative liberty at the expense of other forms. Without much thought Joe likely accepts an understanding of private property in which property is primarily an individual right of some sort, not, as it ought to be understood, as a tool society uses to promote the common good.

Guided by this understanding of private property Joe thinks it natural when an owner of vacant land sells it to a developer at a substantial profit, reaping a rise in value that was, in reality, created by the community, not by the individual land owner. He thinks it natural that government is routinely called upon to justify its limits on what landowners can do, rather than expecting landowners to justify how and why their exercise of power contributes to the common good.

Simple living can take many forms. For it to come about, people as individuals need to take stock of who they are and how they live, and imagine better ways. Some steps can be taken in daily life to shift toward greater simplicity, and they should be taken. But other steps require collective action.

They require people to come together and work together to craft collective lives and to give shape to sensible landscapes, where they all might thrive.

Collective action is no easy path and the possible mistakes are many. It is a path, though, that must be taken. In preparation, we need to rethink the fundamentals of modern liberal society, particularly the economic libertarianism of free-market thought. Liberty, democracy, private property – they all come in many shapes and sizes. New lives, greater health and happiness, will likely require that we reconsider and reshape these inherited fundamentals. In its current political, legal, and economic forms, the modern world makes simple living a difficult option. That world can change. Thoughtful, dedicated people can change it.

Chapter Sixteen

THE NEW POLITICS OF CONSUMPTION

Juliet Schor

In contemporary American culture, consuming is as authentic as it gets. Advertisements, getting a bargain, garage sales, and credit cards are firmly entrenched pillars of our way of life. We shop on our lunch hours, patronize outlet malls on vacation, and satisfy our latest desires with a late-night click of the mouse.[1]

Yet for all its popularity, the shopping mania provokes considerable dis-ease: many Americans and other westerners worry about our preoccupation with getting and spending. They fear we are losing touch with more worthwhile values and ways of living. But the discomfort rarely goes much further than that; it never coheres into a persuasive, well-articulated critique of consumerism. By contrast, in the 1960s and early '70s, a far-reaching critique of consumer culture was a part of our political discourse. Elements of the New Left, influenced by the Frankfurt School, as well as by John Kenneth Galbraith and others, put forward a scathing indictment. They argued that Americans had been manipulated into participating in a dumbed-down, artificial consumer culture, which yielded few true human satisfactions.

For reasons that are not hard to imagine, this particular approach was short-lived, even among critics of American society and culture. It seemed too patronizing to talk about manipulation or the 'true needs' of average Americans. In its stead, critics adopted a more liberal point of view, and deferred to individuals on consumer issues. Social critics again emphasized the distribution of resources, with the more economistic goal of maximizing the incomes of working people. The good life, they suggested, could be achieved by attaining a comfortable, middle-class standard of living. This outlook was particularly prevalent in economics, where even radical economists have long believed that income is the key to well-being. While radical political economy, as it came to be called, retained a powerful critique of alienation in production and the distribution of property, it abandoned the nascent intellectual project of analyzing the consumer sphere. Few economists now think about how we consume, and whether it reproduces class inequality, alienation, or power. 'Stuff' is the part of the equation that the system is thought to have gotten nearly right.

Of course, many Americans retained a critical stance toward our consumer culture. They embody that stance in their daily lives — in the ways they live and raise their kids. But the rejection of consumerism, if you will, has taken place principally at an individual level. It is not associated with a widely accepted intellectual analysis, and an associated *critical politics of consumption.*

But such a politics has become an urgent need. The average American now finds it harder to achieve a satisfying standard of living than 25 years ago. Work requires longer hours, jobs are less secure, and pressures to spend more intense. Consumption-induced environmental damage remains pervasive, and we are in the midst of widespread failures of public provision. While the current economic boom has allayed consumers' fears for the moment, many Americans have long-term worries about their ability to meet basic needs, ensure a decent standard of living for their children, and keep up with an ever-escalating consumption norm.

In response to these developments, social critics continue to focus on income. In his impressive analysis of the problems of contemporary American capitalism, *Fat and Mean*, economist David Gordon emphasized income *adequacy*. The 'vast majority of US households,' he argues, 'can barely make ends meet.... Meager livelihoods are a *typical* condition, an *average* circumstance.' Meanwhile, the Economic Policy Institute focuses on the distribution of income and wealth, arguing that the gains of the top 20 percent have jeopardized the well-being of the bottom 80 percent. Incomes have stagnated and the robust 3 percent growth rates of the 1950s and '60s are long gone. If we have a consumption problem, this view implicitly states, we can solve it by getting more income into more people's hands. The goals are redistribution and growth.

It is difficult to take exception to this view. It combines a deep respect for individual choice (the liberal part) with a commitment to justice and equality (the egalitarian part). I held it myself for many years. But I now believe that by failing to look deeper – to examine the very nature of consumption – it has become too limiting. In short, I do not think that the 'income solution' addresses some of the most profound failures of the current consumption regime.

Why not? First, consuming is part of the problem. Income (the solution) leads to consumption practices that exacerbate and reproduce class and social inequalities, resulting in – and perhaps even worsening – an unequal distribution of income. Second, the system is structured such that an *adequate* income is an elusive goal. That is because adequacy is relative-defined by reference to the incomes of others. Without an analysis of consumer desire and need, and a different framework for understanding what is adequate, we are likely to find ourselves, twenty years from now, arguing that a median income of $100,000 – rather than half that – is adequate. These arguments underscore the social context of consumption: the ways in which our sense of social standing and belonging comes from what we consume. If true, they suggest that attempts to achieve equality or adequacy of individual incomes without changing consumption patterns will be self-defeating.

Finally, it is difficult to make an ethical argument that people in the world's richest country need more when the global income gap is so wide, the disparity in world resource use so enormous, and the possibility that we are already consuming beyond the earth's ecological carrying capacity so likely. This third critique will get less attention in this essay – because it is more familiar, not because it is less important – but I will return to it in the conclusion.

I agree that justice requires a vastly more equal society, in terms of income and wealth. The question is whether we should also aim for a society in which our relationship to consuming changes, a society in which we consume *differently*. I argue here for such a perspective: for a critique of consumer culture and practices. Somebody needs to be for quality of life, not just quantity of stuff. And to do so requires an approach that does not trivialize consumption, but accords it the respect and centrality it deserves.

The New Consumerism

A new politics of consumption should begin with daily life, and recent developments in the sphere of consumption. I describe these developments as 'the new consumerism,' by which I mean an upscaling of lifestyle norms; the pervasiveness of conspicuous, status goods and of competition for acquiring them; and the growing disconnect between consumer desires and incomes.

Social comparison and its dynamic manifestation – the need to 'keep up' – have long been part of American culture. My term is 'competitive consumption,' the idea that spending is in large part driven by a comparative or competitive process in which individuals try to keep up with the norms of the social group with which they identify – a 'reference group.' Although the term is new, the idea is not. Thorstein Veblen, James Duesenberry, Fred Hirsch, and Robert Frank have all written about the importance of relative position as a dominant spending motive. What's new is the redefinition of reference groups: today's comparisons are less likely to take place between or among households of similar means. Instead, the lifestyles of the upper middle class and the rich have become a more salient point of reference for people throughout the income distribution. Luxury, rather than mere comfort, is a widespread aspiration.

One reason for this shift to 'upscale emulation' is the decline of the neighborhood as a focus of comparison. Economically speaking, neighborhoods are relatively homogeneous groupings. In the 1950s and '60s, when Americans were keeping up with the Joneses down the street, they typically compared themselves to other households of similar incomes. Because of this focus on neighbors, the gap between aspirations and means tended to be moderate.

But as married women entered the workforce in larger numbers – particularly in white collar jobs – they were exposed to a more economically diverse group of people, and became more likely to gaze upward. Neighborhood contacts correspondingly declined, and the workplace became a more prominent point of reference. Moreover, as people spent less time with neighbors and friends, and more time on the family-room couch, television became more important as a source of consumer cues and information. Because television shows are so heavily skewed to the 'lifestyles of the rich and upper middle class,' they inflate the viewer's perceptions of what others have, and by extension what is worth acquiring – what one must have in order to avoid being 'out of it.'

Trends in inequality also helped to create the new consumerism. Since the 1970s, the distribution of income and wealth have shifted decisively in the direction of the top 20 percent. The share of after-tax family income going to the top 20 percent rose from 41.4 percent in 1979 to 46.8 percent in 1996. The share of wealth controlled by the top 20 percent rose from 81.3 percent in 1983 to 84.3 percent in 1997. This windfall resulted in a surge in conspicuous spending at the top. Remember the 1980s – the decade of greed and excess? Beginning with the super-rich, whose gains have been disproportionately higher, and trickling down to the merely affluent, visible status spending was the order of the day. Slowed down temporarily by the recession during the early 1990s, conspicuous luxury consumption has intensified during the current boom. Trophy homes, diamonds of a carat or more, granite countertops, and sport utility vehicles are the primary consumer symbols of the late-1990s. Television, as well as films, magazines, and newspapers ensure that the remaining 80 percent of the nation is aware of the status purchasing that has swept the upper echelons.

In the meantime, upscale emulation had become well-established. Researchers Susan Fournier and Michael Guiry found that 35 percent of their sample aspired to reach the top 6 percent of the income distribution, and another 49 percent aspired to the next 12 percent. Only 15 percent reported that they would be satisfied with 'living a comfortable life' – that is, being middle class. But 85 percent of the population cannot earn the six-figure incomes necessary to support upper-middle-class lifestyles. The result is a growing aspirational gap: with desires persistently outrunning incomes, many consumers find themselves frustrated. One survey of US households found that the level of income needed to fulfill one's dreams doubled between 1986 and 1994, and is currently more than twice the median household income.

The rapid escalation of desire and need, relative to income, also may help to explain the precipitous decline in the savings rate – from roughly 8 percent in 1980, to 4 percent in the early 1990s, to the current level of zero. (The stock market boom may also be inducing households not to save; but financial assets are still highly concentrated, with half of all households at net worths of $10,000 or less, including the value of their homes.) About two-thirds of American households do not save in a typical year. Credit card debt has skyrocketed, with unpaid balances now averaging about $7,000 and the typical household paying $1,000 each year in interest and penalties. These are not just low-income households. Bankruptcy rates continue to set new records, rising from 200,000 a year in 1980 to 1.4 million in 1998.

★ ★ ★

The new consumerism, with its growing aspirational gap, has begun to jeopardize the quality of American life. Within the middle class – and even the upper middle class – many families experience an almost threatening pressure to keep up, both for themselves and their children. They are deeply concerned about the rigors of the global economy, and the need to have their children attend 'good' schools. This means living in a community with relatively high housing costs. For some households this also means providing their children with advantages purchased on the private market (computers, lessons, extra-curriculars, private schooling). Keeping two adults in the labor market – as so many families do, to earn the incomes to stay middle class – is expensive, not only because of the second car, child-care costs, and career wardrobe. It also creates the need for time-saving, but costly, commodities and services, such as take-out food and dry cleaning, as well as stress-relieving experiences. Finally, the financial tightrope that so many households walk – high expenses, low savings – is a constant source of stress and worry. While precise estimates are difficult to come by, one can argue that somewhere between a quarter and half of all households live paycheck-to-paycheck.

These problems are magnified for low-income households. Their sources of income have become increasingly erratic and inadequate, on account of employment instability, the proliferation of part-time jobs, and restrictions on welfare payments. Yet most low-income households remain firmly integrated within consumerism. They are targets for credit card companies, who find them an easy mark. They watch more television, and are more exposed to its desire-creating properties. Low-income children are more likely to be exposed to commercials at school, as well as home. The growing prominence of the values of the market, materialism, and economic success make financial failure more consequential and painful.

These are the effects at the household level. The new consumerism has also set in motion another dynamic: it siphons off resources that could be used for alternatives to private consumption. We use our income in four basic ways: private consumption, public consumption, private savings, and leisure. When consumption standards can be met easily out of current income, there is greater willingness to support public goods, save privately, and cut back on time spent at work (in other words, to 'buy leisure'). Conversely, when lifestyle norms are upscaled more rapidly than income, private consumption 'crowds out' alternative uses of income. That is arguably what happened in the 1980s and 1990s: resources shifting into private consumption, and away from free time, the public sector, and saving. Hours of work have risen dramatically, saving rates have plummeted, public funds for education, recreation, and the arts have fallen in the wake of a grass-roots tax revolt. The timing suggests a strong coincidence between these developments and the intensification of competitive consumption – though I would have to do more systematic research before arguing causality. Indeed, this scenario makes good sense of an otherwise surprising finding: that indicators of 'social health' or 'genuine progress' (i.e., basic quality-of-life measures) began to diverge from GDP in the mid-1970s, after moving in tandem for decades. Can it be that consuming and prospering are no longer compatible states?

To be sure, other social critics have noted some of these trends. But they often draw radically different conclusions. For example, there is now a conservative jeremiad that points to the recent tremendous increases in consumption and concludes that Americans just don't realize how good they have it, that they have become overly entitled and spoiled. Reduced expectations, they say, will cure our discontents. A second, related perspective suggests that the solution lies in an act of psychological independence – individuals can just ignore the upward shift in consumption norms, remaining perfectly content to descend in the social hierarchy.

These perspectives miss the essence of consumption dynamics. Americans did not suddenly become greedy. The aspirational gap has been created by structural changes – such as the decline of community and social connection, the intensification of inequality, the growing role of mass media, and heightened penalties for failing in the labor market. Upscaling is mainly defensive, and has both psychological and practical dimensions.

Similarly, the profoundly social nature of consumption ensures that these issues cannot be resolved by pure acts of will. Our notions of what is adequate, necessary, or luxurious are shaped by the larger social context. Most of us are deeply tied into our particular class and other group identities, and our spending patterns help reproduce them.

Thus, a collective, not just an individual, response is necessary. Someone needs to address the larger question of the consumer culture itself. But doing so risks complaints about being intrusive, patronizing, or elitist. We need to understand better the ideas that fuel those complaints.

Consumer Knows Best

The current consumer boom rests on growth in incomes, wealth, and credit. But it also rests on something more intangible: social attitudes toward consumer decision-making and choices. Ours is an ideology of non-interference – the view that one should be able to buy what one likes, where one likes, and as much as one likes, with nary a glance from the government, neighbors, ministers, or political parties. Consumption is perhaps the clearest example of an individual behavior which our society takes to be almost wholly personal, completely outside the purview of social concern and policy. The consumer is king. And queen.

This view has much to recommend it. After all, who would relish the idea of sumptuary legislation, rationing, or government controls on what can be produced or purchased? The liberal approach to consumption combines a deep respect for the consumer's ability to act in her own best interest and an emphasis on the efficiency gains of unregulated consumer markets: a commitment to liberty and the general welfare.

Cogent as it is, however, this view is vulnerable on a number of grounds. Structural biases and market failures in the operation of consumer markets undermine its general validity; consumer markets are neither so free nor so efficient as the conventional story suggests. The basis of a new consumer policy should be an understanding of the presence of structural distortions in consumers' choices, the importance of social inequalities and power in consumption practices, a more sophisticated understanding of consumer motivations, and serious analysis of the processes that form our preferences. To appreciate the force of these criticisms, we need a sharper statement of the position they reject.

The Conventional View

The liberal view on markets for consumer goods has adherents in many disciplines, but its core analytic argument comes from standard economic theory, which begins from some well-known assumptions about consumers and the markets in which they operate.

1. *Consumers are rational.* They act to maximize their own well-being. They know what they prefer, and make decisions accordingly. Their 'preferences' are taken as given, as relatively unchanging, and as unproblematic in a normative sense. They do not act capriciously, impulsively, or self-destructively.

2. *Consumers are well-informed.* They have perfect information about the products offered in the market. They know about all relevant (to the consumer) characteristics pertaining to the production and use of the product.

3. *Consumer preferences are consistent (both at a point in time and over time).* Consistency at a point in time means transitivity: If A is preferred to B and B to C then A will be preferred to C. (In other words, if roast beef is preferred to hamburgers and hamburgers to hot-dogs, then roast beef is preferred to hot dogs.) Consistency over time can be thought of as a 'no regrets' assumption. If the consumer is faced with a choice of a product that yields satisfaction in the present, but has adverse consequences in the future–eat chocolate today and feel great, but gain five unwanted pounds by next week–and the consumer chooses that product today, he or she will not regret the choice when the future arrives. (This does not mean the extra pounds are welcomed, only that the pleasure of the chocolate continues to outweigh the pain of the pounds.)

4. *Each consumer's preferences are independent of other consumers' preferences.* We are self-contained in a social sense. If I want a sport utility vehicle, it is because I like them, not because my neighbor does. The trendiness of a product does not affect my desire to have it, either positively or negatively.

5. *The production and consumption of goods have no 'external' effects.* There are no consequences for the welfare of others that are unreflected in product prices. (A well-known example of external effects is pollution, which imposes costs on others that are not reflected in the price of the good that produces the pollution.)

6. *There are complete and competitive markets in alternatives to consumption.* Alternatives to consumption include savings, public goods, and the 'purchase' of leisure. Unless these alternatives are available, the choice of consumption – over other uses of economic resources – may not be the optimal outcome.

Taken together, and combined with conditions of free entry and exit of firms providing consumer goods, these assumptions imply that no consumer policy is the best consumer policy. Individual consumers know best and will act in their own interest. Firms will provide what the consumers want; those that don't will not survive a competitive marketplace. Competition and rationality together ensure that consumers will be sovereign – that is, that their interests will 'rule.' And the results will be better than any we could achieve through government regulation or political action.

To be sure, conventional theory and policy have always admitted some deviations from these highly idealized conditions. In some areas interventionist policy has been long-standing. First, some consumers are not considered to be fully rational – for example, children or, in an earlier era, women. Because kids are not thought to be capable of acting in their own interest, the state justifies protective policies, such as the restricting advertising aimed at them. Second, the state has traditionally regulated highly addictive or harmful commodities, such as drugs, alcohol, and explosives. (As the debates surrounding the legalization of drugs make clear, the analytical basis for this policy is by no means universally accepted.) A third class of highly regulated commodities involve sex: pornography, contraceptives, sexual paraphernalia, and so forth. Here the rationale is more puritanical. American society has always been uncomfortable about sex and willing to override its bias against consumer regulation because of that. Finally, the government has for much of this century – though less forcefully since the Reagan administration – attempted to ensure minimum standards of product safety and quality.

These exceptions aside, the standard model holds strongly to the idea that unfettered markets yield the optimal outcomes, a conclusion that follows logically and inexorably from the initial assumptions. Obviously, the assumptions of the standard model are extreme, and the real world deviates from them. On that everyone agrees. The question is by how much, how often, and under what conditions? Is the world sufficiently different from this model that its conclusions are misguided?

Serious empirical investigations suggest that these assumptions do not adequately describe a wide range of consumer behaviors. The simple rational-economic model is reasonable for predicting some fraction of choice behavior for some class of goods – apples versus oranges, milk versus orange juice – but it is inadequate when we are led to more consequential issues: consumption versus leisure, products with high symbolic content, fashion, consumer credit, and so on. In particular, it exaggerates how rational, informed, and consistent people are. It overstates their independence. And it fails to address the pressures that consumerism imposes on individuals with respect to available choices and the consequences of various consumption decisions. Understand those pressures, and you may well arrive at very different conclusions about politics and policy.

Rational, Deliberative, and In Control?

The economic model presents the typical consumer as deliberative and highly forward-looking, not subject to impulsive behavior. Shopping is seen as an information-gathering exercise in which the buyer looks for the best possible deal for product she has decided to purchase. Consumption choices represent optimizing within an environment of deliberation, control, and long-term planning.

Were such a picture accurate it would be news (and news of a very bad sort) to a whole industry of advertisers, marketers, and consultants whose research on consumer behavior tells a very different story. Indeed, their findings are difficult to reconcile with the picture of the consumer as highly deliberative and purposive.

Consider some of the stylized facts of modern marketing. For example, the 'law of the invariant right': shoppers overwhelmingly turn right, rather than left, upon entering a store. This is only consistent with the rational search model if products are disproportionately to be found on the right side of the aisle. Or consider the fact that products placed in the so-called 'decompression zone' at the entrance to a store are 30 percent less likely to be purchased than those placed beyond it. Or that the number of feet into a store the customer walks is correlated with the number of items purchased. It's far harder to square these findings with 'rational' behavior than with an unplanned and contingent action. Finally, the standard model has a very hard time explaining the fact that if, while shopping, a woman is accidentally brushed from behind, her propensity to purchase falls precipitously.

Credit cards present another set of anomalies for the reigning assumptions. Surveys suggest that most people who acquire credit cards say that they do not intend to borrow on them; yet roughly two-thirds do. The use of credit cards leads to higher expenditures. Psychological research suggests that even the visual cue of a credit card logo spurs spending. Survey data shows that many people are in denial about the level of credit card debt that they hold, on average underestimating by a factor of two. And the explosion of personal bankruptcies, now running at roughly 1.5 million a year, can be taken as evidence of a lack of foresight, planning, and control for at least some consumers.

More generally, credit card habits are one example of what economists call 'hyperbolic discounting,' that is, an extreme tendency to discount the future. Such a perspective calls into question the idea of time consistency – the ability of individuals to plan spending optimally throughout their lifetimes, to save enough for the future, or to delay gratification. If people are constitutionally inclined to be hyperbolic discounters, as some are now arguing, then forced-saving programs such as Social Security and government-sponsored retirement accounts, restriction on access to credit, waiting periods for major purchases, and a variety of other approaches might improve well-being. Compulsive buying, as well as the milder and far more pervasive control problems that many consumers manifest, can also be incorporated into this framework.

The model of deliberative and informed rationality is also ill-adapted to account for the phenomenon of brand-preference, perhaps the backbone of the modern consumer market. As any beginning student of advertising knows, much of what advertising does is take functionally identical or similar goods and differentiate them on the basis of a variety of non-operational traits. The consumer is urged to buy Pepsi because it represents the future, or Reebok shoes because the company stands for strong women. The consumer develops a brand preference, and believes that his brand is superior in quality. The difficulty for the standard model arises because, absent the labels, consumers are often unable to distinguish among brands, or fail to choose their favorites. From the famous beer taste test of the 1960s (brand loyalists misidentified their beers), to cosmetics, garments, and other tests of more recent vintage, it seems that we love our brands, but we often can't tell which brands are which.

What can we conclude from consumers' inability to tell one washing powder, lipstick, sweater, or toothpaste from another? Not necessarily that they are foolishly paying a brand premium for goods. (Although there are some consumers who do fall into this category – they wouldn't pay the brand premium, as distinct from a true quality premium, if they knew it existed.) What is more generally true, I believe, is that many consumers do not understand why they prefer one brand over another, or desire particular products. This is because there is a significant dimension of consumer desire which operates at the non-rational level. Consumers believe their brand loyalties are driven by functional dimensions, but a whole host of other motivators are at work–for example, social meanings as constructed by advertisers; personal fantasies projected onto goods; competitive pressures. While this behavior is not properly termed 'irrational,' neither is it conscious, deliberative, and narrowly purposive. Consumers are not deluded, duped, or completely manipulated. But neither do they act like profit-maximizing entrepreneurs or scientific management experts. The realm of consumption, as a rich historical literature has taught us, has long been a 'dream world,' where fantasy, play, inner desire, escape, and emotion loom large. This is a significant part of what draws us to it.

Consumption is Social

Within economics, the major alternative to the assumption that individuals' preferences are independent – that people do not want things because others want them – is the 'relative' income, positional, or 'competitive consumption' perspective noted above. In this model, a person's well-being depends on his or her relative consumption – how it compares to some selected group of others. Such positioning is one of the hallmarks of the new consumerism.

Of course, social comparison predates the 1980s. In 1984, French sociologist Pierre Bourdieu explored the social patterning of consumption and taste in *Distinction: A Social Critique of the Judgment of Taste*. Bourdieu found that family socialization processes and educational experiences are the primary determinants of taste for a wide range of cultural goods, including food, dress, and home decor. In contrast to the liberal approach, in which consumption choices are both personal and trivialized – that is, socially inconsequential – Bourdieu argues that class status is gained, lost, and reproduced in part through everyday acts of consumer behavior. Being dressed incorrectly or displaying 'vulgar' manners can cost a person a management or professional job. Conversely, one can gain entry into social circles, or build lucrative business contacts, by revealing appropriate tastes, manners, and culture. Thus, consumption practices become important in maintaining the basic structures of power and inequality which characterize our world. Such a perspective helps to illuminate why we invest so much meaning in consumer goods – for the middle class its very existence is at stake. And it suggests that people who care about inequality should talk explicitly about the stratification of consumption practices.

If we accept that what we buy is deeply implicated in the structures of social inequality, then the idea that unregulated consumption promotes the general welfare collapses. When people care only about relative position, then general increases in income and consumption do not yield gains in well-being. If my ultimate consumer goal is to maintain parity with my sister, or my neighbor, or Frasier, and our consumption moves in tandem, my well-being is not improved. I am on a 'positional treadmill.' Indeed, because consuming has costs (in terms of time, effort, and natural resources), positional treadmills can have serious negative effects on well-being. The 'working harder to stay in place' mantra of the early 1990s expresses some of this sentiment. In a pure reversal of the standard prescription, collective interventions which stabilize norms, through government policy or other mechanisms, raise rather than lower welfare. People should welcome initiatives that reduce the pressure to keep up with a rising standard.

Free and Structurally Unbiased?

The dynamic of positionally driven spending suggests that Americans are 'overconsuming' at least those private goods that figure in our consumption comparisons. There is another reason we may be overconsuming, which has to do with the problems in markets for alternatives to status or positional goods. In particular, I am referring to non-positional private consumption, household savings, public goods, and leisure. Generally speaking, if the markets for these alternatives are incomplete, non-competitive, or do not fully account for social benefits and costs, then overconsumption with respect to private consumption may result. I do not believe this is the case with household savings: financial markets are highly competitive and offer households a wide range of ways to save. (The deceptive and aggressive tactics of consumer credit companies might be reckoned a distortion in this market, but I'll leave that aside.) Similarly, I do not argue that the markets for private consumer goods which we tend not to compete about are terribly flawed. Still, there are two markets in which the standard assumptions do not apply: the market for public goods and the market for time. Here I believe the deviations from the assumptions are large, and extremely significant.

In the case of public goods there are at least two big problems. The first is the underproduction of a clean environment. Because environmental damage is typically not included in the price of the product which causes it (e.g., cars, toxic chemicals, pesticides), we overconsume environmentally damaging commodities. Indeed, because all production has an impact on the environment, we overconsume virtually all commodities. This means that we consume too much in toto, in comparison to non-environmentally damaging human activities.

The second problem arises from the fact that business interests – the interests of the producers of private goods – have privileged access to the government and disproportionately influence policy. Because they are typically opposed to public provision, the 'market' for public goods is structurally biased against provision. In comparison to what a truly democratic state might provide, we find that a business-dominated government skews outcomes in the direction of private production. We don't get enough, or good enough, education, arts, recreation, mass transport, and other conventional public goods. We get too many cars, too many clothes, too many collectibles.

For those public goods that are complementary with private spending (roads and cars versus bicycle lanes and bicycles) this bias constrains the choices available to individuals. Without the bicycle lanes or mass transport, private cars are unavoidable. Because so much of our consumption is linked to larger collective decisions, the individual consumer is always operating under particular constraints. Once we move to HDTV, our current televisions will become obsolete. As public telephone booths disappear, mobile phones become more necessary. Without adequate public libraries, I need to purchase more books.

★ ★ ★

We also under-produce 'leisure.' That's because employers make it difficult to choose free time, rather than long hours and higher incomes. To use the economist's jargon, the labor market offerings are incomplete with respect to trade-offs of time and money. Employers can exact severe penalties when individuals want to work part-time or forego raises in favor of more vacations or days off. In some jobs the options are just not available; in others the sacrifices in terms of career mobility and benefits are disproportionate to any productivity costs to the employer.

This is not a minor point. The standard model assumes that employees are free to vary their hours, and that whatever combination of hours and income results represents the preferences of employees. But if employees lack the opportunity to vary their working hours, or to use improvements in productivity to reduce their work-time, then we can in no way assume that the trajectory of consumption reflects people's preferences. There may well be a path for the economy that involves less work and less stuff, and is preferred by people to the high-work/high-consumption track. But if that option is blocked, then the fact that we buy a lot can no longer be taken *ipso facto* as proof of our inherent consumer desires. We may merely be doing what is on offer. Because free time is now a strongly desired alternative to income for large numbers of employees, this argument is more than a theoretical possibility. It has become one of the most pressing failures of the current moment.

A Politics of Consumption

The idea that consumption is private should not, then, be a conversation-stopper. But what should a politics of consumption look like? To start the discussion – not to provide final answers – I suggest seven basic elements:

1. *A right to a decent standard of living.* This familiar idea is especially important now because it points us to a fundamental distinction between what people need and what they want. In the not very distant past, this dichotomy was not only well-understood, but the basis of data collection and social policy. Need was a social concept with real force. All that's left now is an economy of desire. This is reflected in polling data. Just over 40 percent of adults earning $50,000 to $100,000 a year, and 27 percent of those earning more than $100,000, agree that 'I cannot afford to buy everything I really need.' One third and 19 percent, respectively, agree that 'I spend nearly all of my money on the basic necessities of life.' I believe that our politics would profit from reviving a discourse of need, in which we talk about the material requirements for every person and household to participate fully in society. Of course, there are many ways in which such a right might be enforced: government income transfers or vouchers, direct provision of basic needs, employment guarantees, and the like. For reasons of space, I leave that discussion aside; the main point is to revive the distinction between needs and desires.

2. *Quality of life rather than quantity of stuff.* Twenty-five years ago quality-of-life indicators began moving in an opposite direction from our measures of income, or Gross Domestic Product, a striking divergence from historic trends. Moreover, the accumulating evidence on well-being, at least its subjective measures (and to some extent objective measures, such as health), suggests that above the poverty line, income is relatively unimportant in affecting well-being. This may be because what people care about

is relative, not absolute income. Or it may be because increases in output undermine precisely those factors which do yield welfare. Here I have in mind the growing work-time requirements of the market economy, and the concomitant decline in family, leisure, and community time; the adverse impacts of growth on the natural environment; and the potential link between growth and social capital.

This argument that consumption is not the same as well-being has great potential to resonate with millions of Americans. Large majorities hold ambivalent views about consumerism. They struggle with ongoing conflicts between materialism and an alternative set of values stressing family, religion, community, social commitment, equity, and personal meaning. We should be articulating an alternative vision of a quality of life, rather than a quantity of stuff. That is a basis on which to argue for a re-structuring of the labor market to allow people to choose for time, or to penalize companies that require excessive hours for employees. It is also a basis for creating alternative indicators to the GNP, positive policies to encourage civic engagement, support for parents, and so forth.

3. *Ecologically sustainable consumption.* Current consumption patterns are wreaking havoc on the planetary ecology. Global warming is perhaps the best known, but many other consumption habits have major environmental impacts. Sport utility vehicles, air conditioning, and foreign travel are all energy-intensive, and contribute to global warming. Larger homes use more energy and building resources, destroy open space, and increase the use of toxic chemicals. All those granite counter-tops being installed in American kitchens were carved out of mountains around the world, leaving in their wake a blighted landscape. Our daily newspaper and coffee is contributing to deforestation and loss of species diversity. Something as simple as a T-shirt plays its part, since cotton cultivation accounts for a significant fraction of world pesticide use. Consumers know far less about the environmental impacts of their daily consumption habits than they should. And while the solution lies in greater part with corporate and governmental practices, people who are concerned about equality should be joining forces with environmentalists who are trying to educate, mobilize, and change practices at the neighborhood and household level.

4. *Democratize consumption practices.* One of the central arguments I have made is that consumption practices reflect and perpetuate structures of inequality and power. This is particularly true in the 'new consumerism,' with its emphasis on luxury, expensiveness, exclusivity, rarity, uniqueness, and distinction. These are the values which consumer markets are plying, to the middle and lower middle class. (That is what Martha Stewart is doing at K-Mart.)

But who needs to accept these values? Why not stand for consumption that is democratic, egalitarian, and available to all? How about making 'access,' rather than exclusivity, cool, by exposing the industries such as fashion, home decor, or tourism, which are pushing the upscaling of desire? This point speaks to the need for both cultural change, as well as policies which might facilitate it. Why not tax high-end 'status' versions of products while allowing the low-end models to be sold tax-free?

5. *A politics of retailing and the 'cultural environment.'* The new consumerism has been associated with the homogenization of retail environments and a pervasive shift toward the commercialization of culture. The same mega-stores can be found everywhere, creating a blandness in the cultural environment. Advertising and marketing is also pervading hitherto relatively protected spaces, such as schools, doctors' offices, media programming (rather than commercial time), and so on. In my local mall, the main restaurant offers a book-like menu comprising advertisements for unrelated products. The daily paper looks more like a consumer's guide to food, wine, computer electronics, and tourism and less like a purveyor of news. We should be talking about these issues, and the ways in which corporations are re-making our public institutions and space. Do we value diversity in retailing? Do we want to preserve small retail outlets? How about ad-free zones? Commercial-free public education? Here too public policy can play a role by outlawing certain advertising in certain places and institutions, by financing publicly-controlled media, and enacting zoning regulations which take diversity as a positive value.

6. *Expose commodity 'fetishism.'* Everything we consume has been produced. So a new politics of consumption must take into account the labor, environmental, and other conditions under which products are made, and argue for high standards. This argument has been of great political importance in recent years, with public exposure of the so-called 'global sweatshop' in the apparel, footwear, and fashion industries. Companies fear their public images, and consumers appear willing to pay a little more for products when they know they have been produced responsibly. There are fruitful and essential linkages between production, consumption, and the environment that we should be making.

7. *A consumer movement and governmental policy.* Much of what I have been arguing for could occur as a result of a consumer's movement. Indeed, the revitalization of the labor movement calls out for an analogous revitalization of long dormant consumers. We need independent organizations of consumers to pressure companies, influence the political agenda, provide objective product information, and articulate a vision of an appealing and humane consumer sphere. We also need a consumer movement to pressure the state to enact the kinds of policies that the foregoing analysis suggests are needed. These include taxes on luxury and status consumption, green taxes and subsidies, new policies toward advertising, more sophisticated regulations on consumer credit, international labor and environmental

standards, revamping of zoning regulations to favor retail diversity, and the preservation of open space. There is a vast consumer policy agenda which has been mainly off the table. It's time to put it back on.

(Endnotes)

1 Sources for much of the data cited in this article can be found in the notes to *The Overspent American: Why We Want What We Don't Need* (HarperPerennial, 1999) or by contacting the author.

Chapter Seventeen

POLITICAL PRESCRIPTIONS[1]

John de Graaf

Our country is set up structurally to oppose voluntary simplicity.[2]

– Michael Jackobson, *Marketing Madness*

We are today paying the debt for the material growth that characterized the postwar 'Golden Age:' disfigured landscapes, polluted air and water, erosion of the ozone layer, the greenhouse effect. Since the Third World also needs significant growth of its material production, only a reorientation of the overdeveloped countries towards a model of development centered on the immaterial growth of free time is capable of guaranteeing our common future.

– Alain Lipietz, French Green Party economist

Sometimes an epidemic reaches such proportions that political action is called for, usually in the form of a quarantine. We believe that point has been reached in the case of affluenza, the disease of over-consumption in the world's wealthy countries.

Thomas Naylor (one of the co-authors of *Affluenza*) even wants the quarantine to begin around his state, Vermont. He's been leading a campaign called The Second Vermont Republic, which actually calls for that state to secede from the United States to protect its unique quality of life. Vermont may be less infected by affluenza than any other state. It's almost Wal-Mart-free, and few other big box stores or tacky mini-malls mar its quiet beauty. Vermont towns still have the feel of permanence and liveability; citizens still participate regularly in public forums; everybody in the state has a guaranteed right to health insurance (not true elsewhere in the US). Shopping locally and buying wholesome food is encouraged. Many Vermonters, like Thomas, who moved there because of Vermont's quality of life, want to prevent their good life from being overtaken by affluenza.

But we can't all live in Vermont so we've got to figure out policies to turn back affluenza wherever we live.

Despite twenty five years of bad-mouthing that has left the American public and people in many other countries deeply cynical about whether government can ever do anything right, I believe it can play an important role in helping create a society that is affluenza-unfriendly, or, to put it in more positive terms, simplicity-friendly. Our social ills won't be cured by personal action alone. Just as the symptoms of affluenza are many and interconnected, so must be public efforts to quarantine it. There is no silver bullet that by itself will do the trick. It will take a comprehensive strategy, at all levels of government, built around several key areas of action:

★ Reducing annual working hours, trading money and stuff for time;
★ Restructuring the tax and earnings systems;
★ Corporate reform, including responsibility for entire product cycles;
★ Investment in a sustainable infrastructure;
★ Redirection of government subsidies;
★ A new concept of child protection; and finally
★ New ideas about economic growth.

Many of these ideas will be familiar to readers in western European countries where such policies have already been enacted, but none of yet even been on the radar screens of prominent American political leaders.

Bread and Roses

The first step in solving the problems of over-consumption and moving to a more simplicity-friendly society lies in making it possible for more and more people to trade money for time. It must be made clear that this will not be a sacrifice. The sacrifice is now as we surrender so many aspects of our quality of life to the growing work demands brought on by consumerism.

In 1912, when thousands of women walked out of the textile mills of Lawrence, Massachusetts, in a famous strike, they carried banners that read: WE WANT BREAD, AND ROSES TOO. Bread and roses – symbols for the material and non-material sides of life. The Lawrence strikers needed bread – higher wages. They could barely afford to feed themselves at the time. But they also knew they needed roses – shorter hours of work, allowing time for families, art, love, beauty, spirit: time to 'smell the roses.' Until World War II, American labor always fought for both higher wages and shorter hours, for both bread and roses. But somehow, after the war, we got what was called 'bread and butter unionism.' Notice the difference. Now, suddenly, the unions were only about wages; the roses were left to wilt. By contrast, in Europe, the issue of working hours remained near the top of organized labor's agenda.

Since the Second World War, Americans have been offered what economist Juliet Schor calls 'a remarkable choice.' As our productivity more than doubled, we could have chosen to work half as much – or even less – and still produce the same material lifestyle we found 'affluent' in the '50s. We could have split the difference, letting our material aspirations rise somewhat but also taking an important portion of our productivity gains in the form of more free time. Instead, we put all our apples into making and consuming more.

Our friends in Europe made a difference choice. They took a big part of their gains in labor productivity in the form of time. In his book, *Happiness*, British economist and House of Lords member Richard Layard shows that, as a result, general happiness in Europe continues to increase while in the U.S. it stagnated after the 1950s. At the same time, general health in every European country is better than that in the U.S. Even in the United Kingdom, whose residents are a bit less healthy than those of continental Europe, the comparison with the US is striking. A study by the British health service and the U.S. National Institutes of Health found that after age 55 residents of the United Kingdom are only about half as likely to suffer from chronic diseases such as heart disease, hypertension and diabetes as those in the United States. Shorter working time in the UK seemed to be the major contributor to the difference. British citizens find more time for exercise and socializing with friends and family, and suffer less from stress and insecurity, al factors which strongly influence health outcomes.

In the United States, the forty-hour workweek, established by law in 1938, is still the standard (though most full-time American workers average closer to 45 hours a week.). By law, we could set a different standard, and we should. It need not be a one-size-fits-all standard, like a 30-hour week of six-hour days as proposed in the 1930s or the 35-hour work week which is the law in France, though for many working Americans either of those choices would be ideal.

More important, perhaps, is to get annual working hours – now averaging about 1,850 per year and exceeding those even of the workaholic Japanese (though the Australians and New Zealanders are now working hours similar to ours) – under control. Were the average workday to be six hours, we'd be putting in only about 1500 hours a year. This is about the norm in a number of countries in western Europe and it means an additional 350 hours – nine full weeks! – of free time. The Dutch and Norwegians actually work less than 1400 hours a year.

Flexible Work Reduction

Let's set a standard working year of 1500 hours for fulltime, keeping the forty-hour a week maximum. Then allow workers to find flexible ways to fill the 1500 hours.

Many excellent international ideas for shortening working hours can be found in Anders Hayden's book, *Sharing the Work, Sparing the Planet.* Any of these scenarios could be voluntarily agreed upon between worker and employer, but shorter hours legislation would include stiff employer penalties for work required beyond the 1500-hour maximum per year. We ought not to fear trading income for free time. Beyond the reduction to 1500 hours per year, legislation could ensure the right of workers to choose further reductions in working hours – instead of increased pay – when productivity rises, or further reductions in working hours at reduced pay, when productivity is stagnant.

A 2000 Dutch law called the Hours Adjustment Act, now also in place in Germany, goes even further. It allows workers to reduce their hours to part time simply by asking their employers. Unless there is a clear hardship for the firm – something shown in less than 5% of cases – the employer must grant the reduction in hours. Workers keep the same hourly salary, full health care, and pro-rated additional benefits like vacation time and pensions. This law, in the most concrete terms, allows workers to trade money for time, without losing their jobs or health care. As a result more than a third of Dutch employees work part-time, the highest ratio in the world.

Polls have shown that half of all American workers would accept a commensurate cut in pay in return for shorter working hours. The same is probably true in many other rich countries. But the cut needn't be based on a one-to-one ratio. Workers are more productive per hour when they work fewer hours. Absenteeism is reduced and health improves.

Work Sharing when Recession Comes

Plans for spreading work around by shortening hours should begin now for another reason: When recessions come should we simply say 'sayonara, tough luck' to those whose jobs are lost? There is a better way. Say a company needs to reduce production by twenty percent and believes it must lay off one-fifth of its workforce. What if, instead, it cut everybody's workweek by one day?

Sure, all workers would have to learn to live with less – not a bad idea anyway – but no one would be tossed to the wolves. And we predict that everyone would soon love the time off. On the other hand, if we don't make such plans and millions suddenly face unemployment, then all other negative social indicators – crime, family breakdown, suicide, depression, and so forth – can be expected to skyrocket again.

American Exceptionalism

While work reduction is an admirable goal in all wealthy nations, American public policies protecting family and personal time are particularly weak. A recent study released by the Harvard School of Public Health (www.globalworkingfamilies.org), covering 168 of the world's nations concluded that 'the United States lags dramatically behind all high-income countries, as well as many middle- and low-income countries when it comes to public policies designed to guarantee adequate working conditions for families.' The study found that:

- ★ 163 of 168 countries guarantee paid leave for mothers in connection with childbirth. 45 countries offer such leave to fathers. The U.S. does neither.
- ★ 139 countries guarantee paid sick leave. The U.S. does not.
- ★ 96 countries guarantee paid annual (vacation) leave. The U.S. does not.
- ★ 84 countries have laws that fix a maximum limit on the workweek. The U.S. does not.
- ★ 37 countries guarantee parents paid time off when children are sick. The U.S. does not.

Corporate leaders in other developed countries often look to the United States as an economic model. But in practically every measurement of quality of life (health outcomes, security, social mobility, equality, environmental protection, leisure time, education, personal savings etc.) the U.S. falls far short of the results achieved in other countries with more social democratic economic policies and more protections for workers and consumers. Clearly, the United States is not a model for others; to the contrary it is increasingly, a disaster waiting to happen. Even in traditional terms, the U.S. at the time I write this, is in serious trouble, with a collapsing housing market, falling stock market, major banks going under, 50 million Americans without health care, a negative personal savings rate, and enormous trade deficit and a dollar that has shrunk in value to 60% that of the Euro, after being worth the same in 2000.

Retiring Step by Step

There are other ways of exchanging money for time. Many academics receive 'sabbaticals,' anything from a quarter to a year off every several years, usually accepting a reduced salary during the period. Why not a system of sabbaticals every seven to ten years for all workers who desire them and are willing to take moderate salary reductions when they are on sabbatical? We all need to recharge our batteries every so often.

Or how about a system of graduated retirement? For many of us, self-esteem takes a hit and boredom a bounce when we suddenly go from forty-hour weeks to zero upon retiring. Instead, we could design a pension and social security system that would allow us to retire gradually. Let's say that at fifty we cut 300 hours from our work year – nearly eight weeks. Then at fifty-five we cut 300 more. At sixty, 300 more. And at sixty-five, 300 more. Now, we're down to 800 (given no change in the present annual pattern). We might then have the option to stop paid labor entirely, or to keep working 800 hours for as long as we are capable. Several European countries are experimenting with forms of phased retirement.

What this would do is allow us to begin learning to appreciate leisure, volunteer more, and broaden our minds long before final retirement. It would allow more young workers to find positions and allow older workers to stay on longer to mentor them. It would allow older workers to both stay involved with their careers and also find time for more balance in their lives.

A variation on this idea that also has merit is to allow workers to take some of their 'early retirement' at different stages of their careers, perhaps when they need more parenting time, for example. Belgium has created a unique policy which allows workers to take a year off at five different times in their working lives, with government financial support made possible by the reduced unemployment these job openings create.

The ultimate idea, promoted in some European countries, is that a certain number of hours would constitute a total paid work life, with considerable flexibility around when the hours are worked.

Taxes

In one sense, the 2000 and 2004 American elections were about taxes. Gore and Kerry wanted to tax Americans less, and Bush wanted to tax them even less than Gore and Kerry did. As I am writing this, Republican candidate John McCain wants to make Bush's sharp tax cuts for wealthy American, including abolition of the inheritance tax, permanent. But as Richard Layard points out in *Happiness*, higher taxes actually help to slow the 'rat race' and lead to more overall life satisfaction. What we need is a discussion about the kinds of taxes and what they might do.

A change in the tax system, similar to one already underway in parts of Europe, could help considerably to contain affluenza. The first step toward a change could come through an idea called the progressive consumption tax. Proposed by economist Robert Frank in his book *Luxury Fever*, the tax would replace at least a portion of the personal income tax. Instead, people would be taxed on what they consume, at a rate rising from twenty percent (on annual spending under $40,000) to seventy percent (on annual spending over $500,000). Basically the idea is to tax those with the most serious cases of 'luxury fever' (which seems to be Frank's synonym for affluenza) at the highest rates, thus encouraging saving instead of spending.

At the same time, we must make it possible for lower-income workers to meet their basic needs without working several jobs. The old Catholic idea of, a family or living wage, championed by Pope Leo XIII in his 1891 Encyclical Rerum Novarum, could be accomplished by a negative income tax or tax credits that guarantee all citizens a simple but sufficient standard of living above the poverty line.

Equally promising are so-called 'green taxes.' Their proponents would replace a portion of taxes on 'goods' such as income – and payroll taxes, which discourage increased employment – with taxes on 'bads' such as pollution or waste of nonrenewable resources. The point would be to make the market reflect the true costs of our purchases. We'd pay much more to drive a gas-guzzler, for example, and a little more for this book (to cover the true costs of paper), but no more for a music lesson or theater ticket.

Additional carbon taxes would discourage the burning of fossil fuels. Pollution taxes would discourage contamination of water and air. The costs of cleaning up pollution would be added as a tax on goods whose production causes it. Such a tax could make organic foods as cheap as pesticide-laced produce. Depletion taxes would increase the price of nonrenewable resources and lower the comparative price of goods made to last.

While such a green tax system would be complicated, it could go a long way toward discouraging environmentally or socially harmful consumption, while encouraging benign alternatives. As things currently stand, in the United States we more often subsidize what we should be taxing – extractive industries like mining ($2.6 billion in subsidies a year), and air and auto travel, for example. We could, and should, turn that around, subsidizing clean technologies and activities like wind and solar power or organic family farms (for example) instead of oil and agribusiness.

Corporate Responsibility

Another way to reduce the impact of consumption is to require that corporations take full responsibility for the entire life cycle of their products, an idea now gaining widespread acceptance in Europe. The concept is simple, and well-explained in the book *Natural Capitalism* by Paul Hawken and Amory and Hunter Lovins. In effect, companies would no longer sell us products but lease them. Then, when the products reach the end of their useful lives, the same companies would take them back to re-use and recycle them, saving precious resources.

This cradle-to-the-grave idea is winning considerable corporate support already, with leadership from Ray Anderson, CEO of Interface Corporation, an industrial carpet company, and from businesses that have joined the 'Natural Step' movement, agreeing to full life-cycle responsibility for their products. The Natural Step movement seems to be spreading rapidly in Europe, and is also gaining adherents, including the governors of several states, in the U.S.

If companies take such full responsibility, they will have to include the attendant costs in the prices of their goods.

Going Dutch

Such responsibility will soon be made law in the European Union, for automobile companies at least. But with so many companies and so many products traveling all over the world, a Dutch law may provide a more effective solution. In the Netherlands, car buyers pay an additional 'disassembly tax' when they buy their vehicle. When the car reaches the end of its useful life, they take it to an auto disassembly plant, where it is carefully stripped of anything that can still be used. Then only the metal shell is crushed and recycled (in the United States everything – wires, plastic, and so forth – just gets crushed, and a large percentage is simply lost as waste). By 2001, the Dutch plants were taking 90% of all end-of-life vehicles and recycling 86% of the materials from them.

The plants, which are cheap and low-tech, employ many workers and take any cars. The disassembly tax is part of the Dutch National Environmental Policy Plan (or 'Green Plan') and is now being extended to include many other consumer goods.[3] Among the most important: computers, which are now replaced every eighteen months on average. The old models, full of dangerous toxic chemicals, are usually just thrown away and then exported to poor countries like China and Nigeria, where pollute rivers and poison people. Of course, such a law will increase the price of computers, but then perhaps we won't throw them away so easily.

Stopping Child Abuse

In all rich countries there has been a recent upsurge in marketing targeting children, trying to train them to be voracious consumers from the earliest ages – two and three year olds are now targeted. American consumer advocate Ralph Nader has called this a form of 'corporate child abuse.' It's as if marketers have set out knowingly to infect our children with affluenza by spreading the virus everywhere kids congregate. It's time to protect our kids. At a minimum, we can begin to restrict television advertising to children. Already, places like Sweden and the Province of Quebec don't allow it. If you're a parent like I am, you probably long for relief from TV advertising's manipulation of your kids.

Moreover, a stiff tax on all advertising would send a strong message that curbing the spread of affluenza is serious business.

The Politics of Well-Being

An exciting development along the lines we'll be taking is now happening in the United Kingdom, where economists and ordinary citizens of different political persuasions are working to create a 'Politics of Well-Being.' Based in part on the ideas of Jeremy Bentham, who argued that the goal of government was to seek the greatest happiness for the greatest number of people, the new politics is centered on creating tax and other policies that give people more time and support for important non-material sources of happiness, such as friendships, family and good health. These ideas are well-explored in the books *Happiness*, by Richard Layard, and *Willing Slaves: How the Overwork Culture is Ruling Our Lives*, by Madeleine Bunting. Many of the examples in the books are British, but wholly appropriate to the situation in other rich countries. The new movement in the UK also has an excellent Web site (www.neweconomics.org) and a Manifesto.

Sometimes the case for such change comes from surprising quarters. A new policy plan, released – believe it or not – by the Conservative Party in the United Kingdom, offers perhaps the most far-reaching and sophisticated political policy ideas released anywhere in the world. In 2005, David Cameron, leader of the Tories, commissioned a 'Quality of Life Policy Group' to, in the words of the group's director, Jules Peck, 'rethink the whole way we look at the world.' Cameron pointed out that despite rapid gains in material wealth during the past several decades, life satisfaction in the UK had actually fallen. 'To reconnect with younger generations and the electorate as a whole,' Cameron declared, 'we need to recognize that for people today, the quality of life matters just as much as the quantity of money.'

In September, 2007, after extensive conversations with people from all walks of British life, the policy group released its 550 page report, *Blueprint for a Green Economy*, to enormous fanfare in the British press. Though littered with praise for Margaret Thatcher and other bones thrown to the Tory faithful, the document is a radical departure from Conservative orthodoxy. 'The effective system we call the market must be our servant and not our master. Treating it as a god and doing its bidding does not make men and women happy. The market is only valuable as a tool; it is not an end in itself...Pursued as an ideology, it induces social poverty. Conservatives have a real vocation to develop a society that can use the mechanisms of capitalism without being consumed by them.' (page 58).

At times, the criticism of the market is harsh: 'Unrestrained it will catch till the last fish is landed, drill till there is no more oil and pollute till the planet is destroyed... If markets are not to master us then governments have to intervene to ensure that they keep their place and remain our servants.' (page 17).

Much of the easily-readable document is a call for Green Taxes and national mobilization against Global Warming, recognized by the Policy Group as the greatest threat to our common future. It proposes massive investments in solar and wind technology, reductions in air travel, promotion of walking and cycling, support for green building and new less auto-dependent urban design. The document clearly recognizes the importance of work/life balance to well being, encouraging a shift from economy-friendly families to family-friendly economies, an effort to 'slow things down for the sake of our well-being' and focus on relationships rather than greater material affluence. It suggests that a 'time increase' is more important than a tax cut. Welfare of children is given high priority, with the recognition that the UK ranked last among 21 industrial countries in a recent UNICEF study of child welfare. The U.S. was barely better at 20th place.

Repeatedly, the Blueprint challenges the notion that Gross Domestic Product is a measure of economic success – 'consumption growth may actually be causing harms, particularly when the pursuit of wealth takes away from the quality of personal relationships or proper balance between work and life.' (page 40). The plan advocates the creation of new indices of economic success.

Not surprisingly, the Blueprint has been widely criticized in the UK, especially from the Conservative Party's powerful financial interests, which condemned it as 'subversive and socialistic.' Environmentalists and the Left have been much more favorable, but David Cameron has backed away from the document, knowing he needs his financial backers in the next election. Nonetheless, the fact that the document exists at all is a welcome development and points a clear programmatic way forward in the fight against rampant consumerism. Let the 'politics of well-being' be taken up everywhere!

But Won't our Economy Collapse?

What if we all started buying smaller, more fuel-efficient cars, driving them less and keeping them longer? What if we took fewer long-distance vacations? What if we simplified our lives, spent less money, bought less stuff, worked less, and enjoyed more leisure time? What if government began to reward thrift and punish waste, legislated shorter work hours, and taxed advertisers? What if we made consumers and corporations pay the real costs of their products? What would happen to our economies? Would they collapse, as some economists suggest?

Truthfully, we don't know exactly, since no major industrial nation has yet embarked on such a journey. But there's plenty of reason to suspect that the road will be passable, if bumpy, at first, and smoother later. If we continue on the current freeway, however, we'll find out it ends impassable and in ruins.

Surely we can't deny that if every American, for example, took up voluntary simplicity tomorrow, massive economic disruption would result. But that won't happen. A shift away from affluenza, if we're lucky enough to witness one, will come gradually, over a generation perhaps. Economic growth, as measured by Gross Domestic Product, will slow down and might even become negative. But as economist Juliet Schor points out, there are many European countries (including Holland, Denmark, Sweden, and Norway) whose economies have grown far more slowly than ours, yet whose quality of life – measured by many of the indicators we say we want, including free time, citizen participation, lower crime, greater job security, income-equality, health, and overall life contentment – is higher than our own. Such economies show no sign of collapse. Indeed, their savings rates are high, their deficits are low, and their currencies, especially the Euro, are increasing in value while the dollar plummets. Their emphasis on balancing growth with sustainability is widely accepted across the political spectrum. As former Dutch Prime Minister Ruud Lubbers, a conservative, put it:

> It is true that the Dutch are not aiming to maximize gross national product per capita. Rather, we are seeking to attain a high quality of life, a just, participatory and sustainable society. While the Dutch economy is very efficient per working hour, the number of working hours per citizen are rather limited. We like it that way. Needless to say, there is more room for all those important aspects of our lives that are not part of our jobs, for which we are not paid and for which there is never enough time.[4]

Time for an Attitude Adjustment

If anti-affluenza legislation leads to slower rates of economic growth or a 'steady state' economy that does not grow at all, so be it (growth of GDP is a poor measure of social health anyway). Beating the affluenza bug will also lead to less stress, more leisure time, better health, and longer lives. It will offer more time for family, friends, and community. And it will lead to less traffic, less road rage, less noise, less pollution, and a kinder, gentler, more meaningful way of life.

In a '60s TV American commercial, an actor claims that Kool cigarettes are 'as cool and clean as a breath of fresh air.' We watch that commercial today and can't keep a straight face, but when it first aired, nobody laughed. Since that time, we've come to understand that cigarettes are unhealthy, silent killers. We've banned TV ads for them. We tax them severely, limit smoking areas, and seek to make tobacco companies pay the full costs of the damage cigarettes cause. We once thought them sexy, but today most of us think they're gross.

Where smoking is concerned, our attitudes have certainly changed. Now, with growing evidence that affluenza is also hazardous, it's surely time for another attitude adjustment.

(Endnotes)

1 Parts of this essay appeared in the book *Affluenza: The All-consuming Epidemic*, by John de Graaf, David Wann, and Thomas Naylor (Berrett-Koehler Publishers, 2005.) While the original essay was written with an almost entirely United States-based focus, much of its content applies throughout the developed industrial world. It is still somewhat US-centric, but in this revised essay the focus has been broadened as much as possible.

2 In this quote Jackobson is referring to the United States. If you do not live in the United States, ask yourself, as you read this essay, whether or in what ways your country too may be structurally set up to oppose voluntary simplicity.

3 From the TV documentary *Green Plans*, 1995.

4 Anders Hayden, *Sharing the Work, Sparing the Planet*, 2000.

Chapter Eighteen

EXTENDING THE MOVEMENT

Mary Grigsby

Whether Voluntary Simplicity Movement groups will branch out to more systematically organized collective action, take on more traditional political agendas, build coalitions with a diverse range of other groups, or continue to keep the focus primarily on self-change will be influenced by the political context and actions of people in the movement, and remains to be seen. There are indications that formation of a still loosely bounded but somewhat more cohesive and identifiable network of people involved in voluntary simplicity is underway.

The line between cultural and political transformation is not clean or definitive among movement participants. Research suggests that dichotomizing cultural and political protest may not be helpful in understanding the transformative capacity of movements such as voluntary simplicity. Though the circles I studied have not organized for political action in the traditional sense, some members of circles do participate in networks that are more oriented toward political action and they don't draw clear lines between their voluntary simplicity practices and politics. Movement leaders are increasingly interested in developing a movement policy agenda and ability to mobilize movement participants to support policy initiatives. How successful their efforts will be also remains to be seen.

I chose to study voluntary simplicity because it resonated with me as hopeful. It still does. But I don't believe, as many simple livers, at least at times, do, that self-change in keeping with the prescriptions of voluntary simplicity will result in an evolutionary shift to an ecological era without major political and economic shifts that will need to be achieved through policies aimed at structural and cultural change as well. Voluntary simplicity, as it is lived by the simple livers I studied, offers support for taking action daily, encourages people to look for alternative ways of organizing community, and offers critique of some aspects of the capitalist economy, patriarchy, and consumerist culture. The critique is more powerful, though still incomplete in my view, than the ability of the prescribed solutions to deliver the desired results.

Corporations regularly overproduce, dump the overproduction, and still make a profit. Buying less may produce change in production practices over time, but large numbers of people will have to participate in organized consumer boycotts to put greater pressure on corporations to improve their practices. Quitting midlevel professional jobs is unlikely to open up jobs for the poor since they often lack the educational credentials and cultural capital necessary to be hired for such jobs.

Legislation to limit the ownership capacities of transnational corporations and monopolies needs to be brought about if the economy is going to be moved away from pursuit of profit to social democratic aims, and this will require political action, which can take many forms, among them diffusion of voluntary simplicity ideas through media which has already begun. But the ideas of voluntary simplicity need to be developed to link their complaints and demands to clearly articulated and plausible policies that can be carried into existing political structures to bring about institutional change, as unwieldy and frustrating as such work may be, and as much as we may wish those structures were already different. Protestors against the World Trade Organization and corporate accountability advocates offer such links for Voluntary Simplicity Movement participants. Other movements also offer possible alliances and networking opportunities for people in voluntary simplicity. Greater efforts to organize new workers by the AFL-CIO; increasing anti-sweatshop organizing by students and labor advocates; increased attention to environmental racism and emerging alliances with labor advocates; and the relative rise in welfare rights and antipoverty activism are presently taking place.[1]

The challenge for people in the Voluntary Simplicity Movement, who are committed to achieving the broader goals they claim, is to hold onto their commitment to personal change while they shift their concerns outward to the institutional level to engage in organized resistance and in their communities to engage in a higher level of recognition of difference and commonality. Underestimating the importance of difference all too easily results in slipping into reproducing the inequalities associated with the differences. It all too easily results in discounting the need for input from those situated differently from ourselves in devising our solutions. Too easily we are then able to view ourselves as the given norm. Too easily the solutions arrived at fit what is comfortable for us as a group. Reflexivity benefits our understanding of ourselves as social beings whose very sense of self, group belonging, and others is culturally and economically constructed. If simplicity groups grapple with how to bring about the changes they desire at the institutional level and to find common ground with other groups in the same concrete ways they have used to achieve personal-level change, the movement has great promise.

This sociological analysis points to further actions that those who envision the kind of relationships and practices that voluntary simplicity at the highest level of meaning represents can take to contribute to the shifts they say they want to make.[2] In this concluding analysis I offer the following ideas for improving the emancipatory capacity of the movement in the hopes that they may be useful in bringing us closer to goals we share.

Coalition Building

1. Build an institutional infrastructure that links existing voluntary simplicity organizations and can provide the base for creating networks and coalitions with other groups.
2. Share knowledge and build coalitions with the poor and racial and ethnic minorities based on common concerns such as environmental pollution, environmental dumping, exposure to hazardous materials, and adequate social services. Recognize that the poor and ethnic and racial minorities can contribute to the ideas, practices, and agendas of voluntary simplicity in significant ways and actively seek ways to bring them into the discussions within the movement.
3. Recognize and use overlapping concerns of labor and voluntary simplicity, since working-class laborers are often the victims of the toxic effects of industry, and labor would benefit from a shorter work week and higher levels of control over the aims to which industry is put.
4. Link with political parties that have platforms consistent with voluntary simplicity values and goals without giving up a focus on self and grassroots change and community building. The New Party and Green Party are two that have platforms that are compatible with many of the ideas held by people in the movement.[3]
5. Build coalitions with the academic community and invite research and teaching about voluntary simplicity.
6. Build networks and coalitions with nongovernmental organizations with common concerns.

Improving Participation and Recognition Across Difference Within the Movement

7. Institute methods for increasing the awareness of difference in circles and create ways of building strength across differences rather than just tolerating, denying, or glossing over them. Figure out ways to use recognition of differences to strengthen the movement and to bring marginalized people, including the poor and racial and ethnic minorities, into the movement as full participants.[4]
8. Recognize the importance of race and analyze whiteness as a feature that is significant to the movement and the people attracted to it. Recognize more completely the relative advantage whiteness provides. Instead of discounting it as significant for the movement, keep the question of being privileged open for review.

9. Recognize the importance of gender inequality as a barrier to equitable decision making about access to and distribution of resources. Problematize the institutions of patriarchy, not just the dominant cultural roles and behaviors of men and women. Question the heterosexual norm and other forms of institutionalized gender inequality..
10. Recognize gender power tensions within the movement and the implications they have for the way the movement is organized and the form it may take if it expands. Follow the women-centered model[5] of organizing and question the emergence of competitive, hierarchical ways of organizing so that a voluntary simplicity community will be a model of process that continues to strive to be inclusive, respectful of difference and autonomy, cooperative, and noncompetitive. This is, of course, an ideal that is never perfectly achieved but it is worth striving for. In the short run, those who value the women-centered model which is at the heart of voluntary simplicity ideology[6] need to stand up for their desired approach and encourage those who try to dominate circle agendas to be reflexive and to stop.

Extending the Politics of the Movement

11. Open movement ideology up to recognition of the connections between inequality and sex- and race-segregated work. Recognize how racial and ethnic minorities and women are systematically used as the source for generating surplus value for capitalist corporations as one way of producing profit and investment dividends. Develop practices to reduce participation in these modes of exploitation.
12. Demand the right for all to have work that provides a living wage and humane working conditions with reasonable hours of work. Don't focus just on the right of the affluent to reject undesirable long hours of work and ways of helping them figure out how to opt out.
13. Recognize that in the present economy chances are that your survival and having enough comes from resources derived not only from the earth but at least in part from work — if not your own, then someone else's. Gain a more complete understanding of the relations between investment income and the oppression of others through inhumane work conditions and environmentally damaging practices. Recognize and problematize how simple livers continue to be dependent on a profit-and-growth-driven economy. Adopt socially and environmentally conscious investing if you invest. Imperfect though the options may be, it is potentially just as effective a signal to the market as environmentally sustainable consumption practices are.
14. Recognize that while avoiding consumerist practices is important and helpful, it won't necessarily be enough to change the profit-driven

economy or cause corporations to adopt environmentally sensitive production methods in a timely way. Policies that legally limit corporate practices are necessary too. Add boycotts of products and specific corporations to the already highly elaborated guidelines for sustainable consumption practices of the movement. Link with other groups engaged in such boycotts.[7]

15. Develop an important role in crafting policy (perhaps even establish a political party that has a policy agenda based on the values of voluntary simplicity) at the grassroots and more broadly, joining with other groups with similar concerns to advocate beneficial policy changes such as legally limiting corporate practices that damage the environment and are unjust.[8]

The participation in community life, volunteer work, and economic transactions of simple livers – who at the same time take an oppositional stance toward a taken-for-granted profit-driven economy, rationalized waged work, and consumerist culture – is a stance that can generate change since it brings simple livers into contact with many nonsimple livers. It is a balancing act for movement participants since they must constantly do ideological work to establish their difference at the same time they depend on many features of the dominant culture for their survival and sense of identity and draw upon it to elaborate the alternative they are advocating.

Audre Lorde says you can't dismantle the master's house using the master's tools.[9] But any tools we make, even those that are aimed at opposition, are, at least in part, created in the context of our relations to that house. The people in the Voluntary Simplicity Movement deserve credit for their struggle to fashion new tools. I have tried to acknowledge the limitations of these tools, in their present forms, since in their present embodiment within the lives of simple livers they only partially fulfill the goals simple livers have for emancipatory change. Simple livers are resourceful people with good intentions. They take from the culture pieces that they perceive to fit their purposes, combine them in new ways, craft new meanings with them, and create something new that does shift and transform some relationships. But they don't bring with them only their intended and chosen tools. Their own relative power brings with it aspects of the dominant culture and economy that remain hidden from the full view of simple livers. Even when a group creates an oppositional safe space from which to speak, as those in voluntary simplicity are doing, there are forces at the biographical, cultural, and institutional levels that impinge on the oppositional impulses. At the present moment they are engaged in a dialectical process of changing understandings and material relations[10] that holds the possibility of taking many different directions.

Those playing major roles in institutionalizing the movement have begun to create organizations aimed at cultural change through voluntary simplicity and to direct the resources they have toward diffusion of the ideas. The resources they have include their creative use of culture in constructing an alternative ideology and innovative alternative practices that resonate well with increasing numbers of participants whose biographical histories and current social and economic circumstances it both reflects and responds to. Other resources are monies from book sales, highly skilled volunteers who work for no wage, and networks that give them broad access for diffusion of ideas about voluntary simplicity. These are powerful resources.

The voluntary simplicity cultural movement is struggling with dominant cultural definitions of what constitutes right livelihood and what values should direct the economy and culture. This suggests that, at least in the case of this cultural movement, efforts to generate change extend beyond identity work into a struggle to define what right livelihood is and what constitutes desirable community, culture, and economy. At the highest level of meaning people in voluntary simplicity are engaged in a cultural struggle over the power to say what constitutes moral action for those they define as affluent people. People in the movement carry their voluntary simplicity values and practices into their communities. They elaborate the ideology, practices, and agendas of the movement and institutionalization of it is underway.

When I show *Escape from Affluenza* in my classes at the midwestern university where I teach, the students often say they believe the ideas are good and right but that they could never adopt such extreme practices. These practices do not seem extreme to me anymore. I have to remind myself that voluntary simplicity represents a major shift that is presently unthinkable for most people in my sociology classes and the larger society. The breadth of the influence of voluntary simplicity in twentieth century America and beyond remains to be seen. Much depends on how efforts at diffusion proceed, whether deeper recognition of difference is addressed, and how simple livers elaborate the ideology and practices. Much also depends on changes in the broader culture and economy, how the process of globalization impacts the United States, and how other groups seeking change make meaning of these changes and respond to them.

The energy that adopting voluntary simplicity generates in informants and the emergent quality of the ideas and practices of the movement suggest we will be hearing more from the voluntary simplicity cultural movement in the months and years to come.

(Endnotes)

1 (Reese 2000, 1, 2001).

2 Alain Touraine, 'An Introduction to the Study of Social Movements,' *Social Research* (1985) 52(4) 749–87.

3 Three respondents were Green Party members and two had worked on the campaign of a Green Party candidate in Seattle. Juliet Schor, whose work is read by some in the Voluntary Simplicity Movement and whose ideas about changes needed in the economy and culture are compatible with voluntary simplicity, is a member of the New Party, which works primarily at the local level and was organized as a response to the grassroots political efforts of the Christian right. The New Party platform (http://www.newparty.org/) includes among its many goals the creation of a sustainable economy based on 'the responsible and reverent use of the earth's resources;' full employment, a shorter work week, and a guaranteed minimum income for all adults; a universal social wage to include basic health care, child care, vacation time, and life-long access to education and training, and comparable worth. The platform outlines policies to achieve these goals.

4 In the fall 2001 issue of *Seeds & Circles* Carol Holst reported on a new program initiated by Seeds of Simplicity and Dr. Lourdes Arguelles of Claremont Graduate University held early in 2002 setting up discussion between simplicity circles and 'marginalized' communities. The goals of these dialogues, according to Holst, were to strengthen the social-justice pillar of the simplicity movement, and to broaden its predominantly middle-class focus by linking the practitioners of voluntary simplicity with those involved in involuntary simplicity. In a telephone conversation on December 12, 2002, Holst said, "Strengthening the social justice component of voluntary simplicity has always been in the Seeds of Simplicity's planning and it is now blossoming thanks to the opportunity brought forward by Claremont University and as a response to critiques.' This suggests that key people in the movement such as Carol Holst are looking for opportunities to broaden the base of the movement and are quite open to constructive critiques aimed at enhancing the transformative capacity of the movement. It suggests a vital and responsive approach to bringing new ideas into the movement.

5 Susan Stall and Randy Stoecker, 'Community Organizing or Organizing Community? Gender and Crafts of Empowerment,' *Gender & Society* (1998) 12(6) 729–56.

6 Cecile Andrews, *The Circle of Simplicity: Return to the Good Life* (1997).

7 The participation of some highly respected circle members in the World Trade Organization protests in Seattle in November 1999 offers an example an opportunity for collective action that has engaged some in the movement in political activism and shifted the focus of grass roots participants.

8 In 2001 fifty people drawn from the Voluntary Simplicity Movement, the private sector, and research institutions met to begin the process of developing a policy research agenda for the movement. A second meeting to include a broader representation of people was held in 2002, and a third scheduled for 2003.

9 Audre Lorde, *Sister Outsider* (1984).

10 Kenneth J. Benson, 'Organizations: A Dialectical View' *Administrative Science Quarterly* (1977) 22, 1–21.

Chapter Nineteen

TRANSCENDENTAL SIMPLICITY

David E. Shi

Not all advocates of simple living during the first half of the nineteenth century were intent upon institutionalizing traditional moral and social values. As Ralph Waldo Emerson observed in 1844, there 'was in all the practical activities of New England for the last quarter of a century, a gradual withdrawal of tender consciences from the social organizations.' These 'tender consciences,' imbued with a romantic emphasis on naturalism, immediatism, individualism, and perfectionism, espoused a more spontaneous and liberating version of the simple life than that promoted by conservative moralists. The romantics viewed simplicity as a personally chosen, rather than a socially imposed, way of living. Full of burning enthusiasm and millennialist expectations, these visionary nonconformists were more interested in perfecting individuals than in perfecting institutions, and they insisted on the sufficiency of their own standards of happiness and virtue. In practice this meant that romantic simplicity was less a societal ethic than a spiritual ethic, and many of its excited practitioners were deemed eccentric, naive, or utopian by their peers.[1]

The romantics were indeed more extreme and diverse in their interpretation of simplicity than their Puritan, Quaker, or Revolutionary era predecessors. They inclined toward the party of rebellion and innovation rather than of preservation. Some followed the advice of Sylvester Graham, a charismatic minister and self-taught nutritionist who advocated sexual moderation, chaste reading, meatlessness, and a bran bread diet as the prescription for moral improvement and physical health. Others promoted the simplification of clothing, favoring Byron collars, loose, flowing garments, and gaily colored blouses. A few professed a sweeping disavowal of the cash nexus and the factory system or assailed particular professions such as law and commerce. Many joined utopian communities designed to avoid the snares and temptations of laissez-faire individualism and cosmopolitan living.[2]

Such attitudes and practices proved quite disconcerting to defenders of the status quo. In 1841 William Ellery Channing, the inspiring Unitarian minister and social activist, noted the fears expressed by many public spokesmen upon learning that there were 'enthusiastic romantic reformers' preaching the virtues of 'quaker plainness of dress' in a nation devoted to superfluous finery. Channing, however, was not worried by such activities:

> What! Danger from romance and enthusiasm in this money-getting, self-seeking, self-indulging, self-displaying land? I confess that to me it is a comfort to see some outbreak of enthusiasm, whether transcendental, philanthropic, or religious, as a proof that the human spirit is not wholly engulfed in matter and business, that it can lift up a little the mountains of worldliness and sense with which it is so borne down.

Channing saw great potential in a romantic movement dedicated to simplicity, spirituality, and societal change. There is 'an element – spiritual, moral, and tending towards perfection – in the present movement; and that is my great hope.' He was overjoyed that there were young Americans moved not by dreams of material success but by 'ideas, by principles, by the conception of a better state of society!'[3]

Among the many romantic 'enthusiasts' preaching the virtues of simple living in the Middle Period, the most articulate were the Transcendentalists, that colorful group of inspired poets and philosophers centered in Concord. While other Americans were clamoring for internal improvements in the form of canals, railroads, and harbors, the Transcendentalists wanted infernal improvements in man himself. Emerson, Thoreau, Theodore Parker, Frederic Hedge, Bronson Alcott, George Ripley, Margaret Fuller, Elizabeth Peabody, Orestes Brownson, and other like-minded thinkers literally sought to *transcend* the limitations of Lockean rationalism and penetrate the inner recesses of the self. To them, intuitive truths were ultimately more meaningful than empirical facts or entrenched conventions. The Transcendentalist, Emerson explained, 'believes in miracle, in the perpetual openness of the human mind to new influx of light and power; he believes in inspiration, and in ecstasy.' Religious freethinkers, philosophic idealists, and literary romantics, they sought to experience the same felt spirituality that had energized the early Quakers. This mystical emphasis led them to promote the ideal of self-culture already being so eloquently espoused by the Reverend Dr. Channing. In seeking the good life, Channing had argued, one must begin with the conviction that 'there is something greater within him than in the whole material creation, than in all the worlds which press on the eye and ear; and that inward improvements have a worth and dignity in themselves.'[4]

As interpreted by the Transcendentalists, Channing's ethic of self-culture entailed a Pythagorean simple life of material self-control and intellectual exertion. It also implied a reverential attitude toward the natural world. Where Enlightenment simplicity found its guiding impulse primarily in classical philosophy and Protestant simplicity looked to Jesus' example, the romantic sensibility saw nature as the source of aesthetic pleasure, moral goodness, and spiritual inspiration. Jefferson, Crevecoeur, Philip Freneau, William Bartram, and other eighteenth-century agrarians had foreshadowed such an attitude. For them, however, nature primarily represented earth to be worked and planted. The farmer's labor was itself an ennobling enterprise. During the nineteenth century, however, farming was frequently a life of 'quiet desperation' rather than Homeric or Jeffersonian contemplation, and thus the romantics tended to view nature more in pastoral than agrarian terms. They found in the woods both a retreat from modern complexity and an opportunity for soul-searching introspection. The divine energies at work in the countryside had an ecstatic effect on them, elevating and expanding their vision of the possible and clarifying their understanding of themselves. For the romantic naturalists, therefore, the path to the good life began with self-discovery and then led to an organic synthesis of that self with the natural world surrounding it.[5]

This ideal, of course, had been commonly espoused by Old World romantics for years. But the American Transcendentalists differed from their European counterparts in that they grafted a romantic naturalism onto the tough and springy root of Puritan moralism. 'The moral law,' Emerson wrote, 'lies at the center of nature and radiates to the circumference.' He and other like-minded Transcendentalists translated that nature-inspired moral law into a personal ethic of material restraint and profound thinking. With Wordsworth they believed that 'there is no real happiness in life but in intellect and virtue.' But with Winthrop and Edwards they insisted that the moral life entailed a spartan-like control of the baser instincts.[6]

The Transcendentalist appeal for a more enlightened and spiritual approach to getting and spending, however, evoked little sympathy among the New England social and economic elite. 'The view taken of Transcendentalism in State Street,' Emerson remarked in his journal in 1841, 'is that it threatens to invalidate contracts.' To many members of the New England business and religious establishment, the Transcendentalist outlook smacked of antinomianism, and most commentators declared its reformist message subversive; it challenged both social stability and economic progress. Consequently, the Transcendentalists, like the Quaker enthusiasts of the mideighteenth century who had also found their ideas rebuffed by the larger society, were forced to turn back on themselves for fellowship and support. It was a 'sign of our times,' Emerson observed, that 'many intellectual and religious persons' withdrew from the 'market and the caucus' in order to find something 'worthy to do.'[7]

Since the Transcendentalists were convinced that life was too precious to waste on the mere pursuit and enjoyment of things, their common goal was to develop modes of living that reduced their material and institutional needs to a minimum so that they could more easily pursue spiritual truths, moral ideals, and aesthetic impulses. William Henry Channing, the nephew of the Reverend Dr. Channing, succinctly expressed their credo: 'To live content with small means; to seek elegance rather than luxury, and refinement rather than fashion; to be worthy, not respectable, and wealthy, not rich; to study hard, think quietly, talk gently, act frankly. . . This is my symphony.' The Transcendentalist symphony included many variations on this theme, ranging from the communal experiments in simple living at Brook Farm and Fruitlands to the more individual and reclusive patterns of living practiced respectively by Emerson and Thoreau. Whatever the arrangement, it was a difficult symphony to play. The Congregationalist minister Horace Bushnell pointed out in 1843 that only 'a few towering trunks alone' were successfully practicing such a romantic simplicity. In the Transcendental forest, the two most 'towering trunks' were Emerson and Thoreau, one a majestic oak, the other an aloof elm.[8]

'Life is a selection, no more.' So wrote Emerson in 1846. It was one of those deceptively simple pronouncements that he was a master at composing. In those six words he captured the essence of his own moral outlook and that of the Transcendentalists. The selections Emerson made during his life were almost always intended to reduce the complexity of his life and to enhance his ability to engage in contemplation. 'Great men,' he once maintained, 'are they that see that [the] spiritual is stronger than any material force; that thoughts rule the world.' Thoughts certainly ruled Emerson's universe, and the sources of his thinking were numerous and diverse, ranging from Greek and Roman philosophy to German idealism and English romanticism to Quaker and Oriental mysticism. Often overlooked but equally influential in shaping his moral philosophy was the combined influence of his difficult childhood and his Puritan heritage.[9]

In 1811, when Emerson was only eight, his minister father died of tuberculosis, leaving the family destitute and dependent on charity. The congregation provided widower Ruth Haskins Emerson with a $500 annual pension and the privilege of living in the parish house for a time. Still, to meet expenses, she was forced to sell the family library at auction and to take in boarders over the years. Growing up in such 'deprived' circumstances taught young Emerson the necessity of hard work, cooperation, frugality, and charity. He and his four brothers helped with the housework, performed odd jobs, and shared overcoats in winter. With few frills to distract him, Waldo, as he was called, developed during his youth a preoccupation with reading and thinking. He later credited the 'iron band of poverty, of necessity, of austerity with steering him and his brothers away from the purely sensual and 'into safe and right channels,' making them, 'despite themselves, reverers of the grand, the beautiful, and the good.'[10]

Family tradition initially led Emerson into the ministry, but by 1832 he had come to find the formalisms of the 'cold and cheerless' Unitarian faith too confining. The tragic death of his young wife in 1831 heightened his disillusionment, and he resigned his pastorate at twenty-nine.

After an excursion to Europe that included visits with Wordsworth and Carlyle, Emerson settled with his mother in Concord in 1834, living in the 'Manse' that his grandfather had built before the Revolution. The next year he and his new wife, Lidian Jackson, relocated to a house on the Lexington road. There he was soon 'imparadised.' The house was nestled among two acres of stately pine and fir trees near the Concord River. It was also surrounded by an inviting countryside, and there Emerson found both solitude and solace. 'In the woods,' he discovered, 'is perpetual youth.'[11]

Emerson took walks almost daily. From his house he strolled down the river to Peter's Field or sauntered to Walden Pond, where he would sit on the bank for enchanted hours reading Goethe. The meadows, streams, hemlocks, and pines around Concord filled him with a sense of Providential immanence. All nature was metaphor to him, freighted with meaning and mystery. The countryside was indeed the poet's province, and in its beauty and wonder Emerson surmounted his melancholy and achieved the organic unity between the mental and the spiritual, the human and the universal, that characterized the romantic temperament. He thus rejected the Puritan idea that nature was 'a howling wilderness,' inhabited by the unredeemed, and therefore a force to be fought and subdued. Instead, he came to see the woods as a source of inner harmony and moral strength, a place suffused with divinity and beauty, waiting to enlighten and enliven all visitors. To Emerson, who always valued the seeing eye over the shaping hand, nature was to be contemplated, not conquered. By communing with nature, he wrote, man became 'part and parcel with God,' thereby approaching the ultimate simplification of life. Having discovered himself through nature, Emerson would now be the spokesman for young America, exchanging the gown of pastor for the frock coat of lecturer, ministering to 'all who would live in the spirit.'[12]

Thanks largely to the $1200 a year he received from a legacy provided by his first wife, Emerson developed in Concord the scholarly routine of introspection, writing, community service, occasional preaching, and frequent lecturing, for which he quickly became famous. Occasionally he felt some uneasiness about his unexpected source of income. 'I please myself,' he reassured his conscience in one of his journal entries, 'with the thought that my accidental freedom by means of a permanent income is no wise essential to my habits.' Emerson's Puritan strain ensured that he led a life of enlightened material restraint. His wife Lidian once said: 'No one should take any more than his own share, let him be even so rich,' and he later labeled this the 'true doctrine.' Inured to simple pleasures as a youth, he was easily contented as an adult. Emerson compensated for his own good fortune by sharing it with others, frequently inviting needy friends such as the Alcotts or Henry Thoreau to share his house and his beneficence.[13]

The moral philosophy that Emerson formulated in Concord was based on the same duality of man and hierarchy of values developed by the Greeks and later modified by the Puritans and Quakers. Like Aristotle, Winthrop, and Woolman, he believed that there were two selves – inner and outer, spiritual and material, imaginative and physical. Each is an essential aspect of human experience, but Emerson insisted that the inner self was ultimately superior. The care and culture of man's spirit was far more important than satisfying the political economy of his senses. This is not to say that he dismissed the material side of life lightly. At times in his essays, in fact, Emerson could be rhapsodic about the benefits of prosperity and technology, leading some readers over the years to label him a bourgeois apologist. In one of his most exuberant moods, Emerson found 'money in its effects and laws, as beautiful as roses.' He often heaped praise on the nation's entrepreneurial and engineering achievements, noting that American technology promised to 'make the world plastic and to lift human life out of its beggary to a god-like ease and power.'[14]

But this was the aesthetic, not the moralistic, side of Emerson speaking. He always maintained that money and technology were to be valued only for their *instrumental* qualities, for what they could contribute to the more noble pursuits of self-culture. 'Trade was one instrument,' he wrote in 'The Young American,' but 'Trade is also but for a time, and must give way to somewhat broader and better, whose signs are already dawning in the sky.' Though recognizing that the world of business was not intrinsically evil, he noted that it was too often considered an end in itself. The 'general system of our trade... is a system of selfishness; is not dictated by the high sentiments of human nature; is not measured by the exact law of reciprocity; much less by the sentiments of love and heroism, but is a system of distrust, of concealment, of superior keenness, not of giving but of taking advantage.' The 'true thrift,' he cautioned, 'is always to spend on the higher plane; to invest and invest, with keener avarice, that he may spend in spiritual creation and not in augmenting animal existence.'[15]

Emerson called this his 'gradational ethic.' In an essay on Plato he wrote that all 'things are in a scale, and begin where we will, ascend and ascend.' Emerson repeatedly explained to his listeners and readers that in stressing the primacy of thoughts over things he was not asking them to abandon their coarse labors and flee to the woods like Rousseau's 'noble savage.' The good life, he stressed, required more than 'the crust of bread and the roof.' It should include 'the freedom of the city, freedom of the earth, traveling, machinery, the benefits of science, music and fine arts, the best culture and the best company.' Emerson clearly recognized the benefits of a capitalist economy. The 'end of culture,' he explained, 'is not to destroy this, God forbid!' Americans needed not to overthrow the economic order but to redress the imbalance that had developed between materialism and idealism in their pursuit of happiness. This meant instituting a thoroughgoing reform of domestic habits that 'must correct the whole system of our social living.' And such reform must 'come with plain living and high thinking.' By placing work and its rewards in the proper perspective, subordinating the material to the spiritual, man could achieve the higher level of being advocated earlier by Puritans, Quakers, and classical republicans.[16]

Emerson therefore shared Woolman's belief that leading the good life required neither external legislation nor institutional reforms but inner self-control, the ability to live within one's means in order to afford the luxury of contemplation and creativity. In his 'Lecture on the Times' (1841), he praised the conservative reformers for their objectives but criticized them for their methods. They were relying too much on institutions, legislation, peer pressure, and other external 'circumstances' to promote republican simplicity. Most of the self-appointed improvers of society, Emerson felt, apparently forgetting his own sermonizing tendencies, were so busy pointing out the faults of others that they neglected their own moral deficiencies. He referred to most reformers as 'narrow, self-pleasing, conceited men, [who] affect us as the insane do. They bite us, and we run mad also.'[17]

Emerson was especially sceptical of the many educational reformers dotting the New England landscape. 'A treatise on education, a lecture, a system,' he wrote, 'affects us with a slight paralysis and a certain yawning of jaws.' Nor was he enamored of those moral guardians advocating the domestication of manners and mores. 'I suffer whenever I see that common sight of a parent or a senior imposing his opinion and way of thinking on a young soul to which they are totally unfit.' His own family had taught him how to think rather than what to think, and this was Emerson's preferred approach, for his ideal of self-culture required the freedom of self-discovery. The domestication of culture 'in the high sense does not consist in polishing and varnishing,' but in 'liberating oneself from acquired habits.' He himself refused to specify any precise code of conduct that could be used as a universal standard in American homes and classrooms. Since to him intuition was the fount of truth, man needed to free himself as much as possible from external restraints in order to allow 'new infusions' of the spirit of God to transform him.'[18]

Here Emerson was obviously parting company with his Puritan forebears and reflecting the individualism so visible in his Aunt Mary. Moral instruction was done best, he argued, by benign example rather than by coercive dogmatism. 'Cannot we let people be themselves and enjoy life in their own way?' While the conservators of culture were demanding conformity to their version of republican simplicity, Emerson was urging that 'Whoso would be a man, must be a nonconformist.' In a land of abundant opportunities and social diversity, the American, Emerson assumed, had the luxury of freedom of choice. If he wanted to engage in a life devoted to pursuits higher than the merely material, it was his choice to make. He 'may fix his inventories of necessities and enjoyments on what scale he pleases, but if he wishes the power and privilege of thought, the chalking out of his own career and having society on his own terms, he must bring his wants within his proper power to satisfy.'[19]

The self-reliance Emerson preached was in this sense quite distinct from tooth-and-claw individualism, for the thoughtful individual in his scheme must place clearly defined limits on economic activity where the latter did not. 'It is better to go without,' he asserted, 'than to have them [possessions] at too great a cost. Let us learn the meaning of Economy.' For him, frugality was merely a means to a noble end. Plain living was designed to lead to high thinking of one sort or another – intellectual, moral, spiritual. 'Economy is a high, humane office, a sacrament, when its aim is grand; when it is the prudence of simple tastes, when it is practiced for freedom, or love, or devotion.'[20]

Despite his frequent criticism of professional reformers, Emerson, like so many other spokesmen for simple living, could be interpreted as a social conservative preaching to those below him to be content with their material lot. He once advised, 'If we will take the good we find, asking no questions, we shall have heaping measures.' He never could identify with the intense practical problems of those who were literally hungry or physically mistreated by callous foremen. Yet to interpret Emerson as merely reflecting class bias is to ignore the fact that he spent much of his time lecturing those already successful on their need for simpler living. His experience dealing with Boston's social and cultural elite, for example, convinced him that possessions held in excess tended to become barriers to honest human relationships. People of means too often preferred to show visitors what they owned rather than what they thought. Emerson once imagined in his journal that if 'Socrates were here, we could go and walk with him; but Longfellow, we cannot talk with; there is a palace, and servants, and a row of bottles of different colored wines, and fine coats.'[21]

As he viewed American society in the 1830s and 1840s, Emerson saw far too many Longfellows cluttering their lives with the trappings of wealth. 'It is a sufficient accusation of our way of living,' he maintained, '...that our idea of domestic well-being now needs wealth to execute it.' He agreed with those foreign observers who highlighted the excessive materialism of Americans: 'We... set a higher value on wealth, victory and coarse superiority of all kinds, than other men, have less tranquility of mind, are less easily contented.' A 'vulgar prosperity' was corrupting the nation's moral vision, and it was largely to help remedy such a situation that Emerson directed much of his oratory and prose. In an early issue of the Transcendentalist journal, the *Dial*, he promised that the new magazine would serve as a forum for promoting 'the new heroic life of man, the now unbelieved possibility of simple living, and of clean and noble relations with men.'[22]

Emerson was an eloquent spokesman for contemplative simple living, and his words helped inspire a wide array of individual and group efforts to put into practice the ethic he preached. Like Channing, he took great pleasure in the 'few hermits' who were expressing 'thoughts and principles' that went against the grain of larger society's materialist conformity. But he was somewhat taken aback by the explosive manifestations of romantic simplicity. In a letter to Thomas Carlyle in 1840 he reported: 'We are all a little wild here with numberless projects of social reform. Not a reading man but has a draft of a new community in his waistcoat pocket. George Ripley is talking up a colony of agriculturalists & scholars with whom he threatens to take the field & the book. One man renounces the use of animal food; and another of coin; and another of domestic hired service, and another of the State.' Emerson himself retreated from such extremes and panaceas. 'I do not wish to be absurd and pedantic in reform. I do not wish to push my criticism on the state of things around me to that extravagant mark, that shall compel me to suicide or to absolute isolation from the advantages of civil society.'[23]

Emerson revealed his consternation at the eclectic applications of Transcendental simplicity in his response to the communal experiments at Brook Farm and Fruitlands. Brook Farm, founded in 1841 in West Roxbury, was ostensibly designed to put into practice the ideals that Emerson had promoted. Its residents were determined, as one of them wrote, 'to secure as many hours as possible from necessary toil' in order to spend more leisure time 'for the production of intellectual goods.' The Brook Farmers were not countenancing primitivism, but hoped to provide 'all the elegances desirable for bodily and spiritual health: books, apparatus, collections for science, works of art, means of beautiful amusements.' Brook Farm's organizer, George Ripley, declared that the community was not intended to be a pastoral retreat but a revived 'city on a hill.' If 'wisely executed,' he promised Emerson, Brook Farm 'will be a light over this country and age. If not the sunrise, it will be the morning star.' Genuinely convinced that such enlightened communalism was the wave of the future, Ripley saw Brook Farm as providing a practical alternative for Americans oppressed by competitive capitalism and eager to pursue self-culture within a community of like-minded souls. Brook Farm, one visitor wrote, 'aims to be rich, not in the metallic representation of wealth, but in wealth itself, which money should represent, namely, *leisure to live in all the faculties of the soul*.'[24]

Certainly Emerson could not find fault with such elevated aspirations. He sympathized with Ripley's 'noble and humane' intentions and initially was tempted to participate if he could be 'sure of compeers of the right stamp.' But when Ripley refused to give him such assurances and stressed his intention to promote a diverse group of settlers, Emerson balked. 'I wish to break all prisons,' he pointed out, and to him the eclectic collectivism of Brook Farm promised to be a 'larger prison than his present domestic life.' Moreover, Emerson disliked the idea of living in a community intentionally isolated from society. In Concord he already lived 'in an agreeable neighborhood, in a town which I have many reasons to love.'[25]

Utopian reformers such as Ripley, Emerson felt, failed to recognize that 'we do not make a world of our own but fall into institutions already made & have to accommodate ourselves to be useful at all.' He then admitted that such accommodation represented 'a loss of so much integrity & of course of so much power.' Obviously, Emerson's earlier praise of nonconformity had its limits. He did not intend to be taken so literally. Practically speaking, he asked, how 'shall the world get on if all its *beaux esprits* recalcitrate upon its approved forms & accepted institutions & quit them all in order to be singleminded?' He feared that such perfectionist communities would inevitably become asylums. Emerson concluded that instead of turning their backs on the world, Ripley and his followers should disperse 'and so leaven the whole clump of society.'[26]

Perhaps Emerson was right. Or maybe he was being hypocritical. Whatever the case, Brook Farm was a significant expression of the romantic desire to pursue simplicity as an actual way of life, and the efforts of its residents should not be lightly dismissed. Most of them found considerable happiness and improvement there. Work was shared, compensation was equalized, and leisure time was devoted to contemplation and artistic creation. Although Nathaniel Hawthorne left the community because he felt overworked shoveling manure and found little time or energy to write, he was the exception. A Brook Farmer expressed the view of most of the residents when he wrote: 'We were happy, contented, well-off and carefree; doing a great work in the world, enthusiastic and faithful, we enjoyed every moment of every day, dominated every moment of every day by the spirit of Brook Farm.' Even Hawthorne later spoke of his 'old and affectionately remembered home at Brook Farm' as being 'certainly the most romantic episode in his life.' Posterity, he predicted, 'may dig it up and profit by it.' Indeed, even though the Brook Farm experiment officially ended in 1849, it served thereafter as an inspiration for many later idealists interested in practicing communal simplicity.[27]

Brook Farm, Fruitlands, and the many other individual expressions of Transcendental ethics revealed the continuing ambiguity and power of the simple life. Plain living and high thinking encompassed a wide spectrum of behavior, and it was only a slight step from misplaced simplicity to mere eccentricity. One man's self-restraint was another's asceticism; one man's self-reliance was another's isolationism. Emerson's observations of such eclectic forms of the good life only reinforced his belief that his own version of temperate self-reliance was best. 'Everything runs to excess,' he contended, and a 'sweet and sound life' required adopting the golden mean of the Greeks as the standard to follow. 'The mid-world is best.'[28]

Yet Emerson concluded that such a middle way could not be imposed effectively by legislative statute or public decree. Since we 'boil at different degrees,' each person must establish priorities and boundaries for himself. If that meant the creation of Brook Farms and Fruitlands and the emergence of dogmatic enthusiasts such as Charles Lane, Emerson was willing to accept such diversity. Thus, in speaking of Brook Farm, he remarked: 'Let it live. Its merit is that it is a new life. Why should we have only two or three ways of life & not thousands and millions.' He still preferred idealistic radicalism to materialist conformity. The impulse motivating such utopians, Emerson correctly recognized, was quite admirable, even though they occasionally expressed themselves in destructive ways. All the 'forms of ultraism, blind and headlong as they seem, have yet a meaning which, if it cannot command assent, must at least preclude contempt.'[29]

It was this attitude of respectful criticism that Emerson adopted in his relationship with Henry Thoreau. Initially, he thought that Thoreau had the potential to personify his ideal of a balanced life of self-sustaining work and self-examining thought. Emerson, the sedentary seer, was always inspired by men of practical abilities. 'I like people who can do things,' he said, and young Henry Thoreau, fifteen years his junior, could do a lot of things well – carpentry, masonry, painting, surveying, gardening. Short, lean, inwardly frail but outwardly tough and sinewy, he was a master of the woodland arts. Emerson admired his 'muscle,' his determination, and his simplicity. 'My good Henry Thoreau made this else solitary afternoon,' he noted in his journal, 'sunny with his simplicity and clear perception.' Emerson realized early on that despite Thoreau's 'peculiarities,' he 'gives me in flesh & blood & pertinacious Saxon belief, my own ethics. He is far more real, & daily practically obeying them, than I.' Indeed it was the growing disparity between Emerson's profession of Transcendental simplicity and Thoreau's pertinacious practice of it that eventually contributed to the growing rift between them during the 1850s. The two Concord philosophers agreed that the goal of life was to subordinate lower impulses to higher purposes; how best to do so was another matter.[30]

'Simplicity, simplicity, simplicity.' This was Thoreau's repeated advice to his society. But he himself was by no means a simple man. From the pronunciation of his name to the enunciation of his beliefs, the author of *Walden* bequeathed a confusing legacy. Even Emerson never truly understood him. Over the years scholars have authoritatively portrayed Thoreau as a skulking misanthropist and a lover of humanity; as an individualist, collectivist, activist, recluse, pacifist, militant, stoic, epicurean.[31] Thoreau encouraged such contrasting interpretations. 'Use me,' he wrote, '...if by any means ye may find me serviceable.' The dramatic, yet elusive quality of Thoreau's prose was accentuated by his consciously extravagant use of hyperbole and paradox. In a letter to a friend he once confessed: 'I trust that you realize what an exaggerator I am – that I lay myself out to exaggerate whenever I have an opportunity.' In part Thoreau used artful exaggeration and contradiction to mask his own uncertainties. But he also employed such dramatic effects to get the attention of his reader, since 'you must speak loud to those who are hard of hearing.'[32]

Thoreau's intentionally provocative and contradictory mode of expression makes using him as an example of simple living somewhat treacherous. Several of his more extreme statements in his journal, lectures, and published writings do make him sound at times like a hermit and an ascetic rather than a prophet of the 'middle way.' Understanding Thoreau requires taking his words seriously but not always literally. As he once confessed, 'Those things I say, others I do.' By looking at what he *did* as well as what he *said*, one can see that his moral philosophy had more in common with the tradition of Protestant and republican simplicity than with the tradition of ascetic fanaticism.[33]

Admittedly, Thoreau did have a reclusive, iconoclastic temperament; he relished solitude far more than Emerson. That he showed no ambition for public accomplishment was always a distinct disappointment to Emerson, as was his lack of compassion. Unlike John Woolman, Thoreau was prickly as a hedgehog. His nature was acidic, and he had little patience with those who did not share his outlook. Thoreau's rugged idiosyncrasies and demanding personality made it hard, even for his friends, to feel comfortably close to him. As Emerson once said, many loved Henry, but few liked him.[34]

Yet with all his waywardness and dogmatism, exaggeration and contradiction, Thoreau remains the most conspicuous and persuasive exponent of simple living in the American experience. Why? Certainly the dramatic nature of his experience at Walden Pond has contributed greatly to his reputation. Perhaps even more important in explaining Thoreau's sustained influence is that he was a man who acted on his ideals rather than passively submit to social convention. Where Emerson spoke of self-reliance while surviving on a legacy, Thoreau earned his way, by using his practical skills and by controlling his desires. 'To be a philosopher,' he argued in *Walden*, 'is not merely to found a school, but to love wisdom so as to live according to its dictates a life of simplicity, independence, magnanimity, and trust. It is to solve some of the problems of life, not only theoretically, but practically.'[35]

The living philosophy that Thoreau fastened upon as a young man grew out of the same basic sources that had shaped Emerson's outlook. His family circumstances and his Protestant heritage provided the raw ore for a moral ethic that would later be refined by his reading of Greek philosophy, Oriental religion, and Romantic literature. He grew up in a family whose economic straits were as pinched as Emerson's. His father, John Thoreau, began his career as a successful shopkeeper but went bankrupt in 1817. The 'poor and hard pressed' Thoreau family then moved to Concord in 1823, where John began anew as a pencil-maker, sign painter, and jack-of-all-trades. But it was not until the 1840s that he enjoyed a stable and comfortable income. Henry remembered that his father had 'pecuniary difficulties to contend with the greater part of his life.'[36]

It may have been John Thoreau's life of 'quiet desperation' in search of vocational success and financial solvency that in part influenced Henry to cut a different path. Unlike so many of his countrymen in similar circumstances, young Thoreau did not develop a consuming passion to work his way above his given condition. Instead, he came to appreciate how free and satisfying a life could be led with a minimum of money and status. In middle age he recalled that his greatest skill since childhood had been 'to want but little.' He was able early on to find pleasure in simple things and activities. He loved to hunt and fish and while away the afternoons in dreamy reverie. 'I love to see anything,' he later wrote, 'that implies a simpler mode of life and a greater nearness to the earth.'[37]

Thoreau's preference for rustic simplicity was in part the result of his complex relationship with his parents. Without pressing the psychological point too much, there does seem to be a connection between Thoreau's adult behavior and his ambivalent relationships with his father and mother. Cynthia Thoreau often expressed her desire that Henry become the social success his father was not. Assertive, outspoken, and conventionally ambitious for her children, Mrs. Thoreau apparently wanted them to achieve the stature of her father, Asa Dunbar, a Harvard graduate, lawyer, and civic leader. Henry was clearly dependent on his mother for attention and love, but at the same time he resisted her efforts to steer him toward a 'respectable' career. By keeping his economic desires to a minimum and adopting a plain and frugal ethic, he could chart an independent course while at the same time avoiding his father's crippling indebtedness. And, by withdrawing to nature, he perhaps could find in Mother Earth the tender consolation and approval that he so much desired from Cynthia Thoreau.[38]

But other sources, of course, also contributed to the making of Thoreau's philosophy of living. As a young man, he immersed himself in Greek and Oriental writings, discovering in the process that the great exemplars of simple living were the 'ancient philosophers, Chinese, Hindoo, Persian, and Greek.' For such contemplative saints, he noted, virtue was 'an intellectual exercise, not a social and practical one. It is a knowing, not a doing.' Yet, at the same time that he came to admire such a contemplative simplicity, Thoreau, like Emerson, was also attracted to the strenuous piety of the Puritans. He was a hungry reader of William Bradford's history of Plymouth and other accounts of New England life, and he developed an intense admiration for the Puritans as a people of 'simple... straightforward, prayerful' habits. Although he could not abide the institutional church, and quickly discarded the Calvinist emphasis on original sin, predestination, and Biblical sufficiency, Thoreau remained nonetheless deeply influenced by the Puritan conscience. 'Our whole life is startlingly moral,' he once asserted. Like the early colonists, he believed that body and soul were in a perpetual struggle for man's heart. True virtue resided with those who successfully resisted needless material and sensual temptations in order to concentrate on spiritual or inward development. The distinctive quality of a man's life 'consists not in his obedience, but in his opposition, to his instincts.' More than anything else, it was this Puritan strain of moral toughness leading to self-control that differentiated Thoreau, and, to a lesser extent Emerson, from most European romantics and later American 'hippies' who preached instinctual liberation.[39]

Imbued with this Transcendental version of the Puritan ethic, Thoreau surveyed American life and concluded that the nation's fundamental problem was a loss of moral identity and proportion. While still a student at Harvard in the 1830s, he described the 'commercial spirit' as a virus infecting his age. The United States was tragically becoming a society without moral distinction or unity, bent only on the 'blind and unmanly pursuit of wealth.' Thoreau sharply criticized those material optimists whose sole aim was to 'secure the greatest degrees of gross comfort and pleasure merely.' Cultural progress, he felt, was not keeping pace with mechanical progress. He could no longer even buy a blank note pad; all of them had lines for ledgerbooks. He was determined himself to avoid such short-sighted materialism, for he had a 'desire to soar.'[40]

Instead of seeking more wealth and more machines, man would do better, Thoreau contended, if he elevated his moral character. Doing so required an individual decision to revive the sense of 'Puritan toughness' and higher purpose that he found so inspiring among his colonial ancestors.

Yet it also required modifying the glorification of work itself. The emphasis of the founding generation on the duty of diligent work at one's calling may have been necessary during the starving time of the first settlements or the critical decades after the Revolution, but not in the midst of a thriving young America. Thoreau believed that national prosperity now offered Americans an ideal opportunity to work less in order to spend more time on the 'things of the intellect and the soul.'

This was a significant alteration of the traditional role played by work in both Protestant and republican simplicity. In a Class Day conference at Harvard in 1837 Thoreau indicated how different his perspective was from that of earlier American prophets of the simple life when he suggested that the 'order of things should be somewhat reversed, the seventh should be man's day of toil, wherein to earn his living by the sweat of his brow; and the other six his Sabbath of the affections and the soul, – in which to range this widespread garden.' Several years later, he repeated his theme: 'Work, work, work. It would be glorious to see mankind at leisure for once.'[41]

Young Thoreau was bent on devoting most of his time to his thoughts rather than his labors, but he had to subsist on something, and gaining even a little income required work of some sort. Thus he, too, confronted the vexing problem of choosing a vocation. When he graduated from Harvard in 1837, religion and business were the two prevailing career options. Unfortunately, he sighed, 'neither the New Testament nor Poor Richard speaks to our condition.' For him, the vocational dilemma was 'how to make the getting of our living poetic! If it is not poetic it is not life but death we get.' His father and too many others among his Concord townsmen, he had observed, were making themselves virtual slaves to the acquisition of money and things.[42]

Thoreau was determined not to follow the same worn path. But how? According to his close friend Ellery Channing, Thoreau asked his mother what profession he should choose. Always eager to shape his ambitions, she replied, 'You can buckle on your knapsack, and roam about and seek your fortune.' It was not what he wanted to hear. Tears welled up in his eyes, causing his sister Helen, who was standing nearby, to embrace him and say, 'No, Henry, you shall not go! You shall stay at home and live with us.' Henry had come to depend a great deal on his mother and sisters and the familiar community of Concord. It was his home, and he saw no reason to live elsewhere, despite his mother's advice. To this end he returned to Concord from Cambridge, and after a short stint as a public school teacher, he, along with his brother John, started a private academy. Thoreau took his students walking, rowing, and swimming, demonstrating in the process that learning was as much an experiential as intellectual activity. In 1841, however, his brother's failing health forced the closing of the schoo1.[43]

It was just as well, for Thoreau had already grown tired of the mundane tasks of formal education. 'I have thoroughly tried school-keeping,' he reported, 'but as I did not teach for the good of my fellow-men, but simply for a livelihood, this was a failure.' The New England schools designed by Horace Mann and others, he believed, were intended more for vocational and disciplinary training than for true self-enlightenment. As he 'later said, 'How vain to try to teach youth, or anybody, truths! They can only learn them after their own fashion, and when they get ready. I do not mean this to condemn our system of education, but to show what it amounts to.' How much better than the standardized curriculum was 'a constant intercourse with nature and the contemplation of natural phenomena.' His own intuitive experience in the huckleberry-field 'was some of the best schooling I got, and paid for itself.'[44]

Yet if Thoreau was not satisfied with being an educator, what could he do to make a living? At this point Emerson intervened. He had come to know Thoreau very well since his return from college and was quite impressed by his thoughtful, yet spartan personality. 'I delight much in my young friend,' Emerson wrote in his journal, 'who seems to have as free and erect a mind as any I have ever met.' He invited Thoreau to participate in the Transcendental Club meetings in his home, and their relationship deepened as the years passed. By the early 1840s Emerson was lecturing so much out of town that he found his household chores too taxing. He was also worried about leaving his family alone for extended periods. So he offered Thoreau 'his board for what work he chooses to do,' and in April 1841 Henry moved in with the Emersons. There he occupied a small room at the head of the stairs, tended the garden, took frequent walks with his host, played with little Waldo, helped edit the *Dial,* and sampled widely in Emerson's large library.[45]

Still, Thoreau was not completely comfortable in the midst of such genteel domesticity. In the fall of 1841 he wrote to a friend that he was 'living with Mr. Emerson in very dangerous prosperity.' The problem of discovering a self-sustaining, yet liberating vocation remained acute for Thoreau, and after a short stint in New York trying to make a living as a writer, he began to consider a life of simple sufficiency in the woods as a temporary option. His Harvard classmate Stearns Wheeler had earlier built a shanty at Flint's Pond, and Ellery Channing, even more daringly, had gone to live on the Illinois prairie for a time. Although Thoreau had been invited to join Brook Farm and Fruitlands, he, like Emerson, had declined. Thoreau admired Alcott, calling him the 'best-natured man' he had ever met, but he had no interest in joining the settlers at Fruitlands. 'I had rather keep bachelor's hall in hell than go to board in heaven.' He recognized the value of working together to achieve common goals, but he was suspicious of the value of living together in such corporate, regimented fashion.'[46]

Since communal living in nature was not for him, Thoreau began looking for a small farm to buy, only to discover that his meager capital was insufficient. Then, in October 1844, when Emerson bought fourteen acres of woodland sweeping down to the north shore of Walden Pond, Thoreau saw his chance. Although sceptical of Thoreau's experiment in isolated simplicity, Emerson eventually agreed that Henry could 'squat' on the property in exchange for clearing part of it. Thus believing that a 'man is rich in proportion to the number of things he can do without,' Thoreau began building his cabin in the woods in March 1845 and moved in on Independence Day. Nature would now provide his path to an ideal world and an inner discovery. In this sense his Walden episode entailed an honest introspection that earlier prophets of simple living – Oriental, classical, Puritan, Quaker, republican – had repeatedly deemed necessary. The Revolutionary poet Philip Freneau, for instance, had written in 1782 that such self-reflection was essential to the maintenance of republican virtue. 'Every rational man, let his business or station in life be what it may, should... at least once a year withdraw himself from the numerous connections and allurements that are apt to give us a too great a fondness for life; he should take time to reflect, as a rational being ought to do, and consider well the end of his being.' Thoreau saw his Walden experience as accomplishing the same purpose. In the woods he could 'live deep and suck out the marrow of life.'[47]

Those who know *Walden* only by reputation too often assume that Thoreau lived at Walden Pond the life of a hermit bent on returning to the isolated condition of Adam. Yet it is important to remember that his famous hut was only a mile or so from town, within earshot of Concord church bells and the Fitchburg railroad, and so close to the Lincoln highway that he could smell the pipe smoke of passing travelers. By his own account he had 'more visitors while I lived in the woods than any other period of my life.' His little cabin rang 'with boisterous mirth' on many an occasion. Almost every Saturday his mother and sisters made a special trip out to the pond to bring him something to eat. Thoreau kept up with life in Concord by reading the newspaper and by making trips to the town himself. 'Every day or two,' he remembered, 'I strolled to the village to hear some of the gossip which is incessantly going on there.... I was even accustomed to make an irruption into some houses, where I was well entertained.' Thoreau may have been a deliberately singular character, but he was not an anchorite.[48]

Nor was Thoreau's life in the woods as primitive as its popular image might suggest. He did not go to the Pond to 'live cheaply nor to live dearly there, but to transact some private business with the fewest obstacles.' The 'private business' was initially the writing of his first book, *A Week on the Concord and Merrimack Rivers.* His broader purpose was to discover how many of the so-called necessities of life he could do without in order to experience the wonders of nature and the joys of self-culture. By setting out on his own and stripping away all pretense and superfluity, he could 'first learn what are the gross necessaries of life and what methods have been taken to obtain them.' Then he could begin to 'entertain the true problems of life.' If some mechanical aids or modern conveniences contributed to this goal, he saw nothing wrong with using them, as long as one did not become used by them. 'Though we are not so degenerate but that we might possibly live in a cave or a wigwam or wear skins to-day,' he wrote, 'it is certainly better to accept the advantages, though so dearly bought, which the invention and industry of mankind offer.' Since he had no desire to be truly primitive, he decided to make 'the most of what means were already got.' So, he borrowed Alcott's axe – which he conscientiously returned with a sharper edge – cleared his site, and then he built a cozy cabin of milled boards and brick, inserted two glass windows, shingled the roof and walls, and stocked the interior with a bed, desk, and books.[49]

Before moving to Walden Pond, Thoreau, like so many of the Transcendentalists, had often praised the simple life close to nature without specifying its practical meaning or appreciating its practical difficulties. In his journal he used the terms 'poverty,' 'simplicity,' 'savagery,' and 'primitive' interchangeably. During his two-year bivouac, however, he learned that many of his preconceptions about life in nature were in fact misconceptions. Savagery and poverty and primitivism were not necessarily the conditions most conducive to virtuous living or elevated thinking. The Indians he met during his 1846 excursion in the Maine woods, for instance, were hardly the model examples of the good life he had once supposed. Earlier he had referred to the Indians' life as representing 'practical poetry.' They stood 'free and unconstrained in Nature.' That may have been the case centuries before, but the Indians he saw in Maine were 'sinister and slouching fellows' who made but a 'coarse and imperfect use... of Nature.' He found them generally to be unreliable and slovenly characters. The savage, Thoreau admitted, was not the 'child of Nature' he had pictured. 'The fact is, the history of the white man is a history of improvement, that of the red man a history of fixed habits of stagnation.' For all their simplicity, the Maine Indians lacked imagination and nobility.[50]

Nor did Thoreau find much nobility in the white woodsmen he met while at Walden. As he was walking across Baker Farm one day, a sudden rainstorm led him to take cover in a ramshackle but rented by the Irish immigrant John Field and his family. Thoreau was shocked at the condition of Field's residence. The roof leaked, and chickens roamed freely about the hut's filthy interior. Field and his perspiring wife apparently worked hard but for nought. According to their own testimony, they remained constantly on the bare edge of survival. Thoreau took the opportunity of his unexpected visit to lecture Field 'as if he were a philosopher, or desired to be one.' He suggested that his Irish host could build his own but for much less than he paid in rent. Moreover, by recognizing that coffee, butter, milk, fresh meat, and other expensive foods were not daily necessities, they would not have to work so hard and lead such a grueling life. 'If he and his family would live simply,' Thoreau felt, 'they might all go a-huckleberrying in the summer for their amusement.' Yet Field and his wife were not philosophers, and they could not see the advantages of the life Thoreau suggested. The simple life 'was dead reckoning to them, and they saw not clearly how to make their port so.' Thoreau finally decided that the Fields were born and bred for such myopic poverty, and there was little chance of broadening their vision. 'Through want of enterprise and faith men are what they are, buying and selling, and spending their lives like serfs.'[51]

Thoreau initially had a much higher opinion of Alek Therien, the French Canadian woodchopper and post-maker. The two met in the woods shortly after Thoreau finished his cabin. Therien was a skilled woodsman who, unlike John Field, could do without tea and coffee – even money itself – and still lead a genuinely joyful, self-sustaining existence. A man of 'unalloyed mirth,' he displayed a childlike exuberance for nature and a true satisfaction with his livelihood. 'A more simple and natural man it would be hard to find,' Thoreau remarked. Therien seemed to be the ideal Homeric peasant. And he was literate. If 'it were not for books,' he told Thoreau, he 'would not know what to do [on] rainy days.' The Canadian was unaffected in his manner and simple in his tastes, and Thoreau greatly enjoyed his company.[52]

Yet the longer Thoreau observed Therien, the more he came to realize that his new friend's aspirations were not much more elevated than Field's. The animal in him was not truly counterbalanced by an intellectual or spiritual side. His only books turned out to be an 'almanac and an arithmetic,' and the Canadian was ignorant of every major social issue, from the factory system to monetary reform to antislavery. Thoreau commented that 'I never, by any maneuvering, could get him to take the spiritual view of things; the highest that he appeared to conceive of was a simple expediency such as you might expect an animal to appreciate.' And, he concluded, such 'is true of most men.'[53]

This was a frustrating realization for Thoreau. The Transcendental outlook saw a moral or spiritual sentiment inherent in all people, regardless of station or circumstance. If such 'low and primitive' men, he pined, would only 'feel the influence of the spring of springs arousing them, they would of necessity rise to a higher and more ethical life.' Heretofore, he had tended to interpret such untapped sensibilities as the result of materialism's smothering spiritualism. But Field and Therien demonstrated that even people leading simple lives could lack an enlivened moral sense and intellectual curiosity. Simplicity could mean barrenness; plain living did not necessarily lead to high thinking.[54]

Thoreau's observations of Indian life and his encounters with Field and Therien helped him begin to recognize the complexity of the simple life as an actual way of living. After leaving Walden in 1847, he gradually decided that there was indeed more to simplicity than living a spartan existence in the woods. 'There are two kinds of simplicity,' he explained; 'one that is akin to foolishness, the other to wisdom. The philosopher's style of living is outwardly simple, but inwardly complex. The savage's style of living is both outwardly and inwardly simple.' The savage, he went on to say, 'lives simply through ignorance and idleness or laziness, but the philosopher lives simply through wisdom.' Thoreau clearly preferred the philosopher's version. The truly 'heroic spirit' could never be satisfied *merely* with the 'innocent pleasures of country life.'[55]

Thus, like Rousseau before him, Thoreau concluded that the wilderness and the primitive life it afforded were periodically necessary but not permanently sufficient conditions for the good life. This revelation in part led him to return to Concord. The wilds provided inspiration and physical challenge, but a 'civilized man must at length pine there, like a cultivated plant, which clasps its fibres about a crude and undissolved mass of peat.' Thoreau still found in himself 'an instinct toward a higher, or, as it is named, spiritual life, and another toward a primitive rank and savage one, and I reverence them both.' Satisfying both instincts, however, required that he live not in permanent isolation at Walden Pond but in what he called a 'border life' between primitivism and civilization. That way he could 'combine the hardiness of the savages with the intellectualness of the civilized man.'[56]

Ideally, then, the simple life could best be led not in the wild or in the city, but in 'partially cultivated country' like Concord. Periodic excursions into the wilderness would provide necessary raw materials for the soul, and civilization would provide necessary finished products. Total immersion in either, however, was dangerous. In this way, Thoreau approached the golden mean of the Greeks. The 'temperate zone,' he wrote, 'is found to be most favorable to the growth and ripening of men.' Until his death in 1862, Thoreau would live a simple life in Concord, helping manage the family business during his father's illness, and earning his own income as a part-time surveyor, all the while saving most of his time for sauntering, writing, and reading. He had found, he told Horace Greeley, that six weeks of manual labor would support him for a year.[57]

Thoreau's twenty-six months of camping, hiking, gardening, and thinking at Walden Pond had given him a more profound appreciation of himself, the simple life, and Concord. His town and family provided him with much needed emotional warmth. 'Here are all the friends I ever had or shall have, and as friendly as ever,' he wrote in his journal. 'A man dwells in his native valley like a corolla in its calyx, like an acorn in its cup. *Here*, of course, is all that you love, all that you expect, all that you are.' Though he still needed the 'tonic of wildness,' he now recognized that civilization did represent 'a real advance in the condition of man... though only the wise improve their advantages.' As long as he could keep his wants under control and thereby keep his workday requirements to a minimum, he would be satisfied living in larger society. 'I am grateful for what I am and have,' he acknowledged to a friend in 1856. 'My thanksgiving is perpetual.... O how I laugh when I think of my vague indefinite riches. No run on my bank can drain it – for my wealth is not possession but enjoyment.'[58]

Thoreau still believed that a person would be better off 'raising what you eat, making what you wear, building what you inhabit, burning what you cut or dig.' And it was this spartan strenuosity that made him increasingly impatient with Emerson's genteel simplicity, just as Emerson in turn had been critical of Longfellow's affluence. But Thoreau had come to see by the 1850s that most Americans no longer had the luxury of pursuing his version of self-sufficiency, even if they were so inclined. Modern mass society constantly warred against pure simplicity. 'Those to whom you are allied insanely want and will have a thousand other things which neither you nor they can raise and nobody else, perchance, will pay for.' Hence he published *Walden* in 1854 not in order to convince everyone to abandon their factory jobs and city homes and build isolated cabins in the forest. Too many reformers, he believed, were intent on imposing their prescription for moral reformation on others. 'Alas! this is the crying sin of the age, this want of faith in the prevalence of a man. Nothing can be effected but by one man.'[59]

Although in his dealings with others, Thoreau frequently appeared sanctimonious, in *Walden* he explicitly denied having any single program for simple living that could be universally applied. 'I would not have anyone adopt *my* mode of living on my account.... I would have each one be very careful to find out and pursue *his own* way, and not his fathers or mother's or neighbor's instead.' His expressed purpose was not so much the specification of means as it was the elevation of ends. As he had learned from watching John Field and Alek Therien, the standard of living was not nearly as important as the object of living. Responding to a young disciple's request to '*teach* men in detail how to live a simpler life,' Thoreau again emphasized that he had 'no scheme about it, – no designs on men at all; and, if I had, my mode would be to tempt them with fruit, and not with the manure.' In elaborating on this point, he observed:

> To what end do I lead a simple life at all, pray? That I may teach others to simplify their lives? – and so all our lives may be simplified merely, like an algebraic formula? Or not, rather, that I may make use of the ground I have cleared, to live more worthily and profitably? I would fain lay the most stress forever on that which is most important–imports the most to me, though it were only (what it is likely to be) a vibration in the air. As a preacher, I should be prompted to tell men, not so much how to get their wheat bread cheaper, as of the bread of life compared to which that is bran.

In *Walden*, therefore, Thoreau was fundamentally preaching the advantages of self-culture, not writing a how-to book. Simplify your life, yes, he said over and over again, but do it in your own way.[60]

(ENDNOTES)

1 RWE, 'New England Reformers,' in Edward W. Emerson, ed., *The Complete Works of Ralph Waldo Emerson*, 12 vols. (Boston, 1903 -4), 3:225 (hereafter cited as RWE, *Works)*.

2 On Graham and other health reformers see Stephen Nissenbaum, *Sex, Diet & Debility in Jacksonian America: Sylvester Graham & Health Reform* (Westport, Ct., 1980); James C. Whorton, *Crusaders for Fitness: The History of American Health Reformers* (Princeton, 1982). The communitarian alternative is treated in Arthur Bestor, *Backwoods Utopias: The Sectarian and Owenite Phases of Communitarian Socialism in America, 1663–1829* (Philadelphia, 1950); Alice Felt Tyler, *Freedom's Ferment: Phases of American Social History from the Colonial Period to the Outbreak of the Civil War* (New York, 1962).

3 William Ellery Channing, 'The Present Age,' in *The Works of William Ellery Charming, 6 vols.* (Boston, 1849), 6:171–72 (hereafter cited as Channing, *Works)*.

4 RWE, 'The Transcendentalist,' *Works*, 1:335; Channing, 'Self-Culture,' *Works*, 2:372–75. The literature on Transcendentalism is extensive and uneven. The best recent treatments are Paul F. Boller, Jr., *American Transcendentalism, 1830–1860: An Intellectual Inquiry* (New York, 1974) and Anne Rose, *Transcendentalism as a Social Movement* (New Haven, 1981). Older, but still useful studies are Octavius B. Frothingham, *Transcendentalism in New England: A History* (New York, 1876), and Harold C. Goddard, *Studies in New England Transcendentalism* (New York, 1908).

5 See Arthur A. Ekirch, Jr., *Man and Nature in America* (Lincoln, Neb., 1973), 47–69.

6 RWE, 'Nature,' *Works*, 1:41–42; RWE, 'Society and Solitude,' ibid., 7:179.

7 William H. Gilman, et al., eds., *The Journals and Miscellaneous Notebooks of Ralph Waldo Emerson*, 16 vols. to date (Cambridge, Mass., 1960), 8:108 (hereafter cited as RWE, *Journals)*; RWE, 'The Transcendentalist,' *Works*, 1:340–41.

8 Octavius Brooks Frothingham, *Memoir of William Henry Channing* (Boston, 1886), 166; Henry W. Bellows, 'The Influence of the Trading Spirit upon the Social and Moral Life of America,' *The American Review* 1 (Jan. 1845):98.

9 RWE, *Journals*, 9:428; RWE, 'Progress of Culture,' *Works*, 8:229. On Emerson's debt to Puritanism, see Perry Miller, 'From Edwards to Emerson,' *New England Quarterly* 13 (1940):587–617; Wesley T. Mott, 'Emerson and Thoreau as Heirs to the Tradition of New

England Puritanism' (Ph.D. diss., Boston University, 1975).
10 RWE, 'Domestic Life,' *Works,* 7:121. For biographical information on RWE, I have relied primarily on Gay Wilson Allen, *Waldo Emerson: A Biography* (New York, 1981), and Ralph L. Rusk, *The Life of Ralph Waldo Emerson* (New York, 1949).
11 RWE, 'Nature,' *Works,* 1:9.
12 Ibid., 1:10.
13 RWE, *Journals,* 7:71, 404. RWE's ambivalence about his calling is perceptively discussed in Henry Nash Smith, 'Emerson's Problem of Vocation,' *New England Quarterly* 12 (1939):52-67.
14 Mott, 'Emerson and Thoreau,' 107; RWE, 'Works and Days,' *Works,* 7:158.
15 RWE, 'The Young American,' *Works,* 1:379; 'Man the Reformer,' ibid., 1:232; 'The Conduct of Life,' ibid., 6:126.
16 RWE, 'Plato,' *Works,* 4:53-58; 'The Conduct *of* Life,' ibid., 6:89, 134; 'Society and Solitude,' ibid., 7:116.
17 RWE, 'Lecture on the Times,' ibid., 1:227.
18 RWE, 'Education,' ibid., 10:133, 137; RWE, 'Experience,' ibid., 3:83.
19 RWE, 'Self-Reliance,' ibid., 2:50; RWE, 'The Conduct *of* Life,' ibid., 6:91.
20 RWE, 'Man the Reformer,' ibid., 1:245.
21 RWE, 'Experience,' ibid., 3:62; RWE, *Journals,* 13:38.
22 RWE, 'Domestic Life, *Works,* 7:113; RWE, 'Society and Solitude,' ibid., 7:287; RWE, 'Thoughts on Modern Literature,' *The Dial 1* (Oct. 1840):158.
23 RWE to Thomas Carlyle, 30 Oct. 1840, in Joseph Slater, ed., *The Correspondence of Emerson and Carlyle* (New York, 1964), 283-84; RWE, 'Man the Reformer,' *Works,* 1:247.
24 'Plan of the West Roxbury Community,' *The Dial 2* (Jan. 1842):364; Henry L. Golemba, *George Ripley* (Boston, 1977), 66; 'Plan of the Roxbury Community,' 364. On Brook Farm, see Georgiana Bruce Kirby, *Years of Experience, An Autobiographical Narrative* (Boston, 1887), 98-105; John Van Der Zee Sears, *My Friends at Brook Farm* (New York, 1912); Lindsay Swift, *Brook Farm* (New York, 1900); Zoltan Haraszti, *The Idyll of Brook Farm* (Boston, 1937).
25 RWE to George Ripley, 15 Dec. 1840, in Ralph L. Rusk, ed., *The Letters of Ralph Waldo Emerson,* 6 vols. (New York, 1939), 2:368-71 (hereafter cited as RWE, *Letters);* RWE, *Journals,* 7:408.
26 RWE, *Journals,* 3:319; 7:401; RWE, *Works,* 6:64.
27 Octavius Frothingham, *George Ripley* (Boston, 1883), 153; Sears, *My Friends,* 162. See also Caroline Dail, *Transcendentalism in New England* (Boston, 1897).
28 RWE, 'Experience,' *Works,* 3:64-66.
29 RWE, *Journals,* 9:69.
30 RWE, *Journals,* 5:453; 13:66.
31 The best survey of H DT's changing reputation is Wendell Glick, *The Recognition of Henry Thoreau* (Ann Arbor, 1969). See also Michael Meyer's excellent overview of twentieth-century attitudes toward HDT, *Several More Lives To Live: Thoreau's Political Reputation in America* (Westport, Ct., 1977). On HDT's concept of simple living see John C. Broderick, 'Thoreau's Principle of Simplicity as Shown in His Attitudes Toward Cities, Government and Industrialism' (Ph.D. diss., University of North Carolina, 1953); Leo Stoller, 'Thoreau's Doctrine of Simplicity,' *New England Quarterly* 29 (1956):443-61.
32 Bradford Torrey, ed., *The Writings of Henry David Thoreau,* 20 vols. (Boston, 1906), 1:304-5 (hereafter cited as HDT, *Writings);* JB, 'Henry D. Thoreau,' *Century* (July 1882):375.
33 HDT, *Writings,* 15:155.
34 RWE, *Journals,* 7:498.
35 HDT, *Writings,* 2:16.
36 Mary Hosmer Brown, *Memories of Concord* (Boston, 1926), 101.
37 HDT, *Writings,* 8:319; 20:88.
38 For a provocative, if at times irritatingly speculative, analysis of HDT's childhood and adolescence, see Richard Lebeaux, *Young Man Thoreau* (Amherst, Mass., 1977).

39 HDT, *Writings*, 2:15; 12:426; 8:4; 2:241; 8:46. On HDT's Puritan strain, see Mott, 'Emerson and Thoreau'; Egbert S. Oliver, 'Thoreau and the Puritan Tradition,' *ESQ 44* (1966):79–86.

40 Edwin Moser, 'Henry David Thoreau: The College Essays' (M.A. thesis, New York University, 1951), 183– 85; HDT, *Reform Papers*, ed. Wendell Glick (Princeton, 1973), 156.

41 Franklin Sanborn, *The Life of Henry David Thoreau* (Boston, 1917), 288.

42 HDT, *Writings*, 8:164.

43 William Ellery Channing, *Thoreau the Poet-Naturalist* (New York, 1902), 18.

44 HDT, *Writings*, *2:76* 77; 19:67 68; 8:193; 18:299.

45 RWE, *Journals*, 5:452.

46 Walter Harding and Carl Bode, eds., *The Correspondence of Henry David Thoreau* (New York, 1958), 53 (hereafter cited as HDT, *Correspondence)*; Rose, *Transcendentalism*, 298.

47 Freneau, 'The Pilgrim,' in Philip M. Marsh, ed., *The Prose of Philip Freneau* (New Brunswick, N.J., 1955), 43.

48 HDT, *Writings*, 2:159, 185, 187.

49 Ibid., 21, 12, 44.

50 HDT, *Writings*, 7:253; 3:133, 9, 78. See also Philip Gura, 'Thoreau's Maine Woods Indians: More Representative Men.' *American Literature 49* (1977):366–84; Albert Keiser, *The Indian in American Literature* (New York, 1933), 226; Roderick Nash, *Wilderness and the American Mind* (New Haven, 1967), 91– 93; Robert Sayre, *Thoreau and the American Indians* (Princeton, 1977).

51 HDT, *Writings*, 14:8; 4:229.

52 Ibid., 159–68.

53 Ibid., 166

54 Ibid., 110–23.

55 HDT, *Writings*, 11:410–12.

56 Ibid., 9:296–97; 2:14. See also Nash, *Wilderness and the American Mind*, 92–95.

57 Ibid., 3:172; 18:334–35.

58 Ibid., 17:275; 2:34; HDT, *Correspondence*, 444.

59 HDT, *Writings*, 14:8; 4:229.

60 Ibid., 2:78–79; 6:260.

Chapter Twenty

'ECONOMY'

(from *Walden*)

Henry David Thoreau

When I wrote the following pages, or rather the bulk of them, I lived alone, in the woods, a mile from any neighbor, in a house which I had built myself, on the shore of Walden Pond, in Concord, Massachusetts, and earned my living by the labor of my hands only. I lived there two years and two months. At present I am a sojourner in civilized life again.

I should not obtrude my affairs so much on the notice of my readers if very particular inquiries had not been made by my townsmen concerning my mode of life, which some would call impertinent, though they do not appear to me at all impertinent, but, considering the circumstances, very natural and pertinent. Some have asked what I got to eat; if I did not feel lonesome; if I was not afraid; and the like. Others have been curious to learn what portion of my income I devoted to charitable purposes; and some, who have large families, how many poor children I maintained. I will therefore ask those of my readers who feel no particular interest in me to pardon me if I undertake to answer some of these questions in this book. In most books, the I, or first person, is omitted; in this it will be retained; that, in respect to egotism, is the main difference. We commonly do not remember that it is, after all, always the first person that is speaking. I should not talk so much about myself if there were anybody else whom I knew as well. Unfortunately, I am confined to this theme by the narrowness of my experience. Moreover, I, on my side, require of every writer, first or last, a simple and sincere account of his own life, and not merely what he has heard of other men's lives; some such account as he would send to his kindred from a distant land; for if he has lived sincerely, it must have been in a distant land to me. Perhaps these pages are more particularly addressed to poor students. As for the rest of my readers, they will accept such portions as apply to them. I trust that none will stretch the seams in putting on the coat, for it may do good service to him whom it fits.

I would fain say something, not so much concerning the Chinese and Sandwich Islanders as you who read these pages, who are said to live in New England; something about your condition, especially your outward condition or circumstances in this world, in this town, what it is, whether it is necessary that it be as bad as it is, whether it cannot be improved as well as not. I have travelled a good deal in Concord; and everywhere, in shops, and offices, and fields, the inhabitants have appeared to me to be doing penance in a thousand remarkable ways. What I have heard of Bramins sitting exposed to four fires and looking in the face of the sun; or hanging suspended, with their heads downward, over flames; or looking at the heavens over their shoulders "until it becomes impossible for them to resume their natural position, while from the twist of the neck nothing but liquids can pass into the stomach"; or dwelling, chained for life, at the foot of a tree; or measuring with their bodies, like caterpillars, the breadth of vast empires; or standing on one leg on the tops of pillars – even these forms of conscious penance are hardly more incredible and astonishing than the scenes which I daily witness. The twelve labors of Hercules were trifling in comparison with those which my neighbors have undertaken; for they were only twelve, and had an end; but I could never see that these men slew or captured any monster or finished any labor. They have no friend Iolaus to burn with a hot iron the root of the hydra's head, but as soon as one head is crushed, two spring up.

I see young men, my townsmen, whose misfortune it is to have inherited farms, houses, barns, cattle, and farming tools; for these are more easily acquired than got rid of. Better if they had been born in the open pasture and suckled by a wolf, that they might have seen with clearer eyes what field they were called to labor in. Who made them serfs of the soil? Why should they eat their sixty acres, when man is condemned to eat only his peck of dirt? Why should they begin digging their graves as soon as they are born? They have got to live a man's life, pushing all these things before them, and get on as well as they can. How many a poor immortal soul have I met well-nigh crushed and smothered under its load, creeping down the road of life, pushing before it a barn seventy-five feet by forty, its Augean stables never cleansed, and one hundred acres of land, tillage, mowing, pasture, and woodlot! The portionless, who struggle with no such unnecessary inherited encumbrances, find it labor enough to subdue and cultivate a few cubic feet of flesh.

But men labor under a mistake. The better part of the man is soon plowed into the soil for compost. By a seeming fate, commonly called necessity, they are employed, as it says in an old book, laying up treasures which moth and rust will corrupt and thieves break through and steal. It is a fool's life, as they will find when they get to the end of it, if not before.

Most men, even in this comparatively free country, through mere ignorance and mistake, are so occupied with the factitious cares and superfluously coarse labors of life that its finer fruits cannot be plucked by them. Their fingers, from excessive toil, are too clumsy and tremble too much for that. Actually, the laboring man has not leisure for a true integrity day by day; he cannot afford to sustain the manliest relations to men; his labor would be depreciated in the market. He has no time to be anything but a machine. How can he remember well his ignorance – which his growth requires – who has so often to use his knowledge? We should feed and clothe him gratuitously sometimes, and recruit him with our cordials, before we judge of him. The finest qualities of our nature, like the bloom on fruits, can be preserved only by the most delicate handling. Yet we do not treat ourselves nor one another thus tenderly.

I sometimes wonder that we can be so frivolous, I may almost say, as to attend to the gross but somewhat foreign form of servitude called Negro Slavery, there are so many keen and subtle masters that enslave both North and South. It is hard to have a Southern overseer; it is worse to have a Northern one; but worst of all when you are the slave-driver of yourself. Talk of a divinity in man! Look at the teamster on the highway, wending to market by day or night; does any divinity stir within him? His highest duty to fodder and water his horses! What is his destiny to him compared with the shipping interests? Does not he drive for Squire Make-a-stir? How godlike, how immortal, is he? See how he cowers and sneaks, how vaguely all the day he fears, not being immortal nor divine, but the slave and prisoner of his own opinion of himself, a fame won by his own deeds. Public opinion is a weak tyrant compared with our own private opinion. What a man thinks of himself, that it is which determines, or rather indicates, his fate. Self-emancipation even in the West Indian provinces of the fancy and imagination – what Wilberforce is there to bring that about? Think, also, of the ladies of the land weaving toilet cushions against the last day, not to betray too green an interest in their fates! As if you could kill time without injuring eternity.

The mass of men lead lives of quiet desperation. What is called resignation is confirmed desperation. From the desperate city you go into the desperate country, and have to console yourself with the bravery of minks and muskrats. A stereotyped but unconscious despair is concealed even under what are called the games and amusements of mankind. There is no play in them, for this comes after work. But it is a characteristic of wisdom not to do desperate things.

When we consider what, to use the words of the catechism, is the chief end of man, and what are the true necessaries and means of life, it appears as if men had deliberately chosen the common mode of living because they preferred it to any other. Yet they honestly think there is no choice left. But alert and healthy natures remember that the sun rose clear. It is never too late to give up our prejudices. No way of thinking or doing, however ancient, can be trusted without proof. What everybody echoes or in silence passes by as true today may turn out to be falsehood tomorrow, mere smoke of opinion, which some had trusted for a cloud that would sprinkle fertilizing rain on their fields. What old people say you cannot do, you try and find that you can. Old deeds for old people, and new deeds for new. Old people did not know enough once, perchance, to fetch fresh fuel to keep the fire a-going; new people put a little dry wood under a pot, and are whirled round the globe with the speed of birds, in a way to kill old people, as the phrase is. Age is no better, hardly so well, qualified for an instructor as youth, for it has not profited so much as it has lost. One may almost doubt if the wisest man has learned anything of absolute value by living. Practically, the old have no very important advice to give the young, their own experience has been so partial, and their lives have been such miserable failures, for private reasons, as they must believe; and it may be that they have some faith left which belies that experience, and they are only less young than they were. I have lived some thirty years on this planet, and I have yet to hear the first syllable of valuable or even earnest advice from my seniors. They have told me nothing, and probably cannot tell me anything to the purpose. Here is life, an experiment to a great extent untried by me; but it does not avail me that they have tried it. If I have any experience which I think valuable, I am sure to reflect that this my Mentors said nothing about.

One farmer says to me, "You cannot live on vegetable food solely, for it furnishes nothing to make bones with"; and so he religiously devotes a part of his day to supplying his system with the raw material of bones; walking all the while he talks behind his oxen, which, with vegetable-made bones, jerk him and his lumbering plow along in spite of every obstacle. Some things are really necessaries of life in some circles, the most helpless and diseased, which in others are luxuries merely, and in others still are entirely unknown.

The whole ground of human life seems to some to have been gone over by their predecessors, both the heights and the valleys, and all things to have been cared for. According to Evelyn, "the wise Solomon prescribed ordinances for the very distances of trees; and the Roman praetors have decided how often you may go into your neighbor's land to gather the acorns which fall on it without trespass, and what share belongs to that neighbor." Hippocrates has even left directions how we should cut our nails; that is, even with the ends of the fingers, neither shorter nor longer. Undoubtedly the very tedium and ennui which presume to have exhausted the variety and the joys of life are as old as Adam. But man's capacities have never been measured; nor are we to judge of what he can do by any precedents, so little has been tried. Whatever have been thy failures hitherto, "be not afflicted, my child, for who shall assign to thee what thou hast left undone?"

We might try our lives by a thousand simple tests; as, for instance, that the same sun which ripens my beans illumines at once a system of earths like ours. If I had remembered this it would have prevented some mistakes. This was not the light in which I hoed them. The stars are the apexes of what wonderful triangles! What distant and different beings in the various mansions of the universe are contemplating the same one at the same moment! Nature and human life are as various as our several constitutions. Who shall say what prospect life offers to another? Could a greater miracle take place than for us to look through each other's eyes for an instant? We should live in all the ages of the world in an hour; ay, in all the worlds of the ages. History, Poetry, Mythology! – I know of no reading of another's experience so startling and informing as this would be.

The greater part of what my neighbors call good I believe in my soul to be bad, and if I repent of anything, it is very likely to be my good behavior. What demon possessed me that I behaved so well? You may say the wisest thing you can, old man – you who have lived seventy years, not without honor of a kind – I hear an irresistible voice which invites me away from all that. One generation abandons the enterprises of another like stranded vessels.

I think that we may safely trust a good deal more than we do. We may waive just so much care of ourselves as we honestly bestow elsewhere. Nature is as well adapted to our weakness as to our strength. The incessant anxiety and strain of some is a well-nigh incurable form of disease. We are made to exaggerate the importance of what work we do; and yet how much is not done by us! Or, what if we had been taken sick? How vigilant we are! determined not to live by faith if we can avoid it; all the day long on the alert, at night we unwillingly say our prayers and commit ourselves to uncertainties. So thoroughly and sincerely are we compelled to live, reverencing our life, and denying the possibility of change. This is the only way, we say; but there are as many ways as there can be drawn radii from one centre. All change is a miracle to contemplate; but it is a miracle which is taking place every instant. Confucius said, "To know that we know what we know, and that we do not know what we do not know, that is true knowledge." When one man has reduced a fact of the imagination to be a fact to his understanding, I foresee that all men at length establish their lives on that basis.

Let us consider for a moment what most of the trouble and anxiety which I have referred to is about, and how much it is necessary that we be troubled, or at least careful. It would be some advantage to live a primitive and frontier life, though in the midst of an outward civilization, if only to learn what are the gross necessaries of life and what methods have been taken to obtain them; or even to look over the old day-books of the merchants, to see what it was that men most commonly bought at the stores, what they stored, that is, what are the grossest groceries. For the improvements of ages have had but little influence on the essential laws of man's existence: as our skeletons, probably, are not to be distinguished from those of our ancestors.

By the words, *necessary of life*, I mean whatever, of all that man obtains by his own exertions, has been from the first, or from long use has become, so important to human life that few, if any, whether from savageness, or poverty, or philosophy, ever attempt to do without it. To many creatures there is in this sense but one necessary of life, Food. To the bison of the prairie it is a few inches of palatable grass, with water to drink; unless he seeks the Shelter of the forest or the mountain's shadow. None of the brute creation requires more than Food and Shelter. The necessaries of life for man in this climate may, accurately enough, be distributed under the several heads of Food, Shelter, Clothing, and Fuel; for not till we have secured these are we prepared to entertain the true problems of life with freedom and a prospect of success. Man has invented, not only houses, but clothes and cooked food; and possibly from the accidental discovery of the warmth of fire, and the consequent use of it, at first a luxury, arose the present necessity to sit by it. We observe cats and dogs acquiring the same second nature. By proper Shelter and Clothing we legitimately retain our own internal heat; but with an excess of these, or of Fuel, that is, with an external heat greater than our own internal, may not cookery properly be said to begin? Darwin, the naturalist, says of the inhabitants of Tierra del Fuego, that while his own party, who were well clothed and sitting close to a fire, were far from too warm, these naked savages, who were farther off, were observed, to his great surprise, "to be streaming with perspiration at undergoing such a roasting." So, we are told, the New Hollander goes naked with impunity, while the European shivers in his clothes. Is it impossible to combine the hardiness of these savages with the intellectualness of the civilized man? According to Liebig, man's body is a stove, and food the fuel which keeps up the internal combustion in the lungs. In cold weather we eat more, in warm less. The animal heat is the result of a slow combustion, and disease and death take place when this is too rapid; or for want of fuel, or from some defect in the draught, the fire goes out. Of course the vital heat is not to be confounded with fire; but so much for analogy. It appears, therefore, from the above list, that the expression, *animal life*, is nearly synonymous with the expression, *animal heat*; for while Food may be regarded as the Fuel which keeps up the fire within us – and Fuel serves only to prepare that Food or to increase the warmth of our bodies by addition from without – Shelter and Clothing also serve only to retain the *heat* thus generated and absorbed.

The grand necessity, then, for our bodies, is to keep warm, to keep the vital heat in us. What pains we accordingly take, not only with our Food, and Clothing, and Shelter, but with our beds, which are our night-clothes, robbing the nests and breasts of birds to prepare this shelter within a shelter, as the mole has its bed of grass and leaves at the end of its burrow! The poor man is wont to complain that this is a cold world; and to cold, no less physical than social, we refer directly a great part of our ails. The summer, in some climates, makes possible to man a sort of Elysian life. Fuel, except to cook his Food, is then unnecessary; the sun is his fire, and many of the fruits are sufficiently cooked by its rays; while Food generally is more various, and more easily obtained, and Clothing and Shelter are wholly or half unnecessary. At the present day, and in this country, as I find by my own experience, a few implements, a knife, an axe, a spade, a wheelbarrow, etc., and for the studious, lamplight, stationery, and access to a few books, rank next to necessaries, and can all be obtained at a trifling cost. Yet some, not wise, go to the other side of the globe, to barbarous and unhealthy regions, and devote themselves to trade for ten or twenty years, in order that they may live – that is, keep comfortably warm – and die in New England at last. The luxuriously rich are not simply kept comfortably warm, but unnaturally hot; as I implied before, they are cooked, of course a la mode.

Most of the luxuries, and many of the so-called comforts of life, are not only not indispensable, but positive hindrances to the elevation of mankind. With respect to luxuries and comforts, the wisest have ever lived a more simple and meagre life than the poor. The ancient philosophers, Chinese, Hindoo, Persian, and Greek, were a class than which none has been poorer in outward riches, none so rich in inward. We know not much about them. It is remarkable that we know so much of them as we do. The same is true of the more modern reformers and benefactors of their race. None can be an impartial or wise observer of human life but from the vantage ground of what we should call voluntary poverty. Of a life of luxury the fruit is luxury, whether in agriculture, or commerce, or literature, or art. There are nowadays professors of philosophy, but not philosophers. Yet it is admirable to profess because it was once admirable to live. To be a philosopher is not merely to have subtle thoughts, nor even to found a school, but so to love wisdom as to live according to its dictates, a life of simplicity, independence, magnanimity, and trust. It is to solve some of the problems of life, not only theoretically, but practically. The success of great scholars and thinkers is commonly a courtier-like success, not kingly, not manly. They make shift to live merely by conformity, practically as their fathers did, and are in no sense the progenitors of a noble race of men. But why do men degenerate ever? What makes families run out? What is the nature of the luxury which enervates and destroys nations? Are we sure that there is none of it in our own lives? The philosopher is in advance of his age even in the outward form of his life. He is not fed, sheltered, clothed, warmed, like his contemporaries. How can a man be a philosopher and not maintain his vital heat by better methods than other men?

When a man is warmed by the several modes which I have described, what does he want next? Surely not more warmth of the same kind, as more and richer food, larger and more splendid houses, finer and more abundant clothing, more numerous, incessant, and hotter fires, and the like. When he has obtained those things which are necessary to life, there is another alternative than to obtain the superfluities; and that is, to adventure on life now, his vacation from humbler toil having commenced. The soil, it appears, is suited to the seed, for it has sent its radicle downward, and it may now send its shoot upward also with confidence. Why has man rooted himself thus firmly in the earth, but that he may rise in the same proportion into the heavens above? – for the nobler plants are valued for the fruit they bear at last in the air and light, far from the ground, and are not treated like the humbler esculents, which, though they may be biennials, are cultivated only till they have perfected their root, and often cut down at top for this purpose, so that most would not know them in their flowering season.

I do not mean to prescribe rules to strong and valiant natures, who will mind their own affairs whether in heaven or hell, and perchance build more magnificently and spend more lavishly than the richest, without ever impoverishing themselves, not knowing how they live – if, indeed, there are any such, as has been dreamed; nor to those who find their encouragement and inspiration in precisely the present condition of things, and cherish it with the fondness and enthusiasm of lovers – and, to some extent, I reckon myself in this number; I do not speak to those who are well employed, in whatever circumstances, and they know whether they are well employed or not; but mainly to the mass of men who are discontented, and idly complaining of the hardness of their lot or of the times, when they might improve them. There are some who complain most energetically and inconsolably of any, because they are, as they say, doing their duty. I also have in my mind that seemingly wealthy, but most terribly impoverished class of all, who have accumulated dross, but know not how to use it, or get rid of it, and thus have forged their own golden or silver fetters.

If I should attempt to tell how I have desired to spend my life in years past, it would probably surprise those of my readers who are somewhat acquainted with its actual history; it would certainly astonish those who know nothing about it. I will only hint at some of the enterprises which I have cherished.

In any weather, at any hour of the day or night, I have been anxious to improve the nick of time, and notch it on my stick too; to stand on the meeting of two eternities, the past and future, which is precisely the present moment; to toe that line. You will pardon some obscurities, for there are more secrets in my trade than in most men's, and yet not voluntarily kept, but inseparable from its very nature. I would gladly tell all that I know about it, and never paint "No Admittance" on my gate.

I long ago lost a hound, a bay horse, and a turtle-dove, and am still on their trail. Many are the travellers I have spoken concerning them, describing their tracks and what calls they answered to. I have met one or two who had heard the hound, and the tramp of the horse, and even seen the dove disappear behind a cloud, and they seemed as anxious to recover them as if they had lost them themselves.

To anticipate, not the sunrise and the dawn merely, but, if possible, Nature herself! How many mornings, summer and winter, before yet any neighbor was stirring about his business, have I been about mine! No doubt, many of my townsmen have met me returning from this enterprise, farmers starting for Boston in the twilight, or woodchoppers going to their work. It is true, I never assisted the sun materially in his rising, but, doubt not, it was of the last importance only to be present at it.

So many autumn, ay, and winter days, spent outside the town, trying to hear what was in the wind, to hear and carry it express! I well-nigh sunk all my capital in it, and lost my own breath into the bargain, running in the face of it. If it had concerned either of the political parties, depend upon it, it would have appeared in the Gazette with the earliest intelligence. At other times watching from the observatory of some cliff or tree, to telegraph any new arrival; or waiting at evening on the hill-tops for the sky to fall, that I might catch something, though I never caught much, and that, manna-wise, would dissolve again in the sun.

For a long time I was reporter to a journal, of no very wide circulation, whose editor has never yet seen fit to print the bulk of my contributions, and, as is too common with writers, I got only my labor for my pains. However, in this case my pains were their own reward.

For many years I was self-appointed inspector of snow-storms and rain-storms, and did my duty faithfully; surveyor, if not of highways, then of forest paths and all across – lot routes, keeping them open, and ravines bridged and passable at all seasons, where the public heel had testified to their utility.

I have looked after the wild stock of the town, which give a faithful herdsman a good deal of trouble by leaping fences; and I have had an eye to the unfrequented nooks and corners of the farm; though I did not always know whether Jonas or Solomon worked in a particular field today; that was none of my business. I have watered the red huckleberry, the sand cherry and the nettle-tree, the red pine and the black ash, the white grape and the yellow violet, which might have withered else in dry seasons.

In short, I went on thus for a long time (I may say it without boasting), faithfully minding my business, till it became more and more evident that my townsmen would not after all admit me into the list of town officers, nor make my place a sinecure with a moderate allowance. My accounts, which I can swear to have kept faithfully, I have, indeed, never got audited, still less accepted, still less paid and settled. However, I have not set my heart on that.

Not long since, a strolling Indian went to sell baskets at the house of a well-known lawyer in my neighborhood. "Do you wish to buy any baskets?" he asked. "No, we do not want any," was the reply. "What!" exclaimed the Indian as he went out the gate, "do you mean to starve us?" Having seen his industrious white neighbors so well off – that the lawyer had only to weave arguments, and, by some magic, wealth and standing followed – he had said to himself: I will go into business; I will weave baskets; it is a thing which I can do. Thinking that when he had made the baskets he would have done his part, and then it would be the white man's to buy them. He had not discovered that it was necessary for him to make it worth the other's while to buy them, or at least make him think that it was so, or to make something else which it would be worth his while to buy. I too had woven a kind of basket of a delicate texture, but I had not made it worth any one's while to buy them. Yet not the less, in my case, did I think it worth my while to weave them, and instead of studying how to make it worth men's while to buy my baskets, I studied rather how to avoid the necessity of selling them. The life which men praise and regard as successful is but one kind. Why should we exaggerate any one kind at the expense of the others?

Finding that my fellow-citizens were not likely to offer me any room in the court house, or any curacy or living anywhere else, but I must shift for myself, I turned my face more exclusively than ever to the woods, where I was better known. I determined to go into business at once, and not wait to acquire the usual capital, using such slender means as I had already got. My purpose in going to Walden Pond was not to live cheaply nor to live dearly there, but to transact some private business with the fewest obstacles; to be hindered from accomplishing which for want of a little common sense, a little enterprise and business talent, appeared not so sad as foolish.

I have always endeavored to acquire strict business habits; they are indispensable to every man. If your trade is with the Celestial Empire, then some small counting house on the coast, in some Salem harbor, will be fixture enough. You will export such articles as the country affords, purely native products, much ice and pine timber and a little granite, always in native bottoms. These will be good ventures. To oversee all the details yourself in person; to be at once pilot and captain, and owner and underwriter; to buy and sell and keep the accounts; to read every letter received, and write or read every letter sent; to superintend the discharge of imports night and day; to be upon many parts of the coast almost at the same time – often the richest freight will be discharged upon a Jersey shore; to be your own telegraph, unweariedly sweeping the horizon, speaking all passing vessels bound coastwise; to keep up a steady despatch of commodities, for the supply of such a distant and exorbitant market; to keep yourself informed of the state of the markets, prospects of war and peace everywhere, and anticipate the tendencies of trade and civilization – taking advantage of the results of all exploring expeditions, using new passages and all improvements in navigation; charts to be studied, the position of reefs and new lights and buoys to be ascertained, and ever, and ever, the logarithmic tables to be corrected, for by the error of some calculator the vessel often splits upon a rock that should have reached a friendly pier – there is the untold fate of La Perouse; universal science to be kept pace with, studying the lives of all great discoverers and navigators, great adventurers and merchants, from Hanno and the Phoenicians down to our day; in fine, account of stock to be taken from time to time, to know how you stand. It is a labor to task the faculties of a man – such problems of profit and loss, of interest, of tare and tret, and gauging of all kinds in it, as demand a universal knowledge.

I have thought that Walden Pond would be a good place for business, not solely on account of the railroad and the ice trade; it offers advantages which it may not be good policy to divulge; it is a good port and a good foundation. No Neva marshes to be filled; though you must everywhere build on piles of your own driving. It is said that a flood-tide, with a westerly wind, and ice in the Neva, would sweep St. Petersburg from the face of the earth.

As this business was to be entered into without the usual capital, it may not be easy to conjecture where those means, that will still be indispensable to every such undertaking, were to be obtained. As for Clothing, to come at once to the practical part of the question, perhaps we are led oftener by the love of novelty and a regard for the opinions of men, in procuring it, than by a true utility. Let him who has work to do recollect that the object of clothing is, first, to retain the vital heat, and secondly, in this state of society, to cover nakedness, and he may judge how much of any necessary or important work may be accomplished without adding to his wardrobe. Kings and queens who wear a suit but once, though made by some tailor or dressmaker to their majesties, cannot know the comfort of wearing a suit that fits. They are no better than wooden horses to hang the clean clothes on. Every day our garments become more assimilated to ourselves, receiving the impress of the wearer's character, until we hesitate to lay them aside without such delay and medical appliances and some such solemnity even as our bodies. No man ever stood the lower in my estimation for having a patch in his clothes; yet I am sure that there is greater anxiety, commonly, to have fashionable, or at least clean and unpatched clothes, than to have a sound conscience. But even if the rent is not mended, perhaps the worst vice betrayed is improvidence. I sometimes try my acquaintances by such tests as this – Who could wear a patch, or two extra seams only, over the knee? Most behave as if they believed that their prospects for life would be ruined if they should do it. It would be easier for them to hobble to town with a broken leg than with a broken pantaloon. Often if an accident happens to a gentleman's legs, they can be mended; but if a similar accident happens to the legs of his pantaloons, there is no help for it; for he considers, not what is truly respectable, but what is respected. We know but few men, a great many coats and breeches. Dress a scarecrow in your last shift, you standing shiftless by, who would not soonest salute the scarecrow? Passing a cornfield the other day, close by a hat and coat on a stake, I recognized the owner of the farm. He was only a little more weather-beaten than when I saw him last. I have heard of a dog that barked at every stranger who approached his master's premises with clothes on, but was easily quieted by a naked thief. It is an interesting question how far men would retain their relative rank if they were divested of their clothes. Could you, in such a case, tell surely of any company of civilized men which belonged to the most respected class? When Madam Pfeiffer, in her adventurous travels round the world, from east to west, had got so near home as Asiatic Russia, she says that she felt the necessity of wearing other than a travelling dress, when she went to meet the authorities, for she "was now in a civilized country, where... people are judged of by their clothes." Even in our democratic New England towns the accidental possession of wealth, and its manifestation in dress and equipage alone, obtain for the possessor almost universal respect. But they yield such respect, numerous as they are, are so far heathen, and need to have a missionary sent to them. Beside, clothes introduced sewing, a kind of work which you may call endless; a woman's dress, at least, is never done.

A man who has at length found something to do will not need to get a new suit to do it in; for him the old will do, that has lain dusty in the garret for an indeterminate period. Old shoes will serve a hero longer than they have served his valet – if a hero ever has a valet – bare feet are older than shoes, and he can make them do. Only they who go to soirees and legislative balls must have new coats, coats to change as often as the man changes in them. But if my jacket and trousers, my hat and shoes, are fit to worship God in, they will do; will they not? Who ever saw his old clothes – his old coat, actually worn out, resolved into its primitive elements, so that it was not a deed of charity to bestow it on some poor boy, by him perchance to be bestowed on some poorer still, or shall we say richer, who could do with less? I say, beware of all enterprises that require new clothes, and not rather a new wearer of clothes. If there is not a new man, how can the new clothes be made to fit? If you have any enterprise before you, try it in your old clothes. All men want, not something to *do with*, but something to *do*, or rather something to *be*. Perhaps we should never procure a new suit, however ragged or dirty the old, until we have so conducted, so enterprized or sailed in some way, that we feel like new men in the old, and that to retain it would be like keeping new wine in old bottles. Our moulting season, like that of the fowls, must be a crisis in our lives. The loon retires to solitary ponds to spend it. Thus also the snake casts its slough, and the caterpillar its wormy coat, by an internal industry and expansion; for clothes are but our outmost cuticle and mortal coil. Otherwise we shall be found sailing under false colors, and be inevitably cashiered at last by our own opinion, as well as that of mankind.

We don garment after garment, as if we grew like exogenous plants by addition without. Our outside and often thin and fanciful clothes are our epidermis, or false skin, which partakes not of our life, and may be stripped off here and there without fatal injury; our thicker garments, constantly worn, are our cellular integument, or cortex; but our shirts are our liber, or true bark, which cannot be removed without girdling and so destroying the man. I believe that all races at some seasons wear something equivalent to the shirt. It is desirable that a man be clad so simply that he can lay his hands on himself in the dark, and that he live in all respects so compactly and preparedly that, if an enemy take the town, he can, like the old philosopher, walk out the gate empty-handed without anxiety. While one thick garment is, for most purposes, as good as three thin ones, and cheap clothing can be obtained at prices really to suit customers; while a thick coat can be bought for five dollars, which will last as many years, thick pantaloons for two dollars, cowhide boots for a dollar and a half a pair, a summer hat for a quarter of a dollar, and a winter cap for sixty-two and a half cents, or a better be made at home at a nominal cost, where is he so poor that, clad in such a suit, *of his own earning*, there will not be found wise men to do him reverence?

When I ask for a garment of a particular form, my tailoress tells me gravely, "They do not make them so now," not emphasizing the "They" at all, as if she quoted an authority as impersonal as the Fates, and I find it difficult to get made what I want, simply because she cannot believe that I mean what I say, that I am so rash. When I hear this oracular sentence, I am for a moment absorbed in thought, emphasizing to myself each word separately that I may come at the meaning of it, that I may find out by what degree of consanguinity *They* are related to *me*, and what authority they may have in an affair which affects me so nearly; and, finally, I am inclined to answer her with equal mystery, and without any more emphasis of the "they" – "It is true, they did not make them so recently, but they do now." Of what use this measuring of me if she does not measure my character, but only the breadth of my shoulders, as it were a peg to bang the coat on? We worship not the Graces, nor the Parcee, but Fashion. She spins and weaves and cuts with full authority. The head monkey at Paris puts on a traveller's cap, and all the monkeys in America do the same. I sometimes despair of getting anything quite simple and honest done in this world by the help of men. They would have to be passed through a powerful press first, to squeeze their old notions out of them, so that they would not soon get upon their legs again; and then there would be some one in the company with a maggot in his head, hatched from an egg deposited there nobody knows when, for not even fire kills these things, and you would have lost your labor. Nevertheless, we will not forget that some Egyptian wheat was handed down to us by a mummy.

On the whole, I think that it cannot be maintained that dressing has in this or any country risen to the dignity of an art. At present men make shift to wear what they can get. Like shipwrecked sailors, they put on what they can find on the beach, and at a little distance, whether of space or time, laugh at each other's masquerade. Every generation laughs at the old fashions, but follows religiously the new. We are amused at beholding the costume of Henry VIII, or Queen Elizabeth, as much as if it was that of the King and Queen of the Cannibal Islands. All costume off a man is pitiful or grotesque. It is only the serious eye peering from and the sincere life passed within it which restrain laughter and consecrate the costume of any people. Let Harlequin be taken with a fit of the colic and his trappings will have to serve that mood too. When the soldier is hit by a cannon-ball, rags are as becoming as purple.

The childish and savage taste of men and women for new patterns keeps how many shaking and squinting through kaleidoscopes that they may discover the particular figure which this generation requires today. The manufacturers have learned that this taste is merely whimsical. Of two patterns which differ only by a few threads more or less of a particular color, the one will be sold readily, the other lie on the shelf, though it frequently happens that after the lapse of a season the latter becomes the most fashionable. Comparatively, tattooing is not the hideous custom which it is called. It is not barbarous merely because the printing is skin-deep and unalterable.

I cannot believe that our factory system is the best mode by which men may get clothing. The condition of the operatives is becoming every day more like that of the English; and it cannot be wondered at, since, as far as I have heard or observed, the principal object is, not that mankind may be well and honestly clad, but, unquestionably, that corporations may be enriched. In the long run men hit only what they aim at. Therefore, though they should fail immediately, they had better aim at something high.

As for a Shelter, I will not deny that this is now a necessary of life, though there are instances of men having done without it for long periods in colder countries than this. Samuel Laing says that "the Laplander in his skin dress, and in a skin bag which he puts over his head and shoulders, will sleep night after night on the snow... in a degree of cold which would extinguish the life of one exposed to it in any woollen clothing." He had seen them asleep thus. Yet he adds, "They are not hardier than other people." But, probably, man did not live long on the earth without discovering the convenience which there is in a house, the domestic comforts, which phrase may have originally signified the satisfactions of the house more than of the family; though these must be extremely partial and occasional in those climates where the house is associated in our thoughts with winter or the rainy season chiefly, and two thirds of the year, except for a parasol, is unnecessary. In our climate, in the summer, it was formerly almost solely a covering at night. In the Indian gazettes a wigwam was the symbol of a day's march, and a row of them cut or painted on the bark of a tree signified that so many times they had camped. Man was not made so large limbed and robust but that he must seek to narrow his world and wall in a space such as fitted him. He was at first bare and out of doors; but though this was pleasant enough in serene and warm weather, by daylight, the rainy season and the winter, to say nothing of the torrid sun, would perhaps have nipped his race in the bud if he had not made haste to clothe himself with the shelter of a house. Adam and Eve, according to the fable, wore the bower before other clothes. Man wanted a home, a place of warmth, or comfort, first of warmth, then the warmth of the affections.

We may imagine a time when, in the infancy of the human race, some enterprising mortal crept into a hollow in a rock for shelter. Every child begins the world again, to some extent, and loves to stay outdoors, even in wet and cold. It plays house, as well as horse, having an instinct for it. Who does not remember the interest with which, when young, he looked at shelving rocks, or any approach to a cave? It was the natural yearning of that portion, any portion of our most primitive ancestor which still survived in us. From the cave we have advanced to roofs of palm leaves, of bark and boughs, of linen woven and stretched, of grass and straw, of boards and shingles, of stones and tiles. At last, we know not what it is to live in the open air, and our lives are domestic in more senses than we think. From the hearth the field is a great distance. It would be well, perhaps, if we were to spend more of our days and nights without any obstruction between us and the celestial bodies, if the poet did not speak so much from under a roof, or the saint dwell there so long. Birds do not sing in caves, nor do doves cherish their innocence in dovecots.

However, if one designs to construct a dwelling-house, it behooves him to exercise a little Yankee shrewdness, lest after all he find himself in a workhouse, a labyrinth without a clue, a museum, an almshouse, a prison, or a splendid mausoleum instead. Consider first how slight a shelter is absolutely necessary. I have seen Penobscot Indians, in this town, living in tents of thin cotton cloth, while the snow was nearly a foot deep around them, and I thought that they would be glad to have it deeper to keep out the wind. Formerly, when how to get my living honestly, with freedom left for my proper pursuits, was a question which vexed me even more than it does now, for unfortunately I am become somewhat callous, I used to see a large box by the railroad, six feet long by three wide, in which the laborers locked up their tools at night; and it suggested to me that every man who was hard pushed might get such a one for a dollar, and, having bored a few auger holes in it, to admit the air at least, get into it when it rained and at night, and hook down the lid, and so have freedom in his love, and in his soul be free. This did not appear the worst, nor by any means a despicable alternative. You could sit up as late as you pleased, and, whenever you got up, go abroad without any landlord or house-lord dogging you for rent. Many a man is harassed to death to pay the rent of a larger and more luxurious box who would not have frozen to death in such a box as this. I am far from jesting. Economy is a subject which admits of being treated with levity, but it cannot so be disposed of. A comfortable house for a rude and hardy race, that lived mostly out of doors, was once made here almost entirely of such materials as Nature furnished ready to their hands. Gookin, who was superintendent of the Indians subject to the Massachusetts Colony, writing in 1674, says, "The best of their houses are covered very neatly, tight and warm, with barks of trees, slipped from their bodies at those seasons when the sap is up, and made into great flakes, with pressure of weighty timber, when they are green.... The meaner sort are covered with mats which they make of a kind of bulrush, and are also indifferently tight and warm, but not so good as the former.... Some I have seen, sixty or a hundred feet long and thirty feet broad.... I have often lodged in their wigwams, and found them as warm as the best English houses." He adds that they were commonly carpeted and lined within with well-wrought embroidered mats, and were furnished with various utensils. The Indians had advanced so far as to regulate the effect of the wind by a mat suspended over the hole in the roof and moved by a string. Such a lodge was in the first instance constructed in a day or two at most, and taken down and put up in a few hours; and every family owned one, or its apartment in one.

In the savage state every family owns a shelter as good as the best, and sufficient for its coarser and simpler wants; but I think that I speak within bounds when I say that, though the birds of the air have their nests, and the foxes their holes, and the savages their wigwams, in modern civilized society not more than one half the families own a shelter. In the large towns and cities, where civilization especially prevails, the number of those who own a shelter is a very small fraction of the whole. The rest pay an annual tax for this outside garment of all, become indispensable summer and winter, which would buy a village of Indian wigwams, but now helps to keep them poor as long as they live. I do not mean to insist here on the disadvantage of hiring compared with owning, but it is evident that the savage owns his shelter because it costs so little, while the civilized man hires his commonly because he cannot afford to own it; nor can he, in the long run, any better afford to hire. But, answers one, by merely paying this tax, the *poor* civilized man secures an abode which is a palace compared with the savage's. An annual rent of from twenty-five to a hundred dollars (these are the country rates) entitles him to the benefit of the improvements of centuries, spacious apartments, clean paint and paper, Rumford fireplace, back plastering, Venetian blinds, copper pump, spring lock, a commodious cellar, and many other things. But how happens it that he who is said to enjoy these things is so commonly a poor civilized man, while the savage, who has them not, is rich as a savage? If it is asserted that civilization is a real advance in the condition of man – and I think that it is, though only the wise improve their advantages – it must be shown that it has produced better dwellings without making them more costly; and the cost of a thing is the amount of what I will call life which is required to be exchanged for it, immediately or in the long run. An average house in this neighborhood costs perhaps eight hundred dollars, and to lay up this sum will take from ten to fifteen years of the laborer's life, even if he is not encumbered with a family – estimating the pecuniary value of every man's labor at one dollar a day, for if some receive more, others receive less; so that he must have spent more than half his life commonly before *his* wigwam will be earned. If we suppose him to pay a rent instead, this is but a doubtful choice of evils. Would the savage have been wise to exchange his wigwam for a palace on these terms?

It may be guessed that I reduce almost the whole advantage of holding this superfluous property as a fund in store against the future, so far as the individual is concerned, mainly to the defraying of funeral expenses. But perhaps a man is not required to bury himself. Nevertheless this points to an important distinction between the civilized man and the savage; and, no doubt, they have designs on us for our benefit, in making the life of a civilized people an *institution*, in which the life of the individual is to a great extent absorbed, in order to preserve and perfect that of the race. But I wish to show at what a sacrifice this advantage is at present obtained, and to suggest that we may possibly so live as to secure all the advantage without suffering any of the disadvantage. What mean ye by saying that the poor ye have always with you, or that the fathers have eaten sour grapes, and the children's teeth are set on edge?

"As I live, saith the Lord God, ye shall not have occasion any more to use this proverb in Israel."

"Behold all souls are mine; as the soul of the father, so also the soul of the son is mine: the soul that sinneth, it shall die."

When I consider my neighbors, the farmers of Concord, who are at least as well off as the other classes, I find that for the most part they have been toiling twenty, thirty, or forty years, that they may become the real owners of their farms, which commonly they have inherited with encumbrances, or else bought with hired money – and we may regard one third of that toil as the cost of their houses – but commonly they have not paid for them yet. It is true, the encumbrances sometimes outweigh the value of the farm, so that the farm itself becomes one great encumbrance, and still a man is found to inherit it, being well acquainted with it, as he says. On applying to the assessors, I am surprised to learn that they cannot at once name a dozen in the town who own their farms free and clear. If you would know the history of these homesteads, inquire at the bank where they are mortgaged. The man who has actually paid for his farm with labor on it is so rare that every neighbor can point to him. I doubt if there are three such men in Concord. What has been said of the merchants, that a very large majority, even ninety-seven in a hundred, are sure to fail, is equally true of the farmers. With regard to the merchants, however, one of them says pertinently that a great part of their failures are not genuine pecuniary failures, but merely failures to fulfill their engagements, because it is inconvenient; that is, it is the moral character that breaks down. But this puts an infinitely worse face on the matter, and suggests, beside, that probably not even the other three succeed in saving their souls, but are perchance bankrupt in a worse sense than they who fail honestly. Bankruptcy and repudiation are the springboards from which much of our civilization vaults and turns its somersets, but the savage stands on the unelastic plank of famine. Yet the Middlesex Cattle Show goes off here with eclat annually, as if all the joints of the agricultural machine were suent.

The farmer is endeavoring to solve the problem of a livelihood by a formula more complicated than the problem itself. To get his shoestrings he speculates in herds of cattle. With consummate skill he has set his trap with a hair springe to catch comfort and independence, and then, as he turned away, got his own leg into it. This is the reason he is poor; and for a similar reason we are all poor in respect to a thousand savage comforts, though surrounded by luxuries. As Chapman sings,

"The false society of men –
– for earthly greatness
All heavenly comforts rarefies to air."

And when the farmer has got his house, he may not be the richer but the poorer for it, and it be the house that has got him. As I understand it, that was a valid objection urged by Momus against the house which Minerva made, that she "had not made it movable, by which means a bad neighborhood might be avoided"; and it may still be urged, for our houses are such unwieldy property that we are often imprisoned rather than housed in them; and the bad neighborhood to be avoided is our own scurvy selves. I know one or two families, at least, in this town, who, for nearly a generation, have been wishing to sell their houses in the outskirts and move into the village, but have not been able to accomplish it, and only death will set them free.

Granted that the *majority* are able at last either to own or hire the modern house with all its improvements. While civilization has been improving our houses, it has not equally improved the men who are to inhabit them. It has created palaces, but it was not so easy to create noblemen and kings. *And if the civilized man's pursuits are no worthier than the savage's, if he is employed the greater part of his life in obtaining gross necessaries and comforts merely, why should he have a better dwelling than the former?*

But how do the poor *minority* fare? Perhaps it will be found that just in proportion as some have been placed in outward circumstances above the savage, others have been degraded below him. The luxury of one class is counterbalanced by the indigence of another. On the one side is the palace, on the other are the almshouse and "silent poor." The myriads who built the pyramids to be the tombs of the Pharaohs were fed on garlic, and it may be were not decently buried themselves. The mason who finishes the cornice of the palace returns at night perchance to a hut not so good as a wigwam. It is a mistake to suppose that, in a country where the usual evidences of civilization exist, the condition of a very large body of the inhabitants may not be as degraded as that of savages. I refer to the degraded poor, not now to the degraded rich. To know this I should not need to look farther than to the shanties which everywhere border our railroads, that last improvement in civilization; where I see in my daily walks human beings living in sties, and all winter with an open door, for the sake of light, without any visible, often imaginable, wood-pile, and the forms of both old and young are permanently contracted by the long habit of shrinking from cold and misery, and the development of all their limbs and faculties is checked. It certainly is fair to look at that class by whose labor the works which distinguish this generation are accomplished. Such too, to a greater or less extent, is the condition of the operatives of every denomination in England, which is the great workhouse of the world. Or I could refer you to Ireland, which is marked as one of the white or enlightened spots on the map. Contrast the physical condition of the Irish with that of the North American Indian, or the South Sea Islander, or any other savage race before it was degraded by contact with the civilized man. Yet I have no doubt that that people's rulers are as wise as the average of civilized rulers. Their condition only proves what squalidness may consist with civilization. I hardly need refer now to the laborers in our Southern States who produce the staple exports of this country, and are themselves a staple production of the South. But to confine myself to those who are said to be in moderate circumstances.

Most men appear never to have considered what a house is, and are actually though needlessly poor all their lives because they think that they must have such a one as their neighbors have. As if one were to wear any sort of coat which the tailor might cut out for him, or, gradually leaving off palm-leaf hat or cap of woodchuck skin, complain of hard times because he could not afford to buy him a crown! It is possible to invent a house still more convenient and luxurious than we have, which yet all would admit that man could not afford to pay for. Shall we always study to obtain more of these things, and not sometimes to be content with less? Shall the respectable citizen thus gravely teach, by precept and example, the necessity of the young man's providing a certain number of superfluous glow-shoes, and umbrellas, and empty guest chambers for empty guests, before he dies? Why should not our furniture be as simple as the Arab's or the Indian's? When I think of the benefactors of the race, whom we have apotheosized as messengers from heaven, bearers of divine gifts to man, I do not see in my mind any retinue at their heels, any carload of fashionable furniture. Or what if I were to allow – would it not be a singular allowance? – that our furniture should be more complex than the Arab's, in proportion as we are morally and intellectually his superiors! At present our houses are cluttered and defiled with it, and a good housewife would sweep out the greater part into the dust hole, and not leave her morning's work undone. Morning work! By the blushes of Aurora and the music of Memnon, what should be man's *morning work* in this world? I had three pieces of limestone on my desk, but I was terrified to find that they required to be dusted daily, when the furniture of my mind was all undusted still, and threw them out the window in disgust. How, then, could I have a furnished house? I would rather sit in the open air, for no dust gathers on the grass, unless where man has broken ground.

It is the luxurious and dissipated who set the fashions which the herd so diligently follow. The traveller who stops at the best houses, so called, soon discovers this, for the publicans presume him to be a Sardanapalus, and if he resigned himself to their tender mercies he would soon be completely emasculated. I think that in the railroad car we are inclined to spend more on luxury than on safety and convenience, and it threatens without attaining these to become no better than a modern drawing-room, with its divans, and ottomans, and sun-shades, and a hundred other oriental things, which we are taking west with us, invented for the ladies of the harem and the effeminate natives of the Celestial Empire, which Jonathan should be ashamed to know the names of. I would rather sit on a pumpkin and have it all to myself than be crowded on a velvet cushion. I would rather ride on earth in an ox cart, with a free circulation, than go to heaven in the fancy car of an excursion train and breathe a *malaria* all the way.

The very simplicity and nakedness of man's life in the primitive ages imply this advantage, at least, that they left him still but a sojourner in nature. When he was refreshed with food and sleep, he contemplated his journey again. He dwelt, as it were, in a tent in this world, and was either threading the valleys, or crossing the plains, or climbing the mountain-tops. But lo! men have become the tools of their tools. The man who independently plucked the fruits when he was hungry is become a farmer; and he who stood under a tree for shelter, a housekeeper. We now no longer camp as for a night, but have settled down on earth and forgotten heaven. We have adopted Christianity merely as an improved method of agriculture. We have built for this world a family mansion, and for the next a family tomb. The best works of art are the expression of man's struggle to free himself from this condition, but the effect of our art is merely to make this low state comfortable and that higher state to be forgotten. There is actually no place in this village for a work of fine art, if any had come down to us, to stand, for our lives, our houses and streets, furnish no proper pedestal for it. There is not a nail to hang a picture on, nor a shelf to receive the bust of a hero or a saint. When I consider how our houses are built and paid for, or not paid for, and their internal economy managed and sustained, I wonder that the floor does not give way under the visitor while he is admiring the gewgaws upon the mantelpiece, and let him through into the cellar, to some solid and honest though earthy foundation. I cannot but perceive that this so-called rich and refined life is a thing jumped at, and I do not get on in the enjoyment of the *fine* arts which adorn it, my attention being wholly occupied with the jump; for I remember that the greatest genuine leap, due to human muscles alone, on record, is that of certain wandering Arabs, who are said to have cleared twenty-five feet on level ground. Without factitious support, man is sure to come to earth again beyond that distance. The first question which I am tempted to put to the proprietor of such great impropriety is, Who bolsters you? Are you one of the ninety-seven who fail, or the three who succeed? Answer me these questions, and then perhaps I may look at your bawbles and find them ornamental. The cart before the horse is neither beautiful nor useful. Before we can adorn our houses with beautiful objects the walls must be stripped, and our lives must be stripped, and beautiful housekeeping and beautiful living be laid for a foundation: now, a taste for the beautiful is most cultivated out of doors, where there is no house and no housekeeper.

Old Johnson, in his "Wonder-Working Providence," speaking of the first settlers of this town, with whom he was contemporary, tells us that "they burrow themselves in the earth for their first shelter under some hillside, and, casting the soil aloft upon timber, they make a smoky fire against the earth, at the highest side." They did not "provide them houses," says he, "till the earth, by the Lord's blessing, brought forth bread to feed them," and the first year's crop was so light that "they were forced to cut their bread very thin for a long season." The secretary of the Province of New Netherland, writing in Dutch, in 1650, for the information of those who wished to take up land there, states more particularly that "those in New Netherland, and especially in New England, who have no means to build farmhouses at first according to their wishes, dig a square pit in the ground, cellar fashion, six or seven feet deep, as long and as broad as they think proper, case the earth inside with wood all round the wall, and line the wood with the bark of trees or something else to prevent the caving in of the earth; floor this cellar with plank, and wainscot it overhead for a ceiling, raise a roof of spars clear up, and cover the spars with bark or green sods, so that they can live dry and warm in these houses with their entire families for two, three, and four years, it being understood that partitions are run through those cellars which are adapted to the size of the family. The wealthy and principal men in New England, in the beginning of the colonies, commenced their first dwelling-houses in this fashion for two reasons: firstly, in order not to waste time in building, and not to want food the next season; secondly, in order not to discourage poor laboring people whom they brought over in numbers from

Fatherland. In the course of three or four years, when the country became adapted to agriculture, they built themselves handsome houses, spending on them several thousands."

In this course which our ancestors took there was a show of prudence at least, as if their principle were to satisfy the more pressing wants first. But are the more pressing wants satisfied now? When I think of acquiring for myself one of our luxurious dwellings, I am deterred, for, so to speak, the country is not yet adapted to *human* culture, and we are still forced to cut our *spiritual* bread far thinner than our forefathers did their wheaten. Not that all architectural ornament is to be neglected even in the rudest periods; but let our houses first be lined with beauty, where they come in contact with our lives, like the tenement of the shellfish, and not overlaid with it. But, alas! I have been inside one or two of them, and know what they are lined with.

Though we are not so degenerate but that we might possibly live in a cave or a wigwam or wear skins today, it certainly is better to accept the advantages, though so dearly bought, which the invention and industry of mankind offer. In such a neighborhood as this, boards and shingles, lime and bricks, are cheaper and more easily obtained than suitable caves, or whole logs, or bark in sufficient quantities, or even well-tempered clay or flat stones. I speak understandingly on this subject, for I have made myself acquainted with it both theoretically and practically. With a little more wit we might use these materials so as to become richer than the richest now are, and make our civilization a blessing. The civilized man is a more experienced and wiser savage. But to make haste to my own experiment.

Near the end of March, 1845, I borrowed an axe and went down to the woods by Walden Pond, nearest to where I intended to build my house, and began to cut down some tall, arrowy white pines, still in their youth, for timber. It is difficult to begin without borrowing, but perhaps it is the most generous course thus to permit your fellow-men to have an interest in your enterprise. The owner of the axe, as he released his hold on it, said that it was the apple of his eye; but I returned it sharper than I received it. It was a pleasant hillside where I worked, covered with pine woods, through which I looked out on the pond, and a small open field in the woods where pines and hickories were springing up. The ice in the pond was not yet dissolved, though there were some open spaces, and it was all dark-colored and saturated with water. There were some slight flurries of snow during the days that I worked there; but for the most part when I came out on to the railroad, on my way home, its yellow sand-heap stretched away gleaming in the hazy atmosphere, and the rails shone in the spring sun, and I heard the lark and pewee and other birds already come to commence another year with us. They were pleasant spring days, in which the winter of man's discontent was thawing as well as the earth, and the life that had lain torpid began to stretch itself. One day, when my axe had come off and I had cut a green hickory for a wedge, driving it with a stone, and had placed the whole to soak in a pond-hole in order to swell the wood, I saw a striped snake run into the water, and he lay on the bottom, apparently without inconvenience, as long as I stayed there, or more than a quarter of an hour; perhaps because he had not yet fairly come out of the torpid state. It appeared to me that for a like reason men remain in their present low and primitive condition; but if they should feel the influence of the spring of springs arousing them, they would of necessity rise to a higher and more ethereal life. I had previously seen the snakes in frosty mornings in my path with portions of their bodies still numb and inflexible, waiting for the sun to thaw them. On the 1st of April it rained and melted the ice, and in the early part of the day, which was very foggy, I heard a stray goose groping about over the pond and cackling as if lost, or like the spirit of the fog.

So I went on for some days cutting and hewing timber, and also studs and rafters, all with my narrow axe, not having many communicable or scholar-like thoughts, singing to myself:

Men say they know many things;
But lo! they have taken wings –
The arts and sciences,
And a thousand appliances;
The wind that blows
Is all that anybody knows.

I hewed the main timbers six inches square, most of the studs on two sides only, and the rafters and floor timbers on one side, leaving the rest of the bark on, so that they were just as straight and much stronger than sawed ones. Each stick was carefully mortised or tenoned by its stump, for I had borrowed other tools by this time. My days in the woods were not very long ones; yet I usually carried my dinner of bread and butter, and read the newspaper in which it was wrapped, at noon, sitting amid the green pine boughs which I had cut off, and to my bread was imparted some of their fragrance, for my hands were covered with a thick coat of pitch. Before I had done I was more the friend than the foe of the pine tree, though I had cut down some of them, having become better acquainted with it. Sometimes a rambler in the wood was attracted by the sound of my axe, and we chatted pleasantly over the chips which I had made.

By the middle of April, for I made no haste in my work, but rather made the most of it, my house was framed and ready for the raising. I had already bought the shanty of James Collins, an Irishman who worked on the Fitchburg Railroad, for boards. James Collins' shanty was considered an uncommonly fine one. When I called to see it he was not at home. I walked about the outside, at first unobserved from within, the window was so deep and high. It was of small dimensions, with a peaked cottage roof, and not much else to be seen, the dirt being raised five feet all around as if it were a compost heap. The roof was the soundest part, though a good deal warped and made brittle by the sun. Doorsill there was none, but a perennial passage for the hens under the door-board. Mrs. C. came to the door and asked me to view it from the inside. The hens were driven in by my approach. It was dark, and had a dirt floor for the most part, dank, clammy, and aguish, only here a board and there a board which would not bear removal. She lighted a lamp to show me the inside of the roof and the walls, and also that the board floor extended under the bed, warning me not to step into the cellar, a sort of dust hole two feet deep. In her own words, they were good boards overhead, good boards all around, and a good window" – of two whole squares originally, only the cat had passed out that way lately. There was a stove, a bed, and a place to sit, an infant in the house where it was born, a silk parasol, gilt-framed looking-glass, and a patent new coffee-mill nailed to an oak sapling, all told. The bargain was soon concluded, for James had in the meanwhile returned. I to pay four dollars and twenty-five cents tonight, he to vacate at five tomorrow morning, selling to nobody else meanwhile: I to take possession at six. It were well, he said, to be there early, and anticipate certain indistinct but wholly unjust claims on the score of ground rent and fuel. This he assured me was the only encumbrance. At six I passed him and his family on the road. One large bundle held their all – bed, coffee-mill, looking-glass, hens – all but the cat; she took to the woods and became a wild cat, and, as I learned afterward, trod in a trap set for woodchucks, and so became a dead cat at last.

I took down this dwelling the same morning, drawing the nails, and removed it to the pond-side by small cartloads, spreading the boards on the grass there to bleach and warp back again in the sun. One early thrush gave me a note or two as I drove along the woodland path. I was informed treacherously by a young Patrick that neighbor Seeley, an Irishman, in the intervals of the carting, transferred the still tolerable, straight, and drivable nails, staples, and spikes to his pocket, and then stood when I came back to pass the time of day, and look freshly up, unconcerned, with spring thoughts, at the devastation; there being a dearth of work, as he said. He was there to represent spectatordom, and help make this seemingly insignificant event one with the removal of the gods of Troy.

I dug my cellar in the side of a hill sloping to the south, where a woodchuck had formerly dug his burrow, down through sumach and blackberry roots, and the lowest stain of vegetation, six feet square by seven deep, to a fine sand where potatoes would not freeze in any winter. The sides were left shelving, and not stoned; but the sun having never shone on them, the sand still keeps its place. It was but two hours' work. I took particular pleasure in this breaking of ground, for in almost all latitudes men dig into the earth for an equable temperature. Under the most splendid house in the city is still to be found the cellar where they store their roots as of old, and long after the superstructure has disappeared posterity remark its dent in the earth. The house is still but a sort of porch at the entrance of a burrow.

At length, in the beginning of May, with the help of some of my acquaintances, rather to improve so good an occasion for neighborliness than from any necessity, I set up the frame of my house. No man was ever more honored in the character of his raisers than I. They are destined, I trust, to assist at the raising of loftier structures one day. I began to occupy my house on the 4th of July, as soon as it was boarded and roofed, for the boards were carefully feather-edged and lapped, so that it was perfectly impervious to rain, but before boarding I laid the foundation of a chimney at one end, bringing two cartloads of stones up the hill from the pond in my arms. I built the chimney after my hoeing in the fall, before a fire became necessary for warmth, doing my cooking in the meanwhile out of doors on the ground, early in the morning: which mode I still think is in some respects more convenient and agreeable than the usual one. When it stormed before my bread was baked, I fixed a few boards over the fire, and sat under them to watch my loaf, and passed some pleasant hours in that way. In those days, when my hands were much employed, I read but little, but the least scraps of paper which lay on the ground, my holder, or tablecloth, afforded me as much entertainment, in fact answered the same purpose as the Iliad.

It would be worth the while to build still more deliberately than I did, considering, for instance, what foundation a door, a window, a cellar, a garret, have in the nature of man, and perchance never raising any superstructure until we found a better reason for it than our temporal necessities even. There is some of the same fitness in a man's building his own house that there is in a bird's building its own nest. Who knows but if men constructed their dwellings with their own hands, and provided food for themselves and families simply and honestly enough, the poetic faculty would be universally developed, as birds universally sing when they are so engaged? But alas! we do like cowbirds and cuckoos, which lay their eggs in nests which other birds have built, and cheer no traveller with their chattering and unmusical notes. Shall we forever resign the pleasure of construction to the carpenter? What does architecture amount to in the experience of the mass of men? I never in all my walks came across a man engaged in so simple and natural an occupation as building his house. We belong to the community. It is not the tailor alone who is the ninth part of a man; it is as much the preacher, and the merchant, and the farmer. Where is this division of labor to end? And what object does it finally serve? No doubt another *may* also think for me; but it is not therefore desirable that he should do so to the exclusion of my thinking for myself.

Before winter I built a chimney, and shingled the sides of my house, which were already impervious to rain, with imperfect and sappy shingles made of the first slice of the log, whose edges I was obliged to straighten with a plane.

I have thus a tight shingled and plastered house, ten feet wide by fifteen long, and eight-feet posts, with a garret and a closet, a large window on each side, two trap-doors, one door at the end, and a brick fireplace opposite. The exact cost of my house, paying the usual price for such materials as I used, but not counting the work, all of which was done by myself, was as follows; and I give the details because very few are able to tell exactly what their houses cost, and fewer still, if any, the separate cost of the various materials which compose them:

Boards	$8.03 ½,	(mostly shanty boards)
Refuse shingles for roof and sides	$4.00	
Laths	$1.25	
Two second-hand windows with glass	$2.43	
One thousand old brick	$4.00	
Two casks of lime	$2.40	(That was high.)
Hair	$0.31	(More than I needed.)
Mantle-tree iron	$0.15	
Nails	$3.90	
Hinges and screws	$0.14	
Latch	$0.10	
Chalk	$0.01	
Transportation	$1.40	(I carried a good part on my back)
In all	$28.12 ½	

These are all the materials, excepting the timber, stones, and sand, which I claimed by squatter's right. I have also a small woodshed adjoining, made chiefly of the stuff which was left after building the house.

I intend to build me a house which will surpass any on the main street in Concord in grandeur and luxury, as soon as it pleases me as much and will cost me no more than my present one.

I thus found that the student who wishes for a shelter can obtain one for a lifetime at an expense not greater than the rent which he now pays annually. If I seem to boast more than is becoming, my excuse is that I brag for humanity rather than for myself; and my shortcomings and inconsistencies do not affect the truth of my statement. Notwithstanding much cant and hypocrisy – chaff which I find it difficult to separate from my wheat, but for which I am as sorry as any man – I will breathe freely and stretch myself in this respect, it is such a relief to both the moral and physical system; and I am resolved that I will not through humility become the devil's attorney. I will endeavor to speak a good word for the truth. At Cambridge College the mere rent of a student's room, which is only a little larger than my own, is thirty dollars each year, though the corporation had the advantage of building thirty-two side by side and under one roof, and the occupant suffers the inconvenience of many and noisy neighbors, and perhaps a residence in the fourth story. I cannot but think that if we had more true wisdom in these respects, not only less education would be needed, because, forsooth, more would already have been acquired, but the pecuniary expense of getting an education would in a great measure vanish. Those conveniences which the student requires at Cambridge or elsewhere cost him or somebody else ten times as great a sacrifice of life as they would with proper management on both sides. Those things for which the most money is demanded are never the things which the student most wants. Tuition, for instance, is an important item in the term bill, while for the far more valuable education which he gets by associating with the most cultivated of his contemporaries no charge is made. The mode of founding a college is, commonly, to get up a subscription of dollars and cents, and then, following blindly the principles of a division of labor to its extreme – a principle which should never be followed but with circumspection – to call in a contractor who makes this a subject of speculation, and he employs Irishmen or other operatives actually to lay the foundations, while the students that are to be are said to be fitting themselves for it; and for these oversights successive generations have to pay. I think that it would be *better than this*, for the students, or those who desire to be benefited by it, even to lay the foundation themselves. The student who secures his coveted leisure and retirement by systematically shirking any labor necessary to man obtains but an ignoble and unprofitable leisure, defrauding himself of the experience which alone can make leisure fruitful. "But," says one, "you do not mean that the students should go to work with their hands instead of their heads?" I do not mean that exactly, but I mean something which he might think a good deal like that; I mean that they should not *play* life, or *study* it merely, while the community supports them at this expensive game, but earnestly *live* it from beginning to end. How could youths better learn to live than by at once trying the experiment of living? Methinks this would exercise their minds as much as mathematics. If I wished a boy to know something about the arts and sciences, for instance, I would not pursue the common course, which is merely to send him into the neighborhood of some professor, where anything is professed and practised but the art of life; to survey the world through a telescope or a microscope, and never with his natural eye; to study chemistry, and not learn how his bread is made, or mechanics, and not learn how it is earned; to discover new satellites to Neptune, and not detect the motes in his eyes, or to what vagabond he is a satellite himself; or to be devoured by the monsters that swarm all around him, while contemplating the monsters in a drop of vinegar. Which would have advanced the most at the end of a month – the boy who had made his own jackknife from the ore which he had dug and smelted, reading as much as would be necessary for this – or the boy who had attended the lectures on metallurgy at the Institute in the meanwhile, and had received a Rodgers penknife from his father? Which would be most likely to cut his fingers?... To my astonishment I was informed on leaving college that I had studied navigation! – why, if I had taken one turn down the harbor I should have known more about it. Even the *poor* student studies and is taught only *political* economy, while that economy of living which is synonymous with philosophy is not even sincerely professed in our colleges. The consequence is, that while he is reading Adam Smith, Ricardo, and Say, he runs his father in debt irretrievably.

As with our colleges, so with a hundred "modern improvements"; there is an illusion about them; there is not always a positive advance. The devil goes on exacting compound interest to the last for his early share and numerous succeeding investments in them. Our inventions are wont to be pretty toys, which distract our attention from serious things. They are but improved means to an unimproved end, an end which it was already but too easy to arrive at; as railroads lead to Boston or New York. We are in great haste to construct a magnetic telegraph from Maine to Texas; but Maine and Texas, it may be, have nothing important to communicate. Either is in such a predicament as the man who was earnest to be introduced to a distinguished deaf woman, but when he was presented, and one end of her ear trumpet was put into his hand, had nothing to say. As if the main object were to talk fast and not to talk sensibly. We are eager to tunnel under the Atlantic and bring the Old World some weeks nearer to the New; but perchance the first news that will leak through into the broad, flapping American ear will be that the Princess Adelaide has the whooping cough. After all, the man whose horse trots a mile in a minute does not carry the most important messages; he is not an evangelist, nor does he come round eating locusts and wild honey. I doubt if Flying Childers ever carried a peck of corn to mill.

One says to me, "I wonder that you do not lay up money; you love to travel; you might take the cars and go to Fitchburg today and see the country." But I am wiser than that. I have learned that the swiftest traveller is he that goes afoot. I say to my friend, Suppose we try who will get there first. The distance is thirty miles; the fare ninety cents. That is almost a day's wages. I remember when wages were sixty cents a day for laborers on this very road. Well, I start now on foot, and get there before night; I have travelled at that rate by the week together. You will in the meanwhile have earned your fare, and arrive there some time tomorrow, or possibly this evening, if you are lucky enough to get a job in season. Instead of going to

Fitchburg, you will be working here the greater part of the day. And so, if the railroad reached round the world, I think that I should keep ahead of you; and as for seeing the country and getting experience of that kind, I should have to cut your acquaintance altogether.

Such is the universal law, which no man can ever outwit, and with regard to the railroad even we may say it is as broad as it is long. To make a railroad round the world available to all mankind is equivalent to grading the whole surface of the planet. Men have an indistinct notion that if they keep up this activity of joint stocks and spades long enough all will at length ride somewhere, in next to no time, and for nothing; but though a crowd rushes to the depot, and the conductor shouts "All aboard!" when the smoke is blown away and the vapor condensed, it will be perceived that a few are riding, but the rest are run over – and it will be called, and will be, "A melancholy accident." No doubt they can ride at last who shall have earned their fare, that is, if they survive so long, but they will probably have lost their elasticity and desire to travel by that time. This spending of the best part of one's life earning money in order to enjoy a questionable liberty during the least valuable part of it reminds me of the Englishman who went to India to make a fortune first, in order that he might return to England and live the life of a poet. He should have gone up garret at once. "What!" exclaim a million Irishmen starting up from all the shanties in the land, "is not this railroad which we have built a good thing?" Yes, I answer, *comparatively* good, that is, you might have done worse; but I wish, as you are brothers of mine, that you could have spent your time better than digging in this dirt.

Before I finished my house, wishing to earn ten or twelve dollars by some honest and agreeable method, in order to meet my unusual expenses, I planted about two acres and a half of light and sandy soil near it chiefly with beans, but also a small part with potatoes, corn, peas, and turnips. The whole lot contains eleven acres, mostly growing up to pines and hickories, and was sold the preceding season for eight dollars and eight cents an acre. One farmer said that it was "good for nothing but to raise cheeping squirrels on." I put no manure whatever on this land, not being the owner, but merely a squatter, and not expecting to cultivate so much again, and I did not quite hoe it all once. I got out several cords of stumps in plowing, which supplied me with fuel for a long time, and left small circles of virgin mould, easily distinguishable through the summer by the greater luxuriance of the beans there. The dead and for the most part unmerchantable wood behind my house, and the driftwood from the pond, have supplied the remainder of my fuel. I was obliged to hire a team and a man for the plowing, though I held the plow myself. My farm outgoes for the first season were, for implements, seed, work, etc., $14.72 ½. The seed corn was given me. This never costs anything to speak of, unless you plant more than enough. I got twelve bushels of beans, and eighteen bushels of potatoes, beside some peas and sweet corn. The yellow corn and turnips were too late to come to anything. My whole income from the farm was:

	$23.44
Deducting the outgoes..................	$14.72 1/2
There are left..................................	$8.71 1/2

Beside produce consumed and on hand at the time this estimate was made of the value of $4.50 – the amount on hand much more than balancing a little grass which I did not raise. All things considered, that is, considering the importance of a man's soul and of today, notwithstanding the short time occupied by my experiment, nay, partly even because of its transient character, I believe that that was doing better than any farmer in Concord did that year.

The next year I did better still, for I spaded up all the land which I required, about a third of an acre, and I learned from the experience of both years, not being in the least awed by many celebrated works on husbandry, Arthur Young among the rest, that if one would live simply and eat only the crop which he raised, and raise no more than he ate, and not exchange it for an insufficient quantity of more luxurious and expensive things, he would need to cultivate only a few rods of ground, and that it would be cheaper to spade up that than to use oxen to plow it, and to select a fresh spot from time to time than to manure the old, and he could do all his necessary farm work as it were with his left hand at odd hours in the summer; and thus he would not be tied to an ox, or horse, or cow, or pig, as at present. I desire to speak impartially on this point, and as one not interested in the success or failure of the present economical and social arrangements. I was more independent than any farmer in Concord, for I was not anchored to a house or farm, but could follow the bent of my genius, which is a very crooked one, every moment. Beside being better off than they already, if my house had been burned or my crops had failed, I should have been nearly as well off as before.

I am wont to think that men are not so much the keepers of herds as herds are the keepers of men, the former are so much the freer. Men and oxen exchange work; but if we consider necessary work only, the oxen will be seen to have greatly the advantage, their farm is so much the larger. Man does some of his part of the exchange work in his six weeks of haying, and it is no boy's play. Certainly no nation that lived simply in all respects, that is, no nation of philosophers, would commit so great a blunder as to use the labor of animals. True, there never was and is not likely soon to be a nation of philosophers, nor am I certain it is desirable that there should be. However, *I* should never have broken a horse or bull and taken him to board for any work he might do for me, for fear I should become a horseman or a herdsman merely; and if society seems to be the gainer by so doing, are we certain that what is one man's gain is not another's loss, and that the stable-boy has equal cause with his master to be satisfied? Granted that some public works would not have been constructed without this aid, and let man share the glory of such with the ox and horse; does it follow that he could not have accomplished works yet more worthy of himself in that case? When men begin to do, not merely unnecessary or artistic, but luxurious and idle work, with their assistance, it is inevitable that a few do all the exchange work with the oxen, or, in other words, become the slaves of the strongest. Man thus not only works for the animal within him, but, for a symbol of this, he works for the animal without him. Though we have many substantial houses of brick or stone, the prosperity of the farmer is still measured by the degree to which the barn overshadows the house. This town is said to have the largest houses for oxen, cows, and horses hereabouts, and it is not behindhand in its public buildings; but there are very few halls for free worship or free speech in this county. It should not be by their architecture, but why not even by their power of abstract thought, that nations should seek to commemorate themselves? How much more admirable the Bhagvat-Geeta than all the ruins of the East! Towers and temples are the luxury of princes. A simple and independent mind does not toil at the bidding of any prince. Genius is not a retainer to any emperor, nor is its material silver, or gold, or marble, except to a trifling extent. To what end, pray, is so much stone hammered? In Arcadia, when I was there, I did not see any hammering stone. Nations are possessed with an insane ambition to perpetuate the memory of themselves by the amount of hammered stone they leave. What if equal pains were taken to smooth and polish their manners? One piece of good sense would be more memorable than a monument as high as the moon. I love better to see stones in place. The grandeur of Thebes was a vulgar grandeur. More sensible is a rod of stone wall that bounds an honest man's field than a hundred-gated Thebes that has wandered farther from the true end of life. The religion and civilization which are barbaric and heathenish build splendid temples; but what you might call Christianity does not. Most of the stone a nation hammers goes toward its tomb only. It buries itself alive. As for the Pyramids, there is nothing to wonder at in them so much as the fact that so many men could be found degraded enough to spend their lives constructing a tomb for some ambitious booby, whom it would have been wiser and manlier to have drowned in the Nile, and then given his body to the dogs. I might possibly invent some excuse for them and him, but I have no time for it. As for the religion and love of art of the builders, it is much the same all the world over, whether the building be an Egyptian temple or the United States Bank. It costs more than it comes to. The mainspring is vanity, assisted by the love of garlic and bread and butter. Mr. Balcom, a promising young architect, designs it on the back of his Vitruvius, with hard pencil and ruler, and the job is let out to Dobson & Sons, stonecutters. When the thirty centuries begin to look down on it, mankind begin to look up at it. As for your high towers and monuments, there was a crazy fellow once in this town who undertook to dig through to China, and he got so far that, as he said, he heard the Chinese pots and kettles rattle; but I think that I shall not go out of my way to admire the hole which he made. Many are concerned about the monuments of the West and the East – to know who built them. For my part, I should like to know who in those days did not build them – who were above such trifling. But to proceed with my statistics.

By surveying, carpentry, and day-labor of various other kinds in the village in the meanwhile, for I have as many trades as fingers, I had earned $13.34. The expense of food for eight months, namely, from July 4th to March 1st, the time when these estimates were made, though I lived there more than two years – not counting potatoes, a little green corn, and some peas, which I had raised, nor considering the value of what was on hand at the last date, was:

Rice	$1.74 1/2	
Molasses	$1.73	(Cheapest form of the saccharine)
Rye meal	$1.04 3/4	
Indian meal	$0.99 3/4	(Cheaper than rye)
Pork	$0.22	
Flour	$0.88	(Costs more than Indian meal, both money and trouble.)
Sugar	$0.80	
Lard	$0.65	
Apples	$0.25	
Dried apple	$0.22	
Sweet potatoes	$0.10	
One pumpkin	$0.06	
One watermelon	$0.02	
Salt	$0.03	

Yes, I did eat $8.74, all told; but I should not thus unblushingly publish my guilt, if I did not know that most of my readers were equally guilty with myself, and that their deeds would look no better in print. The next year I sometimes caught a mess of fish for my dinner, and once I went so far as to slaughter a woodchuck which ravaged my bean-field – effect his transmigration, as a Tartar would say – and devour him, partly for experiment's sake; but though it afforded me a momentary enjoyment, notwithstanding a musky flavor, I saw that the longest use would not make that a good practice, however it might seem to have your woodchucks ready dressed by the village butcher.

Clothing and some incidental expenses within the same dates, though little can be inferred from this item, amounted to:

$8.40 3/4
Oil and some household utensils... $2.00

So that all the pecuniary outgoes, excepting for washing and mending, which for the most part were done out of the house, and their bills have not yet been received – and these are all and more than all the ways by which money necessarily goes out in this part of the world – were:

House.. $28.12 1/2
Farm one year.................................. $14.72 1/2
Food eight months.......................... $8.74
Clothing, etc, eight months........... $8.40 3/4
Oil, etc., eight months.................... $2.00

In all.. $61.99 3/4

I address myself now to those of my readers who have a living to get. And to meet this I have for farm produce sold:

For farm produce sold.................... $23.44
Earned by day-labor........................ $13.34

In all.. $36.78

Which subtracted from the sum of the outgoes leaves a balance of $25.21 3/4 on the one side – this being very nearly the means with which I started, and the measure of expenses to be incurred – and on the other, beside the leisure and independence and health thus secured, a comfortable house for me as long as I choose to occupy it.

These statistics, however accidental and therefore uninstructive they may appear, as they have a certain completeness, have a certain value also. Nothing was given me of which I have not rendered some account. It appears from the above estimate, that my food alone cost me in money about twenty-seven cents a week. It was, for nearly two years after this, rye and Indian meal without yeast, potatoes, rice, a very little salt pork, molasses, and salt; and my drink, water. It was fit that I should live on rice, mainly, who love so well the philosophy of India. To meet the objections of some inveterate cavillers, I may as well state, that if I dined out occasionally, as I always had done, and I trust shall have opportunities to do again, it was frequently to the detriment of my domestic arrangements. But the dining out, being, as

I have stated, a constant element, does not in the least affect a comparative statement like this.

I learned from my two years' experience that it would cost incredibly little trouble to obtain one's necessary food, even in this latitude; that a man may use as simple a diet as the animals, and yet retain health and strength. I have made a satisfactory dinner, satisfactory on several accounts, simply off a dish of purslane *(Portulaca oleracea)* which I gathered in my cornfield, boiled and salted. I give the Latin on account of the savoriness of the trivial name. And pray what more can a reasonable man desire, in peaceful times, in ordinary noons, than a sufficient number of ears of green sweet corn boiled, with the addition of salt? Even the little variety which I used was a yielding to the demands of appetite, and not of health. Yet men have come to such a pass that they frequently starve, not for want of necessaries, but for want of luxuries; and I know a good woman who thinks that her son lost his life because he took to drinking water only.

The reader will perceive that I am treating the subject rather from an economic than a dietetic point of view, and he will not venture to put my abstemiousness to the test unless he has a well-stocked larder.

Every New Englander might easily raise all his own breadstuffs in this land of rye and Indian corn, and not depend on distant and fluctuating markets for them. Yet so far are we from simplicity and independence that, in Concord, fresh and sweet meal is rarely sold in the shops, and hominy and corn in a still coarser form are hardly used by any. For the most part the farmer gives to his cattle and hogs the grain of his own producing, and buys flour, which is at least no more wholesome, at a greater cost, at the store. I saw that I could easily raise my bushel or two of rye and Indian corn, for the former will grow on the poorest land, and the latter does not require the best, and grind them in a hand-mill, and so do without rice and pork; and if I must have some concentrated sweet, I found by experiment that I could make a very good molasses either of pumpkins or beets, and I knew that I needed only to set out a few maples to obtain it more easily still, and while these were growing I could use various substitutes beside those which I have named. "For," as the Forefathers sang, "we can make liquor to sweeten our lips, Of pumpkins and parsnips and walnut-tree chips."

Finally, as for salt, that grossest of groceries, to obtain this might be a fit occasion for a visit to the seashore, or, if I did without it altogether, I should probably drink the less water. I do not learn that the Indians ever troubled themselves to go after it.

Thus I could avoid all trade and barter, so far as my food was concerned, and having a shelter already, it would only remain to get clothing and fuel. The pantaloons which I now wear were woven in a farmer's family – thank Heaven there is so much virtue still in man; for I think the fall from the farmer to the operative as great and memorable as that from the man to the farmer; and in a new country, fuel is an encumbrance. As for a habitat, if I were not permitted still to squat, I might purchase one acre at the same price for which the land I cultivated was sold – namely, eight dollars and eight cents. But as it was, I considered that I enhanced the value of the land by squatting on it.

There is a certain class of unbelievers who sometimes ask me such questions as, if I think that I can live on vegetable food alone; and to strike at the root of the matter at once – for the root is faith – I am accustomed to answer such, that I can live on board nails. If they cannot understand that, they cannot understand much that I have to say. For my part, I am glad to bear of experiments of this kind being tried; as that a young man tried for a fortnight to live on hard, raw corn on the ear, using his teeth for all mortar. The squirrel tribe tried the same and succeeded. The human race is interested in these experiments, though a few old women who are incapacitated for them, or who own their thirds in mills, may be alarmed.

My furniture, part of which I made myself – and the rest cost me nothing of which I have not rendered an account – consisted of a bed, a table, a desk, three chairs, a looking-glass three inches in diameter, a pair of tongs and andirons, a kettle, a skillet, and a frying-pan, a dipper, a wash-bowl, two knives and forks, three plates, one cup, one spoon, a jug for oil, a jug for molasses, and a japanned lamp. None is so poor that he need sit on a pumpkin. That is shiftlessness. There is a plenty of such chairs as I like best in the village garrets to be had for taking them away. Furniture! Thank God, I can sit and I can stand without the aid of a furniture warehouse. What man but a philosopher would not be ashamed to see his furniture packed in a cart and going up country exposed to the light of heaven and the eyes of men, a beggarly account of empty boxes? That is Spaulding's furniture. I could never tell from inspecting such a load whether it belonged to a so-called rich man or a poor one; the owner always seemed poverty-stricken. Indeed, the more you have of such things the poorer you are. Each load looks as if it contained the contents of a dozen shanties; and if one shanty is poor, this is a dozen times as poor. Pray, for what do we *move* ever but to get rid of our furniture, our *exuviae*; at last to go from this world to another newly furnished, and leave this to be burned? It is the same as if all these traps were buckled to a man's belt, and he could not move over the rough country where our lines are cast without dragging them – dragging his trap. He was a lucky fox that left his tail in the trap. The muskrat will gnaw his third leg off to be free. No wonder man has lost his elasticity. How often he is at a dead set! "Sir, if I may be so bold, what do you mean by a dead set?" If you are a seer, whenever you meet a man you will see all that he owns, ay, and much that he pretends to disown, behind him, even to his kitchen furniture and all the trumpery which he saves and will not burn, and he will appear to be harnessed to it and making what headway he can. I think that the man is at a dead set who has got through a knot-hole or gateway where his sledge load of furniture cannot follow him. I cannot but feel compassion when I hear some trig, compact-looking man, seemingly free, all girded and ready, speak of his "furniture," as whether it is insured or not. "But what shall I do with my furniture?" – My gay butterfly is entangled in a spider's web then. Even those who seem for a long while not to have any, if you inquire more narrowly you will find have some stored in somebody's barn. I look upon England today as an old gentleman who is travelling with a great deal of baggage, trumpery which has accumulated from long housekeeping, which he has not the courage to burn; great trunk, little trunk, bandbox, and bundle. Throw away the first three at least. It would surpass the powers of a well man nowadays to take up his bed and walk, and I should certainly advise a sick one to lay down his bed and run. When I have met an immigrant tottering under a bundle which contained his all – looking like an enormous well which had grown out of the nape of his neck – I have pitied him, not because that was his all, but because he had all that to carry. If I have got to drag my trap, I will take care that it be a light one and do not nip me in a vital part. But perchance it would be wisest never to put one's paw into it.

I would observe, by the way, that it costs me nothing for curtains, for I have no gazers to shut out but the sun and moon, and I am willing that they should look in. The moon will not sour milk nor taint meat of mine, nor will the sun injure my furniture or fade my carpet; and if he is sometimes too warm a friend, I find it still better economy to retreat behind some curtain which nature has provided, than to add a single item to the details of housekeeping. A lady once offered me a mat, but as I had no room to spare within the house, nor time to spare within or without to shake it, I declined it, preferring to wipe my feet on the sod before my door. It is best to avoid the beginnings of evil.

For more than five years I maintained myself thus solely by the labor of my hands, and I found that, by working about six weeks in a year, I could meet all the expenses of living. The whole of my winters, as well as most of my summers, I had free and clear for study. I have thoroughly tried school-keeping, and found that my expenses were in proportion, or rather out of proportion, to my income, for I was obliged to dress and train, not to say think and believe, accordingly, and I lost my time into the bargain. As I did not teach for the good of my fellow-men, but simply for a livelihood, this was a failure. I have tried trade; but I found that it would take ten years to get under way in that, and that then I should probably be on my way to the devil. I was actually afraid that I might by that time be doing what is called a good business. When formerly I was looking about to see what I could do for a living, some sad experience in conforming to the wishes of friends being fresh in my mind to tax my ingenuity, I thought often and seriously of picking huckleberries; that surely I could do, and its small profits might suffice – for my greatest skill has been to want but little – so little capital it required, so little distraction from my wonted moods, I foolishly thought. While my acquaintances went unhesitatingly into trade or the professions, I contemplated this occupation as most like theirs; ranging the hills all summer to pick the berries which came in my way, and thereafter carelessly dispose of them; so, to keep the flocks of Admetus. I also dreamed that I might gather the wild herbs, or carry evergreens to such villagers as loved to be reminded of the woods, even to the city, by hay-cart loads. But I have since learned that trade curses everything it handles; and though you trade in messages from heaven, the whole curse of trade attaches to the business.

As I preferred some things to others, and especially valued my freedom, as I could fare hard and yet succeed well, I did not wish to spend my time in earning rich carpets or other fine furniture, or delicate cookery, or a house in the Grecian or the Gothic style just yet. If there are any to whom it is no interruption to acquire these things, and who know how to use them when acquired, I relinquish to them the pursuit. Some are "industrious," and appear to love labor for its own sake, or perhaps because it keeps them out of worse mischief; to such I have at present nothing to say. Those who would not know what to do with more leisure than they now enjoy, I might advise to work twice as hard as they do – work till they pay for themselves, and get their free papers. For myself I found that the occupation of a day-laborer was the most independent of any, especially as it required only thirty or forty days in a year to support one. The laborer's day ends with the going down of the sun, and he is then free to devote himself to his chosen pursuit, independent of his labor; but his employer, who speculates from month to month, has no respite from one end of the year to the other.

In short, I am convinced, both by faith and experience, that to maintain one's self on this earth is not a hardship but a pastime, if we will live simply and wisely; as the pursuits of the simpler nations are still the sports of the more artificial. It is not necessary that a man should earn his living by the sweat of his brow, unless he sweats easier than I do.

One young man of my acquaintance, who has inherited some acres, told me that he thought he should live as I did, *if he had the means.* I would not have any one adopt my mode of living on any account; for, beside that before he has fairly learned it I may have found out another for myself, I desire that there may be as many different persons in the world as possible; but I would have each one be very careful to find out and pursue *his own* way, and not his father's or his mother's or his neighbor's instead. The youth may build or plant or sail, only let him not be hindered from doing that which he tells me he would like to do. It is by a mathematical point only that we are wise, as the sailor or the fugitive slave keeps the polestar in his eye; but that is sufficient guidance for all our life. We may not arrive at our port within a calculable period, but we would preserve the true course.

Undoubtedly, in this case, what is true for one is truer still for a thousand, as a large house is not proportionally more expensive than a small one, since one roof may cover, one cellar underlie, and one wall separate several apartments. But for my part, I preferred the solitary dwelling. Moreover, it will commonly be cheaper to build the whole yourself than to convince another of the advantage of the common wall; and when you have done this, the common partition, to be much cheaper, must be a thin one, and that other may prove a bad neighbor, and also not keep his side in repair. The only cooperation which is commonly possible is exceedingly partial and superficial; and what little true cooperation there is, is as if it were not, being a harmony inaudible to men. If a man has faith, he will cooperate with equal faith everywhere; if he has not faith, he will continue to live like the rest of the world, whatever company he is joined to. To cooperate in the highest as well as the lowest sense, means *to get our living together.* I heard it proposed lately that two young men should travel together over the world, the one without money, earning his means as he went, before the mast and behind the plow, the other carrying a bill of exchange in his pocket. It was easy to see that they could not long be companions or cooperate, since one would not *operate* at all. They would part at the first interesting crisis in their adventures. Above all, as I have implied, the man who goes alone can start today; but he who travels with another must wait till that other is ready, and it may be a long time before they get off.

One and the same subject who wants a new state of affairs,
a better reality… also brings it forth.

– Max Horkheimer

Hope is the difference between *probability* and *possibility.*

– Isabelle Stengers

Conclusion

MEDITATIONS ON SIMPLICITY

Samuel Alexander

> All truly wise thoughts have been thought already thousands of times; but to make them truly ours, we must think them over again honestly, till they take root in our personal experience. – Goethe

This conclusion was written primarily for those readers who find themselves in a Goethean mood – that is to say, for those readers who, with a mixture of curiosity, hope, and perhaps a degree of apprehension, are now prepared to think over the preceding chapters slowly and honestly, and who are at least open to the possibility that the insights those chapters contain could take root in personal experience. Comprising of thought experiments and discussion questions, this conclusion aims to facilitate further introspection and provoke conversation about the central themes of this anthology, in the hope that this leads to a more direct and practical understanding of voluntary simplicity *in relation to one's own life*. It follows that this may be the most challenging chapter, since it leaves you, the thinker, doing all the hard work and taking all the risks. But however unsettling it can at times be to examine our own lives, we should remember that confronting ourselves honestly can also be profoundly liberating in the most unexpected ways. And so with honesty as our driving force and liberation as our goal, let us dare continue the exploration our subject.

What follows is divided into ten 'meditations' – a term only meant to imply a certain seriousness of thought – each of which is intended to provide enough material for an evening's alternative entertainment. While there may be distinct advantages to considering this material in quiet solitude, there may also be benefits to discussing it with friends or in a small group of interested individuals. To do both would be ideal. If the material is to be considered in solitude, have a pen and paper at hand, for there is no better way to clarify thought when contemplating an issue than to write down ideas and feelings as they arise. Follow your thoughts and feelings wherever they may take you and try not to stop writing until you run out of words or ink. If the following material is to be considered with others, put some time into thinking about who is going to organize the occasions, where and when they could be held, and how the discussions will be conducted. Needless to say, it is important that participants in any such discussion express themselves respectfully and that everyone is given the opportunity to contribute. The aim should be to establish a conversational forum that is friendly, informal, and open.

Enjoying yourself is permitted. Trusting yourself is imperative.

First Meditation – Defining the Subject

Overview: If we are to engage ourselves in a discussion of a subject, or enquire into the merit or justification of an idea, it is important to have a clear understanding of what it is we are considering. Accordingly, it makes sense to begin with a close analysis of what voluntary simplicity might mean.

1. How would you define voluntary simplicity? What do you think it involves? (As an exercise in self-restraint – almost like resisting a consumer good – try answering these questions without being prompted by the definitions given immediately below.)

2. Here are six short definitions of voluntary simplicity given by contributors to this anthology. Spend some time going over them slowly:

   ★ *Voluntary simplicity is a manner of living that is outwardly simple and inwardly rich, a deliberate choice to live with less in the belief that more of life will be returned to us in the process. (Elgin)*

   ★ *Voluntary simplicity refers to the decision to limit expenditures on consumer goods and services and to cultivate non-materialistic sources of satisfaction and meaning. (Etzioni)*

   ★ *Voluntary simplicity involves directing progressively more time and energy toward pursuing non-material aspirations while providing for material needs as simply, directly, and efficiently as possible. It measures personal and social progress by increases in the qualitative richness of daily living, the cultivation of relationships, and the development of personal and spiritual potentials. Simple living does not denigrate the material aspects of life but rather, by attending to quality, it values material things more highly than a society that merely consumes them. ... Simplicity is about knowing how much consumption is enough. (Burch)*

- ★ *Voluntary simplicity involves the quest for calm, balanced, integrated lives; less clutter, less artificiality, and lessened impact on nature; and the elevation of quality over quantity, time over money, and community over competition. (Freyfogle)*

- ★ *Voluntary simplicity involves both inner and outer condition. It means singleness of purpose, sincerity and honesty within, as well as avoidance of exterior clutter, of many possessions irrelevant to the chief purpose of life. It means an ordering and guiding of our energy and our desires, a partial restraint in some directions in order to secure greater abundance of life in other directions. It involves a deliberate organization of life for a purpose. (Gregg)*

- ★ *Voluntary simplicity often involves making a conscious decision to accept a lower income and a lower level of consumption to pursue other life goals. (Hamilton and Denniss)*

3. Read or re-read chapter one ('Voluntary Simplicity: The "Middle Way" to Sustainability') and chapter nine ('Voluntary Simplicity') of this anthology, both of which are extended definitional statements of voluntary simplicity. Are there any aspects of those statements which you disagree with or are uncomfortable with? Which aspects speak loudest to you? Can you refine or add to them in any way?

4. How is voluntary simplicity different from poverty or deprivation?

5. Is voluntary simplicity just about consuming less?

6. Does voluntary simplicity involve renouncing all the advantages of science and technology?

7. A wide variety of people and communities practice voluntary simplicity, in some form or another, but who do not necessarily call it by that name. Can you think of some examples?

8. At the close of chapter nine, Elgin and Mitchell claim that through voluntary simplicity, 'the need of the individual uniquely matches the need of the society.' Do you agree? Are there any other emergent life patterns that could be described in this way?

9. Craft a short personalized statement of what voluntary simplicity means.

10. Make a list of ways your life may already be consistent with voluntary simplicity.

11. Read or re-read the two appendixes to this anthology. (The first appendix, 'The Manifesto,' is a collection of quotations expressing, in various ways, the philosophy of voluntary simplicity. The second appendix, 'Peaceful Acts of Opposition,' is an attempt to reduce the philosophy of voluntary simplicity to a list of broad proposals for personal action.)

12. Theory of practice: Creatively interpret clauses 48–52 of 'The Manifesto.'

13. Practice of theory: Creatively interpret the first ten 'Peaceful Acts of Opposition.'

14. Closing thought: *Those who know they have enough are rich.*
    – Lao Tzu

Second Meditation – Consumer Culture

Overview: Voluntary simplicity has been presented in this anthology as an 'alternative' to the materialistic form of life widely celebrated within consumer culture. Let us try to sharpen our understanding of voluntary simplicity by taking a closer look at the form of life it is reacting against.

1. What is meant by 'consumer culture'? (The fact that we are deeply embedded in consumer culture – whether we like it or not – can make this an extremely challenging question. Try to dig beneath the surface of what is 'obviously' consumer culture, and see if you cannot uncover certain features of it that might be easily taken for granted, features that we might ordinarily assume are 'facts of life' or 'just the way the world is,' but which on closer analysis turn out to be contingent upon *choices* we have made – choices we could perhaps remake?)

2. Read or re-read chapter four ('What is Affluenza?') and chapter five ('The Conundrum of Consumption') of this anthology. What are the characteristics of consumer culture presented in those chapters?

3. Do you agree with Hamilton and Denniss that western society is in the grip of a collective psychological disorder ('affluenza')?

4. Interpret the following proverb: *Do not be like the fish that doesn't know it's in water.*

5. If it is true, as some existentialists have argued, that we can always make something new out of what we have been made into, then it might be interesting to inquire: Did you choose your mode of living because you preferred it to any other? Or did you honestly think that it was the only way?

6. Compare life within consumer culture to the life of a self-sufficient peasant farmer in Brazil or a Buddhist monk in the Himalayas. Imagine you (along with some friends and family) exchanged roles with either for five years: How would your life be different? What would you miss the most? How might you benefit from the change? Could there be a 'middle way' that secures the advantages of both without the disadvantages of either?

7. Below are four ways of thinking about the difficult term 'ideology.' Consider them with reference to the meanings of 'wealth,' 'progress,' 'enough' and 'the good life' in consumer culture.

   ★ *To study ideology is to study the ways in which meaning serves to establish and sustain relations of domination, including self-domination. (John Thompson)*

   ★ *To study ideology is to study the ways in which people may come to invest in their own unhappiness. (Terry Eagleton)*

   ★ *To study ideology is study the ways people fail to see some instance of oppression at all, or fail to see it as improper or unjust because they believe it has been consented to or legitimated in some way. (Michael Robertson)*

   ★ *To study ideology is to study the ways we might need to free ourselves from ourselves. (Terry Eagleton)*

8. Consider the meaning of 'status.' (a) What is it to have status in consumer culture? (b) What do you think should confer status in a society? (c) How important is status in your life, and, if you value/seek status, of what sort do you value/seek? (d) What could meant by the phrase 'status anxiety'? (e) What is it to be free from status anxiety?

9. Learn Diderot's lesson! In the 18th century, the French philosopher Denis Diderot wrote an essay entitled *Regrets on Parting with My Old Dress*

ing Gown. Juliet Schor (a contributor in this anthology) has summarized the point and relevance of that essay as follows:

> Diderot's regrets were prompted by a gift of a beautiful scarlet dressing gown. Delighted with his new acquisition, Diderot quickly discarded his old gown. But in a short time, his pleasure turned sour as he began to sense that the surroundings within which the gown was worn did not properly reflect the garment's elegance. He grew dissatisfied with his study, with its threadbare tapestry, the desk, his chairs and even room's bookshelves. One by one, the familiar but well-worn furnishings of the study were replaced. In the end, Diderot found himself seated uncomfortably in the stylish formality of his new surroundings, regretting the work of this 'impervious scarlet robe [that] forced everything else to conform with its own elegant tone.'
>
> Today consumer researchers call such striving for conformity the 'Diderot effect.' And, while Diderot effects can be constraining (some people foresee the problem and refuse the initial upgrading), in a world of growing income the pressure to enter and follow the cycle are overwhelming. The purchase of a new home is the impetus for replacing old furniture; a new jacket makes little sense without the right skirt to match; an upgrade in china can't really be enjoyed without a corresponding upgrade in glassware. This need for unity and conformity in our lifestyle choices is part of what keeps the consumer escalator moving ever upward. And 'escalator' is the operative metaphor: when the acquisition of each item on a wish list adds another item, and more, to our 'must-have' list, the pressure to upgrade our stock of stuff is relentlessly unidirectional, always ascending.[1]

10. Many of the world's most sophisticated psychologists are today hired as 'marketers.' They spend all day thinking up ways to make us feel dissatisfied with what we have, despite our plenty, in order to get us buy things we didn't even know we wanted. In relation to the idea of voluntary simplicity, think critically about the function of advertising / television / mass media in modern life.

11. The process of getting richer is now causing the very problems that we seem to think getting richer will solve. Discuss.

12. Theory of practice: Creatively interpret clauses 53–57 of 'The Manifesto.'

13. Practice of theory: Creatively interpret 'Peaceful Acts of Opposition,' numbers 11–20.

14. Closing thought: *How we spend our money is how we vote on what exists in the world.* – Vicki Robin.

Third Meditation – Henry David Thoreau

Overview: At age 28, Henry David Thoreau left his town of Concord and went to live alone in the woods, on the shores of Walden Pond, a mile from any neighbor. He there built himself a modest cabin, and for two years and two months earned a simple living by the labor of his own hands. 'I went to the woods because I wished to live deliberately,' wrote Thoreau, 'to front only the essential facts of life, and see if I could not learn what they had to teach, and not, when I came to die, discover that I had not lived.' While at the pond he wrote *Walden*, perhaps the greatest statement ever made on the subject of voluntary simplicity – one more relevant today than ever before and deserving of our closest attention.

1. Read or re-read chapter ten ('Thoreau's Alternative Economics'), chapter nineteen ('Transcendental Simplicity'), and chapter twenty ('Economy'). Reduce each chapter to ten central insights. Also, try to get your hands on a complete copy of *Walden* and set out to read it as deliberately as it was written. (As a last resort, *Walden* can be read online for free at www.gutenberg.org/catelog/. Another relevant essay of Thoreau's, also available online, is 'Life Without Principle.')

2. 'The necessaries of life of life,' wrote Thoreau in *Walden*, 'may, accurately enough, be distributed under the several heads of Food, Shelter, Clothing, and Fuel; for not till we have secured these are we prepared to entertain the true problems of life with freedom and a prospect of success.' In all seriousness, what do you consider to be the necessaries of life? (Try to be as detailed as you can.)

3. Housing is typically life's greatest expense, so we should think especially carefully about where we live and why. 'Consider how slight a shelter is absolutely necessary,' asks Thoreau. 'Most people appear never to have considered what a house is, and are actually though needlessly poor all their lives because they think that they must have such a one as their neighbors have.' Carefully reconsider your housing from this perspective and, then, in exactly the same vein, reconsider your consumption habits relating to food, clothing, and fuel.

4. Imagine you won a prize that provided you with the necessaries of life for the rest of your life, plus $5,000 to buy a few extra things. The only

condition to accepting the prize was that you were prohibited from ever earning more money. Would you accept it? Could you live a happy and fulfilling life? How would you spend the $5,000 dollars? And, of particular interest, what would you do with a life of 'free time'?

5. Can you think of examples where some of your material *wants* have come to feel like *needs*? If so, what is the significance this transformation? What might cause it?

6. By consciously reducing his material wants and choosing to live simply, Thoreau was able to live a healthy and fulfilling life on six weeks work per year. Perhaps he was exceptional? Perhaps he had it easy? Whatever the case, six weeks gives us at least a rough guide as to how much time is required for human beings to provide for their most basic material needs. In your social circumstances today, how much time would you need to secure the necessaries of life (and perhaps a few simple comforts)? In what ways might reducing your material wants / working hours enhance your freedom and/or contentment?

7. Mull over what is perhaps the central passage in *Walden*: 'When we have obtained those things necessary to life, there is another alternative than to obtain superfluities; and that is to adventure on life now, our vacation from humbler toil having commenced.' How does this 'alternative' living strategy of Thoreau's sit in relation to the living strategy normally employed within advanced capitalist society today?

8. Thoreau does not think that we should only ever obtain the mere necessaries of life and no more. Rather, he is trying to get us to think about the *true cost* of 'superfluities.' According to Thoreau, 'The cost of a thing is the amount of what I will call life which is required to be exchanged for it.' What do you think he meant by this? Try to apply this type of economic analysis to purchases you have made (or might make) in your life.

9. In the passage below, Thoreau offers some justification for his approach to life. Consider its merits:

> Those slight labors which afford me a livelihood, and by which it is allowed that I am to some extent serviceable to my contemporaries, are as yet commonly a pleasure to me, and I am not often reminded that they are a necessity. So far I am successful. But I foresee that if my wants should be much increased, the labor required to supply them would become a drudgery. If I should sell both my forenoons and afternoons to society, as most appear to do, I am sure that for

me there would be nothing left worth living for. I trust that I shall never thus sell my birthright for a mess of pottage. *I wish to suggest that a man may be very industrious, and yet not spend his time well. There is no more fatal blunderer than he who consumes the greater part of his life getting a living.*[2]

10. Thoreau believed that the high-consumption life which is praised and regarded as successful is but one kind. Why, then, he asks of us, should we exaggerate any one kind at the expense of others? Put otherwise, Thoreau is asking us to consider, 'What kinds of "success" can be achieved outside of or beyond the consuming middle-class?'

11. Consider 'declaring independence' by isolating yourself from consumer culture for long enough to gain a new perspective on it – for long enough to unlearn it, so that it may be relearned. Retreating to a quiet, natural setting for an extended period of time is a self-conscious attempt to rouse oneself from the daze of unexamined habit, which, if successful, might bring about a surprisingly fresh interpretation of the form of life left behind, as well as provoke a new appreciation of the possibilities of an alternative existence. One need not go to the extremes of Thoreau, but his justification for temporarily escaping society might provide an incentive for us all: 'My purpose in going to Walden Pond was not to live cheaply nor to live dearly there, but to transact some private business with the fewest obstacles.'[3] Think of places that could be your own 'Walden Pond.' Plan an excursion there. Stay until your 'private business' is complete.

12. Theory of practice: Creatively interpret clauses 58–62 of 'The Manifesto.'

13. Practice of theory: Creatively interpret 'Peaceful Acts of Opposition,' numbers 21–30.

14. Closing thought: *The individual who goes it alone can start today.*
    – Henry David Thoreau

Fourth Meditation – How Much Consumption is 'Enough'?

Overview: The idea of voluntary simplicity urges us to ask ourselves: 'How much consumption is "enough."'? But when we ask ourselves this question we discover that there is a prior and even more important question to consider first: 'Enough for *what?*' Let us consider both of these difficult questions in some detail, for if we do not know where we are going, or why we are heading in one direction rather than another, we will not be able to tell if we are lost.

1. What is your chief purpose in life?

    ★ *Terrifying though it can be to admit, no one, no thing, no book, no logic, no universe, can answer this question for us. Consequently, we should trust ourselves, live in good faith, and make no excuses.*

    ★ *Make a list of 4–5 of your most important life aspirations. ('It is better to travel than to arrive.' – Aristotle)*

    ★ *Hypothetically reflect on your life from the vantage point of a very old age: What kind of life would you like to remember? What attitudes would you hope defined it?*

2. We all want the material resources needed to pursue our chief purpose in life – whatever that purpose might be – but might there be times when our pursuit of material resources does not support but actually interferes with our chief purpose? (Again, if we do not know what our chief purpose *is*, we will not be able to tell if it is getting interfered with.)

3. Can you specify how much consumption is 'enough' for you? How much would be 'too much'?

4. Read or re-read chapter three ('Two Ways of Thinking About Money') and chapter six ('The Value of Voluntary Simplicity') of this anthology.

5. Consider the following thought experiment: Imagine that you are climbing a huge mountain and your chief purpose in life awaits you at the top. You have concentrated all your thoughts and energies on the planning of this expedition for several years, acquiring all the equipment you thought you might need, but in the actual attempt you find that some of the equipment is just hindering your ascent. Do you discard the equipment which is not needed to attain your chief purpose in life? Or will your possessive tendencies put the entire exhibition in jeopardy? (Apply to life.)

6. The great difficulty with the above thought experiment (when applied to life) lies in knowing which possessions are indeed 'irrelevant' to our

chief purpose in life, since thousands of cultural messages bombard us daily insisting that we need *more* than we have, not less – and we are easily persuaded. So not only are we at risk of spending too much of our precious time thoughtlessly acquiring more and 'better' possessions – nicer cars, bigger houses, finer clothes, etc. – but, through mere ignorance and mistake, we are forever unwilling to let those possessions go. Thoreau, however, was not to be fooled: 'I had three pieces of limestone on my desk, but was terrified to find that they required to be dusted daily, when the furniture of my mind was all undusted still, and I threw them out the window in disgust.' Dig beneath the surface of this obscure insight, dwell on its subtleties, and, with respect to your own life, reflect upon the insidious nature of 'stuff.'

7. Important: What is the difference between 'standard of living' and 'quality of life'?

8. Does an increased 'standard of living' necessarily mean a better 'quality of life'? Could increasing your 'standard of living' ever impact *negatively* on your 'quality of life'? Could decreasing your 'standard of living' ever impact *positively* on your 'quality of life'?

9. Clive Hamilton and Richard Denniss have conducted extensive research into Australian attitudes to consumption. Consider the significance of their following conclusion (from chapter four of this volume):

   When asked whether they can afford to buy everything they really need, nearly two-thirds of Australians say 'no'. If we remember that Australia is one of the world's richest countries and that Australians today have real incomes three times higher than in 1950, it is remarkable that such a high proportion feel so deprived. Average earnings exceed $50,000 a year, yet a substantial majority of Australians who experience no real hardship – and indeed live lives of abundance – believe that they have difficulty making ends meet and that they qualify as 'battlers.'

10. Imagine that the economy of your society doubled over night. Do you think people would have 'enough' then? What if it tripled? Or even quadrupled? Can you imagine a time when a society might collectively say, 'Surely we have acquired enough stuff! Let's do something else, for we've begun laying waste our powers.' Or is human nature such that too much consumption is never enough?

11. Marcus Aurelius, the great stoic philosopher, once said: 'Always bear in mind that very little indeed is necessary for living a happy life.' What is the *minimum* you would need to be happy?

12. Theory of Practice: Creatively interpret clauses 63–67 of 'The Manifesto.'

13. Practice of Theory: Creatively interpret 'Peaceful Acts of Opposition,' numbers 31–40.

14. Closing thought: *Lately in the wreck of a California ship, one of the passengers fastened a belt about him with two hundred pounds of gold in it, with which he was afterward found at the bottom. Now, as he was sinking – had he the gold? Or had the gold him?* – John Ruskin

Fifth Meditation – To Have or To Be?

Overview: The social psychologist / political theorist, Erich Fromm, has drawn an important distinction between two 'modes of existence'– namely, *having* and *being*. In the *having* mode, the meaning of one's identity is defined by and dependent upon material factors external to oneself. In the *being* mode, the meaning of one's identity is defined by and dependent upon existential factors internal to oneself. These modes are not 'either/or' alternatives, but rather they sit upon a spectrum, with pure *having* at one extreme (insanity), pure *being* at the other (saintliness), and with shades of degree in between. Fromm argues that advanced capitalist society is heavily characterized by the *having* mode. The question he provokes, and which we will now consider, is what individual and/or collective life would be like if the *being* mode was privileged over the *having* mode.

1. On the spectrum between *pure being* (1) and *pure having* (10), where would you place our society? Where would you place your life? Give reasons.

2. What types of actions or attitudes in your life could bring about an 'immaterial shift' toward the *being* mode? List twenty 'simple luxuries.'

3. Imagine that tomorrow your employer advises you that due to [insert reason] your position must be reduced to part-time (one day less per week) and your total wages reduced by twenty percent. How would you cope? Could there be benefits to such a change?

4. Now imagine, instead, that tomorrow your employer offered you *either* a twenty percent pay rise *or* an extra day off per week at the same income *or* two extra days off per week with a twenty percent reduction in pay. Which would you prefer and why? Compare options.

5. Read or re-read chapter two ('A New Social Movement?') and chapter thirteen ('The Downshifters) of this anthology. In what ways do those chapters support (explicitly or implicitly) the privileging of *being* over *having*?

6. How does Amatai Etzioni think that the 'cyber age' might help advance the Voluntary Simplicity Movement?

7. Over the last half a century, most westerners have been offered a remarkable choice, as John de Graaf explains in the following passage. Consider what the world would be like if we had made a different choice:

   ★ *As our productivity has more than doubled [since World War II], we could have chosen to work half as much – or even less – and still produce the same material lifestyle we found 'affluent' in the 1950s. We could have split the difference, letting our material aspirations rise somewhat but also taking an important portion our productivity gains in the form of more free time. Instead, we put all our apples into making and consuming more.*[4]

8. With reference to the above quotation, consider the following statement by the French philosopher, Michel Foucault: 'We are freer than we think we are.'

9. In terms of acquiring material things, how far are you influenced by what your neighbors have or think? To what extent do you define 'success' by what lies outside of yourself, outside of your control?

10. In the following passage, Duane Elgin speculates insightfully about what a society that privileges *being* over *having* might be like. Consider his ideas and then develop them further:

A conscious simplicity, then, is not self-denying but life affirming. Voluntary simplicity is not an 'ascetic simplicity' (of strict austerity); rather it is an 'aesthetic simplicity' where each person considers whether his or her level and pattern of consumption fits with grace and integrity into the practical art of daily living on this planet. The possessions that seemed so important and appealing during the industrial era would gradually lose much of their allure. The individual or family who, in the past, was admired for a large and luxurious home would find that the mainstream culture increasingly admired those who had learned how to combine functional simplicity and beauty in a smaller house. The person who was previously envied for his or her expensive car would find that a growing number of people were uninterested in displays of conspicuous consumption. The person who was previously recognized for always wearing the latest in clothing styles would find that more and more people viewed high fashion as tasteless ostentation that was no longer fitting in a world of great human need. This does not mean that people would turn away from the material side of life; rather, they would place a premium on living ever more lightly and aesthetically.[5]

11. Voluntary simplicity is misunderstood if it is thought to be about just consuming less *and no more*. Consider what might be called the 'immaterial dimension' or 'spiritual dimension' of voluntary simplicity.

12. What do you love doing but don't do enough of? Could voluntary simplicity help free up some more time and energy?

13. When we come to draw our last breath, what attitude might we have towards our possessions? Would we ever wish that we had spent more time in the office?

14. Theory of practice: Creatively interpret clauses 68–72 of 'The Manifesto.'

15. Practice of theory: Creatively interpret 'Peaceful Acts of Opposition,' numbers 41–50.

16. Closing thought: *Most people, even in this comparatively free country, through mere ignorance and mistake, are so occupied with the factitious cares and superfluously coarse labors of life that its finer fruits cannot be plucked by them.* – Henry David Thoreau

Sixth Meditation – Poverty and Distributive Justice

Overview: What follows is not about guilt or blame. Rather, it is about our shared hope for a world in which everybody has 'enough' to live a simple, dignified life of material sufficiency. On that basis, let us begin by stating the facts bluntly: (1) More than three billion of our fellow human beings live lives of material destitution;[6] (2) More than 10,000 people die everyday for want of life's most basic necessities, such as access to clean drinking water.[7]

There is a sense in which these grim figures are utterly incomprehensible to our intellectual and emotional faculties – we could not possibly grasp their true significance, and perhaps we would not want to. But the fact we cannot fully understand them doesn't lessen the objective tragedy of this very real human situation, this very real human challenge. What is to be done?

1. Consider Jim Merkel's thought experiment about distributive justice and try to specify an answer to his difficult questions:

   > Imagine you are at a potluck buffet and see that you are the first in line. How do you know how much to take? Imagine that this potluck spread includes not just food and water, but also the materials needed for shelter, clothing, health care and education. It all looks and smells so good and you are hungry. What will you heap on your plate? How much is enough to leave for your neighbors behind you in the line? Now extend this cornucopia to today's global economy, where the necessities for life come from around the world. Six billion people, shoulder to shoulder, form a line that circles around the globe to Cairo, onto Hawaii over ocean bridges, then back, and around the globe again, 180 times more. With plates in hand, they too wait in line, hearty appetites in place. And along with them are giraffes and klipspringers, manatees and spiders, untold millions of species, millions of billions of unique beings, all with the same lusty appetites. And behind them, the soon-to-be-born children, cubs, and larvae.
   >
   > A harmonious feast just might be possible. But it requires a bit of restraint, or shall we say, a tamed appetite, as our plate becomes a shopping cart, becomes a pickup truck – filling our home, attic, basement, garage, and maybe even a rented storage unit with nature transformed into things. As we sit down for a good hearty meal with new friends and creatures from around the world, what is the level of equity that we would feel great about? *At what level of inequity would we say, 'Wait a minute, that's not fair?'*

2. Do you believe that moral obligations stop at the border? Discuss.

3. John Rawls, in his *Theory of Justice* (1972), has argued that our starting position in life is 'arbitrary from a moral perspective.' He means by this that nobody *deserves* to be born into a position of relative advantage any more than someone *deserves* to be born into a position of relative disadvantage. Our starting point in life is the result of what Rawls calls 'the natural lottery.' The outcome of the 'natural lottery' is neither just nor unjust, according to Rawls. That is just a fact of life. What is just or unjust is how we *deal* with this fact. How do you think we should deal with the fact that billions of people, through no fault of their own, are born into positions of poverty? If you were born into the Third World,

for example, what assistance would you reasonably expect from the First World?

4. Read or re-read chapter eight ('Building the Case for Global Living') and chapter eleven ('Why Simplify?') of this anthology. How do those chapters seek to justify voluntary simplicity?

5. A large and growing body of social science supports the thesis that, not far beyond the poverty line, there is only a very weak correlation between having more money and increased wellbeing.[8] In other words, it seems that once human beings have their basic needs securely met, and have acquired a modicum of comforts appropriate for a dignified life, somehow defined, further increases in wealth have a fast diminishing and at times even negative marginal utility. In the United States, for example, where consistent surveys have been conducted since 1946, real incomes have increased by 400 percent, yet, remarkably, even disconcertingly, there has been no increase in reported levels of 'wellbeing' (meaning levels of happiness, fulfillment, and satisfaction with 'life as a whole.')[9] Moreover, there is virtually no reported difference in wellbeing between Americans with incomes of $20,000 and $80,000.[10] And similar conclusions are reflected throughout a substantial and expanding body of social research into many of the developed nations,[11] including Australia,[12] suggesting strongly that above a certain level of individual and national income, more wealth does not tend to increase wellbeing. One expansive study even indicates that there is a threshold level around US$10–15,000 above which a higher average income makes almost no difference to a population's life satisfaction.[13] What do these findings suggest about the distribution of wealth in our world? What do they suggest about the pursuit of ever-more wealth?

6. In chapter four of this anthology, 'What is Affluenza?', Hamilton and Denniss argue that we will not be able to solve the problem of poverty until we solve the problem of affluence. What do you think those authors meant by this?

7. Recall Vicki Robin's insight that, 'How we spend our money is how we vote on what exists in the world.' From that perspective, consider the following:

   ★ *In 2007, the United States alone spent about $700 billion on its military. Imagine what the world would be like if the United States, and other wealthy industrialized countries, redirected half of the resources spent on military to the alleviation of poverty? Or* *imagine if half the global expenditure on advertising and fashion was redirected similarly? Does poverty exist because we don't have enough money?*

8. What is the difference between an act and an omission?

9. Money is power, and with power comes responsibility. On that basis, to what extent is poverty a middle-class responsibility?

10. Could the middle-class become a non-violent revolutionary class simply by using its wealth differently?

11. Earlier you were asked to imagine winning a prize that provided you with the necessaries of life for the rest of your life, plus $5,000 to buy a few extra things. Now imagine that the whole world won this prize? What would the world be like?

12. What link is there between voluntary simplicity and the possibility of distributive justice?

13. Theory of practice: Creatively interpret clauses 78–82 of 'The Manifesto.'

14. Practice of theory: Creatively interpret 'Peaceful Acts of Opposition,' numbers 61–70.

15. Closing thought: *Live simply so that others may simply live.*
    – Mahatma Gandhi

Seventh Meditation – Environmental Sustainability

Overview: Environmental sustainability can be broadly defined as follows: *each generation should meet its needs without jeopardizing the prospects of future generations to meet their own needs.* There is now an overwhelming consensus among scientists that 'ordinary' western consumption habits are *not* sustainable, and certainly not universalizable. On that basis, it is time to reconsider the 'ethics of consumption' and reevaluate cultural understandings of 'the good life.'

1. Reports by the United Nations have predicted that the world's population will be peak in about 100 years somewhere around 9 or 10 billion

people.[14] What do you think the world will be like then? Does everyone have the right to live in the consuming middle–class?

2. If there is an infinite variety of meaningful and satisfying ways of life compatible with living on an equitable share of nature, then it could be argued that consuming an inequitable share is evidence of (among other things) a lack of imagination. Discuss.

3. The Climate Change Program of the New Economics Foundation has published a technical note entitled '100 Months,' which concludes that '100 months from August 2008 atmospheric concentrations of greenhouse gases will begin to exceed a point whereby it is no longer *likely* that we will be able to avert potentially irreversible climate change....' Let us suppose for a moment that the almost unanimous scientific community is more or less correct about its gloomy prospects for the future of our natural environment. What precisely is at stake here?

4. The Union of Concerned Scientists, in their publication, *The Consumer's Guide to Effective Environmental Choices*, recommend that consumers start by reforming the features of their lifestyles that have the *largest* negative impacts on the environment, rather than fretting the small stuff. Some of the largest problems are listed below for consideration:

   ★ *Since automobiles have arguably more impact on the environment than anything else, there is no better place to start than by seriously doubting the need to own your own car. Why not walk, ride a bike, or use public transport? Perhaps you could hire or borrow a car when traveling longer distances? If you seriously think that your own car is a necessity, could you make driving the exception rather than the norm?*

   ★ *Second on the list, in terms of negative environmental impact, might be the consumption of meat and not eating locally. Have you ever considered becoming a vegetarian or reducing meat consumption? Could you eat food that doesn't travel long distances to arrive on your plate? Are you able to cultivate a vegetable garden / grow fruit trees?*

   ★ *Third on the list might be excessive energy use. Could you be more energy efficient? Could you progress towards 'green' / 'renewable' energy?*

- ★ *Fourth may be air travel. Air travel is the world's fastest growing source of carbon-dioxide emissions.*[15] *Why not travel closer to home and avoid air travel? Take the train, perhaps, or consider 'video conferencing' for business, etc.? Or travel inward?*

- ★ *Fifth may be general consumption habits/spending habits. Could you find ways to reform your consumption habits to consume less? Could you find ways to spend more wisely? Use your imagination. (N.B. Beware of times when 'green' marketing might be a sham, for calling something 'green' doesn't necessarily make it so).*

5. Do some research on five other significant causes of environmental damage. How could decisions at the personal level help reduce such damage?

6. Read or re-read chapter seven ('Less is More') and chapter twelve ('Sharing the Earth') of this anthology. What environmental issues are discussed in those chapters?

7. Let us return again to the idea that, 'How we spend our money is how we vote on what exists in the world.' From that perspective, consider the following:

   - ★ *How much renewable energy could be bought for the 700 billion (plus) dollars that has recently been spent bailing out banks? Martin Lloyd has offered a quick calculation: 'Global wind market in 2007 – 37 billion dollars – 19,865 MV added. 700 billion is about 19 times 37 billion, giving us 377 GW of new electricity. So that's 5–6% of global electricity demand switched to clean renewable fuel.'*

8. Consider the difficult phrase 'crimes against our grandchildren' in the context of overconsumption and the prospect of environmental collapse. Should we today be haunted by the gaze of future generations? Could we say we didn't know?

9. Increased consumption is often presumed to be a *good* thing, without question. Political parties, for example, spend most of their time claiming that they would run the economy 'best,' meaning that under their leadership ordinary people would be richer and therefore able to consume more goods and services. On the face of it, this sounds like a reasonable goal – but is it? Might we need to fundamentally reassess

what we mean by 'economic progress'? How much economic growth is 'enough'? Or, again, is too much never enough?

10. Consider the problem of overpopulation: How could it be addressed? How is overpopulation and overconsumption connected?

11. Arnold Toynbee, in his *Study of History* (1972), summarized a lifetime of research into the evolution of civilizations with his 'Law of Progressive Simplification,' which can be expressed as follows: 'This law asserts that as evolution proceeds, a civilization will transfer increasing increments of energy and attention from the material to the nonmaterial side of life and that this will be expressed through developing culture (music, art, drama, literature) and a growing capacity for compassion, caring community, and self-governance.'[16] According to Toynbee, the globalization of consumer culture would obviously reflect a regression, not a progression, of civilization. How do you think we should use the word 'progress'? We are certainly getting richer, but is our society progressing?

12. Theory of practice: Creatively interpret clauses 73–77 of 'The Manifesto.'

13. Practice of theory: Creatively interpret 'Peaceful Acts of Opposition,' numbers 51–60.

14. Closing thought: *If not us, then who? If not now, then when?*

Eighth Meditation – Extending the Movement

Overview: Whether voluntary simplicity is considered from the perspective of personal happiness, the environment, distributive justice, spiritual awakening, opposing global capitalism, fostering human solidarity, etc., the Voluntary Simplicity Movement, though still in its infancy, is arguably the most promising social movement on the planet today. Many of the problems facing humankind seem *connected*, and voluntary simplicity offers a compelling and graceful solution to many of them. The movement is sometimes described as 'the quiet revolution,' and this may indeed indicate its potential. But the problem is that currently, with the environmental clock ticking and the third world expanding, it may be *too* quiet. In other words, if the Voluntary Simplicity Movement remains a small, unorganized, 'subculture,' it will probably fail to have enough impact on the course of history to do much good. If, however, voluntary simplicity one day came to more widely inform 'common sense,' in the same way that the anti-slavery and women's rights movements have come to do so, the Voluntary Simplicity Movement could change the course of history as profoundly as those movements have. An important question, then, is whether or in what ways the Voluntary Simplicity Movement could extend into the mainstream and become a more significant oppositional force.

1. Consider the meaning of voluntary simplicity, not as a personal living strategy, but as a *social movement*? What might it promise?

2. Think about some of the great social movements which have changed / are still changing the world (e.g. anti-slavery, women's rights, environmentalism, etc.). How have they expanded our awareness? Why were they so effective? Could the Voluntary Simplicity Movement learn anything from them?

3. To what extent are children in consumer culture educated about voluntary simplicity? What benefits might there be to giving voluntary simplicity more emphasis? (Were you ever informed about the idea of voluntary simplicity at school? Or by your parents or peers?)

4. How often have you seen or heard voluntary simplicity promoted in the mass media of corporate capitalism? Might there be a conflict of interest at work here?

5. How or in what ways do you think the Voluntary Simplicity Movement could be extended?

6. In what ways could *you* help extend it?

7. Read or re-read chapter fifteen ('Simplicity, Community, and Private Land') and chapter seventeen ('Extending the Movement'). What are the limitations to voluntary simplicity that are described in those chapters?

8. How does Mary Grigsby think the Voluntary Simplicity Movement could be extended?

9. How does Eric Freyfogle conceptualize private property? Does he think private property could be reformed to better reflect social and environmental values? Consider the validity of his arguments.

10. What do you think a voluntarily simplistic society would look like? Exhaust your imagination and be as detailed as possible.

11. Jessie Sampter has argued that voluntary simplicity is the 'peak of civilization.' What do you think he means by this? Do you agree or disagree with his view?

12. Theory of practice: Creatively interpret clauses 83–87 of 'The Manifesto.'

13. Practice of theory: Creatively interpret 'Peaceful Acts of Opposition,' numbers 71–80.

14. Closing thought: *If we do not change direction, we are likely to end up where we are going.* – Chinese Proverb

Ninth Meditation – The Politics of Consumption

Overview: However much we might want to live simply, it is a fact that western society (and increasingly global society) is structurally opposed to voluntary simplicity. That is, our political and economic institutions make living simply much more difficult than it needs to be. This has lead some simplicity theorists to call for a 'politics of consumption.' Let us think about what a 'politics of consumption' might look like by considering what institutional reforms could facilitate the emergence of a society of simple livers.

1. To what extent can *personal action* solve the problems of our age? To what extent is *structural reform through collective political engagement* necessary? What are the strengths and weakness of both modes of opposition?

2. Voluntary simplicity is usually described as a 'social movement.' How would 'politicizing' the movement further its causes)? What does 'politicizing' the movement even mean?

3. Study Appendix III 'Declaration on Degrowth'.

4. Read or re-read chapter sixteen ('The Politics of Consumption') and chapter seventeen ('Political Prescriptions) of this anthology. Take note of the political reforms proposed in those chapters.

5. Consider, in relation to voluntary simplicity, the merits of the following broad political / economic / educational reforms:

- ★ *Introduce legislation limiting working hours per year (e.g. 1,500) to combat unemployment, time poverty, and 'affluenza.' Protect employees who wish to work part-time.*

- ★ *Provide tax incentives for corporations that establish themselves as locally owned worker co-ops to encourage the emergence of a more communitarian and ecologically sensitive capitalism.*

- ★ *Provide an adequate minimum wage.*

- ★ *Establish new 'green taxes' (i.e. taxes which tax environmentally damaging goods and services) in an attempt to encourage sustainable capitalism and price things at their true cost. (For example, imagine high taxes on non-local food or non-electronic cars. Can you think of other examples?)*

- ★ *Create a progressive income tax system culminating in a socially acceptable 'income cap' (i.e. tax the rich progressively more than the poor, and in such a way that all income above a certain level is taxed very heavily or even completely).*

- ★ *Establish new 'luxury taxes' (i.e. taxes which tax luxury goods) in an attempt to foster more socially beneficial spending. The money collected could subsidize the provision of 'basic needs' for all, perhaps, or fund research into green/renewable energy.*

- ★ *Establish new 'wealth taxes' (i.e. taxes which annually tax the very rich) in order to distribute the social product more fairly and provide all with the resources needed to live a simple life.*

- ★ *Increase 'inheritance taxes' to promote a more egalitarian society with equal opportunities.*

- ★ *Reconceive the meaning of private property to prohibit socially and environmentally destructive action (i.e. sensibly limit the 'right to use' in various ways).*

- ★ *Halt the privatization of common resources.*

- ★ *Provide free health care and education for all.*

- ★ *Provide adequate social security.*

- ★ *Create new advertising standards and prohibit corporate advertising to children.*
- ★ *Replace state promotion/subsidization of consumerism with promotion/subsidization of the simple life by redirecting state expenditure. Think up some examples.*
- ★ *Increase aid to the Third World. What would fulfill our humanitarian duties? Be precise.*
- ★ *Establish stricter and more humanitarian standards for fair trade.*
- ★ *Discuss the possibility of voluntary simplicity being promoted in schools.*
- ★ *Limit corporate funding of political campaigns so that political parties are not unduly influenced by corporate interests.*

6. Imagine a society where all of the above reforms were democratically enacted over a fifteen year period. What would it be like? Is such a world possible/desirable?

7. Can you think of other ways voluntary simplicity could be facilitated by political / economic / educational reform?

8. Think of all the good things the above reforms could achieve. Think of all the new problems they could cause. Weigh up the pros and cons. What is a reasonable path forward?

9. The central neoliberal objection to reforms such as those noted above is that such reforms would be 'inefficient,' in the sense that they would not 'maximize wealth.' This may indeed be true, but from the eco-social-democratic perspective of voluntary simplicity, the response would be that the good gained from the reforms (or the evils avoided) would outweigh the costs of their alleged 'inefficiency.' What do you think of this response? Should the aim of political society be to 'maximize wealth' or to 'increase human wellbeing'?

10. Let us return, once again, to the idea that, 'How we spend our money is how we vote on what exists in the world.' Collective spending is a political matter. How could redirecting our collective expenditure change the world?

11. Theory of practice: Creatively interpret clauses 88–92 of 'The Manifesto.'

12. Practice of theory: Creatively interpret 'Peaceful Acts of Opposition,' numbers 81–90.

13. Closing thought: *Our social ills will not be cured by personal action alone.* – John de Graaf

Tenth Meditation – Living the Idea

Overview: Perhaps there are some readers who have already been convinced of the merits of voluntary simplicity and who wish to explore it further, but who haven't yet taken any practical steps? For some people this could be a state that persists over a number of years, a lifetime even. For others, in different circumstances, there could be more urgency. Whatever the case, the first step is unlikely to be easy, since the passion for simplicity leads us in an opposite direction to where most of the world is drifting. But if your heart is so inclined, and if being swept along is no longer enough, why don't you become a pioneer of postmaterialism? Why don't you consider proactively downshifting? A more radical simplicity could follow, perhaps, circumstances permitting? (Only your imagination is needed.)

1. Begin by imagining for yourself, in some detail, a simple life of your own. What would it look like? How would you live? What would you do differently? How might you think differently?

2. What obstacles lie in the way to achieving this life and how could they be overcome? What would you find most difficult about simplifying?

    ★ *If you are concerned about what other people would think, consider that there might be more important things at stake.*

    ★ *If you are concerned about what luxuries you might have to give up, focus on all that you will get back in return.*

    ★ *If you do not think you could do it, make the pioneer's leap of faith.*

3. Earlier you were asked to consider what ways your life might already be consistent with voluntary simplicity. Now make a list of small but

meaningful ways you might like to change your life over coming weeks and months to further increase consistency. (The cumulative result of small actions can be of transformative significance.)

4. What could you do *today*?

5. Would you like to take more radical steps towards simplicity some time in the future? ('What old people say you cannot do, you try and find that you can. Old deeds for old people, and new deeds for new.' – Thoreau.)

6. When living simply it is especially important not to waste money, so make sure you know where it is all going. The following exercise can be enlightening: Over a one month period, record *every* purchase you make, and then categorize your expenses. Multiply each category by twelve to get a rough estimate of the annual cost. Then consider how much of your time and life-energy you spent obtaining the money to buy everything you consumed that month. Question not only the amounts but also the categories. You might find that seemingly little purchases add up to an inordinate amount over a whole year, suggesting that the money might be better spent elsewhere, not at all, or exchanged for more time by working less. (Again, 'The cost of a thing is the amount of life which is required to be exchanged for it.') You may find that some small changes to your spending habits, rather than inducing any sense of deprivation, will instead be life-affirming.[17]

7. Knowing your finances is not just about making sure you don't waste any life. Recall, yet again, Vicki Robin's insight: 'How we spend our money is how we vote on what exists in the world.' Reflect on the kinds of products and corporations you are 'voting' for.

8. Read or re-read chapter fourteen ('A Culture of Permanence').

9. In this anthology it has been argued that any proposed solutions to the problems of poverty, environmental degradation, social decay, and spiritual malaise, are destined to fail unless we first address the role that commodity fetishism plays in creating those problems. Do you agree? How could we protect ourselves from or overcome commodity fetishism? How could we live the solution?

10. Begin compiling your own list of inspiring quotations. (A highly recommended source is the book of quotations on simplicity edited by Gold-

ian Vanenbroeck, entitled *Less is More: An Anthology of Ancient and Modern Voices Raised in Praise of Simplicity.*[18])

11. Rework or refine the 'Peaceful Acts of Opposition' to suit your own situation and condition. What amendments would you make? Add your own commentary. (Please email any suggestions or comments to the author at samuelalexander42@gmail.com).

12. If, as Gandhi believed, 'our life is our message,' what do you want your message to be? Write a letter to yourself addressing this question.

13. Theory of practice: Creatively interpret clauses 93–95 of 'The Manifesto.'

14. Practice of theory: Creatively interpret 'Peaceful Acts of Opposition,' numbers 91–95.

15. Closing thought: *Be the change you wish to see in the world.*
    – Mahatma Gandhi

Endnotes

1 Juliet Schor, 'Learning Diderot's Lesson: Stopping the Upward Creep of Desire,' in Tim Jackson (ed.), *The Earthscan Reader in Sustainable Consumption* (2005) p178.

2 Henry David Thoreau, 'Life Without Principle,' in Carl Bode (ed.) *The Portable Thoreau* (1982) p636. (emphasis added.)

3 Henry David Thoreau, *Walden*, in Carl Bode (ed..) *The Portable Thoreau* (1982) p275.

4 John de Graaf et al, *Affluenza: The All-consuming Epidemic* (2005, 2nd edition) p224.

5 Duane Elgin, *Voluntary Simplicity: Toward a Way of Life that is Outwardly Simple, Inwardly Rich* (1993, revised edition) p150-51.

6 United Nations 'Human Development Report' (2007/8)

7 As noted in a speech by Kofi Annan (then Secretary-General of the United Nations) in July 2004.

8 See, for example, Ed Diener and Martin Seligman, 'Beyond Money: Toward an Economy of Well-Being' (2004) 5(1) *Psychological Science in the Public Interest* 1 (reviewing over 150 studies assessing the correlation between financial wealth and wellbeing). See also, Clive Hamilton, *Growth Fetish* (2003), especially chapters one and two.

9 See D G Myers and E Diener, 'The Pursuit of Happiness' (1996) 274 *Scientific American* 54-6; and D G Myers, 'Does Economic Growth Improve Human Morale?' (1997) Center for a New American Dream, available at www.newdream.org (last retrieved on 12 June 2008).

10 See Bruno Frey and Alois Stutzer, *Happiness and Economics* (2002), 74-6.

11 Data for Japan show that between 1958 and 1991 real GDP per person increased sixfold, yet reported levels of satisfaction with life did not change at all. Ibid, 9-10.

12 Clive Hamilton, 'Overconsumption in Australia: The Rise of the Middle-class Battler' (2002, Australia Institute Discussion Paper No. 49); and 'Tracking Well-being in Australia: The Genuine Progress Indicator' (2000, Australia Institute Discussion Paper No. 35); and (with Richard Denniss), *Affluenza: When Too Much is Never Enough* (2005).

13 See note 10, above, 74-6.

14 United Nations, 'Human Development Report' (2007/8).

15 Tony Jupiter, *How Many Lightbulbs Does it Take to Change a Planet?* (2007) p141.

16 Duane Elgin, *Voluntary Simplicity: Toward a Way of Life that is Outwardly Simple, Inwardly Rich* (1993, revised edition) p195.

17 For more elaborate financial exercises, see Vicki Robin and Joe Dominguez, *Your Money or Your Life: Transforming your relationship with money and achieving financial independence* (1992).

18 I gratefully acknowledge that clauses 50, 53, 63, 64, 79, 80, of the Manifesto were first read in *Less is More: An Anthology of Ancient and Modern Voices Raised in Praise of Simplicity* (1991).

APPENDIX ONE

MANIFESTO OF THE LIFE POETS' SIMPLICITY COLLECTIVE

A THEORETICAL ROMANCE

Let us be pioneers once more

Invitation / Incitation

A respected elder of a small town is strolling one spring evening in the woods. While circling close to the shores of a secluded pond he crosses paths with an apparently disaffected romantic poet, but one who seems temporarily in the mood for society. As the sun calmly ushers itself from the scene, the following civil confrontation takes place.

Elder:

Citizen poetic,
I find deliberately astray,
You seem a being without having,
As if having didn't pay,
Wild mystical enigma,
Is the state of your inside,
It has you even as I speak,
Devouring yourself alive.

Expecting tranquility in gentle soliloquy,
Through wandering woods to this pond,
I left my business alone in the township this eve,
In search of what might lie beyond,
Yet no surprise should it have been,
This far from good society,
That I cross upon a militant romantic,
Of some quiet crossbred variety.

Are you one of those who propose in revolt,
'Find your path that simplicity has broken'?
Don't tell me that you're an inciter of this!
Perhaps we should never have spoken,
I tend to tire of such romance, you see,
Please forgive me my honesty here,
A life lived imagining some 'Other' to gold,
Would explain your kaleidoscope stare.

With eyes of infinite affirmation,
To each their own black hole,
They glisten with free spirit,
And leak of radioactive soul,

Still something in their glow sings,
In melancholy keys,
The tune is of a mind gone diving,
Far too deep for me.

But enough of my impressions,
Which so rudely forth I spew,
I'll bid you now good evening, sir,
And leave you to your view,
Unless of course a bard you are,
Without a place to be?
In which case might you fight twilight,
Inciting verse with me?

LIFE POET:

Witness O mysterious other,
Who wanders in from beyond,
Like mist emerging from the woods,
To settle on the pond,
With etiquette poetic,
Charm refined by some sixth sense,
You seem a gentlemanly brother,
If not a little like Clamence.

As for me a place to be,
Is none but than right where I am,
Passing through in awe,
What commerce cannot understand,
You could too see through this worldview,
If you saw what yours ignores,
Please don't be quick to think I'm lost,
For simply wandering these shores.

Just bathe your eyes in these soft ocean skies,
Of blue, purple, and pink,
And you will find in this sublime,
That there are worse places to sink –
Crass rat race, not to my taste,
Out from the rush I stepped with haste,
It gave me twisted faces,
Only here I find my grace.

A welcome cosmic accident,
Of time and chance I trust,
That we should meet this setting sun,
Among all Nature in the dusk,
So come and join my meditations,
Burning in the dew,
Tonight I'd like to fight twilight,
Inciting verse with you.

A discourse did ignite,
Two lanterns on a kite,
Which we cast out at darkness,
To carry forth light,
This may lead us past yonder,
But before we go too far,
Perhaps you would tell me,
Who on earth you are?

'Who are you?' it is asked of me,
With a seriousness hitherto unseen,
Please may we start with an easier question,
Or next you'll ask me what I mean.

'Tis best methinks you evaded the subject,
Because now my suspicion is this,
If you tried to tell me the truth of your meaning,
You'd never stop changing the script,
So rather than bother you, and cause you the trouble,
To live only a life of review,
Agreed we should start with an easier question,
Why not just tell me what you do?

On the far side of the shore,
Beneath a tree there sits a chair,
Where I front every morning star,
With questions God is meant to hear,
Then later in the day,
Like a mad Dostoyevskian clown,
I chase my butterfly thoughts fragmented,
And try to write them down.

With your ink among the birds,
A sojourner in search of words,
In this strange way to spend your day,
Have you found something new to say?

I have yet found but few new words,
In this sense I'm a flightless bird,
So destiny has me,
Repeating only things I've heard:
– Just enough is plenty –
– Abundance is a state of mind –
Since this can cure the Golden Plague,
My fate is not part–time.

So will you quietly revolt?
This is my soul refrain,
Like Abraham, if you give up,
You'll get more back again,
Compose yourself a simple life,
The poet's leap of faith,
At the edge of the abyss,
Creation seems to be at stake.

Come, let us foresee the starry night,
That perfect economy,
Alone, together,
In silence.

TRAGEDY AND THE POETIC CONCEPTION OF LIFE

1

The bleaker and emptier life becomes under capitalism, the more intense is our yearning after beauty.[1]

2

The paradox of the human situation yields no resolution.[2]

3

Love thy fate.[3]

4

Imagination is more important than knowledge.[4]

5

Poetry can be defined as the expression of the imagination; it is at once the center and circumference of knowledge.[5]

6

We will never arrive at descriptions of reality or the meaning of human existence so perfect that imaginative redescription will become pointless.[6]

7

Take care of freedom and truth will take care of itself.[7]

8

The important thing is not to stop questioning.[8]

9

We absolutely refuse a discourse that would assign us a single code, a single language game, a single context, a single situation; and we claim this right not simply out of caprice or because it is to our taste, but for ethical and political reasons.[9]

10

Deconstruction is not an enclosure in nothingness, but an openness to the other.[10]

11

The most beautiful experience we can have is the mysterious.[11]

12

Let us work out honorable terms upon which philosophy might surrender to poetry. Let us poeticize culture.[12]

13

We must create the taste by which we will be judged.[13]

14

Imagination is the chief end of the good. Art is more moral than moralities.[14]

15

Art has the spiritual quality of religion.[15]

★ ★ ★

16

Creativity can save some who could not be saved any other way.[16]

★ ★ ★

17

God's away on business.[17]

★ ★ ★

18

By mediating between the transcendental sublime and the common, one is able to condense a cloud of metaphysics into a drop of grammar.[18]

★ ★ ★

19

Metaphor is less in the philosophical text than the philosophical text is within metaphor.[19]

★ ★ ★

20

Proceed within aesthetic metaphors.[20]

★ ★ ★

21

The world is but a canvas to the imagination.[21]

★ ★ ★

22

The world may be justified as an aesthetic phenomenon.[22]

★ ★ ★

23

We are citizens of the world.[23]

★ ★ ★

24

We are condemned to be free.[24]

★ ★ ★

25

We will be what we make of ourselves and nothing else.[25]

★ ★ ★

26

We must compose as an aesthetic project the meaning of our own life.[26]

★ ★ ★

27

Aesthetics and ethics are one.[27]

★ ★ ★

28

Our life is our message.[28]

★ ★ ★

29

Life as literature.[29]

★ ★ ★

30

The personal is political.[30]

★ ★ ★

31

The objective of global political society is to create a free association of human beings within which each has an opportunity for self-creation.[31]

★ ★ ★

32

The subject is not a substance; it is a form.[32]

★ ★ ★

33

Give birth to oneself.[33]

★ ★ ★

34

Do not take for granted the distinction between art and life.[34]

★ ★ ★

35

In our society art has become something which is related only to objects and not to individuals, or to life. That art is something which is specialized or which is done by experts who are artists. But couldn't everyone's life become a work of art? Why should the lamp or the house be a work of art, and not our life?[35]

★ ★ ★

36

From the idea that the self is not given to us, there is only one practical consequence: We must create ourselves as a work of art.[36]

★ ★ ★

37

Search for an aesthetics of existence.[37]

★ ★ ★

38

Be the poet of your life.[38]

★ ★ ★

39

If it is not poetic it is not life but death we get.[39]

★ ★ ★

40

Beauty rests on necessities. The line of beauty is the result of perfect economy.[40]

★ ★ ★

41

Art is the elimination of the unnecessary.[41]

★ ★ ★

42

Simplify, simplify.[42]

★ ★ ★

43

If not us, then who? If not now, then when?[43]

★ ★ ★

44

Old deeds for old people, and new deeds for new.[44]

★ ★ ★

45

Poets are the ones who 'make things new,' and thus to fail as a poet is to accept someone else's description of oneself.[45]

★ ★ ★

46

We can always make something new out of what we have been made into.[46]

★ ★ ★

47

Poets are the unacknowledged legislators of the world.[47]

★ ★ ★

Voluntary Simplicity

The Poetics of a Quiet Revolution

48

Getting and spending, we lay waste our powers.[48]

★ ★ ★

49

One day a 'why' arises, and everything begins in that weariness tinged with amazement. 'Begins' – this is important.[49]

★ ★ ★

50

We will be revolutionary when we revolutionize ourselves.[50]

★ ★ ★

51

The individual who goes it alone can start today.[51]

★ ★ ★

52

The inner crisis of our civilization must be resolved if the outer crisis is to be effectively met.[52]

★ ★ ★

53

Let thy walk be an interior one.[53]

★ ★ ★

54

Rouse yourself from the daze of unexamined economic habit.[54]

★ ★ ★

55

Do not be a bourgeois compromise.[55]

★ ★ ★

56

There is no wealth but life.[56]

★ ★ ★

57

Superfluous wealth can buy superfluities only. Money is not required to buy one necessary of the soul.[57]

★ ★ ★

58

People are rich in proportion to the things which they can afford to leave alone.[58]

★ ★ ★

59

The essence of civilization consists not in the multiplication of wants but in their deliberate and voluntary renunciation.[59]

★ ★ ★

60

The cost of a thing is the amount of life which is required to be exchanged for it.[6]

★ ★ ★

61

Most of the luxuries, and many of the so called comforts of life, are not only not indispensable, but positive hindrances to the elevation of humankind.[61]

★ ★ ★

62

How we spend our money is how we vote on what exists in the world.[62]

★ ★ ★

63

Though gold and gems by the world are sought and prized,
To us they seem no more than weeds or chaff.[63]

★ ★ ★

64

It is better to have fewer material wants than to have larger resources.[64]

★ ★ ★

65

Those who know they have enough are rich.[65]

★ ★ ★

66

Economy of means and simplicity of life – voluntarily chosen – have always been the secret to fulfillment, while acquisitiveness and extravagance are a despairing waste of life.[66]

★ ★ ★

67

Abundance is not a specific quantity of goods; it is a state of mind, a set of attitudes.[67]

★ ★ ★

68

By changing our attitudes of mind, we can change the world.[68]

★ ★ ★

69

To solve the problem of poverty, we must first solve the problem of affluence.[69]

70

Voluntary simplicity and non-violence are closely related. To consume material resources heedlessly or extravagantly is an act of violence, and while complete non-violence may not be attainable here on earth, there is nonetheless an ineluctable duty on us to aim at the ideal of non-violence in all we do.[70]

71

The plain fact is that we are starving people, not deliberately in the sense that we want them to die, but willfully in the sense that we prefer their death to our own inconvenience.[71]

★ ★ ★

72

Live simply so that others may simply live.[72]

★ ★ ★

73

Any proposed solutions to the problems of poverty, environmental degradation, social decay, and spiritual malaise, are destined to fail unless we first address the role that commodity fetishism plays in creating those problems.[73]

★ ★ ★

74

Simple living is both a humble, personal endeavor and at the same time a socially, economically, and politically radical form of life.[74]

★ ★ ★

75

Voluntary simplicity is an expression of human freedom, one of whose aims is an increase in that freedom.[75]

★ ★ ★

76

Those who have a *why* to live can bear almost any *how*.[76]

★ ★ ★

77

One does not have to be sad to be militant.[77]

★ ★ ★

78

There is an infinite variety of exhilarating ways of life compatible with living simply on an equitable share of nature.[78]

★ ★ ★

79

Hasn't the artist always kept the true balance between the poverty of riches and the riches of poverty?[79]

★ ★ ★

80

We are lovers of beauty, yet simple in our tastes.[80]

★ ★ ★

81

Always bear in mind that very little indeed is necessary for living a happy life.[81]

★ ★ ★

82

Pleasure and simplicity are two old acquaintances.[82]

★ ★ ★

83

Amazingly small means lead to extraordinarily satisfactory results.[83]

★ ★ ★

84

Less is more.[84]

★ ★ ★

85

Simplicity is the ultimate sophistication.[85]

★ ★ ★

86

Consider the lily; we say unto all that even Solomon in all his glory was not arrayed like it.[86]

★ ★ ★

87

Through voluntary simplicity the needs of the individual uniquely match the needs of society. Of what other emergent life patterns can this be said?[87]

★ ★ ★

88

Western civilization is set up structurally to oppose voluntary simplicity.[88]

★ ★ ★

89

Private property is a concept that has many conceptions. Choosing a conception implies a vision of the social world.[89]

★ ★ ★

90

The ethics of voluntary simplicity provides common ground not only between traditional political oppositions, but between all major world religions. Why not meet there and continue the human conversation?[90]

★ ★ ★

91

A shift in values in relation to the material aspects of life emerges as individuals and societies evolve from a postmodern to a voluntarily simplistic age.[91]

★ ★ ★

92

The foregoing generations beheld God and nature face to face; we, through their eyes. Why should we not also enjoy an original relation to the universe?[92]

★ ★ ★

93

The spirit of simplicity is not an inherited gift, but the result of a laborious conquest.[93]

★ ★ ★

94

Simplicity is the peak of civilization.[94]

★ ★ ★

95

Light dawns gradually over the whole.[95]

★ ★ ★

* Indicates a minor adaptation of original quote.

(ENDNOTES)
1 Georg Lukacs*
2 Avivah Gottlieb Zornberg
3 Friedrich Nietzsche
4 Albert Einstein
5 Percy Bysshe Shelley*
6 Richard Rorty*
7 Richard Rorty
8 Albert Einstein
9 Jacques Derrida*
10 Jacques Derrida
11 Albert Einstein
12 Richard Rorty*
13 Samuel Taylor Coleridge
14 John Dewey
15 Silentio
16 Silentio
17 Tom Waits
18 John Dewey*
19 Jacques Derrida
20 Silentio
21 Henry David Thoreau
22 Friedrich Nietzsche*
23 Diogenes*
24 Jean-Paul Sartre
25 Jean-Paul Sartre
26 Silentio
27 Ludwig Wittgenstein
28 Mahatma Gandhi*
29 Friedrich Nietzsche*
30 Carol Hanisch
31 Silentio
32 Michel Foucault
33 Harold Bloom
34 Silentio
35 Michel Foucault
36 Michel Foucault
37 Michel Foucault
38 Friedrich Nietzsche*
39 Henry David Thoreau
40 Ralph Waldo Emerson
41 Pablo Picasso
42 Henry David Thoreau.
43 Origin Unknown
44 Henry David Thoreau
45 Martin Heidegger / Richard Rorty*
46 Jean-Paul Sartre*
47 Percy Bysshe Shelley
48 William Wordsworth
49 Albert Camus
50 Ludwig Wittgenstein*

51 Henry David Thoreau*
52 Lewis Mumford
53 Blessed Henry Suso
54 Epictetus*
55 The Steppenwolf*
56 John Ruskin
57 Henry David Thoreau
58 Henry David Thoreau*
59 Mahatma Gandhi
60 Henry David Thoreau
61 Henry David Thoreau*
62 Vicki Robin*
63 Fu Hsuan
64 St Augustine
65 Lao-Tzu*
66 Theodore Roszak
67 Robert Theobald
68 William James*
69 Clive Hamilton and Richard Denniss*
70 E.F. Schumacher*
71 Victor Gollancz
72 Mahatma Gandhi
73 Silentio
74 Mark A. Burch*
75 Mark A. Burch
76 Friedrich Nietzsche
77 Michel Foucault*
78 Jim Merkel*
79 Honore de Balzac
80 Thucydides*
81 Marcus Aurelius
82 Charles Wagner
83 E.F. Schumacher
84 Mies Van der Rohe
85 Leonardo da Vinci
86 From the Sermon on the Mount
87 Duane Elgin*
88 Michael Jacobson*
89 Jeremy Waldron / Joseph Singer
90 Silentio
91 Silentio
92 Ralph Waldo Emerson
93 Charles Wagner
94 Jessie Sampter
95 Ludwig Wittgenstein

Appendix two

PEACEFUL ACTS OF OPPOSITION

THE PERSONAL IS POLITICAL

This document is an attempt to reduce the philosophy of voluntary simplicity to a list of broad proposals for personal action. While any such list will be incomplete, to some degree controversial, and everywhere in need of creative interpretation, it is hoped that what follows may nevertheless provide imaginative individuals with the raw material needed to begin practicing simplicity and shaping a simple life.

1

Affirm life.

★ ★ ★

2

Privilege being over having.

★ ★ ★

3

Take a second look.
(Dissatisfaction with our material situations might be the result of failing to look properly at our lives rather than the result of any 'lack.')

★ ★ ★

4

Read and talk about voluntary simplicity.

★ ★ ★

5

Isolate yourself from consumer culture for long enough to unlearn it.
(Find your own 'Walden Pond.' Stay until your private business is complete.)

★ ★ ★

6

Declare independence.

★ ★ ★

7

Remind yourself that those who know they have enough are rich.

★ ★ ★

8

Personally redefine the meaning of wealth.

★ ★ ★

9

Stop the upward creep of material desire.

★ ★ ★

10

Commit to 'downshifting.'
(A more radical simplicity may follow.)

★ ★ ★

11

Create personally fulfilling and meaningful ways to shift your energy and attention from the material to the nonmaterial side of life.

★ ★ ★

12

Dedicate your imagination to thinking up a poeticized life based on an equitable share of nature.
(The possibilities are infinite.)

★ ★ ★

13

Compose yourself.

★ ★ ★

14

Determine what your chief purpose in life is.

★ ★ ★

15

Avoid possessions irrelevant to your chief purpose in life.

★ ★ ★

16

Do not confuse 'standard of living' with 'quality of life.'

★ ★ ★

17

Consume less – for yourself, for others, and for the Earth.

★ ★ ★

18

Be conscious of time poverty.
(Choose time over money or things.)

★ ★ ★

19

Reduce working hours.

★ ★ ★

20

Vote with your time.

★ ★ ★

21

Be mindful of how you earn a living and what it stands for.

★ ★ ★

22

Live beneath your means.

★ ★ ★

23

Save your raise.

★ ★ ★

24

Know your finances and spending habits, precisely.

★ ★ ★

25

Vote with your money.

★ ★ ★

26

Fund sustainable democracy rather than the mega-corporations of advanced capitalism.

★ ★ ★

27

Buy local / green / organic / fair trade.

★ ★ ★

28

Avoid all goods you know or suspect were unjustly manufactured.

★ ★ ★

29

Think very carefully about what housing is necessary.
(Most people appear never to have considered what a house is, and are actually though needlessly poor all their lives because they think that they must have such a one as their neighbors have. – Thoreau)

★ ★ ★

30

The 'conspicuous consumers' are not so much sad as foolish – relinquish to them the pursuit.

★ ★ ★

31

Dress down.

★ ★ ★

32

Cultivate a vegetable garden and grow fruit trees.

★ ★ ★

33

Acquire a taste for minimalism.
(Lose yourself in the unceasingly eloquence of silence. Gaze at the stars on a clear night.)

★ ★ ★

34

Be humble.

★ ★ ★

35

Celebrate art.

★ ★ ★

36

Hold onto that mystical tingle associated with aesthetic experience.

★ ★ ★

37

Meditate and/or create your own spiritual exercises.

★ ★ ★

38

Devour yourself alive.
(Explore your intellectual passions, your aesthetic sensibilities, and your sensuality.)

★ ★ ★

39

Be creative.
(Find your own way.)

★ ★ ★

40

Read.

★ ★ ★

41

Keep a journal.

★ ★ ★

42

Walk in nature.

★ ★ ★

43

Recognize yourself as a citizen of the world.

★ ★ ★

44

Think global, act local.

★ ★ ★

45

Foster community spirit and be open to others.

★ ★ ★

46

Give some of yourself away as an unconditional gift.

★ ★ ★

47

Travel inward.

★ ★ ★

48

Enjoy solitude.

★ ★ ★

49

Take a short 'retirement' every so often to indulge a burning passion. (Retire progressively.)

★ ★ ★

50

Be a thoughtful non-conformist.

★ ★ ★

51

Slow down.

★ ★ ★

52

Seek the infinite in great music.

★ ★ ★

53

Find a way to earn some money doing something you love.

★ ★ ★

54

Avoid unnecessary technology.

★ ★ ★

55

Declutter all aspects of life.

★ ★ ★

56

Value self-reliance.
(Avoid paying people to do things you can do yourself.)

★ ★ ★

57

Entertain yourself for free.

★ ★ ★

58

Share your expertise.

★ ★ ★

59

Lend when asked and borrow when necessary.

★ ★ ★

60

Make your own.

★ ★ ★

61

Buy second-hand.

★ ★ ★

62

Never go shopping without a purpose or for entertainment.

★ ★ ★

63

Avoid television.
(It quickly becomes a general anesthetic that wastes life glamorizing behaviors and values that are poisonous to life.)

★ ★ ★

64

Avoid and reject as much advertising / mass media / consumer culture as possible – or else the product may be you.
(Do not be a corporate advertisement.)

★ ★ ★

65

Destroy some or all of your credit cards.

★ ★ ★

66

Use it up, wear it out, make it do, or do without.

★ ★ ★

67

Reclaim the vast wealth of the commons.

★ ★ ★

68

Protect and respect the commons.
(Oppose further privatization.)

★ ★ ★

69

Reduce your ecological footprint. (Do some research.)

★ ★ ★

70

Become a vegetarian or reduce meat consumption.
(Eating simply and creatively can be cheap.)

★ ★ ★

71

Do not own a car or make driving the exception.
(Walk or ride a bike. Use public transport. When necessary, hire or borrow a vehicle.)

★ ★ ★

72

Avoid air travel.

★ ★ ★

73

Conserve water.

★ ★ ★

74

Progress towards 100% green / renewable energy.

★ ★ ★

75

Take energy reduction / efficiency seriously.

★ ★ ★

76

Explore 'living off the grid,' at least in part. Consider getting a water tank and solar panels.

★ ★ ★

77

Waste not.
(Refuse, reduce, reuse, recycle, and compost. Avoid plastic bags and unnecessary packaging.)

★ ★ ★

78

Be stoic during those times when simple living may be tough.

★ ★ ★

79

Seek inspiration from the greatest simpler livers of the past and present. (Buddha, Diogenes, Socrates, Jesus, Marcus Aurelius, St Francis, Henry David Thoreau, Leo Tolstoy, Mahatma Gandhi, Helen and Scott Nearing, Joe Dominguez, Charles Grey, Jim Merkel, Anastasia etc.)

★ ★ ★

80

Object loudly to the existence of poverty amidst plenty.
(Leftist politics and/or religious belief entails trying to live the solution.)

★ ★ ★

81

Occasionally ask yourself awkward questions.

★ ★ ★

82

Make no excuses.

★ ★ ★

83

Affect the quality of your day.

★ ★ ★

84

Think carefully about the ways our society might be set up structurally to oppose voluntary simplicity and how you might be embedded in that structure. Struggle creatively for reform.
(Individuals are needed.)

★ ★ ★

85

Invest in a book on voluntary simplicity and leave it in your common room at work and/or lend it to curious friends or family members. Ask if you can leave another copy in your local café.
(Alternatively, improve and then distribute this document.)

★ ★ ★

86

Treasure your electoral votes.

★ ★ ★

87

Join your union.

★ ★ ★

88

Protest.
(If necessary, consider civil disobedience. Make non-violence absolute.)

★ ★ ★

89

Raise children to have few material wants.
(Be an example.)

★ ★ ★

90

Stand up.

★ ★ ★

91

Trust thyself.[1]

★ ★ ★

92

Live deliberately.[2]

★ ★ ★

93

March to the beat of your own drummer.[3]

★ ★ ★

94

Advance confidently in the direction of your dreams, and endeavor to live the life which you have imagined.[4]

★ ★ ★

95

Be the change you wish to see in the world.[5]

★ ★ ★

(Endnotes)

1 Ralph Waldo Emerson.

2 Henry David Thoreau.

3 Henry David Thoreau.

4 Henry David Thoreau.

5 Mahatma Gandhi.

We have only this moment, sparkling like a star in our hand –
and melting like a snowflake.

APPENDIX THREE

DECLARATION ON DEGROWTH

This Declaration is the product of a workshop held at the Conference on Economic Degrowth for Ecological Sustainability and Social Equity held in Paris on 18-19 April 2008. It reflects the points of view of the conference participants and articulates the vision of the Decroissance movement.

PARIS, 19 APRIL 2008

WE, PARTICIPANTS IN THE CONFERENCE ON ECONOMIC DEGROWTH FOR ECOLOGICAL SUSTAINABILITY AND SOCIAL EQUITY HELD IN PARIS ON 18-19 APRIL 2008, MAKE THE FOLLOWING DECLARATION:

1. Economic growth (as indicated by increasing real GDP or GNP) represents an increase in production, consumption and investment in the pursuit of economic surplus, inevitably leading to increased use of materials, energy and land.
2. Despite improvements in the ecological efficiency of the production and consumption of goods and services, global economic growth has resulted in increased extraction of natural resources and increased waste and emissions.
3. Global economic growth has not succeeded in reducing poverty substantially, due to unequal exchange in trade and financial markets, which has increased inequality between countries.
4. As the established principles of physics and ecology demonstrate, there is an eventual limit to the scale of global production and consumption, and to the scale national economies can attain without imposing environmental and social costs on others elsewhere or future generations.
5. The best available scientific evidence indicates that the global economy has grown beyond ecologically sustainable limits, as have many national economies, especially those of the wealthiest countries (primarily industrialized countries in the global North).
6. There is also mounting evidence that global growth in production and consumption is socially unsustainable and uneconomic (in the sense that its costs outweigh its benefits).
7. By using more than their legitimate share of global environmental resources, the wealthiest nations are effectively reducing the environmental space available to poorer nations, and imposing adverse environmental impacts on them.
8. If we do not respond to this situation by bringing global economic activity into line with the capacity of our ecosystems, and redistributing wealth and income globally so that they meet our societal needs, the result will be a process of involuntary and uncontrolled economic decline or collapse, with potentially serious social impacts, especially for the most disadvantaged.

WE THEREFORE CALL FOR A PARADIGM SHIFT FROM THE GENERAL AND UNLIMITED PURSUIT OF ECONOMIC GROWTH TO A CONCEPT OF "RIGHT-SIZING" THE GLOBAL AND NATIONAL ECONOMIES.

1. At the global level, "right-sizing" means reducing the global ecological footprint (including the carbon footprint) to a sustainable level.
2. In countries where the per capita footprint is greater than the sustainable global level, right-sizing implies a reduction to this level within a reasonable timeframe.
3. In countries where severe poverty remains, right-sizing implies increasing consumption by those in poverty as quickly as possible, in a sustainable way, to a level adequate for a decent life, following locally determined poverty-reduction paths rather than externally imposed development policies.
4. This will require increasing economic activity in some cases; but redistribution of income and wealth both within and between countries is a more essential part of this process.

THE PARADIGM SHIFT INVOLVES DEGROWTH IN WEALTHY PARTS OF THE WORLD.

1. The process by which right-sizing may be achieved in the wealthiest countries, and in the global economy as a whole, is "degrowth".
2. We define degrowth as a voluntary transition towards a just, participatory, and ecologically sustainable society.
3. The objectives of degrowth are to meet basic human needs and ensure a high quality of life, while reducing the ecological impact of the global economy to a sustainable level, equitably distributed between nations. This will not be achieved by involuntary economic contraction.
4. Degrowth requires a transformation of the global economic system and of the policies promoted and pursued at the national level, to allow the reduction and ultimate eradication of absolute poverty to proceed as the global economy and unsustainable national economies degrow.
5. Once right-sizing has been achieved through the process of degrowth, the aim should be to maintain a "steady state economy" with a relatively stable, mildly fluctuating level of consumption.
6. In general, the process of degrowth is characterized by:

    - ★ an emphasis on quality of life rather than quantity of consumption;
    - ★ the fulfilment of basic human needs for all;
    - ★ societal change based on a range of diverse individual and collective actions and policies;

- ★ substantially reduced dependence on economic activity, and an increase in free time, unremunerated activity, conviviality, sense of community, and individual and collective health;
- ★ encouragement of self-reflection, balance, creativity, flexibility, diversity, good citizenship, generosity, and non-materialism;
- ★ observation of the principles of equity, participatory democracy, respect for human rights, and respect for cultural differences.

7. Progress towards degrowth requires immediate steps towards efforts to mainstream the concept of degrowth into parliamentary and public debate and economic institutions; the development of policies and tools for the practical implementation of degrowth; and the development of new, nonmonetary indicators (including subjective indicators) to identify, measure and compare the benefits and costs of economic activity, in order to assess whether changes in economic activity contribute to or undermine the fulfilment of social and environmental objectives.

NOTES ON CONTRIBUTORS

Samuel Alexander — The editor of this anthology, Samuel Alexander is a sessional lecturer and doctoral student at the University of Melbourne Law School, Australia. He is also the founder of the Life Poets' Simplicity Collective (www.simplicitycollective.com), a grass-roots network of imaginations dedicated to the organization and advancement of the Voluntary Simplicity Movement. Living simply and happily in a small hut that he built himself using mostly abandoned materials, he spends his time quietly planning, with youthful ambition, the non-violent erasure of consumer culture. His pamphlet, 'Peaceful Acts of Opposition,' is included as an appendix to this anthology.

Mark A. Burch — Mark A. Burch is an author, educator, and group facilitator. He has been offering workshops and courses on simple living since 1995. He is currently Director of Campus Sustainability at the University of Winnipeg, as well as Co-Director of the Simplicity Practice and Resource Centre (SPARC). Among other books, he is the author of *Stepping Lightly: Simplicity for People and the Planet* (2000) as well as *Simplicity: Notes, Stories and Exercises for Developing Unimaginable Wealth* (1998). A chapter from each of these texts is included in this anthology.

Philip Cafaro — A former ranger with the U.S. National Park Service, Philip Cafaro is now a member of the Department of Philosophy at Colorado State University. His research interests include environmental ethics, virtue ethics, American philosophy and wild lands preservation. An outstanding Thoreau scholar, he is the author of *Thoreau's Living Ethics:* Walden *and the Pursuit of Virtue* (2004), a chapter from which is included in this anthology. Also included is his paper, 'Less is More.'

Richard Denniss — Richard Denniss is Executive Director of the Australia Institute and an adjunct Associate Professor at the Crawford School of Economics and Government, Australian National University. Among other publications, he is the co-author, with Professor Clive Hamilton (see below), of *Affluenza: When Too Much is Never Enough* (2005), two chapters from which are included in this anthology.

Alan Durning – Alan Durning is the founder and Executive Director of the Sightline Institute (formerly Northwest Environmental Watch), a non-for-profit organization based in Seattle. Prior to this role he worked as a researcher at the Worldwatch Institute, where he wrote *How Much is Enough? The Consumer Society and the Future of the Earth* (1992), which has been translated into seven languages and honored with two awards. Two chapters from that text are included in this anthology.

Duane Elgin – Duane Elgin is an author, educator, and media activist, who has earned himself a central place in the Voluntary Simplicity Movement. He has written extensively on voluntary simplicity, most notably, his book *Voluntary Simplicity: Toward a Way of Life that is Outwardly Simple, Inwardly Rich* (1993, revised ed.), and his famous 1977 essay, 'Voluntary Simplicity,' co-authored with Arnold Mitchell (see below), an excerpt from which is included in this anthology.

Amatai Etzioni – After receiving his PhD in Sociology from the University of California, Berkley in 1958, Amatai Etzioni served as a Professor of Sociology at Columbia University for 20 years, part of that time as Chair of the Department. In 1980, he was named the first University Professor at the George Washington University, where he is the Director of the Institute for Communitarian Policy Studies. In 2001, Etzioni was named among the top 100 American intellectuals, as measured by academic citations. He is the author of thirty books, including *The Moral Dimension: Towards a New Economics* (1988), *The New Golden Rule* (1996), and *The Monochrome Society* (2001).

Eric T. Freyfogle – Eric Freyfogle is a Professor of Law at the University of Illinois, College of Law, where he teaches property, environmental, and land use law. He writes and speaks on basic issues of nature and culture with particular concern for modes of living that sustain the healthy functioning of landscapes. His many writings include *On Private Property: Finding Common Ground on the Ownership of Land* (2007) and *Why Conservation Is Failing and How It Can Regain Ground* (2006). He has long been active in state and local conservation efforts in his home state of Illinois and his written an essay for this anthology entitled 'Simplicity, Community, and Private Land.'

John de Graaf – John de Graaf is a the co-chair of the Public Policy Committee for the Simplicity Forum, a leading think tank for the Voluntary Simplicity Movement. As well as being a multi-award winning film-maker (over one hundred awards), he is also the national coordinator (U.S.) of "Take Back Your Time" day, an annual event scheduled for 24 October, the day Americans would finish work for the year if they worked the hours of the average western European. This anthology includes a chapter from the best-selling book, *Affluenza: The All-Consuming Epidemic* (2005, 2nd ed.), which de Graaf co-authored with David Wann and Thomas Naylor.

Richard Gregg — Richard Gregg (1885–1974) was an American lawyer and social philosopher who coined the term 'voluntary simplicity' in his 1936 essay 'The Value of Voluntary Simplicity,' which is included in this anthology (abridged). A disciple of Gandhi, he also developed a substantial theory of non-violent resistance, in a book called *The Power of Non-Violence* (1934), which Martin Luther King, Jnr, listed as one of the five most influential books he had ever read.

Mary Grigsby — Mary Grigsby is Associate Professor of Rural Sociology at the University of Missouri. Among other writings, she has authored *Buying Time and Getting By: The Voluntary Simplicity Movement* (2004), which is an incisive sociological examination of the Voluntary Simplicity Movement, from which her contribution for this anthology is drawn, and *Life Through the Eyes of College Students* (2009, forthcoming), which analyzes and offers insights into college student culture.

Clive Hamilton — Professor Clive Hamilton is the former Executive Director of The Australia Institute, a progressive think tank he founded. In June 2008 he was appointed to the newly created Vice-Chancellor's Chair at Charles Sturt University and joined the Centre for Applied Philosophy and Public Ethics as Professor of Public Ethics based at Australian National University. His books include *The Freedom Paradox* (2008) and *Growth Fetish* (2003), and he also co-authored (with Richard Denniss) *Affluenza: When Too Much is Never Enough* (2005), two chapters from which are included in this anthology.

Jim Merkel — Jim Merkel has led over 1,000 workshops on sustainable lifestyles and is a member of the Simplicity Forum Steering Committee and the Global Footprint Network. He is also the author of *Radical Simplicity,* two chapters from which are included in this anthology, and has worked as the Sustainability Coordinator at Dartmouth College. Merkel founded and directs the Global Living Project (GLP) in Vermont.

Arnold Mitchell — Arnold Mitchell was a consumer futurist at SRI International when he co-authored 'Voluntary Simplicity' with Duane Elgin (see above). Mitchell's later writings include *The Nine American Lifestyles: Who We Are and Where We're Going.*

Juliet Schor — Juliet Schor taught at Harvard University for 17 years before joining Boston College, where she is currently a Professor of Sociology. She has authored many books, including *The Overworked American: The Unexpected Decline of Leisure* (1992), *The Overspent American: Upscaling, Downshifting and the New Consumer* (1998), and *Born to Buy: The Commercialized Child and the New Consumer Culture* (2004). Her contribution to this anthology, 'The Politics of Consumption,' is based on her 1992 and 1998 publications.

Jerome Segal — Jerome Segal is a Research Scholar at the University of Maryland's School of Public Policy. His book *Graceful Simplicity: Towards a Philosophy and Politics of Simple Living* (1999), of which a chapter is included in this anthology, has received considerable acclaim in the United States. He is also a leading commentator on Israeli–Palestinian relations and has written extensively on this subject.

David E. Shi — David E. Shi is the president of Furman University in Greenville, S.C. Before assuming his present position in 1994, he spent one year as Furman's vice-president for academic affairs and dean and another 17 years teaching history at Davidson College. In 1999, Shi was among a distinguished group of 50 college and university presidents who were recognized by the John Templeton Foundation for their outstanding leadership in the development of student character. One chapter from his book, *The Simple Life: Plain Living and High Thinking in American Culture* (2007, revised ed.), is included in this anthology.

Henry David Thoreau — H.D. Thoreau (1817–1862), the great American poet-philosopher, is most famous for his essay 'Civil Disobedience' and his masterpiece, *Walden*. The latter gives an account of his two year experiment living simply on the shores of Walden Pond. Chapter One from *Walden*, entitled 'Economy,' is included in this anthology.

INTERNET RESOURCES

The Life Poets' Simplicity Collective @ www.simplicitycollective.com

Founded by the editor of this anthology, the Life Poets' Simplicity Collective is a grass-roots network of imaginations dedicated to the organization and advancement of the Voluntary Simplicity Movement. The Collective is founded upon the idea that there is an *infinite variety* of meaningful, fulfilling, and equitable forms of life compatible with living simply on a sustainable share of nature. Accordingly, membership entails dedicating one's imagination to progressively creating such a life and, in the same creative spirit, peacefully facilitating through democratic processes the emergence of a just and sustainable society for all. This website provides important information on voluntary simplicity and invites sympathetic readers to join the Life Poets' Simplicity Collective. Only your imagination is needed.

The Simple Living Network @ www.simpleliving.net

A good place to start exploring voluntary simplicity on the web is through the Simple Living Network. There is an abundance of useful information and features, including essays, advice, discussion forums, online study groups, and a substantial resource directory and library. Under the tab 'Partners' there is a list of other excellent websites dedicated to voluntary simplicity, each with resources and online reading of their own. Under the tab 'Simple Radio' there are some free audio recordings, including a reading of parts of Thoreau's *Walden*, an overview of the vision of voluntary simplicity by Cecile Andrews, and an inspiring interview with 'simple liver' Helen Hearing.

The Simplicity Forum @ www.simplicityforum.org

The Simplicity Forum is a leading think tank of academics and authors, activists and artists, educators and entrepreneurs who seek to promote simplicity in our work and practice it in our lives. Like the Simple Living Network, it is an excellent resource for those wishing to explore simplicity further.

The Global Footprint Network @ www.footprintnetwork.org

In 2003, the Global Footprint Network was established to measure human impact on the Earth so we can make more informed choices. The 'Ecological Footprint' is a resource accounting tool that measures how much nature we have, how much we use, and who uses what. The website aims to provide the scientific data necessary to drive large-scale, social change.

Aussies Living Simply (ALS) @ www.aussieslivingsimply.com.au

ALS is a community focused on sustainability, permaculture, organic gardening, backyard livestock, simple living and stepping lightly on the planet. On this website there is a lot of very practical information, hundreds of links and articles, and very active discussion forums.

In Context: Quarterly of Humane Sustainable Culture @ www.context.org

This website contains over 1000 free articles, many written by distinguished writers, on matters intimately related to the theory and practice of voluntary simplicity. See the tab 'Back Issue Listing,' where there is a list of 44 themes to choose from, such as 'Strategies for Cultural Change,' 'Toward a Sustainable World Order,' 'Reclaiming Politics,' 'What is Enough?' and 'Art and Ceremony in Sustainable Culture.' All the articles are concise and easy to read, so exploring this website can be a fruitful and peaceful way to spend fifteen minutes everyday.

The New Economics Foundation @ www.neweconomics.org

The New Economics Foundation is an independent think-and-do-tank that aims to improve quality of life by promoting innovative solutions that challenge mainstream thinking in economic, environmental, and social issues. This stimulating website has a great deal of useful and insightful reading, especially important given its focus on the political changes needed for society to progress.

Yearning for Balance, by the Harwood Group @ www.iisd.ca/consume/harwood.html

This document details a broad and long term study of the patterns of consumption and the consequences of those patterns for our society and the environment. The study was prepared by the Harwood Group and was sparked by a growing concern that current consumption habits have us on an unsustainable path – one that robs resources from the future generations, generates far too much waste, and undermines community and family life.

The Simple Life, by Vernard Eller @ www.hccentral.com/eller3/index.html

In 1973, Vernard Eller wrote a paper addressing the question of voluntary simplicity from a Christian perspective. The paper is freely available at the above address. (On the same subject, but not online, see, *Simplicity as Compassion: Voluntary Simplicity From a Christian Perspective*, 1996, by Michael Schut.) See also, www.christiansimpleliving.com

LibriVox @ www.libivox.org and/or the Gutenberg Project @ www.gutenberg.org

LibriVox and the Gutenberg Project provide free online books and audiobooks from the public domain. (Books enter the 'public domain' when their copyright expires, meaning that anyone can use the text for free.) Not only can you read or listen to Thoreau's *Walden* (LibriVox), or Emerson's *Nature* (LibriVox), or Wagner's *Simple Life* (Gutenberg Project), but you will have access to almost any literary classic you want – all for free.

Other Internet Resources @ www.google.com

One only needs to do a Google search on 'voluntary simplicity,' 'simple living,' 'the simple life,' or 'downshifting,' etc. to discover a vast array of other internet resources dedicated to the subject. Not all of it is worthwhile – a lot of it is not – but the sheer volume of websites is perhaps the clearest evidence that a social movement is underway.

FURTHER READING

Recommended Places To Start:

★ *Stepping Lightly: Simplicity for People and the Planet*, by Mark A. Burch (2000).

★ *Less is More: An Anthology of Ancient & Modern Voices Raised in Praise of Simplicity*, selected and edited by Goldian Vanenbroeck (1991).

★ *Affluenza: When Too Much is Never Enough*, by Clive Hamilton and Richard Denniss (2005).

★ *The Simple Life: Plain Living and High Thinking in American Culture*, by David E. Shi (2007, revised edition).

★ *Graceful Simplicity: The Philosophy and Politics of the Alternative American Dream* (1999) by Jerome Segal.

★ *Voluntary Simplicity: Responding to Consumer Culture* (2003) edited by Amatai Etzioni and Daniel Doherty.

★ *Walden*, by Henry David Thoreau, (1854).

Select Reading List:

Almedingen, E.M., *St. Francis of Assisi: A Great Life in Brief* (1967).

Andrews, Cecile, *The Circle of Simplicity* (1997).

Brower, Michael and Warren Leon, *The Consumer's Guide to Effective Environmental Choices: Practical Advice from the Union of Concerned Scientists* (1999).

Burch, Mark A., *Simplicity: Notes, Stories and Exercises for Developing Unimaginable Wealth* (1995).

Burch, Mark A., *Stepping Lightly: Simplicity for People and the Planet* (2000).

Cafaro, Philip, *Thoreau's Living Ethics:* Walden *and the Pursuit of Virtue* (2004).

Callenbach, Ellen, *Living Cheaply With Style* (1992).

Clark, Duncan, *Ethical Living* (2006).

Crocker, David A. (ed.), *The Ethics of Consumption* (1998)

Dacyczyn, Amy, *The Tightwad Gazette: Promising Thrift As a Viable Alternative Lifestyle* (1993).

De Graaf, John (ed.), *Take Back Your Time* (2003).

De Graaf, John et al, *Affluenza: The All-consuming Epidemic* (2005).

Dominguez, Joe and Vicki Robin, *Your Money or Your Life: Transforming your relationship with money and achieving financial independence* (1992).

Durning, Alan, *How Much is Enough? The Consumer Society and the Future of the Earth* (1992).

Elgin, Duane, *Voluntary Simplicity: Toward a Way of Life that is Outwardly Simple, Inwardly Rich* (1993).

Etzioni, Amatai, and Daniel Doherty, (eds.), *Voluntary Simplicity: Responding to Consumer Culture* (2003).

Frank, Robert, *Luxury Fever: money and happiness in an era of excess* (1999).

Freyfogle, Eric T., *On Private Property: Finding Common Ground on the Ownership of Land* (2007).

Fromm, Eric, *To Have or To Be?* (1976).

Gray, Charles, *Toward a Nonviolent Economics*, (1989).

Grigsby, Mary, *Buying Time and Getting By: The Voluntary Simplicity Movement* (2004).

Juniper, Tony, *How many lightbulbs does it take to change a planet?* (2007).

Hamilton, Clive, and Richard Denniss, *Affluenza: When Too Much is never Enough* (2005).

Hamilton Clive, *Growth Fetish* (2003).

Jackson, Tim, (ed.), *The EarthScan Reader in Sustainable Consumption* (2006).

James, Oliver, *Affluenza: How to Be Successful and Stay Sane* (2007).

Luhrs, Janet, *The Simple Living Guide* (1997).

McBride, Tracy, *Frugal Luxuries: Simple Pleasures to Enhance Your Life and Comfort Your Soul* (1997).

Merkel, Jim, *The Global Living Handbook* (2000).

Merkel, Jim, *Radical Simplicity: Small Footprints on a Finite Earth* (2003).

Nearing, Helen and Scott, *The Good Life* (1990).

Offer, Avner, *The Challenge of Affluence: Self Control and Well-Being in the United States and Britain since 1950* (2006).

Pierce, Linda Breen, *Simplicity Lessons: A 12-Step Guide to Simpler Living* (2003).

Pierce, Linda Breen, *Simplicity: Real People Finding Peace and Fulfillment in a Complex World* (2003).

Reich, Charles, *The Greening of America* (Revised edition, 1995).

Rohr, Richard, *Simplicity: The Art of Living* (1991).
Roszak, Theodore, *The Making of a Counter Culture: Reflections on the Technocratic Society and Its Youthful Opposition* (1995).
Roszak, Theodore, *Where the Wasteland Ends* (1973).
Talbot, John Michael, *The Lessons of St. Francis*, (1998).
Thoreau, Henry David, *Walden and Other Writings* (1989).
Schor, Juliet, *The Overworked American: The Unexpected Decline of Leisure* (1992).
Schor, Juliet, *The Overspent American: Upscaling, Downshifting, and the New Consumer* (1998).
Schumacher, E.F., *Small is Beautiful: A Study of Economics as if People Mattered* (1993).
Schut, Michael, *Simplicity as Compassion: Voluntary Simplicity From a Christian Perspective* (1996).
Segal, Jerome M., *Graceful Simplicity: The Philosophy and Politics of Voluntary Simplicity* (1999).
Shi, David E., *The Simple Life: Plain Living and High Thinking in American Culture* (Revised edition, 2007).
Smith, Andrea, and Nicola Baird, *Save Cash and Save the Planet* (2005).
Theobald, Robert, *The Challenge of Abundance* (1961).
Thoreau, Henry David, *The Portable Thoreau* (1982).
Vanenbroeck, Goldian, *Less is More: An Anthology of Ancient & Modern Voices Raised in Praise of Simplicity* (1991).
Wachtel, Paul L., *The Poverty of Affluence* (1989).
Wagner, Charles, *Simple Life* (1904).